Great Migration Newsletter

Vols. 16–20

Great Migration Newsletter

Volumes 16–20
(2007–2011)

Robert Charles Anderson

2012
Great Migration Study Project
NEW ENGLAND HISTORIC GENEALOGICAL SOCIETY
Boston, Massachusetts

ISBN-13: 978-0-88082-277-0
Library of Congress Control Number: 2012936270

Printed in the United States of America by King Printing Company, Lowell, Massachusetts

Cover design: Carolyn Sheppard Oakley

NEW ENGLAND HISTORIC
GENEALOGICAL SOCIETY®
99-101 Newbury Street
Boston, MA 02116
www.AmericanAncestors.org

CONTENTS

Note: The Newsletter *has been paginated consecutively for this volume, with the new number at the bottom of each page.*

INTRODUCTION

When the Great Migration Study Project was initiated in 1988, we immediately began to plan for a quarterly newsletter, which would serve a number of purposes. First and foremost, the *Great Migration Newsletter* would provide useful information on the immigrants of the Great Migration, on the towns that they settled, and on the records that they created. Second, the *Newsletter* would provide interested readers with updates on the progress of the Project itself, and would thus generate and maintain interest in the Project.

The original reasons for creating this publication have been more than justified, and the *Newsletter* continues publication to this day. This book comprises Volumes 16 through 20 of the *Newsletter,* supplementing a previous compilation of the first fifteen volumes. (Readers who do not already own the previous compendium can purchase a new comprehensive compendium of Volumes 1 through 20.)

From the beginning, the *Newsletter* has adhered to a regular format. Most issues have been eight pages, with the outer four pages constituting one section of the Newsletter and the inner four pages another section. The outer section includes one or two feature articles, a column with editor's comments, and a review of recent literature on the Great Migration. The inner section is called the FOCUS section, with detailed coverage of one of the towns settled during the Great Migration, or of a specific critical record, or group of records. The FOCUS and feature articles frequently concentrate on a particular class of records for one or another of the early new England towns or colonies.

In the first volume of *The Great Migration Begins* and in each of the volumes of the second *Great Migration* series, a section entitled SOURCES provides brief comments on each of the major categories of records consulted in the writing of these volumes. The many articles in the *Great Migration Newsletter* may be considered an extension of this introductory material in *The Great Migration Begins* and the more recent books, inasmuch as it treats the records of each town and colony in more detail than has been possible in the books. The *Newsletter* articles provide much of the basis for the rules of evidence used in compiling the Great Migration sketches, so this collected set of the *Newsletter* should be used as a companion to the published volumes, to help the reader interpret the conclusions reached in the sketches.

Robert Charles Anderson

Great Migration Newsletter

Vol. 16 January-March 2007 No. 1

JOHN MANNING OF IPSWICH

Some Great Migration sketches may be written in fifteen minutes, while others may consume a week or more of research and writing. The former variety, as one might expect, are those in which there exists a single record for a given immigrant, perhaps nothing more than a passenger list entry or an isolated appearance in court. At the opposite end of the spectrum, the sketches that take many days are generally those of the long-lived leaders of the colony, the governors and ministers.

The length of time required to complete a sketch is not, however, always a simple linear function of the number of records generated. The situation often arises wherein we find a record identifying a Great Migration immigrant, and also find additional later documents for the same name, which may or may not be assignable to the immigrant. In such cases, we may be required to devote many hours of analysis to this collection of records, sometimes connecting several records together to portray the full life of an immigrant who resided for many years in New England.

On other occasions, however, the result of our work may be the conclusion that the record that caused us to identify a Great Migration immigrant cannot be connected with any others. The result of such a circumstance will be a relatively short sketch, for a man or woman who left no posterity.

Several such sketches have been developed in the course of the volume currently in preparation, a volume which will cover the letters M, N, O and P for the years 1634 and 1635. As an example, in 1634 the town of Ipswich

> [g]ranted unto John Maning six acres of land more or less in equal shares with Thomas Howlett, John Gage and others lying on the neck of land at the east end of the town [ITR].

Two years later, in 1636, the town of Ipswich compiled a list of the parcels of land held by John Manning:

> an houselot three rods of ground ... bounded on the east by a houselot of Thomas Howlett, on the west by the high-

> way leading to the river, at the south end by a houselot of Thomas Hardy's, at the north end by the crossway leading towards the mill;
> granted him before Anno 1634 a planting lot of six acres;
> fifty acres of land ... lying beyond the North River [ITR].

The houselot described here was located some distance east of the meeting house green. A diagram published by Thomas F. Waters does not show this lot, but the accompanying text, and the description in the deed, place the lot between those of Thomas Howlett and Thomas Hardy in the bend of the Ipswich river just below the center of the diagram [Ipswich Hist 1:403 and Diagram 3 (between pages 386 and 387)].

On 15 February 1638[/9], the town of Ipswich granted to

> Susan Manning an houselot one acre of ground lying in the swamp area near the Mill Street having an acre of ground of Hugh Sherratt's on the northeast and a highway on the southwest, also six acres of planting ground beyond Muddy River, having a planting lot of Thomas Manning's on the southeast and a planting lot of Thomas Smith's on the northwest, butting upon ten acres of land granted to Robert Lord [ITR].

Some secondary sources claim that Susan was the widow of John Manning. If, however, Susan Manning were the widow of John Manning, there would be no reason for the town to grant her a houselot and other parcels of land; as a widow,

(continued on page 2)

EDITOR'S EFFUSIONS

The two volumes treated at the end of the *Recent Literature* section, *Deep Ancestry* by Spencer Wells and *Saxons, Vikings, and Celts* by Bryan Sykes, may not at first glance seem to have much to do with the Great Migration Study Project. We believe firmly, however, that over the next few years the research activities described in these volumes will mature and expand to the point that direct connections will be made with the detailed genealogical study of modern migrations to the New World.

The two volumes noted above, and many more soon to come, describe an attempt by population geneticists to delineate in more and more detail the full range of human migration over the entire globe for the last fifty thousand years or so. The earliest studies, based on relatively small samples of DNA sequences, divided the human species into a dozen or so major groups. In just the last few years, as the sample sizes have expanded, the researchers have been able to subdivide these broad groups, and trace migration pathways on smaller scales of both space and time. At this point, however, these results are too broad-gauge to be of immediate use to genealogists.

Over the past decade or so, genealogists, using the same techniques, and even the same laboratories, as the population geneticists, have begun to explore smaller samples of individual families. Because of the close correlation between the descent of surnames and Y chromosomes, family associations and interested individuals have initiated hundreds of family studies based on DNA data. These studies have begun to produce results, usually either confirming or casting doubt on suspected relationships.

The full potential of these results has not yet been approached, however. What is most needed is an expansion of sample sizes, on both the genealogical and the population sides, by orders of magnitude. Within a few years, assuming that the data is openly accessible, the information available will allow the two groups to meet in the middle, at which point organized assaults on Great Migration English origins may be undertaken.

Robert Charles Anderson, FASG   Editor
Jean Powers, Production Assistant

The Great Migration Newsletter is published quarterly by the Great Migration Study Project, a project of the New England Historic Genealogical Society, 101 Newbury Street, Boston MA 02116
www.NewEnglandAncestors.org
www.GreatMigration.org
GreatMigration@nehgs.org

(continued from page 1)

she would have been provided for in some way out of the land earlier granted to John Manning. Also, she is not described in the grant as a widow, although, as we shall see, she probably was, although not necessarily widow of John Manning. One might argue that the grant to Susan Manning was a regrant of the land given to John Manning, but one would expect that fact to be more explicit, and furthermore the description of the houselot granted to Susan, incomplete as it is, does not match that of the houselot in the 1636 inventory of the landholding of John Manning.

On 15 March 1647[/8?], "Thomas Maning of Ipswich, husbandman," sold to

> Robert Whitman of the same town, husbandman, & Susan his wife, all that his right & interest (being two parts) in the house where the said Robert now dwelleth, situate & being in Ipswich aforesaid, bounded by land of Edmund Gardner toward the southeast, east and northeast, & by the land of John Anniball toward the northwest, & the street on the southwest [ILR 1:43].

This sale of land by Thomas Manning to Robert Whitman is highly suggestive. The grant of "two parts" of the houselot would be consistent with an eldest son relinquishing his rights in property owned by his father. The inclusion of Susan Whitman, wife of Robert Whitman, as a grantee would be consistent with her also having some right to the land, perhaps as the remarried mother of Thomas, perhaps as sister. In this regard, note that one parcel of land granted to Susan Manning abutted on land of Thomas Manning. All this hints at some relationship between Susan and Thomas, but has nothing to say about John Manning.

The houselot that was the subject of this deed is delineated on the same diagram as the houselot of John Manning, but some distance away. It was located just to the east of the meeting house green, above the center of the diagram [Ipswich Hist 1:413 and Diagram 3]. Also, this houselot, part of which was relinquished to Robert Whitman and his wife Susan, does not match the description of the houselot granted separately to Susan Manning.

Next, on 13 October 1653,

> Thomas Maning of Ipswich having in my possession a parcel of land which is part of a houselot of Mr. Samuel Symonds, which is for the constant maintaining of the whole fence between the houselot of Mr. Symonds and this parcel of land, do hereby sell the said parcel of land to John Woodham [ILR 1:127].

The next day, on 14 October 1653,

> Thomas Manning of Ipswich, husbandman, sold to John Appleton of the same town & county, gentleman, &

(continued on page 8)

Focus on the PLANTER

(continued from page 30)

In some cases, then, the residence of the certifying authorities may not be the actual residence of the emigrants. On the other hand, a large proportion of the emigrants came from communities with a large number of like-minded individuals, including ministers and justices of the peace. For these emigrants, finding a compliant certifying authority would not have been difficult.

7 APRIL 1635

vij° Aprilis 1635 [7 April 1635]

This partie under mencioned is to be imbarqued in the *Planter* bound for New-England, p[er] Cert: from Alderman Fenn of his conformitie. he hath taken the oath of Allegeance & Supremacie.

Richard Fenn   27

No records for this passenger have been found in New England [GM 2:2:516]. We might assume, however, that he was related in some way to Alderman Fenn, who issued the certificate of conformity in his favor. Since the residence of Alderman Fenn is not given in the port book, and since the port book was being compiled in London, he was probably a London town official.

8 APRIL 1635

[8 Aprilis 1635]

Theis p[ar]ties hereunder written are to be transported in the *Planter* pr[e]d[ictus] p[er] Cert: from the Minister of Kingston upon Thames in the County of Surrey of their conformitie: & that they are no Subsedy men.

A Miller Palmer Tingley	21
An ostler Wm Butterick	20
A Miller Tho: Jewell	27

This is an interesting and unusual grouping of passengers, consisting of three young men, all with trades, and all apparently from the same town, Kingston-upon-Thames, Surrey, but, so far as we can tell from this one record, not as yet married, and not obviously connected with one another other than in this listing. As we shall see, they were not directly connected in any later records.

Palmer Tingley settled in Ipswich, where he resided as late as 1639 [Pope 456]. He may have married Hannah Fosdick, daughter of Stephen Fosdick, but this is not certain [GM 2:2:548]. If he was not the husband of Hannah Fosdick, it may be that he died in Ipswich around 1640, or perhaps he returned to England. Since we have a clue from the passenger list as to his English origin, research in Surrey records might tell us whether he did continue his life in old England.

On 13 April 1635, less than a week after the appearance of "W[illia]m Butterick" as a passenger on the *Planter*, the same document contains an entry for "W[illia]m Battrick," aged 18, on the *Susan & Ellen* [Hotten 59]. This may or may not be the same man, but it does demonstrate a common situation. The same name will sometimes appear twice in this port book, with the ages recorded in the two entries being close, enrolling on different vessels a few days or weeks apart. This situation always requires additional analysis, usually without producing a definitive solution. Sometimes this will result in two separate sketches, and sometimes the two entries will be included in a single sketch.

In any case, William Buttrick settled in Concord, where he married three times, having at least seven children with his first two wives. Although he contemplated moving to Chelmsford, in the end he remained in Concord, where he died in 1698 [GM 2:1:522-26].

Thomas Jewell settled in Boston, in that part of the town that was set off as Braintree [GM 2:4:59-62]. On 24 February 1639/40, the town of Boston "granted to Thomas Jewell, of the Mount, miller, for three heads, 12 acres" [BTR 1:49]. Despite the passage of more than four years between the date of the port book entry and the date of this land grant, we conclude that these records pertain to the same man because of the shared occupation of miller.

The "Mount" was Mount Wollaston, the early name for the area just south of Boston, but separated from Boston by sections of Roxbury and Dorchester, that became Braintree. The grant of land "for three heads" indicates a family of three, the simplest explanation for which is that Thomas Jewell had married and had one living child by the date of the land grant, which is consistent with the other information we have on the family.

Although these three young men settled in three different towns, there is a slight hint that William Buttrick and Thomas Jewell may have interacted with one another after their arrival: Thomas Jewell married a woman from Concord, where William Buttrick had settled. Further research in Kingston-upon-Thames could be fruitful.

10 APRIL 1635

x° Aprilis 1635 [10 April 1635]

Theis under written names are to be transported in the *Planter* pr[e]d[ictus] Nico: Trarice Mr bound for New Engl: p[er] Cert: of the Minister of Sudburie in Suffolk & from the Maior of the Towne of his conformitie to the orders & descipline of the Church of England & that he is no Subsedy man. he hath taken the oath of Alleg: & Suprem:

	yeres
Carrier Richard Hasfell	54
uxor Martha	42
Marie Hasfell	17
Sara Hasfell	14
Martha Hasfell	8
Rachell Hasfell	6
Ruth Hasfell	3
Alice Smith	40
Elizabeth Coop[er]	24
Jo: Smith	13
Job Hawkins	15

Hotten added a footnote to this section of the passenger list, commenting on the spelling of the surname of this family, stating that some entries looked like "Hasfell" and some like "Haffell." Examination of a microfilm copy of the original confirms this observation, although the latter spelling is either certain or possible in all cases. Whatever the port clerk may have intended, the spelling in New England was generally "Haffield" or "Halfield," with the former of these two being the more common form.

Richard Haffield, his wife, and five daughters, settled in Ipswich, where he died in early 1639 [GM 2:3:183-87]. His will provides a hint that the two older daughters were born to an earlier wife, and later documents, generated long after the death of Richard Haffield, confirm this.

On 29 April 1668, "Josiah Cobbet and Mary his wife, with John Ilsley and Sarah his wife," petitioned the Court,

> showing that the late Richard Hayfeild, heretofore of Sudbury, England, and Judeth his wife, by whom he had several children, sons and daughters, and his wife departing this life leaving only two daughters, Mary and Sarah, he married a second wife by whom he had several children, three of whom (daughters also) are now living; the said Richard with his second wife removed from Sudbury into New England bringing a considerable estate in goods and ready money, and afterwards he sold a good estate in land, left him by their grandfather,

then proceeded to claim that their stepmother had not distributed to them their fair share of their father's estate, and

asked the court to order a proper distribution [EPR 2:118-19; MA Arch 114b, 115b].

So, although no records for this family have been found in England, later records generated in New England confirm that the family did derive from Sudbury, Suffolk, in accord with the statement in the port book of the issuer of the certificate of conformity.

What, then of the four remaining names in this section of the passenger list, not obviously connected with the Haffield family? Were these four individuals also from Sudbury or vicinity? Were they connected in some way with Richard Haffield and his family, or were they one or more separate groupings? We will not be able to answer all of these questions.

Alice Smith presents a very interesting problem, which we will encounter twice more in later entries for this same ship. First, we will assume the working hypothesis that the John Smith, aged 13, two entries below, was travelling with her, and was probably her son. Under this assumption, we of course want to know where her husband was at this time. Was she a widow? Had her husband already migrated to New England, so she and her son were now joining him? Or were mother and son making the move ahead of the head of household, who was perhaps detained at home for some reason, perhaps to dispose of his land?

Since this is such a common surname, we are not surprised to learn that four early Smith immigrants to New England had wives named Alice, at least some of whom might potentially be identified with these passengers.

Christopher Smith of Providence had wife Alice, but he had no son John. The children credited to them seem to have been born in the early 1630s [Austin 376]. Of the four candidates we are considering, this one has the least evidence in favor of connecting with the 1635 passengers.

Francis Smith of Watertown and Reading had wife Alice, and son John who married in 1647, which would be appropriate for a man who was aged 13 in 1635. Francis and Alice had a son Benjamin born shortly after arrival in New England, at a time when Alice would have been in her early forties, which would be at the very end of her childbearing range [Warner-Harrington 580-81].

John Smith of Lancaster has been stated to have had wife Alice, and did have a son John who also married in 1647 [Miner Anc 158-60]. We have argued elsewhere, however, that the assignment of Alice and John Smith, the *Planter* passengers, to this John Smith was erroneous [TAG 61:24-25].

John Smith, miller, of Providence had wife Alice, and son John, who was by 1649 acting as administrator on his father's estate, which would be consistent with being aged 13 in 1635. This couple also had a daughter Elizabeth who was apparently born in the mid-1630s [Austin 382].

Of our four candidates for husband of Alice and father of John, then, two are tentatively, although not decisively, excluded, leaving us with two who are equally plausible, though not proved: Francis Smith of Watertown and Reading and John Smith, miller, of Providence. Unfortunately, we do not have information on place of English origin for any of these men, so we cannot say whether Alice Smith should be deemed to have been issued a certificate of conformity from the minister of Sudbury, nor can we say whether there was any connection with Richard Haffield.

Elizabeth Cooper cannot be connected confidently with any records in New England [GM 2:2:199]. Pope thought that she might be the woman of that name admitted to Charlestown church on 9 December 1643 [Pope 117; ChChR 10], which may or may not be true, but which, even if true, does not advance our knowledge of this passenger much.

A further interesting point arises, however. Elizabeth is sandwiched between Alice Smith and John Smith. Might she have been part of this family group? Possibly, but not certainly. In many of these passenger lists we find that not all the families' members are collected together in one tight grouping, so this placement of Elizabeth Cooper may have no significance. Nevertheless, should more certain information on the English connections of Alice Smith ever emerge, an effort should be made to see if there is an Elizabeth Cooper in the same place.

Job Hawkins presents a different example of a man arriving without the rest of his family. He probably settled first at Boston, where his elder brother James Hawkins was living in 1635 [GM 2:3:261-66]. A few years later, Job's parents, Richard and Jane Hawkins, also appeared in Boston. And there was a third brother, Thomas, who also came to New England. At the time of the Antinomian upheavals, Richard and Jane removed to Portsmouth, Rhode Island, and Job went with them. He returned to Boston by 1646, where the births of his two children were recorded [GM 2:3:266-70].

In one of his passages on Anne Hutchinson, in 1640, Governor John Winthrop noted that "Hawkins's wife (who continued with her, and was her bosom friend) had much familiarity with the devil in England, when she dwelt at St. Ives, where diverse ministers and others resorted to her and found it true" [WJ 2:10-11; NEHGR 114:207-11].

There are two English parishes named St. Ives, one in Cornwall and one in Huntingdon. The Huntingdon parish is much the closer to Sudbury, but not all that close. By saying "when she dwelt at St. Ives," Winthrop was implying that this was not her native parish. Even so, we find no evidence to connect Job Hawkins and the rest of the Hawkins family with Sudbury.

[10 April 1635]

In the *Planter* pr[e]d[ictus] Theis under names are to be transported to New-England

Eglin Hanford	46
Margaret Hanford	16
Eliz: Hanford	14
Rodolphus Elmes	15
Tho: Stansley	16

Eglin Hanford and her two daughters are another example on this vessel of a family travelling without a male head of household. In this case, Eglin was twice widowed, making the migration with two of her five children. She was sister of Timothy Hatherly, settled near him in Scituate and, two years after her arrival, married Richard Sillis, another Scituate resident [GMB 2:876-81; GM 2:3:205-7].

Eglin (Hatherly) (Downe) Hanford was baptized at Winkleigh, Devonshire, and resided in other Devonshire parishes. Given her association with Hatherly, however, she was probably living in the London area in 1635.

All five of Eglin's children were with her second husband, Jeffrey Hanford. At least one of these children, Lettice Hanford, must have come to New England at least a year before her mother and sisters, as she married Edward Foster at Scituate on 8 April 1635 [GMB 1:690-92], just two days before Eglin and other family members appeared in London to enroll for passage to New England. She may have come to New England in the care of her uncle Timothy Hatherly, who made annual trips between England and New England from 1631 to 1634. The other two Hanford children who are not on the 1635 passenger list, Susanna Hanford and Thomas Hanford, may also have come across in the same manner.

Rhodolphus Elmes also settled in Scituate, where he married in 1644 and resided until his death in 1712. He was son of the widow Sarah Elmes of Southwark, Surrey, who included in her will of 25 August 1653 a bequest to "son Radolphus Elmes (now in parts beyond the seas)" [GM 2:2:424-26].

Timothy Hatherly resided in Southwark prior to coming to New England, and continued to have connections there throughout the 1620s and 1630s, so Rhodolphus was clearly travelling with the Hanfords. No genealogical connection to Hatherly or Hanford has been found, so he may have been a servant rather than a family member.

No records have been found in New England for Thomas Stansley. Like Rhodolphus Elmes, however, he may also have been with the Hanfords. The name does not appear in the extensive early Scituate records. (There was a Thomas Stanley who arrived in New England in 1634, who was baptized in 1601 [TAG 80:220-21], and clearly cannot be this passenger of 1635.)

11 APRIL 1635

[xjo die Aprilis 1635]

In the *Planter* pr[e]d[ictus] Theis under written names are to be transported to New-England p[er] Certificate according to order

Sara Pittnei	22
Sara Pitnei	7
Samuell Pitney	1½
Margaret Pitney	22
Rachell Deane	31

Sarah Pitney and her family represent the last of the instances of a family making the voyage without a male head of household. She was the wife of James Pitney, who resided first at Ipswich, by 1643 had moved to Marshfield, and later lived in Boston. The first New England record for James Pitney himself was on 26 March 1640, when he was hired "to keep a herd of swine" at Ipswich [ITR]. We cannot tell, therefore, whether James Pitney crossed the Atlantic before or after his wife.

On 27 December 1624, James Pitney and Sarah Smith were married at Rotherhithe, Surrey. The date and names of this marriage are consistent with what we know of the New England couple, but this record does not conclusively pertain to them.

No records for Margaret Pitney have been found in New England. She could well have been a sister of James Pitney.

Rachel Deane was a widow, possibly pregnant at the time of sailing, who settled in Marshfield [GM 2:2:335-36]. Since the Pitney family also resided for many years at Marshfield, the families were very likely associated in England before migration.

SUMMARY

The passenger complement of the *Planter* arrived dockside over a period of three weeks, from 22 March 1634/5 to 11 April 1635. A total of one-hundred and nineteen individuals of all ages, from three months to seventy years, were enrolled for passage to New England.

We observe first that most of the passengers, perhaps as many as ninety, came as members of families. None of these families are simple nuclear families, with just father, mother and children. There are multi-generational families and families with stepchildren, and almost all of the kinship groups are accompanied by one or more servants.

The largest family grouping on the *Planter* was that of the Tuttles and their kin. Three brothers, John, William and

Richard Tuttle are all here, with their wives and children. One of these brothers, John Tuttle, had married the widow Joan (Antrobus) Lawrence, who was accompanied aboard ship by her mother (Joan Antrobus), two of her sons, two of her daughters, and a son-in-law (George Giddings). And all of these families included servants. At a minimum, then, thirty of the passengers, or one-quarter of the ship's complement, were from this one kinship network.

Even some of the single men in this list had the appearance of being family men. The three men who were enrolled on 8 April 1635, Palmer Tingley, William Buttrick and Thomas Jewell, were all in their early twenties, with established trades. The same may be said for other passengers, such as Allen Perley, Francis Peabody and William Fellows. Most of these men married soon after arrival in New England, and lived lives very similar to those of the men who had growing or completed families at the time of migration. This is yet another way in which the makeup of the New England passenger lists differs so much from those of the vessels bound for the Chesapeake or the Caribbean. On those latter ships, most of the young men did not yet have trades and were headed to the colony for the purposes of entering servitude.

The servants bound for New England were themselves integral parts of the families. Of those that are identified explicitly on the list as servants, many cannot be traced later in New England. Of those who can be traced, however, some completed their term of servitude, and then moved into the same economic and social strata as those occupied by their masters. Two servants of Nicholas Davis, for example, James Hayward and Judith Phippin, completed their service and then married one another. Hayward was granted land in Charlestown not long before his marriage, and undoubtedly would have acquired more had he not died just a few years later.

Although we have no clear examples from this list, the servants who were brought to New England were often kinsmen of the adult members of a family group making the voyage. We have suggested above that Rhodolphus Elmes came to New England as a servant in the Hanford household. Further research might well reveal that he was related in some way to the Hanfords.

Pregnancy did not prevent women from making sea voyages at this time. At least two women on the *Planter* may have been expecting at the time of the voyage: Jane Giddings and Rachel Deane.

We have asked whether the explicit statement of the parish of issuance of a certificate of conformity at the head of a long list of passengers guarantees that all the persons named in that list were from the one parish. Although we have not proved definitely that this is not true, enough contrary hints have emerged to indicate that we should use these ascriptions of origin with care.

RECENT LITERATURE

Kathleen Canney Barber and Janet Ireland Delorey, "William[1] Varney of Ipswich and Gloucester, Massachusetts," *The American Genealogist* 81 (2006): 161-71. The authors examine the life and family of William Varney, suggesting that he was the man of that name who married at Windsor, Berkshire, in 1629 Bridget Deverell, and, in this first installment, treating in detail the marriages and children of their eldest child, daughter Rachel.

William Wyman Fiske, "The London Origin of Richard[1] Waters of Salem, Massachusetts: Revisited," *The American Genealogist* 81 (2006):172-82. Through close examination of a London parish register, Fiske substantially augments the earlier research of Henry FitzGilbert Waters on the parentage and siblings of the immigrant Richard Waters.

Leslie Mahler, "The Maternal Ancestry of Phebe[1] Bisby, Wife of New England Colonists Thomas[1] Bracy of Ipswich and New Haven and Samuel[1] Martin of New Haven," *The American Genealogist* 81 (2006):224-37. The author demonstrates that William Bisby, father of Phebe Bisby, the second wife of the immigrant Thomas Bracy, married at Childerditch, Essex, Raberge Salmon, daughter of William and Raberge (Thresher) Salmon. He also delineates three generations of Thresher ancestry, and adds information on the Malle (or Maule) family, Margaret Malle being the mother of Raberge Thresher.

Eugene Cole Zubrinsky, "John[2] Cole and Family of Plymouth and Swansea, Massachusetts, and Portsmouth, Rhode Island: With Additional Corrections to the Cole Literature (*concluded*)," *The American Genealogist* 81 (2006):238-45. Zubrinsky concludes his treatment of the family of John[2] Cole of Plymouth and Swansea with a genealogical summary of the family. The author then addresses the question of the date of death of John's father, James[1] Cole, concluding that he died in the early 1680s. Finally, the author adds an appendix, correcting a number of other erroneous statements about the Cole family.

Nathaniel Lane Taylor, "Genealogist John Farmer Discovers His Ancestry: The Warwickshire Family of Edward[1] Farmer, Isabel[1] (Farmer) (Wyman) (Blood) Green, and Thomas[1] Pollard, of Billerica, Massachusetts," *The New England Historical and Genealogical Register* 160 (2006):261-72. The author presents the first installment of a multipart series on the immigrant Edward Farmer and his family. The approach is unusual and intriguing, as it views the family both through the eyes of John Farmer, descendant of Edward Farmer and pioneer genealogist, and through modern research in English records. This first installment presents summaries or transcripts of contemporary documents which came into John Farmer's hands.

Eben W. Graves, "The Ancestry of Alice (Archer) Dummer, Wife of Stephen[1] Dummer and Mother of Jane (Dummer) Sewall," *The New England Historical and Genealogical Register* 160 (2006):273-79. Through the use of a will from one of the so-called Peculiar Courts, Graves has identified the parents and siblings of Alice Archer, wife of the immigrant Stephen Dummer. He then provides evidence for two further generations of Archer ancestry.

Patricia Law Hatcher, "The Edmund Marshall Family of Chebacco, Essex County, Massachusetts," *The New England Historical and Genealogical Register* 160 (2006):282-94. The author completes her study of the immigrant Edmund Marshall with accounts of his two sons Edmund and Benjamin. The article concludes with an appendix on Thomas Marshall of Chebacco, concluding that this man was not related to Edmund Marshall.

Spencer Wells, *Deep Ancestry: Inside the Genographic Project* (Washington, 2006).
Bryan Sykes, *Saxons, Vikings, and Celts: The Genetic Roots of Britain and Ireland* (New York and London, 2006). These two volumes represent the vanguard of a burgeoning genre of studies of human migration pathways based on DNA evidence. Spencer Wells is the Director of the Genographic Project of the National Geographic Society, a project which aspires to collect DNA samples from all quadrants of the globe, focussing especially on indigenous populations. The DNA will be tested for both mitochondrial and Y chromosome variations, enabling both a paternally and a maternally oriented, broad-stroke picture of global migration patterns of the past fifty thousand years or so, since the emergence of *Homo sapiens* from Africa. This volume describes the aims and methods of the project, and provides some prelininary results. Bryan Sykes, a geneticist at Oxford University, looks at a part of the same problem. Using techniques similar to those of the Genographic Project, he tackles the question of the peopling of the British Isles. Examining separately Scotland, Ireland, Wales and England, he attempts to establish the relative contributions to each of these regions made by Celts, Picts, Romans, Vikings, Saxons, Normans and others. As an example, he and his team have found a genetic signature in eastern Scotland, in the neighborhood of Fife and the Grampian Hills, that they associate with the Picts. Here and elsewhere, they observe different paternal and maternal contributions to the population.

(continued from page 2)

Samuell Appleton of the same town & county, gentleman, that my dwelling house situate & being in Ipswich aforesaid near the meeting house, having the meeting house green toward the northwest & the river toward the southeast, having the land of John Woodam toward the northeast, & the land of Mr. Symonds on the south [ILR 1:131].

The houselot described in these deeds was yet another parcel. Thomas F. Waters placed this lot just to the south of the meeting house green, as part of the lot originally granted to William White (or perhaps part of the lot granted to Henry Sewall) [Ipswich Hist 1:334 and Diagram 1 (between pages 318 and 319)].

So what are we left with? Three individuals with the surname Manning (John, Susan and Thomas) were recorded during the first two decades of the existence of the town of Ipswich as holding all or part of what appear to be four different houselots in the center of the town. Are there any connections we can make?

Starting from the end of this series of grants and transactions, we find Thomas Manning in possession of a houselot on the meeting house green. This does not match with land held earlier by John or Susan, and appears to have been acquired by Thomas Manning on his own. There is nothing here to connect him to anyone else.

Next, we look at the sale by Thomas Manning to Rober Whitman and his wife Susan. As noted above, this certa has the appearance of an heir to an estate selling off his of a parcel of land, and the inclusion of Susan Whitman grantee would indicate that she also had some interest i land. Susan might, then, be the mother of Thomas, rece remarried to Robert Whitman.

In his account of Robert Whitman, Pope states that this "[h]as land formerly belonging to Susan Manning in 16 [Pope 495]. The document supporting this statement ha been found, but, if accurate, this would strongly suppor hypothesis that Susan Manning was a widow who had r ried Robert Whitman, and that Thomas was her son. Th would indicate that the location of Susan Manning's pla lot adjacent to that of Thomas Manning was not accide1

But, crucial to the purpose of the sketch, was Susan Ma the widow of John Manning? The argument in favor of hypothesis would be that Susan Manning appeared on I wich records shortly after John Manning disappeared. T arguments against would be that there is nothing to sup such an hypothesis, and that the grant of land to Susan I ning on 15 February 1638[/9] is not what one would ex for a widow, whose presumed recently deceased husba1 had already been granted a full proprietary share. In the sence of further evidence, we conclude that Susan was the widow of John, and that the records for John stand

Great Migration Newsletter

Vol. 16   April-June 2007   No. 2

ENGLISH AS SHE WAS SPOKE

Any researcher who undertakes the study of records and families of seventeenth-century New England soon learns that the English language has changed over the last four centuries. Of greatest concern to the genealogist are the different semantic ranges of some of the terms of kinship, such as brother or sister, niece or nephew, and cousin.

Semantic shift was not limited to kinship terminology, though. Many ordinary words had a different denotation at the time of the Great Migration. If the modern researcher analyzes seventeenth-century documents with a twentieth-first century understanding, misunderstanding and errors will abound. To demonstrate this problem, we will examine some common examples of such words. For each word, we will begin the entry with a modern definition, from the College Edition of *Webster's New World Dictionary of the American Language* (Cleveland and New York, 1966). Other, older definitions will be taken from the *Oxford English Dictionary*.

OUTHOUSE: "a building separate from but located near any main building or dwelling; specifically, an outdoor latrine; privy."

The latter meanings, latrine or privy, are those that come quickest to our minds for the last century or more. In seventeenth-century documents, though, the first, more general meaning is what we find. The word occurs most frequently in probate inventories:

> the dwelling house & outhouses and land thereto adjoining for it in Boston (inventory of the Rev. John Norton of Boston, 24 April 1663 [SPR 4:137-40])

> 36 acres of land with houses, outhouses, gardens & orchard thereupon (inventory of Nicholas Noyes of Newbury, 4 December 1701 [EQC 307:236])

These outhouses might be cattle sheds, brewhouses, and the like. Sometimes a barn might be included among the outhouses, and sometimes the barn would be mentioned separately. The word can also be found in some documents in a dialect form, as "outhousen," which might give a clue to the English dialect spoken by the creator of the document.

CELLAR: "a room or group of rooms below the ground level and usually under a building, often used for storing fuel, provisions, etc."

This word was apparently in transition in the early seventeenth century from an older meaning to our modern understanding of the word.

> On 7 January 1651[/2?], "William Paine of Ipswich ..., merchant," sold to "William Towne of Salem ... Senior ... forty acres of grounds (or thereabouts) lying in Topsfield, whereof six acres is by the cellar which William Howard of Topsfield aforesaid built, and about thirty-two acres joining up to the said six acres eastward of it, part of which is plow ground, another part is meadow and another part upland unplowed" [ILR 2:23-24].

This land description depicts the cellar as an isolated building in a part of Topsfield away from the settled center. This cannot be a "cellarhole," a term not encountered this early. The cellar was "built."

The *OED* gives as the primary definition "A store-house or store-room, whether above or below ground, for provisions." The word appears often in the Boston town records.

> There is liberty granted unto Thomas Joy, carpenter, to set up an house over his cellar by the waterside, in the common way by his dwelling house (26 December 1642 [BTR 1:71])

(continued on page 10)

EDITOR'S EFFUSIONS

As this issue of the *Newsletter* is being completed, the final touches are also being put on the next Great Migration volume, covering the letters M, N, O and P for the years 1635 and 1636 and containing more than two hundred and ten sketches.

The completion of a volume provides an appropriate occasion for looking at some of the broader and enduring aspects of the Great Migration Study Project. First, the discovery of English origins for Great Migration immigrants continues at a steady pace. The pages of the leading genealogical journals carry several such identifications every year, and a number of such discoveries will also appear for the first time in this volume. Joseph Metcalfe of Ipswich was from Strood near Rochester in Kent. The first evidence for this was found in some parish register entries in the International Genealogical Index, and then confirmed by the association of Joseph Metcalfe in New England with another immigrant from that same parish. William Nash of Charlestown was found to be from Maidstone in Kent, the critical clue being a reference to a kinswoman in his widow's will.

Second, we continue to expand our horizons by making more extensive use of familiar sources. In the past, when studying immigrants who settled in Newbury, we have relied on the published version of that town's vital records. In the volume nearing completion, the families of Anthony Morse and James Noyes presented some interesting problems. Examination of a microfilm copy of the original vital records clarified some of the published dates and made our sketches for these two families better as a result.

Third, as we approach the end of this second series of Great Migration volumes, with two more to go, we also approach the halfway point in our coverage of all Great Migration immigrants. We are now seeing many of the children of the immigrants whose sketches we are now compiling marrying children of immigrants whose sketches were done in earlier volumes. This is one of the many ways in which we are obtaining a clearer picture of the entire migration process.

Robert Charles Anderson, FASG   Editor
Jean Powers, Production Assistant

The Great Migration Newsletter is published quarterly by the Great Migration Study Project, a project of the New England Historic Genealogical Society, 101 Newbury Street, Boston MA 02116
www.NewEnglandAncestors.org
www.GreatMigration.org
GreatMigration@nehgs.org

(continued from page 9)

There is liberty granted unto James Oliver to continue his entrance into his cellar, where it now is in the street, laying the nether part of the door flat about 18 inches, or two foot (31 July 1643 [BTR 1:75])

In the first of these two examples, the cellar was initially clearly underground, but not under a building. In the second example, the position of the cellar with relation to any other buildings on the lot is unstated. When we read of a cellar at this time, we should not succumb to our modern preconceptions of what such a structure was.

SQUADRON: "a group of warships assigned to some special duty; unit or subdivision of a fleet"

This word was employed regularly in describing the boundaries of the grants of Farms in the western portion of Watertown. For example, in a deed of 28 June 1697, the north and south bounds of a sixty-acre farm being deeded by Roger Wellington to his children were stated to be the "squadron lines" [MLR 12:143].

The term was also used in the same town

> in laying out the land in Lieu of Township land, it being first laid out into 4 squadrons, the first lot shall begin at the north squadron, each squadron of half a mile in breadth with allowance of highways of 4 rods betwixt squadron & squadron [WaTR 1:60]

In both these examples, a squadron is clearly a strip of land, with one lot laid next to another. A division of land was made of several such strips or squadrons, parallel to one another.

The *OED* provides some quotations from early New England records under the heading "squadron," but not directly related to the division of land. There are also some entries relating to the division of land, with the meaning of a square or right-angled figure. There is a cross-reference to the obsolete word "squadrant," which further leads to "quadrant," emphasizing the connotation of square or rectangular allocations of land.

Only a few New England towns used this term, so again there may be a clue to the region of origin in England.

DISCOVER: "to be the first to find out, see, or know about"

In early New England, we find this word in a wide variety of documents, but we encounter it most frequently at the end of probate inventories:

> Mrs. Mary Norton deposed ... that when she knows more she will discover the same (2 May 1663, inventory of the estate of the Rev. John Norton [SPR 4:140])

(continued on page 16)

Focus on Weymouth

In a previous issue of the *Great Migration Newsletter* we undertook a brief analysis of the surviving records for the earliest grants of land at Weymouth [GMN 5:30]. We noted that there was an inventory of landholding, arranged by proprietor and compiled in late 1643 or early 1644, and that there was only one record of one of the divisions of land prior to that date, a list of sixteen recipients of Great Lots in 1636.

We concluded that because "we have only the short list of 1636 grants of Great Lots, and because so much of the land had changed hands by 1643, a parcel-by-parcel analysis would be necessary to determine what a typical series of grants would have looked like."

We propose to carry out that detailed analysis in a multi-part article, of which this is the first installment. We will analyze each of the dozen or so "fields" which made up the various land divisions, seeking to answer a number of questions. Who were the original grantees in each of these divisions? What would the standard set of land grants be for each individual? When were the grants made? Where were the home-lots? Answers may not be obtainable for these and many other questions, but we will pursue our usual empirical approach and see what emerges.

Our results will necessarily be incomplete, for we know that this inventory of landholding was incomplete. On 26 November 1644, just a few months after the inventory was compiled, Rev. James Parker sold several parcels of Weymouth land to Zaccheus Gould [SLR 1:56]. Neither of these men had an entry in the inventory, although there are traces of Parker's land in other men's entries. (Quoted passages are from Weymouth Hist 1:184-98.)

WEST FIELD

In the 1643 list twelve men held parcels of various size in the West Field, ranging from 21 acres in the hands of John Whitman to one-quarter of an acre held by Richard Walling, and totalling 52½ acres.

To get a feel for how these records were organized, and for the frequency of land changing hands in the period of less than a decade between the original grants and the compilation of 1643, we will look closely at the parcels held by or formerly held by Robert Lovell.

Walter Harris: "An acre and a half in the west field first given to Robert Lovell"

Edward Smith: "Five acres and half in the west field three acres and half first given to Richard Porter and two acres to Robert Lovell"

Robert Lovell: "One acre and a quarter in the west field first given to him"

Each of these land descriptions also lists the abutters on the four principal points of the compass, which allows us to plot out these parcels in order to better understand the original granting process. When we carry out this task for these three parcels, we find that the grant to Robert Lovell was made in two discontiguous pieces. The section owned in 1643 by Walter Harris and the piece retained by Lovell himself were next to one another, and together made up a lot of 2¾ acres. To the south of that parcel were four acres originally held by Thomas Holbrook and John Whitmarsh, and in 1643 in the hands of John Harding. Then came the 1643 holding of Edward Smith, who had combined land originally granted to Richard Porter and Robert Lovell, Lovell's portion being two acres.

Pursuing this same process for the remaining sections of the West Field, we obtain the following list of original grantees, arranged in descending order of the size of the grant (regardless of whether the grant was in one piece or more):

Mr. [Joseph] Hull	21¾
Robert Lovell	4¾
Robert Jeffrey	4
John Rogers	4
William Fry	4
Richard Porter	3½
William Newland	2½
William Hues	2
Thomas Holbrook	2
John Whitmarsh	2
Thomas Baylie	2

Leaving aside the large grant to Joseph Hull, we observe that these grants cluster around what could be standard sizes of two and four acres. Whether the small deviations from these possible norms represent differences introduced at the time of the original grants, or adjustments made during later transfers of land, we do not yet know.

Finally, note that only two out of the original eleven grantees retained any of the land they had been given by the town. John Rogers held his full complement of four acres and Robert Lovell had two acres, less than half his original grant. Thus, nearly ninety percent of the land in this field had changed hands in less than a decade.

EAST FIELD

The East Field was much larger than the West Field. In the 1643 compilation twenty-one different men held twenty-eight parcels, totalling 190¾ acres.

We begin here by simply reshuffling the parcels to obtain the list of original grantees, in the same manner as for the West Field:

James Parker	15
Henry Kingman	13
William Reade	11½
Clement Briggs	11¼
Richard Adams	11
Edmond Hart	11
Zachary Bicknell	10
Stephen French	10
[Br]others Gould	10
Widow Streame	8
Musachiell Bernard	7
William Smith	7
Angel Hollard	5
William Brandon	4
John Gurney	4
Richard Knight	4
Macuth Pratt	4
William Richards	4
George Allin	3
John Allin	3
John Bursley	3
Wife of Thomas Clapp	3
Thomas Rawlins	3
James Rogers	3
Edward Sale	3
Jeffrey Staple	3
John Staple	3
Robert Stone	3
Thomas White	3
Edward Bate	2
Edward Bennett	2
William Hughes	2
Robert Lenthall	2

A third of the grants were for three acres and nearly two-thirds were for two, three or four acres. As with the West Field, the largest single grant was to a minister, Rev. James Parker. On the other hand, one of the smallest grants was to Rev. Robert Lenthall, although the form of the entry for this parcel of land was different from the others, stating not that Lenthall was the original grantee, but that he had sold the parcel, so Lenthall himself may have acquired it by purchase. And John Bursley, a wealthy early settler, only received three acres. The normal fashion was to grant land on the basis of a combination of family size and size of estate, but on these few observations we cannot be certain that this was the policy here.

To examine this point further, we look at a few families where the number in the household is known reasonably well. Recent research by Gail Staples has demonstrated that Jeffrey Staple came from Wendover, Buckinghamshire, and that John Staple was his son [NEHGR 161:95-100]. Jeffrey Staple was born about 1576 and brought with him his wife Margaret and three or four children. We do not know for certain when this family arrived in Weymouth. The eldest of these children, John, had been baptized in 1608 and was married by 1639. Another possible son (or perhaps nephew), Thomas Staple, had settled in Fairfield by 1639, and a daughter, Martha Staple, was buried at Weymouth on 17 February 1639/40. In this context, the date of the granting of the East Field becomes of interest. If the division was made in 1635 or soon after, then the household of Jeffrey Staple could have had as many as six persons, and John Staple may not yet have left the household. On the other hand, if the grant was made in 1640, Jeffrey Staple and his wife would have had only one child remaining at home and John Staple would have established a household of the same size, with himself, his wife and a newborn child. Interestingly, both men received three acres in the East Field.

More briefly, we have already examined most of the families that received ten or eleven acres. Richard Adams arrived in 1635 with a wife and young stepdaughter, and by 1642 he had added three children of his own, making a household of six on that date [GM 2:1:8-11]. Edmond Hart moved from Dorchester to Weymouth in 1636, on which date he was not yet married; by 1642 he was married with at least three children, for a household of five [GMB 2:866-69]. Zachary Bicknell arrived in Weymouth with a wife and son, and was dead by early 1637 [GM 2:1:282-83]. Like Edmond Hart, Stephen French had moved from Dorchester to Weymouth in 1636, with a wife and one or two children [GMB 1:700-3]. Again, these four examples do not produce much of a pattern.

Turning our attention to exchanges of lands between the date of the original grant (whenever that may have been) and the date of the inventory, we notice a slight tendency towards consolidation, with fewer individuals holding land in the East Field than there were original grantees. The listing for Nathaniel Adams, for example, contains five separate parcels of land, four of which were in the East Field. These parcels totalled 42¼ acres and included land originally granted to seven different individuals. Examination of the abutters for these four parcels indicates that they were not contiguous, but were in various places around the field. Interestingly, three of the parcels bordered on the three parcels that had been accumulated by Robert Randall, which parcels were themselves discontiguous. In one case, Nathaniel Adams and Robert Randall had bought land from the same man, each one acquiring two acres from the four-acre grant originally made to John Gurney. There does not seem to be any known genealogical relationship between Nathaniel Adams and Robert Randall, but this pattern is suggestive.

In the East Field nine men held 54½ acres that had been originally granted to them, indicating that nearly three-quarters of the land in the field had been sold at least once since the time of the grant. Note also that only one man was an original grantee in both the East Field and the West Field: William Hughes.

THE PLAIN

At the time of the inventory twelve men held land in The Plain, in fourteen parcels. These parcels totalled 95½ acres. The usual rearrangement of these entries produces the following list of original grants:

John Upham	14
Richard Silvester	11
John Glover	8
Robert Abell	6
Richard Long	6
Thomas Applegate	5
Edward Poole	5
Musachiell Bernard	3½
George Allin	3
Thomas Baylie	3
Stephen French	3
William Fry	3
Thomas Holbrook	3
Henry Kingman	3
Robert Lovell	3
William Newland	3
William Smith	3
Arthur Warren	3
John Whitmarsh	3
William Richards	2
John Rogers	2

Clearly the standard grant size in this field was three acres, with more than half of the grants being of that size. Other possible standard grant sizes were two, five and six acres. (The three largest grants in this list are suspect, as in each case there is a defect in the inventory entry, either a failure to state clearly the name of the original grantee(s) or a failure to allocate precisely the original acreage of each grantee.)

As with the East Field, there were more original grantees (21) than there were landholders in 1643 (12), although the patterns of consolidation are somewhat different. As one interesting example, Musachiell Bernard was granted three and a half acres, all of which he alienated, but during the same period he acquired two parcels totalling nine acres from other original grantees. First the land granted to Bernard. In the 1643 inventory John Fussell held twelve and a half acres which he had gathered from four original grantees, only half an acre of which was from "Mr. Bernard." John Staple had amassed six acres, three from "Mr. Bernard" and three from Henry Kingman. From the description of the group of parcels collected by John Fussell, it would appear that the two parcels disposed of by Musachiell Bernard were originally a single lot. On the other hand, Bernard purchased six acres from Richard Long and three acres from Thomas Baylie. Although these two parcels seem not to have abutted one another, they both were bounded by land of Arthur Warren and John Fussell, indicating that they were in the same part of The Plain. Also, given the adjacency to John Fussell, these two pieces of land may not have been far from the land in the same field originally granted to Musachiell Bernard.

As we noted above, the number of acres given in our list of original grantees for John Upham is suspect. The fourteen acres is made up from two parcels. In 1643 Edward Bate held "eight acres upon the plain, three acres of it first given to John Upham, 3 acres to William Frie, two acres to John Whitmarsh." Enoch Hunt held "twenty-two acres in the plain twenty acres of upland and two acres of salt marsh first given to Richard Silvester and John Upham." It is this second item that is problematic, as the entry does not tell us how much of the original grant was to Richard Silvester and how much to John Upham. These two pieces of The Plain were not adjacent to one another. It may be, then, that the three acres acquired by Edward Bate was a standard three-acre dividend to John Upham, and the indeterminate amount of land that Upham held that was acquired by Enoch Hunt was a separate grant of some sort.

Two of the entries in the 1643 inventory do not tell us who the original grantee was, the eight acres held by John Glover and the five acres held by Edward Polle. Leaving these two parcels aside, not one of the grantees in The Plain continued to hold their original grants.

HARRIS'S RANGE

Nine men held eleven parcels of land in Harris's Range, for a total of 51 acres. This field was apparently named for Walter Harris, who arrived in New England in 1637 [Coldham 185]. We obtain the usual list of original grantees:

John Whitman	11
Walter Harris	8
Jeffrey Staple	6
Musachiell Bernard	5
Henry Kingman	4
Robert Martin	4
William Newland	4
Mr. Joseph Hull	3
John Butterworth	2
Samuel Butterworth	2
John Upham	2

Compared to the other fields we have studied above, there was relatively little turnover of parcels in Harris's Range. Four lots (including the three largest) comprising 27 acres, more than half the total, did not change hands between the date of the grants and the date of the inventory. Most of the lots that did change hands were transferred in their entirety. All of this stability may be one of the reasons there were no lots with fractional acres. If Harris's Range was named for Walter Harris, and if the grants in this field were not made until after his arrival, then there may not have been as much time for the trading of land as there had been in some of the other fields.

Musachiell Bernard again demands special attention. He was granted five acres in Harris's Range, but had disposed of all five acres by the time of the inventory. Two acres went to John Burge and three acres to Richard Webb, the latter combining these three acres with two more acres granted to John Butterworth. Within the timeframe of our study Bernard was the only man to subdivide his lot in Harris's Range.

WESTERN NECK

The Western Neck is the largest of the fields we have analyzed to this point, with seventeen men holding nineteen parcels totalling 211½ acres. The original grantees were:

William Smith	21
John Whitmarsh	21
John Bursley	19½
Joseph Hull	17½
Angel Hollard	17
William Reade	17
Richard Adams	16
Edward Bennett	14
Richard Silvester	14
Thomas White	14
John Upham	12
George Allin	8
Samuel Butterworth	6
John Whitman	4½
Thomas Baylie	4
John Barstow	3
Richard Porter	3

We note first that in none of the other fields studied so far were there as many grants in the fifteen to twenty acre range. The total acreage in the East Field was almost as great as in the Western Neck, but the East Field was divided into a greater number of smaller parcels.

The Western Neck had a number of interesting features. Apparently this field consisted of a mix of upland and meadow. For example, there is an entry in the inventory for Thomas Rawlins for "one acre of salt marsh in the Westerneck," a formulation that suggests that this acre of marsh was in amongst the lands granted in the Western Neck, but not considered an integral part of that grouping of grants. This feature is further supported by the presence of some Western

Neck grants that are mostly bounded by wetlands, rather than by other other Western Neck grants. Robert Martin held "twelve acres and half in the Westerneck first given to Mr. Joseph Hull bounded on the north with the sea, the land of William Richards on the south, the salt marshes on the east and west."

On the other hand, there were large sections of this field that were totally upland. As a result we may piece together several of the grants to recover much of the original layout of the field. We begin with William Smith, who held "eighteen acres in the Westerneck first given to himself, the commons on the east and west, the land of John Tomson and Thomas Holbrook on the north, the land of Richard Adams on the south." There are no entries in the inventory for Tomson and Holbrook, nor are they identified as original grantees in the Western Neck, so the land to the north of William Smith may have been part of another field. To the south was Richard Adams, who held "fourteen acres on the Westerneck first granted to him, bound on the east with the land of Edward Smith, on the west with the land of William Smith, on the north with a swamp, on the south with the commons." (As Adams is south of William Smith, but William Smith is west of Adams, we assume that this sequence of lots was actually aligned on a northwest-southeast axis. This flexibility in the use of the principal points of the compass is often seen in the early New England town land inventories.)

To the south (or southeast) of Richard Adams was Edward Smith, who was credited with "ten acres and half in the Westerneck, eight acres and half first given to William Reade and two acres first given to Richard Addames, bounded on the east and west with the common, on the north with the land of Richard Addames, on the south with the land of William Reade." Next comes the lot of William Reade, "eight acres and half in the Westerneck, the land of Richard Silvester on the east, of Edward Smith on the west, the highway that leadeth to Silvestere's on the north, the commons on the south." From the descriptions of the lots held by Richard Adams, Edward Smith and William Smith we conclude that Richard Adams was granted sixteen acres and William Reade seventeen and that these two parcels were originally adjacent to one another. At some point prior to the creation of the inventory, Edward Smith purchased two acres from the south end of the lot of Richard Adams and eight and a half acres from the north end of the lot of William Reade, thus carving out for himself a lot of ten and a half acres between Adams and Reade.

Proceeding in this manner, we may string together three more lots to the south. Next is the twenty-six acre parcel held by Richard Silvester, followed by nine acres of John Rogers and twenty-two acres of Edward Bennett. These seven parcels, totalling 108 acres, were all bounded east and west with common or highway, making this largest part of the Western Neck a long tongue of large parcels of upland.

(to be continued)

RECENT LITERATURE

R. Andrew Pierce, "Joseph[2] Daggett of Martha's Vineyard, His Native American Wife, and Their Descendants," *The New England Historical and Genealogical Register* 161 (2007):5-21. Although there are many documented cases of illicit liaisons between European men and Native American women in seventeenth-century New England, there may be only one such union that was accepted by contemporary society, that between Joseph Daggett of Martha's Vineyard and a sister of Puttuspaquin, a local sachem. Pierce examines this couple in detail, along with the second consort of Joseph Daggett.

Ernest H. Helliwell, III, "Was Mary, Wife of Nathaniel Barker, A Daughter of George[1] Kilbourne of Rowley, Massachusetts?" *The New England Historical and Genealogical Register* 161 (2007):22-26. Helliwell presents a detailed argument, based on indirect evidence, that the wife of Nathaniel Barker, son of James Barker, immigrant to Rowley by 1640, was a daughter of George Kilbourne, who had settled in the same town by 1639. The author surveyed all known available women of the right age, from whom Mary Kilbourne emerged as best candidate. He then examined chronological and onomastic evidence and the significance of James Barker referring to George Kilbourne as "brother."

Marshall K. Kirk, "A Probable Royal Descent for Thomas Bradbury of Salisbury, Massachusetts," *The New England Historical and Genealogical Register* 161 (2007):27-36. Many royal descents have been proposed over the years for Thomas Bradbury, but none have withstood critical examination. The late Marshall Kirk worked on this problem, and here proposes a different path to royalty, running through the immigrant's mother, Elizabeth Whitgift. Kirk identifies her paternal grandmother as a daughter of William and Katherine (Fulnetby) Dynewell, which connects with a known line from Edward I.

Deborah Kimball Nowers, "Osmund[1] Trask and His Children of Salem and Beverly, Massachusetts," *The New England Historical and Genealogical Register* 161 (2007):47-61. Nowers compiled a careful account of the life and family of Osmund Trask, who had settled in Salem by 1649. There are also separate treatments of each of the five sons of the immigrant who left issue. Osmund Trask is not known to be related to William Trask, an earlier immigrant to Salem [GMB 3:1834-37], although the two men may have been from the same English parish, East Coker in Somerset.

Nathaniel Lane Taylor, "Genealogist John Farmer Discovers His Ancestry: The Warwickshire Family of Edward[1] Farmer, Isabel[1] (Farmer) (Wyman) (Blood) Green, and Thomas[1] Pollard, of Billerica, Massachusetts," *The New England Historical and Genealogical Register* 161 (2007):62-72. In this second installment of his Farmer investigations, Taylor presents correspondence that John Farmer received from an English cousin, and examines some of the claims made in that correspondence.

Robert Leigh Ward, "The Whitney Lineage of John[1] Whitney of Watertown, Massachusetts," *The American Genealogist* 81 (2006):249-62. Ward reexamines the long-contested agnate ancestry of John Whitney of Watertown, focussing on the paternity of the immigrant's father. Accepting Thomas Whitney as the father of the immigrant and, in agreement with other recent scholars, rejecting Sir Robert Whitney of Whitney, Hereford, as the grandfather of this Thomas, the author looks carefully at various pedigrees of the family, extracting what they all agree upon. The result is the emergence of Robert Whitney of Castleton, Hereford, as the likely father of Thomas. Ward then studied all the children of this Robert, at the end of which he concluded that this Robert was the father of Thomas and the grandfather of John Whitney, the immigrant.

Eugene Cole Zubrinsky, "The Immigration and Early Whereabouts in America of Thomas[1] Stanton of Connecticut," *The American Genealogist* 81 (2006):263-73. The author challenges the standard accounts of Thomas Stanton of Connecticut (well known for his employment as an Indian interpreter), which make him the same as a passenger of that name to Virginia in 1635. He first shows that there was a Thomas Stanton in Virginia in the years after 1635, who would have a better claim to be the passenger to Virginia than would the Connecticut man. Zubrinsky then examines the life of the New England settler in detail, demonstrating his early residence at Hartford and his activities at Saybrook, and also showing that the proposed early records for Thomas Stanton in Massachusetts Bay actually pertain to Israel Stoughton of Dorchester. Finally, he explores the early association of Stanton with other Great Migration immigrants, such as John Oldham and Richard Lord, suggesting the possibility that as a single young man, Stanton had resided for a time in Watertown or Cambridge.

Kathleen Canney Barber and Janet Ireland Delorey, "William[1] Varney of Ipswich and Gloucester, Massachusetts," *The American Genealogist* 81 (2006):316-21. The authors conclude their study of William Varney of Ipswich and Gloucester, in this installment treating the immigrant's two sons, Humphrey and Thomas Varney.

(continued from page 10)
Mr. W[illia]m Davis appearing in Court 14 May 1663 deposed that these five pages contain a true inventory of the estate of the late Mr. W[illia]m Paddy that is come to his knowledge, that when he knows more he will discover the same [SPR 4:199].

What is intended here by the word "discover" is that the executor or administrator of the estate, if he learns of more belongings of the deceased, will inform the court of what he learns, will reveal to the court his new knowledge. This older meaning is closer to the etymology of the word, in the sense that the "discoverer" will lift the "cover" from the new knowledge and reveal it to others.

The word "discover" was also used in situations closer to the modern meaning. The group of men who eventually settled the town of Dedham, after obtaining the patent for their new town, held meetings in Watertown during late 1636 and early 1637, prior to their removal to Dedham. At the first meeting held in Dedham, on 23 March 1636/7, the town

> granted unto Samuell Morse & Edward Alleyn one small parcel of meadow lying next above & near unto the former meadow so granted & as the same doth in consideration of their like pains taken in discovery of that side of our town [DeTR 1:29]

The sense of the word here is closer to what we would now call exploration, but still not the modern meaning.

COUNTRYMAN: "1. a man who lives in the country; rustic. 2. a man of one's own country; compatriot"

On 16 April 1659, "An Sawars" testified

> that as she came along the street in Newbury with her masters kinsman Thomas Fowlar and one called John Johnson when they came against Anthony Morse his house the said Thomas Fowlar said he would go in and see his countryman [EQC 2:155].

Anthony Morse and Thomas Fowler were both from Marlborough, Wiltshire, in old England. "Countryman" here means something narrower than that they were just Englishmen. The *OED* notes that before the word "country" gained its modern association with a nation-state, it often referred to a smaller region, such as a county, and that fits the quoted item above much better.

When reading documents of the seventeenth century, or of any time period earlier than our own, we must always be sensitive to these drifts in semantic range. Failing to do so can lead to misunderstandings that could prevent us from making important genealogical discoveries.

Great Migration Newsletter

| Vol. 16 | July–September 2007 | No. 3 |

GREAT MIGRATION TOUR 2008:
ESSEX AND HERTFORDSHIRE

We are pleased to announce the first Great Migration Tour to England. This event will run from Tuesday, 5 August 2008, until Friday, 15 August 2008. The tour will be based at The County Hotel in Chelmsford, and from this location we will visit a number of locations in Essex and Hertfordshire associated with families who migrated to New England in 1631, 1632 and 1633 as a reaction to the ecclesiastical policies of William Laud, at that time Bishop of London.

We will be traveling each day by coach, with most of our walking limited to strolling around town and city centers. Perhaps the greatest demands in this area will be on our day in Cambridge, but the amount of walking you do there is at your discretion. There will be two optional walks of under two miles each, but on both of these occasions the coach will be available as well to get you from point to point.

The tour will provide breakfast on all days, and both lunch and dinner on 5 August (the assembly day) and on 14 August (the final full day). For eight days, from 6 through 13 August the tour will provide either lunch or dinner, but not both. On those days when you will be on your own for lunch, we will be in towns or cities with multiple options for a meal. On those evenings when you will be on your own for dinner, there are many restaurants in Chelmsford within easy walking distance from the hotel, some just across the street and some a walk of about fifteen minutes away.

Although you may make your way to Chelmsford by any path you like, the main gathering point will be at Heathrow Airport on Tuesday, August 5, at 10:30 in the morning. In order to give you a day to recover from jet lag and to make the assembly process more efficient, we recommend that you plan to arrive in England on August 4th and spend that night in the Heathrow area. At the end of the tour, we will depart Chelmsford at 9 on Friday morning, August 15, arriving at Heathrow about 11.

The aim of this first Great Migration Tour is to give you a detailed view of a critical, transitional moment in the Great Migration. The period from 1628 to about 1633 comprises what may be called the Winthrop Migration, in which the immigration process was organized on a top-down basis,

with leading men like John Winthrop and Richard Saltonstall, acting on behalf of the Massachusetts Bay Company, organizing the migration process. They bought or hired the passenger vessels, they gathered the provisions, and they recruited the passengers, including the ministers. The years from 1634 to 1640, on the other hand, may be called the Laudian Migration, during which the migration process was "organized" from the bottom up. Reacting to the Puritan-hunting policies of William Laud, Archbishop of Canterbury, charismatic Puritan ministers decided that they could no longer follow their consciences in old England, and chose to make the move to New England. They were preceded, accompanied or followed by their most ardent adherents, creating what Roger Thompson has called "Clerical Companies" [Roger Thompson, *Mobility & Migration: East Anglian Founders of New England, 1629-1640* (Amherst, Massachusetts, 1994), 186-89].

Before he was elevated to the post of Archbishop of Canterbury, William Laud was Bishop of London from 1628 to 1633. The entire county of Essex was within the Diocese of London, and so Laud began to institute his policies on that smaller stage. Essex had been for decades a hotbed of Puritanism. Among the ministers active in Essex from the 1620s were Thomas Hooker, John Eliot, Thomas Weld and Roger Williams, all of whom came to New England in 1631, 1632 or 1633, accompanied by many other families.

Thus, these first few years of the 1630s in Essex may be viewed as a transitional period from the Winthrop Migration to the Laudian Migration. In the end, more than three-quarters of the English immigrants to New England from 1620 to 1640 were part of the Laudian Migration. By looking closely at Essex in the early 1630s, we will acquire an excellent understanding of the conditions in England that led to the decisions by our ancestors to make the transatlantic crossing.

A typical day for the tour will be Thursday, 7 August, the second full day of the tour. In the morning we will focus on the life of Rev. John Eliot, who came to New England in 1631 and became minister at Roxbury, Massachusetts.

First, we will visit the parish church at Nazeing, Essex, where John Eliot lived as a boy. When Eliot decided to sail for New England, several Nazeing families went with him, or followed in his path over the next few years, among them the families of Giles Payson, Edward Payson, Edward Riggs and George Holmes. In later years, John Eliot referred to these families as "the Nazeing Christians."

The church sits on a prominence, overlooking the valley of the River Lea. The church dates from the twelfth century, at which time it was located at the center of settlement. More recently, the section of the parish about a mile to the west, along the river, has become heavily populated, and the church is now relatively isolated.

Second, we will continue on across the River Lea, to Widford in Hertfordshire, where John Eliot and most of his siblings were born and baptized. The interior of the church has many unusual features. Unlike most churches, the nave (the main part of the church) was built first, probably in the middle of the thirteenth century. The chancel, where the altar is located, was built within the next fifty years.

Very soon after the construction of the chancel, the walls were decorated with paintings depicting various religious scenes. These were painted over during the iconoclastic activities of the early years of the English Reformation. Fragments of some of these paintings have been more recently uncovered <*www.paintedchurch.org/widford.htm*>, and later in the tour we will be able to compare this art with medieval paintings we will see in other churches.

Robert Charles Anderson, FASG   Editor

Jean Powers, Production Assistant

The Great Migration Newsletter is published quarterly by the Great Migration Study Project, a project of the New England Historic Genealogical Society, 101 Newbury Street,

Boston MA 02116

www.NewEnglandAncestors.org

www.GreatMigration.org

GreatMigration@nehgs.org

Of further interest, the churchyard cemetery has expanded to the point that there are large sections on both sides of the road into the village of Widford. There are, therefore, two lychgates, one leading into each of the separate sections of the cemetery. In addition to providing access to a cemetery, a lychgate usually contains a bench, large enough to provide a resting place for the coffin on its way from the church to the cemetery.

Once we are done at Widford, we will penetrate further into Hertfordshire to spend the afternoon at Hatfield House and Hatfield Gardens. For further details on this part of the day, see the article on Gardens and Mazes on the last page of this issue.

On Friday, 8 August, we will make our longest excursion to the north, to the university town of Cambridge. Upon arrival we will embark upon a guided tour of the colleges, with emphasis on Emmanuel College. This college was established by Sir Walter Mildmay, an ardent Puritan. Samuel Eliot Morison identified 130 Great Migration immigrants with college degrees, of whom 100 were Cambridge men. Of those, more than a third had their degrees from Emmanuel. Of the four Essex ministers we are concentrating on, Thomas Hooker was an Emmanuel graduate. This was also the college of John Harvard [Samuel Eliot Morison, *The Founding of Harvard College* (Cambridge 1935), 359-410].

After the tour you will be on your own for lunch, and you may then spend the early afternoon exploring the city, visiting other colleges as well as the many small churches and large bookstores. We will also lead a pilgrimage to the pub frequented by Watson and Crick in the early 1950s when they were unraveling the structure of DNA, certainly unaware of the future contribution they would be making to genealogists.

In the middle of the tour will be two consecutive days that will be organized differently. On Sunday, August 10, we will delay our departure from Chelmsford until mid-morning, and then travel to London. The sites we will visit in London will provide a counterpoint to the heavy doses of Puritanism which we meet with on all other days.

Our first stop will be at Fulham Palace, on the Thames in the western part of London. Fulham Palace was the residence of the Bishop of London, and so would have been the official headquarters for William Laud from 1628 to 1633, during the years that he was attempting to suppress Puritanism in his diocese.

Once we get to Fulham Palace, you will be on your own for a light lunch in the museum cafeteria. After this we will have a guided tour of the museum and the gardens on the palace grounds. Fulham Palace and its grounds have just undergone a complete restoration and should provide an excellent experience.

We will then cross to the south side of the Thames, for an early dinner at Shakespeare's Globe Theatre. After dinner we will attend an evening performance. The Globe Theatre puts on plays by both Shakespeare and by modern writers. The schedule for 2008 will not be available until next spring, but Sunday evening shows are usually Shakespeare plays <www.shakespeares-globe.org>. Whatever play we happen to see, we will be reminded that our Puritan ancestors were opposed to the whole idea of live theatre, and that during their ascendancy in the 1640s and 1650s they closed down the theatres.

Having attended an evening performance in London, we will get back to Chelmsford late in the evening, and, as a result, the following day, Monday, 11 August, will be a slow and quiet day. Several optional activities are available, and you will be able to plan your own day.

Coming as it will just past the midpoint of the tour, you may decide simply to sleep in and spend the day recharging your batteries. The hotel is quite close to the center of town, just a ten-minute walk to the pedestrian mall with shops and cafes of all varieties.

Until 1914 the county of Essex was part of the Diocese of London, and prior to that date the church at Chelmsford was of a size typical for a large market town, very much like the church building we will see later in the tour at Saffron Walden. When the Diocese of Chelmsford was established in 1914, comprising the county of Essex and some sections of East London, Chelmsford church became a cathedral. As a result, the structure is not as imposing as more traditional diocesan cathedrals, such as those at Exeter or Norwich. There are, however, a number of features of interest to us, including a memorial to Rev. Thomas Hooker and a monument to the Mildmays, one of the leading Puritan gentry families. You may visit the cathedral at any time during the day. We will offer a brief walking tour to the cathedral in the late morning.

Another option you may choose on this Monday would be to undertake some genealogical research at the Essex Record Office [ERO] <www.essexcc.gov.uk/ero>. The ERO is located in a modern, spacious building about a mile from our hotel. This record office has the originals or microfilm of Essex parish registers, the original wills for the county, and may other valuable sources. There are abundant separate workstations for microfilm, microfiche and manuscript materials, and about seventy-five computer terminals. On Monday, the ERO is open from nine in the morning until half past eight in the evening. Upon arrival you will be required to obtain a reader's ticket (which provides access to county record offices throughout England), but no reservations or other prior arrangements are needed.

About noon, those who are looking for a little exercise may join in a walk from the hotel to the neighboring village of Writtle. A five-minute walk will bring us to a municipal park. About halfway through the park we will strike out on a public footpath through fields and pastures, which will eventually bring us out at the east end of Writtle. The walk will

take about three-quarters of an hour, over level ground. For those who do not wish to make the walk, but who would like to join us at Writtle, the coach will be available for transportation. At the end of our time at Writtle, you will have the option of walking back or taking the coach.

The village green at Writtle is one of the most beautiful in Essex, with some remarkable Tudor houses among the surrounding buildings. You will be on your own for lunch in one of the many pubs and restaurants surrounding the green, after which we will visit the church.

Writtle was for several generations the home of the Pynchon family and John Pynchon, father of William Pynchon, settler at Roxbury and founder of Springfield, was born there. Toward the end of the sixteenth century John Pynchon moved to Springfield, Essex, on the other side of Chelmsford, and William was born there. The Writtle church contains an impressive monument to Sir Edward Writtle, William's first cousin, from the senior branch of the family. Interestingly, there were a number of marriages between members of the Pynchon family and residents of Terling, Essex, which is also on our tour.

In the evening we will take the coach to Pontlands Park Hotel in Great Baddow, a suburb of Chelmsford, where we will have dinner. The hotel was converted from an impressive Victorian estate, set in well-manicured grounds, which we will have an opportunity to explore before sitting down to our meal <www.pontlandsparkhotel.co.uk>.

On the following day, Tuesday, 12 August, we will resume our usual daily schedule and motor north to the market town of Saffron Walden, in the northwest corner of the county. As was typical for the towns which were commercially prosperous in the late medieval period, the Saffron Walden church is a large and beautiful structure, more impressive in many ways than the structure that became Chelmsford Cathedral. We will begin our time in Saffron Walden with a visit to this church.

The participation of several of the congregation at Saffron Walden in this transitional period of the Great Migration remains something of a mystery. At least four families from this parish had settled in New England by 1633: Samuel Bass and Thomas Pidge in Roxbury, George Minot in Dorchester and Cotton Flack in Boston. The timing of this mini-migration and the residence of two of these four families in Roxbury suggest that these families were stimulated to migrate by some of the same forces that drove Hooker, Eliot, Weld and Williams and their adherents. There were, however, no known connections between Saffron Walden and these four ministers. We hope to have solved this mystery by the time of the tour.

Once we have visited the church, you will have a wide range of other places to visit. On our approach to Saffron Walden, we will have passed by a large open public park, which contains a medieval turf maze. This is an easy walk from the town center, and will take only a few minutes to negotiate.

Adjacent to the church are the Bridge End Gardens, actually a collection of seven gardens, built about 1840 by a family of Quaker merchants <*www.bridgeendgarden.org*>. There is no admission for this recently renovated site, which includes a walled herb garden and a rose garden among its seven sections. There is also a tall hedge maze, at the center of which is an even taller observation platform from which you can examine the construction of the maze and hurl insults at your friends who are still lost in the maze.

Also near the church are the Saffron Walden Museum and the remains of Walden Castle. No admission fee is required to wander the castle grounds and examine the massive remains of the keep. Admission to the museum is one pound. There are exhibits on a wide range of events in the history of Saffron Walden and vicinity. Perhaps the most interesting is a section on the cultivation and uses of saffron, the crop that made the town prosperous and that became a part of the town's name.

Tuesday is market day in Saffron Walden, so the town will be bustling. Between the church and the market square are several streets lined along their whole length by small Tudor buildings with boutiques and antique shops on the ground floor. You will be on your own for lunch while in Saffron Walden.

We will depart Saffron Walden in mid-afternoon and stop along the way at the village of Finchingfield. This village has a town green at least as beautiful as that of Writtle, and somewhat larger. There are many connections between this parish and the United States, largely because of the presence of the Wethersfield Airfield, which was active during World War II and then was reactivated during the Cold War as the home of an American fighter squadron.

We will visit the parish church, which includes a modern plaque commemorating the migration of Daniel Shedd to New England in the 1640s. The west face of the church tower has a beautiful and well-preserved Norman door. In a very unusual feature, the main approach to the church is by way of an arched passageway through the guildhall.

We will then have time to wander about the green, which has a number of small shops. We will also have a proper English tea at the Causeway Tea Cottage, overlooking the green.

The final day of the tour we expect to be a special treat. We will first make a brief stop at the church at Sandon, a parish not far from Pontlands Park and Great Baddow, to admire the architecture. We will then motor a short distance to the north and spend the day at Little Baddow, where Hooker and Eliot operated their school in the early 1630s.

We will be hosted by the Little Baddow History Centre, which is attached to the Restoration-era nonconformist chapel that claims continuity with the Puritan congregation of the time of Hooker and Eliot. Cuckoos Farm, the actual location of the school, is just across the road, and the current owners will welcome us into this building. Less than a quar-

ter of a mile away is the old parish church, which is surrounded by an award-winning garden. We will be treated to lunch by the History Centre.

Our attention will not be limited to the fascinating physical locations we will be visiting. An important part of the tour will be the elaboration of the convoluted relations among the immigrants before they departed for New England, both kinship relations and the interactions of Puritan ministers across all of England.

On the first full day of the tour, Wednesday, 6 August, we will spend the day at Braintree, where Rev. Thomas Hooker preached in the late 1620s. Although he was never instituted to the living at Braintree, many families from that parish came to New England in the early 1630s, many settling in Cambridge and then following Hooker to Hartford in 1635 and 1636.

The vicar at Braintree from 1611 until his death in 1657 was Rev. Samuel Collins, a man of tepid Puritan inclinations, who clearly tolerated Hooker's presence as a lecturer but later cooperated with Archbishop Laud in pursuing other Puritans [Bernard Davies, *Samuel Collins of Braintree: A Seventeenth Century Essex Vicar* [Braintree 1997]. At least one nephew and three nieces of Samuel Collins migrated to New England [NEHGR 89:73-79, 148-51; TAG 23:149-53].

John Collins, elder half-brother of Samuel, had a son Edward who was living at Cambridge by 1636 and a daughter Phebe, who married John Russell and settled in Cambridge by 1635. Abigail Collins, elder half-sister of Samuel, married Samuel Bedle of Wolverston, Suffolk. This couple had at least seven children, the youngest of whom were Dorothy Bedle, who married John Bowles, residents of Roxbury by 1639, and Abigail Bedle, who married Michael Powell, who had settled in Dedham by 1639.

While there were many more families from or connected to Braintree and the adjoining parish of Bocking who came to New England, this little cluster is typical of what we will encounter throughout the tour.

A different sort of connection may be found at Terling. As we have seen, the main interest of this parish is the presence there for several years of Rev. Thomas Weld, early minister at Roxbury, and of several immigrant families associated with him.

William Coddington, an immigrant from Boston, Lincolnshire, and therefore a parishioner of Rev. John Cotton, came to New England and settled in Boston in 1630. His first wife died at Boston during the family's first winter in New England, and Coddington returned to old England in 1631, in search of a wife. He was successful in his quest, and for many years the name of this second wife, Mary Moseley, had been known, but the date and place of this marriage were unknown.

In the research for the first series of Great Migration volumes, while studying Thomas Weld and others from Terling, the marriage record for John [*sic*] Coddington and Mary Moseley on 2 September 1631 at Terling was found [GMB 1:395-401]. All of the circumstances lead to the conclusion that this was actually the marriage for William Coddington. But what was he doing at Terling, many miles from Boston, Lincolnshire? There may have been other, as yet unrevealed family connections. But in late 1631 John Cotton and Thomas Weld were still in old England, and this marriage may have resulted somehow from this ministerial connection.

What should you expect to get from the tour experience? Most immediately, you will learn about a small but very important part of the overall Great Migration experience. You will see many details of the physical setting in which were born and raised those immigrants who, in the early 1630s, came to New England from southwestern Essex and neighboring parts of Hertfordshire. You will encounter their churches and villages, their fields and pastures.

Beyond this, you should gain information on two broader aspects of the Great Migration. First, you will learn not just about the physical environment of the immigrants, but also of their economic and social status, and how this affected their decision to migrate (or, for most Englishmen of the time, not to migrate).

Second, because the period we will be examining was the beginning of the Laudian Migration, you will be able to apply much of this knowledge and experience to the Great Migration immigrants of later years and from all parts of England, whether Lincolnshire or Somerset, Buckinghamshire or Dorset.

RECOMMENDED READING

As the date of the tour approaches, we will post on the Great Migration website further details on the tour, with suggestions for books, articles and other websites that might be of interest. There are a few books that are of critical importance for the overall theme of the tour, and we recommend that you read at least one of the following.

Keith Wrightson and David Levine, *Poverty and Piety in an English Village: Terling, 1525-1700*, second edition [Oxford 1995]. This study was originally published in 1979, as part of the new social history, which emphasized close examination of parish registers, wills, and other local records, and employed the technique of "family reconstitution," a polite academic way of avoiding the word genealogy. The authors had no special interest in Rev. Thomas Weld or his migration to New England, but they have provided excellent insight into the background of migration in the 1630s.

An important part of the presentation is an analysis of the social and economic structure of the village. There were five manors in Terling, and most of the residents were tied to the manors and engaged in mixed husbandry. The authors distinguish four strata in the society: gentry, yeomen, husbandmen and laborers. For our purposes, the important distinction is that between yeomen and husbandmen (a distinction not maintained in New England). Husbandmen generally held fifty acres or less, and were usually able to grow enough only for their own subsistence. Yeomen held a hundred acres or more, and generated an annual surplus which they could convert into various forms of personal wealth. Somewhere between fifty and a hundred acres was the dividing point between subsistence and surplus.

Although not discussed by the authors, most of the immigrants to New England were from the yeomen class, or were craftsmen of a similar economic level, and this was true of the migrants to New England from all parts of England. This circumstance is an important element in the argument that migration to New England was principally motivated by religious reasons, and not because of economic stress.

Tom Webster, *Godly Clergy in Early Stuart England: The Caroline Puritan Movement, c.1620-1643* [Cambridge 1997]. Although intended as a study of Puritan ministers throughout England, the author draws almost all his examples from Essex ministers. The very first sentence of Chapter One tells us that from "28 to 30 December 1625, a fast was held at Hatfield Broad Oak in Essex, the home of the Barrington family." We are then told that at the "Hatfield Broad Oak fast it seems likely that discussions were held regarding the settlement of Thomas Hooker in a preaching post in Essex."

On Saturday, August 9, we will visit Hatfield Broad Oak as part of our examination of the life of Roger Williams. Although not at the 1625 fast, he later lived in the nearby parish of High Laver, and during his years there unsuccessfully courted a Barrington daughter.

William Hunt, *The Puritan Moment: The Coming of Revolution in an English County* [Cambridge, Massachusetts, and London 1983]. In the 1980s a number of English historians published county-wide studies of the years leading up to the English Civil War, and this volume examines that period in the county of Essex. Both the political and the religious background are studied, with emphasis on such episodes as the Forced Loan in the 1620s and Ship Money in the 1630s.

RECENT LITERATURE

George Ely Russell, "John[1] Gatchell Family of Marblehead, Massachusetts," *The Genealogist* 21 (2007):3-41. Russell has compiled a detailed account of the immigrant John Gatchell, his sons and grandsons, with additional data on the children and some of the grandchildren of the grandsons. The author includes in his treatment information on the many societal transgressions of this family. A second wife is given for Thomas Gatchell, the youngest son of the immigrant (compare GM 2:3:30).

Leslie Mahler, "An Addition to the English Ancestry of Thomas[1] Olcott of Hartford, Connecticut," *The Genealogist* 21 (2007):41-42. With the help of an entry in the records of the Merchant Taylors' Company, Mahler has identified the paternal grandfather of the immigrant Thomas Olcott of Hartford.

John Anderson Brayton, "Additions to the Ancestry of Sarah (Hawkredd) (Story) (Cotton) Mather of Boston, Lincolnshire," *The Genealogist* 21 (2007):108-28. Sarah (Hawkredd) (Story) (Cotton) Mather came to New England with her second husband, Rev. John Cotton. Her sister, Elizabeth (Hawkredd) (Coney) (Mellows) Makepeace, also came to New England, with her second husband, Oliver Mellows. In this first installment of a multi-part article, Brayton corrects the previously published Hawkredd pedigree, identifying the grandfather of Andrew Hawkredd, correcting the identity of Andrew's wife and properly identifying Andrew's mother. The continuation of this article will have information on the families of the wives of Andrew Hawkredd and his father, William Hawkredd.

William Wyman Fiske, "Ancestry of Bennet Eliot of Nazeing, Essex, Father of Seven Great Migration Immigrants to Massachusetts," *The New England Historical and Genealogical Register* 161 (2007):85-91. In this first installment of a three-part article, Fiske discusses the difficulties in identifying the agnate ancestry of Bennet Eliot, given the size of the Eliot family of Hertfordshire and Essex. He provides abstracts of some relevant wills, and then a manorial record from Much Hadham, Hertfordshire, that identifies the father of Bennet Eliot as Simon Eliot. Future installments will present an extensive Eliot pedigree.

Brandon Fradd, "Abraham Toppan Was Not a Yorkshire Man," *The New England Historical and Genealogical Register* 161 (2007):92-94. Through the careful analysis of a number of wills, Fradd demonstrates that Abraham Toppan of Great Yarmouth, Norfolk, and Newbury, Massachusetts, cannot be the same as the Abraham Toppan supposed to have been baptized at Coverham, Yorkshire, on 10 April

1606, thereby adding to the list of pedigrees invented by Horatio Gates Somerby.

Gail Staples, "The English Origins of Jeffrey Staple of Weymouth, Massachusetts," *The New England Historical and Genealogical Register* 161 (2007):95-100. Jeffrey Staple and his family had settled in Weymouth by 1639. Following up on a single entry in the IGI, the author has found a number of records in the parish register of Wendover, Buckinghamshire, which clearly identify that parish as the English origin of Jeffrey Staple. These records also show that John Staple of Weymouth was son of Jeffrey. Other early New England settlers were from Wendover, including Jonas Humfrey of Dorchester [TAG 68:14-22].

Peter Ray, "The English Ancestry of Thomas Burton of Portsmouth, Rhode Island, Signer of the Remonstrance of 1646," *The New England Historical and Genealogical Register* 161 (2007):101-12. The author presents evidence that Thomas Burton, who was recorded at Portsmouth, Rhode Island, as early as 1638, was baptized at St. Bartholomew Exchange, London, on 26 May 1588, and that he was also the man of that name who signed the Child Remonstrance in 1646. The father and grandfather of the immigrant are also identified.

Don Blauvelt, "Abigail (Lothrop) Huntington's Second Husband, Samuel Baker, of Windsor, Connecticut," *The New England Historical and Genealogical Register* 161 (2007):123-26. Blauvelt demonstrates that Samuel Baker, second husband of Abigail (Lothrop) Huntington, was son of Jeffrey Baker, who had settled in Windsor by 1642, and not son of Rev. Nicholas Baker of Hingham, thus correcting an identification made by other researchers and incorporated into the Great Migration sketch of Nicholas Baker [GM 2:1:143]. Samuel Baker, son of Nicholas, had only one known wife, Fear Robinson, daughter of Isaac Robinson [GMB 3:1593].

Nathaniel Lane Taylor, "Genealogist John Farmer Discovers His Ancestry: The Warwickshire Family of Edward[1] Farmer, Thomas[1] Pollard, and Isabel[1] (Farmer) (Wyman) (Blood) Green, of Billerica, Massachusetts," *The New England Historical and Genealogical Register* 161 (2007):146-55. In this third of five installments, Taylor presents entries from a number of Warwickshire parish registers and will abstracts from the Diocese of Lichfield and Coventry. This evidence points to the identity of the paternal grandfather and great-grandfather of the immigrant Edward Farmer, as well as the wife of the latter. Evidence is also presented for the marriage of an aunt of Edward Farmer.

ITINERARY

Tuesday, 5 August
    Gather tour group at Heathrow Airport
    Bishops Stortford, Hertfordshire, church
    Lunch at Boars Head, Bishops Stortford
    Arrive at Chelmsford and get settled at hotel
    Welcome dinner

Wednesday, 6 August   Thomas Hooker Day
    Braintree church
    Lunch and murals at Town Hall
    Braintree Museum
    Free time in town market

Thursday, 7 August   John Eliot Day
    Nazeing church
    Widford church
    Lunch at Hatfield Gardens
    Hatfield Gardens and Hatfield House Tour

Friday, 8 August   Cambridge Day
    Emmanuel College, Cambridge, tour
    Lunch on your own in Cambridge
    Free time in Cambridge

Saturday, 9 August   Roger Williams Day
    High Laver
    Hatfield Broadoak
    Lunch at The Swan, Thaxted
    Thaxted church and guildhall

Sunday, 10 August   William Laud Day
    Light lunch at Fulham Palace, London
    Fulham Palace tour – museum and garden
    Dinner at Globe Theatre
    Shakespeare performance at Globe Theatre

Monday, 11 August   Chelmsford Day
    Options:
        Research at Essex Record Office
        Visit Chelmsford Cathedral
        Walk to Writtle (Pynchon territory)
        Lunch at Writtle
        Free time in Chelmsford
    Dinner at Pontlands Park

Tuesday, 12 August   Saffron Walden Day
    Saffron Walden church
    Options:
        Turf maze
        Bridge End Gardens
        Walden Castle
        Saffron Walden Museum
    Lunch on your own
    Free time in market and shopping areas
    Tea at Finchingfield

Wednesday, 13 August   Thomas Weld Day
    Terling church
    Fairsted church (medievel wall paintings)
    Lunch at Six Bells, Boreham
    Cressing Temple Barns (13th-century barns with
        17th-century herb garden)

Thursday, 14 August   Hooker and Eliot Day
    Sandon church
    Little Baddow church (& churchyard garden)
    Little Baddow History Centre (lunch)
    Cuckoos Farm
    Farewell dinner

Friday, 15 August
    Depart for Heathrow Airport

GREAT MIGRATION TOUR 2008 REGISTRATION FORM

Name:_____ Address:_____

City:_____ State:_____ Zip:_____

Telephone:_____ E-mail:_____ NEHGS Member #:_____

Cost per participant: $3995 (includes lodging, all breakfasts, and lunch OR dinner each day).
Deposit of $1000 per participant to be submitted with this form. Remainder due June 1, 2008.

☐ My check is enclosed, payable to NEHGS.

Please charge my: ☐ VISA   ☐ MasterCard   ☐ Discover   ☐ American Express

Card #_____ Expiration date:_____

Signature:_____

Cancellation policy: Written cancellations received before February 1, 2008, will be subject to a $300 per person cancellation fee. No refund is possible after this date.

I have read and understand the NEHGS cancellation policy stated above.

Signature: _____ Date: _____

Please mail registration form and payment to NEHGS, Great Migration Study Project, 101 Newbury, Boston, MA 02116.

GARDENS AND MAZES

As we proceed through our tour of sites of historical and genealogical significance, we will also find ourselves in or near a number of formal gardens, several of which have been incorporated into the tour. Many of these gardens include mazes or labyrinths as well.

Perhaps the most spectacular of these are the gardens at Hatfield House in Hertfordshire. On the second full day of the tour, we will drive first to Nazeing, Essex, and then to Widford, Hertfordshire, two parishes central to the lives of Rev. John Eliot, his family, and many of his followers. We will then move on to Hatfield House, where we will first have lunch, and then have the rest of the day to walk through Hatfield House and the adjacent gardens.

Since 1611 Hatfield House has been the home of the Cecil family, Earls and then Marquesses of Salisbury. For the last thirty-five years, the Dowager Marchioness of Salisbury, widow of the sixth Marquess, has been engaged in reviving the many acres of gardens surrounding Hatfield House, returning them to their former glory. Among the many sections in the gardens are a large yew maze and a smaller knot garden <*www.hatfield-house.co.uk*>.

Toward the end of the tour, we will spend most of the day in Saffron Walden, Essex, a market town which supplied a number of early settlers of Roxbury, although there is no known connection with Eliot, Weld, Pynchon, or any of the other founders of that town. Immediately adjacent to Saffron Walden church are Bridge End Gardens, a collection of seven nineteenth-century gardens that are nearing the end of a major restoration <*www.bridgeendgarden.org*>. One of the gardens is a large hedge-maze, at the center of which is an observation platform which you can climb to observe the entirety of the maze and also other members of the tour who have not yet found the center.

We will also see gardens at Fulham Palace in London, Emmanuel College in Cambridge, Cressing Temple Barns and the church at Little Baddow. At Little Baddow, for example, we will see a small plot of about two dozen varieties of flowers and herbs whose names are associated in some way with the Virgin Mary. Some of these sites also have mazes or labyrinths.

Great Migration Newsletter

Vol. 16   October-December 2007   No. 4

PROBLEM PASSENGERS

The survival of ship passenger lists for the Great Migration is wildly uneven, with no lists at all for some years, and nearly complete lists for others, and many years with only partial records. The year for which the most complete lists survive is 1635, and, as this is one of the years being covered by the current series of Great Migration volumes, one might think that the writing of sketches for immigrants arriving in 1635 becomes easier because of the existence of these lists. Paradoxically, the existence of a name on a passenger list often creates unexpected difficulties in writing a sketch. A few examples taken from the most recently published Great Migration volume may make this point more clearly.

John Marshall, aged 14, sailed from London on the *Hopewell*, having been enrolled for passage on 11 September 1635 [Hotten 130; GM 2:5:41]. Savage proposed that this passenger was the John Marshall of Boston with wife Sarah and several children, including one named Christopher [Savage 3:156].

Another Boston settler of about this time was Christopher Marshall, who was certainly in Boston by 1634, although he does not appear on any passenger list [GM 2:5:30-35]. Research on this immigrant demonstrated that he was from Alford, Lincolnshire, the home also of the many early Hutchinson immigrants to New England, including William Hutchinson and his notorious wife Anne.

Inasmuch as John Marshall of Boston had been a servant of Edward Hutchinson and named a son Christopher, the Marshall family of Alford was studied further. A John Marshall was identified in this family who could well have been the settler at Boston. This John Marshall was baptized at West Keal, not far from Alford, on 21 December 1615. This would make him six years older than the 1635 passenger on the *Hopewell*. Ages entered in the London port books are known to be imprecise, but this gap of six years at such a young age looms quite large, and so the decision was made that the 1635 passenger was not likely to be the Boston inhabitant.

A different problem was presented by Thomas Marshall, aged 22, who was enrolled at London on 13 July 1635 as a passenger for New England on the *James* [Hotten 107; GM 2:5:46-47]. There were two men by the name of Thomas

Marshall in early New England who might have been this passenger. One resided in Lynn, then in Reading, and then back in Lynn, and was usually distinguished by his rank of Lieutenant and later Captain. The other resided in Reading, Ipswich and Andover, and was referred to often as carpenter.

Savage and Pope intermingled the records for these two men and more recently other researchers, including Marcia Wiswall Lindberg and Patricia Law Hatcher, have begun the process of disentangling these records [TEG 16:158-68, 231-34; NEHGR 160:293-94].

In the process of preparing the sketch for this passenger of 1635, we looked closely at the evidence for the ages of each of these two Thomas Marshalls. The passenger gave his age as 22, which would place his birth about 1613. On 28 June 1681, Captain Thomas Marshall of Lynn gave his age as "sixty-six years," which would date his birth at 1615. The other Thomas Marshall, then of Reading, gave his age in 1661 as "about 45 years," and so born about 1616. Thus, the estimated dates of birth for these two men were closer to one another than either was to the age of the 1635 passenger. On this basis, we concluded that there was not sufficient evidence to attach the passenger list entry to either of the men of that name with long histories in New England. This is not to say that such an assignment of the 1635 record to one or another of these men might not have been correct, but

(continued on page 26)

EDITOR'S EFFUSIONS

In the lead article for this issue we describe some problems peculiar to the records available for the year 1635, and so applicable only to the current series of Great Migration sketch volumes. As we begin work on the sixth volume of this seven-volume series, our thoughts begin to stray forward to contemplate what may be different about the third series, the commencement of which is only a few years away.

The first step in starting a new Great Migration series is to compile a checklist of the sketches to be covered in the given time period. This task has not yet begun for the third series, but we can make a few comments. For the current, second series, the checklist contains about fifteen hundred names, which will be covered in seven volumes.

We believe that migration to New England continued at about the same pace from 1634 through 1639, with about 2000 to 2500 immigrants per year. If this rate of migration was indeed consistent, we would expect that the years 1636 and 1637 would have delivered about the same number of settlers as had 1634 and 1635. If this turns out to be the case, then the third series will, like the second series, cover a two-year period.

The truth, however, may be different. Perhaps the pace of migration did vary during the middle and late 1630s. And, with fewer passenger lists available for the years after 1635, we may find that there are fewer immigrants that we can confidently assign to these years, even though the same numbers arrived. Learning whether the migration rate is constant or variable in these years is one of the long-range goals of the Great Migration Study Project. We should have a better answer to this question within a year or two, and we will know whether the third series will cover two years or three.

In the last issue of the *Great Migration Newsletter* we announced our first tour to England, to take place in August of 2008. Response to this announcement has been highly gratifying, and at the time of this writing we are nearly sold out, with only a few slots remaining. We look forward to this event with great excitement.

Robert Charles Anderson, FASG   Editor
Jean Powers, Production Assistant

The Great Migration Newsletter is published quarterly by the Great Migration Study Project, a project of the New England Historic Genealogical Society, 101 Newbury Street, Boston MA 02116
www.newenglandancestors.org
www.GreatMigration.org
GreatMigration@nehgs.org

(continued from page 25)

only that we have no way to choose. We are frequently confronted with decisions of this sort, and choose always to take the more conservative position, pending the discovery of further data.

A third example for the same surname is the entry for William Marshall, aged 40, who was enrolled at London on 17 June 1635 as a passenger for New England on the *Abigail* [Hotten 92; GM 2:5:47-48]. Savage proposed that this man was the same as the William Marshall listed by Felt as having had a grant of land at Salem in 1638 [Savage 3:159; Felt 1:169]. Unfortunately for this theory, no such record exists, because Felt had misreported a town land record that actually pertained to Edmund Marshall of Salem. And so there was no appropriate William Marshall in New England to whom the passenger list entry could be attached.

Our fourth and final example provides yet another variation on the theme. On 15 April 1635, Isaac More, aged 13, was enrolled at London as a passenger for New England on the *Increase* [Hotten 65; GM 2:5:137-45]. Entries of this sort, for young men or women, not yet adults but also not obviously part of a family group migrating on the same ship, are a constant source of difficulty. Such a person as Isaac More, who might be a servant to another passenger, or perhaps related to a family on the same ship, perhaps a stepson or a nephew, would in most cases not be expected to appear in New England records for a decade or so after arrival, until he reached adulthood. How do we determine if such a passenger was the same as a man or woman who did appear in New England records in the 1640s?

In the case of Isaac More, fortunately, we have many clues that permit us to make a strong case for the passenger's connection to a later man of the same name. In the passenger list of the *Increase*, Isaac More appears at the end of the listing of the family of Matthew Marvin, and apparently as a part of that household [Hotten 65; GM 2:5:63-71]. We observe that Isaac More is first seen in New England records in 1645, when he married at Hartford; in that year, the 1635 passenger would have been 23 years old. This was the residence at the time of Matthew Marvin. More then resided in Farmington, where Marvin held land, although he does not seem to have been resident there. In 1651 both More and Marvin moved to Norwalk. These parallel migrations of the two men indicate strongly that the 1635 passenger was the same as the Isaac More of Hartford, Farmington and Norwalk.

In many instances, then, the existence of passenger list entries, especially for men and women with common names, creates new challenges in the writing of sketches, and adds an extra level of analysis to our goal of providing the most accurate information available on the Great Migration immigrants.

Focus on WEYMOUTH

In the first installment of this three-part study of early Weymouth landgranting, we looked closely at the divisions of land in five different "fields" of the town [GMN 16:11-14]. In the present installment we examine the grants in several more "fields" of Weymouth. In the third installment, we will summarize the material in the first two parts of the study to see what a standard set of grants of land looked like in this town.

MILL FIELD

In the 1643 inventory of Weymouth landholding, fourteen different landholders were credited with a total of 93 acres. We provide first a few sample entries from this field.

> James Snooke: "Three acres in the mill field the land of Nicholas Norton on the east, of Thomas Clape on the west, a swamp on the south, the mill foot path on the north."

This entry does not state, as most entries do, whether this parcel was granted to James Snooke by the town, or whether he purchased it from someone else. In such circumstances, we assume by default that the land was granted to Snooke by the town.

> Elizabeth and Mary Fry: "Six acres in the mill field first given to William Frie bounded on the east with a little pond, Steephen French on the north, the Mill River on the west."

William Fry had died at Weymouth in 1642, and Elizabeth and Mary were his only two children, born in 1639 and 1641 respectively [Weymouth Hist 3:244].

With the exception of these two parcels, the entries in the land inventory are explicit in stating the original grantee of each parcel of land. The usual rearrangement of these entries produces the following list of original grants:

Edward Bate	12
Arthur Warren	10
Musachiell Bernard	8
John Harding	8
Macuth Pratt	8
John Dunford	6½
William Fry	6
James Nash	6
Thomas Baylie	4
John Gurney	4
Richard Adams	3
Thomas Clap	3

John Hicks	3
Richard Silvester	3
James Snook	3
Richard Walling	3
John Whitmarsh	2½

Thus, there were seventeen grantees of land in this field, whereas by 1643 these same grants were held by only fourteen persons, indicating a moderate consolidation of parcels in the Mill Field. In nine cases, the original grantees or their heirs still held all or part of the original grant.

We also note that with two exceptions (John Dunford and John Whitmarsh), there seems to be a straightforward range of original grants, of 12, 10, 8, 6, 4 and 3 acres.

EASTERN NECK

The Eastern Neck was comprised of a few relatively large plots, totalling 68 acres. The largest plot in this field supplies an unusual clue to the nature of the landgranting process, at least in this section of town:

> William Torrey: "Two shares and half upon the Easter[n] Neck containing by estimation twenty-five acres first given to Mr. John Buslem bounded on the east with the land of Nicholas Phillipes, on the west with the land of James Ludden, on the north with the bay, on the south with the Back River."

This entry implies, for this field at least, that each grantee would receive ten acres for each share. The broader implication might be that the number of shares associated with a given proprietor might be applied in all the fields. Further evidence on this point is needed.

After the usual analysis, the list of original grantees is as follows:

John Bursley	25
George Allen	20
Clement Briggs	10
William Pitty	10
James Smith	3

The last entry may not belong with the rest, based on the following entry:

> Henry Kingman: "Three acres in the Easterneck of salt marsh first given to Mr. Buslem bounded on the north with the bay, on the south with the Back River."

The lot recorded to James Smith may also be a parcel of marsh located in or close to the larger parcels in the Eastern Neck, which would have been upland.

KING OAK HILL

In the 1643 listing of Weymouth land grants, sixteen men held land at King Oak Hill, in seventeen relatively small parcels, totalling 55¾ acres. This field underwent considerable churning, with only about one-third of the parcels still in the hands of the original grantees. An example of this churning may be seen in two separate entries:

Richard Webb: "Two acres in Kingoke Hill first given to Thomas Rawlines bounded on the east with Mr. Parkere's land, on the west the highway, on the north with the land of John Upham, of Phillip Reade's on the south."

Thomas Rawlins: "Two acres in King Oke Hill first given to Aingle Holard bounded on the east with the land of Tho[mas] Rider, on the west with the street, on the north the land of John Upham, Edward Benet's south."

Examination of the descriptions of some of the neighboring plots indicates that for Richard Webb's lot the orientation of the abutters John Upham and Phillip Reade should be switched. If that assessment is correct, we observe that Thomas Rawlins was originally granted two acres on King Oak Hill just to the north of the land granted to John Upham. Then, at some point prior to 1643, he sold this tract to Richard Webb and purchased another lot at King Oak Hill, also of two acres, on the south side of John Upham's grant. These two parcels held successively by Thomas Rawlins would have been only a few hundred yards apart, if that, so it is not immediately obvious why he felt compelled to make the switch.

Sorting this list of land grants according to the original grantee produces the following results:

Robert Lovell	10½
John Whitmarsh	8
Edward Bennett	7
John Upham	7
Thomas Holbrook	6
Angel Hollard	5
John Reade	3
Thomas Rawlins	2
Phillip Reade	2
Richard Webb	1¾
Richard Walling	1½
Richard Adams	1
John Burrell	1

There were only thirteen parcels at the time of the original grants, as opposed to fourteen in 1643. No obvious pattern of grant sizes is detected and here more than elsewhere the number of parcels with fractional acres is puzzling.

GREAT LOTS

The only surviving list of grants made prior to the land inventory of 1643 was that of the Great Lots on 12 [blank] 1636 [Weymouth Hist 1:199], so we do not need to attempt to reconstruct the grants of the Great Lots, as we have tried to do with the other fields. Also, very few of the entries for the Great Lots in the 1643 list state explicitly who the original grantee was. For all these reasons, we will treat this group of land grants differently, by studying each of the original grants in an attempt to match them up with the appropriate entries in the 1643 land inventory. There were sixteen numbered entries in the 1636 division. The discussion below will begin with the grantee and number of acres from the 1636 list, and then the 1643 entry that seems to match. When appropriate, explanatory comments will be added for some lots.

1) Edward Bennett, 18

Macuth Pratt: "Eighteen acres of upland first given to Edward Bennet now in the possession of Mathew [sic] Pratt bounded on the east with the Mill River, on the west with John Whitman's lot, on the north with the mill ground, on the south with the pond."

William Carpenter: "Eighteen acres near the fresh pond, first given to Edward Benet, bounded on the east with the mill river, on the west with the land of Mr. Hull, the mill and [sic] on the north, with the pond on the south."

These two entries clearly refer to the same lot, the Great Lot granted to Edward Bennett. Since the adjoining lot passed from Joseph Hull to John Whitman, and since the entry for William Carpenter names Mr. Hull as the abutter on the west, whereas the entry for Macuth Pratt has John Whitman in this position, it would seem that Edward Bennet's lot passed first to William Carpenter and then to Macuth Pratt.

2) Mr. Joseph Hull, 54

John Whitman: "Sixty acres by the great pond first given to Mr. Hull bounded on the east with the land of William Carpenter, on the west with a swamp and the pond on the south."

3) Henry Kingman, 42

No match found in 1643 land inventory.

In the listing for Samuel Newman, we find "Twenty acres of upland first granted to Henry Kingman bounded on the south a great pond, on the north with John Rande's marsh." Given the reference to the pond, this may be part of Kingman's Great Lot, but the absence of references to the abutters to the east and west leaves this uncertain. If these twenty acres were part of the Great Lot of Henry Kingman, the other 22 acres have not been found in the 1643 list.

4) Mr. Jener, Senior, 18

No match found in 1643 land inventory (but see comments below under Mr. Jener, Junior).

5) Thomas White, 21

Thomas White: "Twenty and one acres amongst the Great Lots given to himself bounded on the east with the land of Thomas Jener Senior, of Thomas Doget on the west, the commons on the north, the pond on the south."

6) William Fry, 12

"The Land of Thomas Doget During the Life of His Wife and Afterward to Elizabeth and Mary Frie the daughters of William Frie Deceased": "Twelve acres amongst the Great Lots bounded on the east with the great pond, on the west with the common, the north with the land of Thomas White, of Robert Lovell on the south."

7) Robert Lovell, 34

Robert Lovell: "Thirty acres in the Great Lots the pond on the east, Thomas Dogete's land on the north, Edmond Harte's on the south."

8) Edmond Hart, 18

Edmond Hart: "Eighteen acres amongst the Great Lots bounded on the east with the great pond, on the west with the common, on the north with the land of Robert Lovell, on the south with the land of Thomas Rawlines."

9) Thomas Rawling, 12

No match found in 1643 land inventory.

10) Mr. Jener, Junior, 45

No match found in 1643 land inventory.

On 28 December 1649, "Thomas Jenner of Charlstowne" sold to "Elder Edw[ard] Bates & John Whitman of Way-mouth" several parcels of land in Weymouth, including "forty acres which is his own proper lot ..., & eighteen acres which was his father's" [SLR 1:111]. This deed clearly transfers the Great Lots of father and son, allowing for the discrepancy in the acreage of the lot of the younger Thomas Jenner.

11) William Reed, 18

William Reade: "Sixteen acres amongst the Great Lots bounded on the east with a great pond, by the commons on the west."

12) Rich[ar]d Silvester, 24

No match found in 1643 land inventory.

13) Rich[ar]d Addomes, 24

Richard Addames: "Twenty-four acres amongst the Great Lots butted on the east with a great pond, on the west with the common, with the lot of Richard Silvester on the north, with the lot of William Smith on the south."

14) William Smith, 30

William Smith: "Thirty acres in the Great Lots the land of Richard Addames on the east, of Steephen French on the west, the common on the north and the great pond on the south."

15) Stephen French, 21

No match found in 1643 land inventory.

The 1643 listing for Stephen French does contain a parcel said to be in the Great Lots, but it does not correspond with this original grant. Note, though, that the Great Lot entries for William Smith and John Upham properly state that Stephen French was an abutter.

16) John Upham, 30

John Upham: "Thirty acres in the Great Lots the pond on the east, the commons on the west, Steephen French on the north."

Before proceeding to a discussion of these records, we need to take note of four entries for parcels described as Great Lots which can not as yet be matched up with the 1636 grants:

Angel Hollard: "Twenty-three acres amongst the Great Lots bounded with the Hing[h]am line on the east and south, the marsh of Mr. Richards on the north, Mr. Richards his lot on the west."

Stephen French: "Fourteen acres in the Great Lots first given to John Upham bounded on the east with Hing[h]am line, on the west to the mill, the land of Robert Lovell on the north, of Thomas Doget south."

Robert Martin: "Twenty and four acres amongst the Great Lots the land of Edward Sale on the north and of William Hughes on the south."

Robert Martin: "Thirty acres in the Great Lots having the land of Arthure Warren on the north and of James Luddon on the south."

Based on the reference to the mill in the Stephen French item, the first two of these items appear to be a portion of some grants made not far from the main grouping of Great Lots. An entry in the listing for Robert Lovell contains a parcel, distinct from his Great Lot, that abuts this lot of Stephen French. These parcels may all be part of, or close to, the Mill Field.

The two parcels held by Robert Martin and designated as Great Lots have no obvious connection with the other lots so designated.

Looking now at the broader picture of the original sixteen Great Lots, we observe that they were laid out in a long string around the Great Pond, beginning at the Mill River and running along the north and west side of the pond. (The descriptions of the parcels begin with the pond to the south, and then as we move down the chain of lots, the pond is usually to the east. As in many of the early New England towns, the drafters of the land descriptions only employed the four cardinal points of the compass, even though the lots might have been aligned on a northwest-southeast axis, for example. This explains those instances when the descriptions of adjacent parcels sometimes employ seemingly inconsistent abutters.)

For eight of the sixteen parcels, eight remain in 1643 in the hands of the original grantees (Thomas White, Thomas Jenner Junior, Robert Lovell, Edmond Hart, William Reade, Richard Adams, William Smith and John Upham) and two more have passed to the children of the original grantees (William Fry to Thomas Doggett [as trustee for the daughters of William Fry] and Thomas Jenner Senior to Thomas Jenner Junior). Two more of the Great Lots have been sold to other Weymouth inhabitants (Edward Bennett to William Carpenter to Macuth Pratt, and Joseph Hull to John Whitman). Although there are minor discrepancies in acreage for four of these twelve lots, all have remained intact. Four of the sixteen Great Lot grants of 1636 cannot be identified in the 1643 inventory (Henry Kingman, Thomas Rawlins, Richard Silvester and Stephen French [although the latter is referred to in the descriptions of the abutting parcels]).

Of great importance to our further analysis of Weymouth land granting, this discussion of the Great Lots tells us that not all the parcels originally granted by the town will necessarily be found in the 1643 inventory. Furthermore, the deed made by Thomas Jenner Junior in 1649, from which we learn that he still possessed his Great Lot in 1643, indicates that,

unlike the practice at Watertown, for example, no entries were included at Weymouth for absentee landholders. These features of the Weymouth land inventory will place some limits on what we can learn about land granting in that town.

OTHER SMALL FIELDS

There are many entries in this inventory which don't identify the field in which the land lay. With close attention to the abutters, many of these parcels could be stitched together into coherent groupings, but this task is beyond the scope of the present article.

There were a number of other named fields which had only a few owners, and in some cases only a single proprietor is associated with a given locality within the town.

Two men held land at a place called Hockley.

Angel Hollard: "Two acres and half of meadow at Hocklie at first granted to Clement Brigges bounded with a creek and Edward Bennete's marsh on the east and Steephen French his lot on the west."

Edward Bennett: "Six acres at Hockley first given to himself bounded on the east with the river, his meadow on the west, the common on the south."

Edward Bennett: "One acre and a quarter of salt marsh at Hocklie bounded with his own land on the east, Aingell Holard on the west, the river on the north, the land of Steephen French on the south."

These three parcels constitute a contiguous unit. Two of the descriptions name Stephen French as an abutter, but none of the entries in his listing seems to match these descriptions.

Finally, we take note of a few entries naming fields which only appear once in the inventory:

Walter Harris: "Eight acres in the mill furlong first given to him the said Walter Harris bounded on the east by the land of Richard Silvester, on the west by the land of Thomas Rider, on the south by the land of Phillip Reade."

Edward Poole: "Two acres at the stepping stone the swamp on the east, the highway on the west, the land of Ralph Shepherd on the north, of Mr. Newman on the south."

William Pitty: "Five acres of land at London Berge [Bridge?] bounded on the east with the sea, the land of Mr. Torrie on the west, of Mr. Waltham on the north and the round marsh on the south."

(to be continued)

RECENT LITERATURE

Allis Ferguson Edelman and Daniel G. Jenkins, "The English Origins of Edward[1] Jenkins of Scituate, Massachusetts," *The New England Historical and Genealogical Register* 161 (2007):165-66. The authors demonstrate that Edward Jenkins, who sailed to New England in 1635 as a servant of Nathaniel Tilden, and who settled at Scituate, was baptized at Bethersden, Kent, on 14 December 1617, son of Edward Jenkins. In the course of this research, they also found the marriage at Bethersden on 13 October 1606 of Nathaniel Tilden and Lydia Huckstep.

William Wyman Fiske, "Ancestry of Bennet Eliot of Nazeing, Essex, Father of Seven Great Migration Immigrants to Massachusetts," *The New England Historical and Genealogical Register* 161 (2007):186-98. In this installment of his study of the family of Bennet Eliot, Fiske resolves a number of discrepancies in the heralds' visitations that covered the family, and also discusses the coats of arms claimed by various branches of the family. He shows distant connections of Bennet Eliot to two other immigrants to America, Governor John Haynes of Connecticut and Colonel William Claiborne of Maryland and Virginia.

Nathaniel Lane Taylor, "Genealogist John Farmer Discovers His Ancestry: The Warwickshire Family of Edward[1] Farmer, Thomas[1] Pollard, and Isabel[1] (Farmer) (Wyman) (Blood) Green, of Billerica, Massachusetts," *The New England Historical and Genealogical Register* 161 (2007):209-22. In this fourth installment of the Farmer article, Taylor presents a compiled genealogical summary of the Farmer family, including three generations of agnate ancestry, later collateral lines down to the nineteenth-century English cousins who corresponded with John Farmer, and an account of the family of Thomas Pollard, who married a sister of the immigrants Edward and Isabel Farmer.

Jonathan Beecher Field, "A Key for the Gate: Roger Williams, Parliament, and Providence," *The New England Quarterly* 80 (2007):353-82. Field argues that Roger Williams composed his study of the language of the Narragansett Indians, and published it in London shortly after his arrival there, as part of his successful diplomatic mission of obtaining a proper charter for the Rhode Island settlements. *A Key into the Language of America* was written to the standards of similar volumes published by or in imitation of the continental scholar John Comenius, who was admired by many of the Puritan Parliamentarians of the early 1640s.

François Weil, "John Farmer and the Making of American Genealogy," *The New England Quarterly* 80 (2007):408-34. The author traces the early development of scholarly geneal-

ogy in the United States, seen from the perspective of John Farmer, the New Hampshire antiquarian. Before considering Farmer himself, Weil first looks at the attitudes towards ancestry in the early Republic, and at the formation of the earliest historical societies in the 1790s and the early eighteenth century. The focus then turns to the activities of Farmer, in promoting the organization of the New Hampshire Historical Society, and then in proposing and completing *The Genealogical Register of the First Settlers of New England*, which was published in 1829. Weil emphasizes the network of scholars with whom Farmer worked, including such men as Lemuel Shattuck and James Savage. The author concludes with a brief discussion of the influence that John Farmer had, some years after his death, in the formation of the New England Historic Genealogical Society in 1845. This article represents the first fruits of a larger, book-length project, in which Weil will examine "the history of genealogy in American culture."

Mary Beth Norton and Emerson W. Baker, eds., " 'The Names of the Rivers': A New Look at an Old Document," *The New England Quarterly* 80 (2007):459-87. The authors re-examine an early seventeenth-century document, listing the rivers of what would become the Maine, New Hampshire and northern Massachusetts coast, and the area around Cape Cod, Nantucket and Martha's Vineyard. The document also named the sachems of the Indian tribes on each of those rivers. Norton and Baker argue that the document was created in or just before 1611, by someone who had been associated with the 1603 voyage of Martin Pring to New England. They further argue that Pring anchored for some time in the harbor at Edgartown, and that the author of the document may have been Robert Salterne, who sailed with Pring.

Leslie Mahler, "The English Origin of John[1] Baisey/Baysey of Hartford, Connecticut: Cousin of the Olmstead Family of Hartford," *The American Genealogist* 82 (2007):32-38. The author demonstrates that John Baisey, who had settled in Hartford by 1639, was baptized at Dedham, Essex, in 1612, son of John and Mary (Slaney) Baisey. The immigrant's mother's sister was Frances (Slaney) Olmstead, wife of Richard Olmstead and mother of the Olmstead siblings who came to Hartford.

Glade Ian Nelson, "Anthony[1] and Grace (_____) (Hall) White of Watertown, Massachusetts," *The American Genealogist* 82 (2007):39-48. Nelson argues that Anthony White, who came to New England in 1634 and resided in Watertown and Sudbury, married a widow, Grace (_____) Hall. The identity of her Hall husband has not been determined, but she did have a son Christopher Hall with that husband.

Martin E. Hollick, "The English Origin of William[1] Dudley of Guilford, Connecticut," *The American Genealogist* 82 (2007):63-75. Following up on the clue provided by the marriage record for William Dudley of Guilford, Hollick presents extensive extracts from the parish register of Dorking, Surrey, along with a number of English probates, to show that this immigrant was baptized at Dorking on 22 January 1608/9. The author considers four different William Dudleys in coming to this conclusion, and presents three generations of agnate ancestry for the immigrant.

John Anderson Brayton, "Additions to the Ancestry of Sarah (Hawkredd) (Story) (Cotton) Mather of Boston, Lincolnshire," *The Genealogist* 21 (2007):191-217. Brayton presents data on the spouses of the father and paternal grandfather of Sarah Hawkredd, the principal focus of this two-part article. Sarah's mother, and the first wife of Anthony[A] Hawkredd, was Isabell (Bonner) (Earle) Jeffraye, daughter of Robert Bonner and widow of William Earle and William Jeffraye. The first wife of William[B] Hawkredd, and the mother of Anthony, was Cassandra (Claymond) Dowse, daughter of John Claymond and widow of John Dowse. The compiled genealogical summaries for these various families are supported by extensive will abstracts, inquisitions *post mortem* and parish register entries.

Shirley Moore Barnes, "William[1] Loveridge [Leveridge], Hatter of Albany and Ulster County," *The New York Genealogical and Biographical Record* 138 (2007):165-77. Although this immigrant did not arrive in New England until the late 1650s, the delineation of his life and family did necessitate the examination of the life of William Leverich, who was at Dover, New Hampshire, by 1633 [GMB 2:1178-80]. The research on the subject of this article is an excellent example of tracing a family that moved frequently from colony to colony.

Patricia M. Kirwin, "Additions and Corrections to the Kentish Roots of Thomas Baker and Ralph Dayton of East Hampton," *The New York Genealogical and Biographical Record* 138 (2007):178-88. The author presents additional English records, from several parishes in the Weald of Kent, for the families of Thomas Baker, who arrived in Milford, Connecticut, in 1639, and Ralph Dayton, who had settled at New Haven in 1639. Bennett Tritton, the wife of Thomas Stanley of Lynn, Hartford and Hadley, was connected to these two families by the marriages of her parents. Interestingly, Bethersden, Kent, one of the parishes studied here for the Baker family, is the same parish where Edelman and Jenkins found records for the Jenkins and Tilden families (see above).

Great Migration Newsletter

| Vol. 17 | January-March 2008 | No. 1 |

CHECKING THE CHECKLIST

More than twenty years ago, when the Great Migration Study Project was in the planning stages, we compiled a checklist of those persons who should be included in the published volumes. This earliest version of the checklist was derived almost totally from the standard grand compendia, such as Savage, Pope, Austin, and Noyes, Libby and Davis.

In the early years of the Project, this primitive checklist was the basis for research on all sketches. Experience showed, however, that this form of the list was highly inadequate, as it missed many immigrants and at the same time included a number who actually arrived years later. The latter group were an annoyance, but could be excluded as the research process proceeded. The former group were more troublesome, as the omission might not be corrected prior to publication.

As an attempt to correct this problem, an extensive revision to the checklist was undertaken after the publication of the first series of Great Migration volumes, and before work on the second series was too far advanced. The most important part of this revision was the consultation of all relevant primary sources, in addition to the general secondary sources which had been consulted previously. This survey included all available passenger lists, town, church and court records, private correspondence, and other available contemporary records for the period from May 1634 to May 1636, the range of time of arrivals covered by the second series of Great Migration volumes. (A remaining shortcoming of the checklist at this point is that it may not include individuals who did arrive in 1634 or 1635, who did not create a record during those years, but who left a much later deposition or similar record from which we may deduce their arrival during those years.)

Even with this revision, however, the checklist is not yet a finished product. As we begin the research for each new volume, our first step is to "dummy up" each sketch. This involves opening a Word file for each person in the checklist and entering at least those records which were identified as demonstrating that that person had arrived in New England in 1634 or 1635. At this stage we may also enter the material found in Savage or one of the other colony-wide compendia. We also make notes for further research as we notice discrepancies and other problems.

As we make this first pass through the list of sketches to be included in a volume, we inevitably encounter problems with some of the items in the checklist. As we write this article, we are a few months into the preparation of the sixth volume in the second series, covering the letters R and S. We are nearly through with the process of creating the "dummy" sketches, and have made a number of further revisions to the checklist. We present here a few samples of this workings of this process, which will result in changes to the version of the checklist that is currently posted at www.GreatMigration.org.

As a simple example, one of the entries was for William Shetle, who first appeared in Plymouth Colony in 1634. This was based on an entry in the Plymouth Colony court records [PCR 1:31]:

> September 2, 1634. William Shetle hath put himself an apprentice to Thomas Clarke for the term of eleven years from the 16 of May last; and at the end of the said term the said Thomas is to clothe him with two suits fit for such a servant, and also eight bushels of Indian corn.

No other records for a surname spelled this way were found, but it quickly became apparent that this was the first appearance in New England of William Shurtleff, whose surname would eventually be spelled in a wide variety of ways.

Two further entries look suspiciously like they pertain to the same man. "Michael Shaflin" was on a 1635 passenger list, sailing from Southampton [Drake's Founders 56]. "Michael Shavelin" was found in a 1634 Charlestown town record [ChTR 11]. The problem here is that a man who did not sail

(continued on page 2)

EDITOR'S EFFUSIONS

In the lead article of this issue of the *Newsletter,* we discuss the steps we take to refine our checklist of names of individuals who should be included in a given volume. This process is just one facet of the overall decision for or against inclusion in a given volume. The ultimate outcome of this process gives rise to the most frequent question we are asked: *Why was my ancestor not included in this volume?* Since this question is so common, reiteration of our guiding principles is worthwhile.

With respect to the current series, we look first for an explicit record that places the immigrant for the first time in New England in 1634 or 1635. Beyond this, we will include individuals or families who make a reliable, but much later, statement of presence in New England in those years. Beyond that, we enter a fuzzy area where we have a hint that a person might have arrived by 1634 or 1635, but no certainty.

There are undoubtedly many immigrants whom we have excluded from the volumes published to date, who were in fact in New England by the date covered by that volume. This is unfortunate, but conforms to a consistent, conservative principle of selection. We could include persons for whom there was a hint of their presence, and then later be disproved by a record found in England which shows they were still there in 1634 and 1635. So, we exclude such potential immigrants when the possibility of finding a conflicting record exists.

The Great Migration Tour to England, which we announced in a previous *Newsletter* [GMN 16:17-24], is now fully subscribed and will take place in August of this year. We are publishing a monthly online bulletin, called *Tour Talk,* which describes some of the sites we will be visiting on the tour, and some of the history behind what we will be experiencing. You are all invited to visit the website and read each issue of *Tour Talk.* Just go to www.GreatMigration.org and you will find in the middle of the page a link to current and past issues of this bulletin. We hope this material enhances your knowledge and understanding of the Great Migration.

Robert Charles Anderson, FASG   Editor
Jean Powers, Production Assistant

The Great Migration Newsletter is published quarterly by the Great Migration Study Project, a project of the New England Historic Genealogical Society, 101 Newbury Street, Boston MA 02116
www.NewEnglandAncestors.org
www.GreatMigration.org
GreatMigration@nehgs.org

Copyright © 2008
New England Historic Genealogical Society

(continued from page 1)

for New England until 1635 should not appear in New England prior to sailing. The difficulty was relieved by reexamination of the Charlestown records, which showed that we had made an error in the checklist entry, and that "Michael Shavelin" did not appear in Charlestown until 1635. These two entries have been combined into one.

A similar situation was found with "Andrew Story," who was included in a list of 1635 arrivals at Ipswich [Ipswich Hist 1:493], and "Andrew Storyn," who appeared in Massachusetts Bay court records in the same year [MBCR 1:154]:

> 1 September 1635: It was ordered, that Andrewe Storyn shall be whipped, for running from his master.

Search in the Ipswich town records revealed a first appearance in 1638 when he received a grant of land, and then again in 1639 when he was given land for service in the Pequot War in 1637. These Ipswich records are consistent with a man who was still a servant in 1635 and performed military service in 1637, at about which time he attained his majority and began to receive town land grants.

No records other than the 1635 court record used the spelling "Storyn." The author of the Ipswich town history must have been aware of the 1635 record, decided that it pertained to the man he found in Ipswich records, and on that basis entered him as a 1635 arrival. We concur in this conclusion, and have revised the checklist accordingly.

The revised checklist contained two consecutive entries for men first appearing at Ipswich in 1635, "Edmund Sayward" and "Mr. Saywell," both items being from the published Ipswich town records. Closer examination revealed five early entries for these surnames or for other similar surnames:

> Edmund Sayward, 1635, land abutting John Cogswell
> Mr. Seawall, 1635, land abutting William Fuller
> Edmund Sawyer, 1637, land abutting Thomas Clarke
> Edmund Seward, 1638, granted 32 acres
> Edmund Seward, 1639, land abutting Thomas Clarke

Taking the second of these entries first, we note first that this is the same as the item that appears in our checklist as "Mr. Saywell." This record almost certainly pertains to Henry Sewall, who arrived in 1634, lived for one winter in Ipswich, and then in 1635 joined the settlers of the new town of Newbury. Since our checklist already contains Henry Sewall in his proper place, the entry for "Mr. Saywell" or "Mr. Seawall" may be deleted.

The third and fifth items, which appear to refer to the same piece of land, abutting a parcel owned by Thomas Clarke, show that in these records the surnames Sawyer and Seward were interchangeable. We conclude that the first entry and the third through fifth entries refer to the same man, whose surname in early records was most frequently spelled Sayward, so this entry in the checklist will remain unchanged.

Focus on Weymouth

WHERE IS THE HOUSELOT?

The fundamental principle of landgranting in early New England towns was that the grant of a houselot carried with it a proprietary share in the future granting of other types of land in the town. The holder of the proprietary share would then receive over time, perhaps within just a few years and perhaps spread out over decades, several other parcels of land, including meadow or marsh land, planting or arable land, and wood lots or upland lots.

For most of the early Massachusetts Bay towns, we do not have contemporary records of the actual grants of houselots. Either the earliest records have not survived, or the houselots were granted before the town started keeping records. For Watertown, for example, there are surviving records of the grants of arable land and woodlots, but not of the distribution of houselots and marsh and meadow land [WaBOP 3-14]. However, as with Weymouth, a detailed land inventory survives for Watertown, from about the same date as the Weymouth inventory [WaBOP 17-146]. Unlike the Weymouth inventory, though, the Watertown compilation includes detailed descriptions of each proprietor's houselot, allowing a detailed reconstruction of the landgranting process [GMN 1:4-6].

Similar arrangements of records exist for several other early Massachusetts Bay towns, including Cambridge, Charlestown, Boston and Roxbury [GMN 1:4-6, 12-13, 2:6, 13-14].

In the case of Weymouth, we have less to go on. First, only one fragmentary record of landgranting exists prior to the making of the land inventory – a 1636 grant of great lots to only sixteen men, a fraction of the proprietors then resident. Second, the land inventory does not explicity describe any houselots.

Were the houselots excluded from the Weymouth land inventory, or are they there but not described as such? Before we can outline the overall landgranting process, we need to examine other evidence in an attempt to learn more about the houselots.

EVIDENCE FROM DEEDS

One helpful source in solving this mystery is the Suffolk County Registry of Deeds. Although the county was not formed until 1643, just shortly before the Weymouth land inventory was created, several records of transfer of Weymouth property were recorded which reached back into the later 1630s. Our first step, then, will be to present and then analyze these deeds. We begin with three documents in which Henry Waltham, a wealthy Weymouth settler, was the grantor.

> On 12 December 1637, "Henerye Walthame of Waymouth granted unto Jo[hn] Arthur ... one house & land lying in Waymouth aforesaid containing ten acres more or less, bounded on the south with a lot of Peeter de Salinovas on east & west with the river" [SLR 1:27].

> About a year later, "Henerye Walthame of Waymouth granted unto Jo[hn] Arthur of Waymou[th] in England ... six acres of marsh meadow ground lying in Waymouth in New England bounded on the south with the marsh of Will [iam] Jefferay, on the north with Jerimye Goulds, on the west the river" [SLR 1:27].

> On 30 September 1642, "Henery Walthame of Waymouth granted unto Jo[hn] Arthur of Waymouth in England ... all that one half of a grist mill lying in Waymouth in New England aforesaid and also the rooms of the house joining to the mill as it was divided, also a garden paled in divided, more the one half of a hundred acres of ground not yet divided belonging to the said mill with all the other appurtenances, also a new dwelling house erected by the said Henerye the last year" [SLR 1:29].

These three records are more tantalizing than helpful, as there are no entries in the Weymouth land inventory for either Henry Waltham or John Arthur. As late as 1656, Waltham was quitclaiming rights in the mill property, stating then that this land was "late in the possession of Capt. John Arthur of Weimouth in old England" [SLR 3:1].

We do learn, however, that he did own in 1637 "one house & land ... containing ten acres," which we will take provisionally as his houselot.

The next item does involve men who are represented in the Weymouth land inventory, Richard Silvester and John Fussell.

> On 28 September 1640, "Richard Silvester of Waymouth granted unto John Fussell all his home lot containing six acres more or less situate in Waymouth, together with the housing standing thereon" [SLR 1:16].

In the land inventory, John Fussell was credited with only one parcel of land, "twelve acres and half in the plain, six acres of it first given to Robert Able, three acres of it first given to Thomas Holbrooke, half an acre first given to Mr. Barnard, and the other three acres first given to William

Newland" [Weymouth Hist 1:188]. Since Richard Silvester was one of the first settlers of Weymouth, we would expect the six-acre household he sold to Fussell to have been "first given" to him, so no part of the twelve and a half acres described in the land inventory entry for Fussell corresponds to the lot sold by Silvester in 1640.

We would not expect this six-acre parcel to be still in the possession of Silvester at the time of the land inventory, and indeed it is not. So, we can assign a grant of a six-acre houselot to Richard Silvester. Unfortunately, based on the land description which lacks any indicators of location or abuttors, we cannot tell from this deed where in Weymouth this houselot was.

A few months after this sale by Silvester, Thomas Applegate entered into a more informative transaction.

> On [blank] March 1640[/1?], "Tho[mas] Apellgate of Waymouth … hath sold unto George Allen of Waymouth … my house and home lot in Waymouth accounted seven acres, also two acres of salt marsh, also eight acres of planting land at Smelt Brook, & also a great lot belonging to the said Tho[mas] Apellgate['s] house & home lot, and in commons, & all my rate in Waymouth" [SLR 1:17].

Thomas Applegate had moved to Newport by 1641 [GM 2:2:72-75], so there is no entry for him in the Weymouth land inventory. There is an entry for George Allin, but it contains only one parcel of land, which does not correspond with any of the parcels transferred in the deed just above: "Three acres in Kingoke Hill first granted to Robert Lovell" [Weymouth Hist 1:190].

From this document, then, we can assign to Thomas Applegate the grant from the town of Weymouth of a houselot of seven acres, a tract of land which does not appear in the Weymouth land inventory.

These are all the Weymouth land transactions which have been found in the Suffolk deeds prior to the date of the Weymouth land inventory. Immediately after the completion of that inventory, the Weymouth town clerk entered brief records of a few transfers of land which took place shortly thereafter. At a later date these transfers would also have been entered in the county registry of deeds, but at this early date many land transactions between individuals were still recorded at the town level.

These tranfers provide us with some information about the typical early landholding in Weymouth, and so we transcribe them here in full [Weymouth Hist 1:198]:

> Sold by Edward Smith unto Thomas Dyer as followeth five acres and half of land in the west field, three acres and half of it was given first to Richard Porter and two acres of it first given to Robert Lovell and his dwelling house, barn and cellar with the appurtenances thereunto belonging

bounded on the east & west with highways, on the north with the land of John Harding, on the south by John Holbrook land, also three acres of fresh marsh which was first given to Stephen French bounded on the east by Richard Addames marsh, on the west and north with the common, on the south with the fresh brook.

Although undated, this deed must have been executed shortly before the two below, in May 1644. The entry in the Weymouth land inventory for Edward Smith contains three parcels, the first and third of which correspond exactly with the two described in the deed above [Weymouth Hist 1:192]. Although not explicitly stated to be a houselot in the proprietorial sense, Edward Smith noted that the first of these lots included "his dwelling house, barn and cellar with the appurtenances thereunto belonging." This final phrase, "with the appurtenances thereunto belonging," sometimes does designate the future shares in commons connected with a particular piece of land, and may well mean that this parcel in the West Field, assembled by Edward Smith from two original grants made to Richard Porter and Robert Lovell, did include an original houselot grant with proprietorial rights.

> Sold by Thomas Dyer unto Thomas Baylie the 21st of the 3 month [May] 1644 his dwelling house, barn and cellar, his garden and yard both of them containing by estimation one quarter of an acre being more or less bounded on the north with the land of Robert Lovell, on the west with the land of Mr. Webb, on the north with the land of said Thomas Dyer, and on the south a highway.

This deed delineates a single parcel of land, including buildings and a kitchen garden, on a quarter of an acre of land, a description that looks exactly like a houselot in other early Massachusetts Bay towns. There is an entry for Thomas Dyer in the Weymouth land inventory, which lists two parcels, one of seven acres and the other of two acres, the latter being swamp [Weymouth Hist 1:192]. Neither of these tracts of land matches the quarter acre in the 1644 deed, nor does either seem to include that quarter acre.

> Sold by Edward Smith unto William Reade the 25th of the 3 month [May] 1644 ten acres and half of land in the wester neck, eight acres and half of it was first given to him the said William Reade, two acres first given to Richard Addames, bounded in the east with the land of the said William Reade, on the west with the land of Richard Addames, north and south with the commons.

As noted above in the earlier deed made by Edward Smith, his land inventory entry included three pieces of land, two of which were disposed of in that deed. This instrument conveys the remaining parcel credited to Smith in that inventory [Weymouth Hist 1:192]. In these two deeds of 1644, Edward Smith apparently completed the disposal of his Weymouth land. About this time, in company with a number of other Weymouth families, Smith moved to

Rehoboth, where he was propounded for Plymouth Colony freemanship on 4 June 1645 [PCR 2:84].

The first volume of Suffolk deeds also contains some additional Weymouth transactions concluded shortly after the compilation of the Weymouth land inventory, and these may provide us with some additional clues.

> On 26 November 1644, "James Parker of Strawberry Banck granted unto Zaccheus Gould of Ipswich ... a certain house & lands, to wit, one dwelling house & other his houses & ground thereto adjoining, as also nine acres of upland which he bought of Jeremie Gould, & also the commons thereunto belonging & all his meadows in Waymouth aforesaid" [SLR 1:56].

> On 2 April 1645, "Zaccheus Gould of Ipswich being seized in fee of a certain tenement situate in Waymouth with certain arable grounds, meadows, pastures, swamps, & woods thereto belonging lately by him purchased of James Parker of Waymouth ... hath granted the same with all the appurtenances thereto belonging unto Capt. William Perkins" [SLR 1:58].

These two deeds, despite the differences in the descriptions of land transferred, appear to refer to the same collection of land, held by Zaccheus Gould for a few months in the winter of 1644-5. The second parcel of land, nine acres of upland, was first held by Jeremiah Gould and then sold by him to James Parker before the transcations reported above.

The Weymouth land inventory does not have entries for Jeremiah Gould, James Parker or Zaccheus Gould. Jeremiah Gould resided at Weymouth as late as 1640 [SLR 1:16; Lechford 372-73] and James Parker as late as 1642 [GMB 3:1391-93]. Unfortunately, these documents do not tell us either the size or the location of the houselot.

> On 12 April 1648, "W[illia]m Richards of Waimouth" sold to "Henry Kingman of Waymouth his dwelling house in Waymouth together with his lot adjoining to it being twenty acres more or less, as also two acres of salt marsh adjoining to the upland & fourteen rod of upland more joining to the forenamed upland ..., also one acre salt marsh in the town of Braintre lying close by the farm house of Mr. W[illia]m Tyng" [SLR 1:91].

In the Weymouth land inventory, William Richards was credited with three parcels [Weymouth Hist 1:195]:

> Nineteen acres and half in the Westernecke first given to Mr. Buslem ...

> Two acres of salt marsh in the same neck first given to William Smith ...

> Four acres in the same neck first given to himself ...

The twenty acres of the deed apparently matches with the nineteen acres and a half in the land inventory, and the two acres of salt marsh is the same in both. The third parcel in the inventory may or may not correspond in part with the fourteen rods of upland of the deed.

WEYMOUTH HOUSELOTS

Our examination of deeds from the 1630s and 1640s has identified seven parcels which appear to have been houselots. Our best efforts to determine the original grantees and the sizes of these lots may be summarized as follows: 1) Henry Waltham (ten acres); 2) Richard Silvester (six acres); 3) Thomas Applegate (seven acres); 4) Richard Porter (three and a half acres) or Robert Lovell (two acres); 5) Thomas Dyer (one-quarter of an acre); 6) James Parker (unknown); and 7) John Bursley (twenty acres). An unusual feature of this short list is the large size of many of these houselots. In most towns the houselots were much smaller, frequently an acre or less.

In only two of these examples do we have any indication of the location of the houselot. The grant made to John Bursley was in the Wester Neck, while the plot of land sold by Edward Smith, and originally held by Richard Porter and Robert Lovell, was in the West Field. The West Field was presumably arable land, and finding a houselot there seems unusual. This did happen, but most commonly when a proprietor chose not to live in the town center, and converted an outlot into his houselot, contrary to the intent of the grants.

In 1885 Gilbert Nash wrote that

> for the better protection of the various towns in the colony from the Indians, it was ordered by the General Court that no dwelling house should be built more than a mile from the meeting-house. It appears, however, that the latter order was never enforced, or soon became a dead letter, for at this time the people of Weymouth were scattered over a territory from two to three miles in extent. The larger part of the population lived in North Weymouth, commonly known as "Old Spain," extending from the shore of the bay to Burying Hill, more than a mile, while there were quite a number of plantations extending south and east over King Oak Hill as far as Fresh Pond, now Whitman's, in East Weymouth [Weymouth Hist 1:172-73].

Taking all this together, we are left with two possibilities. First, based on the records presented here, we may not yet have enough evidence to make any firm conclusions about the granting of houselots in Weymouth. Second, Weymouth may have deliberately chosen a different manner of granting houselots than did other New England towns, in which case the land inventory may conceal many more houselots. A much more detailed reconstruction of Weymouth land would be required to decide between these two possibilities.

A TYPICAL LAND DISTRIBUTION

In the first two installments of this article, we surveyed the entries in the Weymouth inventory of landholding for nine named "fields," with the goal of identifying the original grantees in each of these fields. As a final step in our current investigation, we will analyze these results in the hope of obtaining a better picture of the process of granting land in the earliest years at Weymouth.

We begin with a few general comments. First, the named fields we have examined were either plowland or woodland, so no marsh or meadow lots are included in our analysis. Second, with the exception of the East Field and West Field, where the grants were mutually exclusive (aside from the minor exception of William Hewes), grantees could receive land in just about any combination of fields. Third, as we have already noted in some places, the inventory is clearly far from complete.

Only two men were granted land in five of these nine fields, and an additional eleven in four fields. We will take a closer look at a few of these, on the assumption that these approach a typical allotment of land. (For each person below, the list consists of the name of the field, the acreage received within that field, and the total acreage from all fields.)

John Whitmarsh: West Field (2); Plain (3); Wester Neck (21); Mill Field (2½); King Oak Hill (8). Total: 36½ acres.

Joseph Hull: West Field (21¾); Harris's Range (3); Wester Neck (17½); Great Lot (18). Total: 60¼ acres.

Robert Lovell: West Field (4¾); Plain (3); King Oak Hill (10½); Great Lot (34). Total: 52¼ acres.

William Fry: West Field (4); Plain (3); Mill Field (6); Great Lot (12). Total: 25 acres.

Thomas Baylie: West Field (2); Plain (3); Wester Neck (4); Mill Field (4). Total: 13 acres.

Henry Kingman: East Field (13); Plain (3); Harris's Range (4); Great Lot (42). Total: 62 acres.

Richard Adams: East Field (11); Wester Neck (16); Mill Field (3); Great Lot (24). Total: 54 acres.

Musachiell Bernard: East Field (7); Plain (3½); Harris's Range (5); Mill Field (8). Total: 23½ acres.

William Smith: East Field (7); Plain (3); Wester Neck (21); Great Lot (30). Total: 51 acres.

George Allin: East Field (3); Plain (3); Wester Neck (8); Easter Neck (20). Total: 34 acres.

Edward Bennett: East Field (2); Wester Neck (14); King Oak Hill (7); Great Lot (18). Total: 41 acres.

John Upham: Plain (14); Harris's Range (2); Wester Neck (12); King Oak Hill (7); Great Lot (30). Total: 65 acres.

Richard Silvester: Plain (11); Wester Neck (14); Mill Field (3); Great Lot (24). Total: 52 acres.

We note first that eight of these thirteen grantees had sailed to New England in 1635 on the vessel that carried Joseph Hull [Hotten 283-86]. Richard Silvester had already been in New England since 1630 [GMB 3:1677-81]. William Fry, Thomas Baylie and Edward Bennett had received grants of Great Lots in 1636 [Weymouth Hist 1:199]. We conclude, then, that the listings above are a fair representation of the earliest round of land grants in Weymouth, in 1635 and 1636, consequent to the arrival of the Hull party.

Second, with one exception, the size of the grants of Great Lots recovered from the analysis of the 1644 inventory of landholding agree with the record of the original grants in 1636. The only difference is for Joseph Hull, who was originally granted 54 acres, only 18 of which are found in the land inventory.

Third, we have already noted that with one exception the grants in the East Field and the West Field are mutually exclusive. Two of the men in the above list did not receive land in either of these fields, but did receive the two largest grants in The Plain (John Upham and Richard Silvester). However, many men who did receive land in the East or West Field did receive smaller parcels of three acres in The Plain. This suggests that the larger grants in The Plain were intended to serve the same purpose as those in the East and West Fields, for those who did not get anything in the latter two fields.

Fourth, the total acreage in these fields ranged from 65 to 13 acres, which is quite typical of what we have found in other towns, where land is granted according to some formula based on wealth and family size. Unfortunately, we do not have enough information to recover what this formula might have been. (We note that the amount of land actually received in these fields by Joseph Hull was actually about 96 acres, based on the size of his Great Lot grant. This again is typical of the special treatment given to the town's minister.)

In the end, our analysis of land granting in early Weymouth is both tantalizing and frustrating. We have learned that the town made grants in the same size range as in other towns, and probably according to a similar formula. On the other hand, we have hints, but not sufficient proof, that the town did not aspire to a tightly nucleated village, but may have permitted a more sprawling settlement pattern for houselots. We conclude that a more extensive analysis of Weymouth land records would produce further useful results.

RECENT LITERATURE

Eben W. Graves, "Notes on the Family of Deacon George Grave of Hartford, Connecticut," *The New England Historical and Genealogical Register* 161 (2007):245-49. Through the examination of family correspondence and of English probate, parish register and livery company records, Eben W. Graves has improved our knowledge of the family of George Grave, who had settled in Hartford by 1639. The author has identified a brother of the immigrant (and a daughter and two grandsons of that brother), the possible apprenticeship record for the immigrant himself, and a second marriage, to Richard Smith of Hartford, for Mary (Grave) Dowe, daughter of the immigrant.

William Wyman Fiske, "Ancestry of Bennet Eliot of Nazeing, Essex, Father of Seven Great Migration Immigrants to Massachusetts," *The New England Historical and Genealogical Register* 161 (2007):250-59. Fiske continues his study of the Eliot family with a compiled genealogical summary of the descendants of William Eliot of Hertfordshire, born about 1540, great-great-grandfather of the immigrants. This installment identifies his children and presents detailed treatments of his three eldest sons, with the fourth son and descendants in later generations to be included in the next installment.

Leslie Mahler, "The London Apprenticeship of Edward[1] Rainsford of Boston, Massachusetts," *The New England Historical and Genealogical Register* 161 (2007):260. Mahler has found in the records of the Haberdashers Company of London the 1626 apprenticeship record of Edward Rainsford, 1630 settler at Boston, to Owen Roe, a London merchant with extensive land and business interests in New England.

William Wyman Fiske, "Joan (_____) (Wylley) Pilston of Bishops Stortford, Hertfordshire," *The New England Historical and Genealogical Register* 161 (2007):280-81. Fiske corrects the ancestry of Thomas[1] Miller of Rowley, Massachusetts, showing that he was almost certainly not son of John Miller of Bishops Stortford, Hertfordshire. The author also presents additional information on Joan (_____) (Wylley) Pilston

Nathaniel Lane Taylor, "Genealogist John Farmer Discovers His Ancestry: The Warwickshire Family of Edward[1] Farmer, Isabel[1] (Farmer) (Wyman) (Blood) Green, and Thomas[1] Pollard, of Billerica, Massachusetts," *The New England Historical and Genealogical Register* 161 (2007):289-99. Farmer concludes his examination of the genealogical connections of Edward Farmer with compiled accounts of the Moore, Burbage and Packwood families, from which families came the wives of Edward Farmer, his father and grandfather. Finally, the author offers suggestions for further lines of research in England on these various families.

William Wyman Fiske, "The Perry Family of Sawbridgeworth, Hertfordshire: Shared Ancestry of Six Massachusetts Immigrants: John[1] Perry of Roxbury, Isaac[1] Perry of Boston, Mary[1] (Perry) Heath of Roxbury, Phebe[1] (Perry) Desborough of Roxbury, John[1] Redding of Topsfield, and Abraham[1] Reddington of Topsfield and Boxford," *The American Genealogist* 82 (2007):81-90. In this first installment of a multi-part article, Fiske publishes a will and more than a hundred parish register entries for the Perry family of Sawbridgeworth, Hertfordshire, ancestral to several early New England immigrants. Based on these and other records, he offers some corrections to material already in print on this Perry family and its connections with other Great Migration families. Most importantly, he argues that the wife of John[1] Perry was not Phebe Cramphorn, sister of the first wife of William[1] Heath, and that the second wife of William Heath was daughter of Abraham Perry and not of John Perry.

Leslie Mahler, "The English Origin of Thomas[1] and Sarah (Scott) Grave(s) of Hartford, Connecticut, and Hadley, Massachusetts," *The American Genealogist* 82 (2007):107-10. Mahler presents records that demonstrate that Thomas Graves, who had settled in Hartford by 1645, had two children baptized at Thundridge, Hertfordshire, in the 1620s and that his wife was the daughter of Christopher Scott of Hatfield Broadoak, Essex, a parish about ten miles east of Thundridge.

Alvy Ray Smith and Robert Charles Anderson, "Proposed Hawkshead, Lancashire, Origins of Edward[1] Riggs of Roxbury, Massachusetts, and Thomas[1] Riggs of Gloucester," *The American Genealogist* 82 (2007):120-29. The authors present documentary evidence for the Hawkshead, Lancashire, origin of Thomas Riggs, who had settled in Gloucester, Massachusetts, by 1658. They then demonstrate that Y-chromosome DNA evidence indicates a close relation between this Thomas Riggs and Edward Riggs, who came to Roxbury by 1633, from Nazeing, Essex. Finally, they publish English records for three men by the name of Edward Riggs, two from Hawkshead and one from Roydon, Essex, immediately adjacent to Nazeing, any one of whom might be the immigrant to New England.

Craig Partridge, "The English Origin of Daniel[1] Kempster of Cambridge, Massachusetts," *The American Genealogist* 82 (2007):142-52. Partridge has collected probate and parish register records which document the Kettlebaston, Suffolk, origin of Daniel Kempster, immigrant to Cambridge by the early 1640s. These records also identify the father and grandfather of the immigrant, as well as the Kempster kin who remained in old England but were named in the New England will of the immigrant. The connections to Thomas Moulton and Samuel Andrews, other New England relatives named in the will of Daniel Kempster, however, remain unresolved.

Emerson W. Baker, *The Devil of Great Island: Witchcraft & Conflict in Early New England* (New York 2007).

In 1682 on Great Island in Portsmouth, New Hampshire, George Walton, his family and his tavern were assaulted for several weeks by a rain of stones and other flying objects. Walton had made his first appearance in New England at Exeter in 1639, moved a few years later to Dover, and by 1649 had settled at Great Island [Lydia Harmon Anc 81-90].

Baker has two main goals: to tell the story of the events of 1682 on Great Island, and to place these events in the larger context of witchcraft in seventeenth-century New England. He has scoured the contemporary documents to delineate in great detail the life and family of George Walton, who emerges as a contentious man who was at odds with the prevailing political and religious leaders of his community.

A major element in the story is the ongoing land dispute with the neighboring Walford family. Thomas Walford may have been in New England as early as 1623, and by 1628 was certainly at Charlestown [GMB 3:1902-6]. By 1634 he was living on the Piscataqua, and ended up owning land adjoining that of George Walton. For many years Walton contended with Walford and his children, and Baker believes that this ongoing feud, combined with Walton's unorthodox religious and political beliefs, were the underlying causes for the entirely natural misfortunes which befell him.

W. Bruce Fairchild, *Thomas Fairchild, Puritan Merchant & Magistrate: The Life and Times of an American Colonizer & Patriarch, c.1610-1670* (New York 2006).

The author has prepared a detailed and exhaustive biography of Thomas Fairchild, a prominent settler of Stratford, Connecticut, by 1639. The material on the immigrant is carefully interwoven with extensive information on the historical circumstances within which he lived. The first chapter, for example, provides a description of the Puritan movement as Fairchild would have come to know it during the reign of James I.

Bruce Fairchild has carefully examined the documentary basis for each phase of the life of the immigrant, and for each major life event along the way. In an early chapter he surveys the several claims that have been made for the English origin of Thomas Fairchild, in the end concluding that we do not yet know that origin.

Thomas Fairchild returned to England and resided in London for about three years in the early 1660s, during which time he married his second wife. The author carefully delineates London during these years, and also describes in detail the courtship and the marriage process experienced by the couple. The volume is enhanced throughout with excellent reproductions of important documents and with other appropriate illustrations.

Great Migration Newsletter

Vol. 17   April-June 2008   No. 2

MANASSEH AND MARY (SALTER) BECK

On a number of occasions in past issues of the *Newsletter* we have discussed the sources and methods employed to identify the spouses of the subjects of Great Migration sketches, and also to identify the spouses of their children. Interestingly, as we approach the end of the second series of Great Migration volumes, covering nearly half of the immigrants of the Great Migration, the published volumes are themselves becoming important sources in making these identifications.

One of the immigrants whose sketch will appear in the next published volume is William Salter, who was admitted to Boston church on 20 September 1635 [BChR 19]. Salter died on 12 August 1675 and in his will named four children: "my son Jabez"; "my daughter Beck"; "my daughter Mehitable"; and "my son Jno." [SPR 6:104]. The immediate problem is identifying "my daughter Beck."

Boston church and vital records provide evidence for either four or five daughters of William Salter. (1) Elizabeth Salter was born on 16 April 1639 and baptized on 26 April 1640 [NEHGR 9:166; BChR 286]; (2) Mary Salter was born on 10 August 1642 and baptized on 30 October 1642 [NEHGR 9:166; BChR 290]; (3) Mehitable Salter was baptized on 30 April 1648 "being about 4 days old" [BChR 310]; (4) Ann Salter was baptized on 15 March 1656/7 [BChR 331]; and (5) Lydia Salter was born on 24 March 1657 [BVR 59].

Before attempting to discover which one of these women had a husband with the surname Beck, we need to comment on some inconsistencies in these records. First, the difference of more than a year between the birth and baptism of Elizabeth, while not impossible, is suspicious. In earlier examinations of Boston records, we have noted that the baptismal records are generally more reliable than the town vital records [GMN 3:4-6]. In addition, some Boston vital records were recorded many years after the event, which provides additional opportunity for error [GMN 12:19-22], and some of the Salter entries, including that for Elizabeth, fall into this category. We suggest that the correct date of birth for Elizabeth should be 16 April 1640.

Second, we note that the baptismal date for Ann may be only nine days before the birth date for daughter Lydia, depending on the resolution of the double-date for the latter. Although the interpretation of the Boston vital records as

published is fraught with multiple difficulties, we observe that for the year 1657 the entries have been published in rough chronological order, with the birth of Lydia sixth in the list, in a group of several others born in March. If this arrangement is accurate, then the Boston town clerk in 1657 counted 1 March rather than 25 March as the first day of the year, and we should represent this date of birth as 24 March 1656/7. This further suggests that Ann and Lydia were the same child, although this is not certain.

As a first step in attempting to identify "my daughter Beck," we will examine all marriages in Clarence Almon Torrey's *New England Marriages Prior to 1700* for men with the surname Beck. The marriage must have taken place by 1675 and the wife's name should be Elizabeth, Mary, Ann or (possibly) Lydia. Since the eldest of these daughters, Elizabeth, was born in 1640, the marriage should not have taken place much before 1660, thus giving us a date range of about fifteen years.

There are only seven male Beck marriages in Torrey's compilation. Three of these might meet the rough criteria given above. (1) Caleb Beck of Portsmouth, New Hampshire, son of Henry Beck, is said to have been married by 1661, with wife named Hannah, perhaps with surname Bowles or Bolles. Caleb did marry Hannah Bolles, daughter of Joseph, but probably not until 1670, as she was born in 1649 [GM 2:1:229; GDMNH 101]. Caleb's wife was most certainly not a daughter of William Salter.

(2) Henry Beck of Great Island, New Hampshire, another son of Henry Beck, is said to have married Elizabeth, perhaps as early as 1675. Closer analysis shows that Henry was

(continued on page 10)

EDITOR'S EFFUSIONS

Careful readers of the last issue of the *Great Migration Newsletter* will have noticed some changes in style and format by comparison with earlier issues, changes that we hope make the *Newsletter* more attractive and easier to read.

In its earliest years the *Newsletter* was published only in print form and was prepared with earlier publishing software, *Ventura*, that was used in many departments of the New England Historic Genealogical Society. After a few years, use of *Ventura* fell by the wayside, and for some time we created the *Newsletter* as a *Word* document.

Early in this decade we began to publish the *Newsletter* in both print and electronic formats. Each issue was first prepared in *Word*, which was submitted to the printer in "camera-ready" form and also used as the basis for the online version of the *Newsletter*. The publishing world has reached the point that printers now want documents submitted directly in electronic form, and so we had to make another change.

With the help of Carolyn Oakley, Jean Powers and Lynn Betlock of the NEHGS staff, we started in the last issue to prepare the *Newsletter* in *Microsoft Publisher*, a distant relative of the earlier *Ventura*. Under this arrangement, once we have completed an issue of the *Newsletter*, a simple conversion to a PDF file may be carried out, and the issue is then ready for publication in both print and electronic format.

The template used as the beginning point for each issue now includes all banner headlines, running heads and sidebar boxes, thus reducing the amount of "post-production" work necessary to complete the issue. Other details were attended to as well. For example, in the Table of Contents box on the first page of each issue, we had not found it easy to arrange the page numbers in the more pleasing right-justified format. That detail has now been attended to, thus making the overall appearance of the *Newsletter* more attractive.

Prompted by these improvements, we have been stimulated to make additional changes, such as formatting all text in the full-justified manner. No changes are being made in the content of the *Newsletter*, but we hope that the format changes will provide a better reading experience.

Robert Charles Anderson, FASG   Editor
Jean Powers, Production Assistant

The Great Migration Newsletter is published quarterly by the Great Migration Study Project, a project of the New England Historic Genealogical Society, 101 Newbury Street, Boston MA 02116
www.NewEnglandAncestors.org
www.GreatMigration.org
GreatMigration@nehgs.org

Copyright © 2008
New England Historic Genealogical Society

(continued from page 9)

nineteen years old in 1673, and so not likely to have been married by 1675. There is no evidence that he was married any earlier than 1686 [GM 2:1:230; GDMNH 86].

Manasseh Beck of Boston, son of Alexander Beck, is said to have married by 1668 a woman named Mary, whose maiden name has been unknown [GMB 1:144].

Up to this point, the methodology used in this process has been in line with that we have used from the beginning of the Great Migration Study Project. But note that these three men of the second generation in New England are sons of two Great Migration immigrants who have already been treated in our published volumes: Alexander Beck, who settled in Boston by 1632 [GMB 1:143-45]; and Henry Beck, who sailed for New England in 1635 and settled in Dover [GM 2:1:228-30]. We have already seen that reference to the Great Migration sketch for Henry Beck has allowed us to eliminate Caleb Beck as the husband of a daughter of William Salter and to cast serious doubt on Henry Beck as the husband of such a daughter.

This leaves us with only Manasseh Beck as a viable candidate to be the son-in-law of William Salter. A standard next step is to compile the list of children of Manasseh Beck and his wife, to see if any onomastic evidence might assist with the identification. This couple had children Ephraim, Manasseh, Mary, Mehitable and Ebenezer [BVR 107, 109, 113, 117, 122, 131, 137, 144, 151, 157]. William Salter had daughters Mary and Mehitable, the first of which is so common as to have little evidentiary value, but the second of which is uncommon, and gives some support to the wife of Manasseh Beck as a daughter of William Salter.

At this point, rather than continue our survey of the records created directly by Manasseh Beck, we chose to look at the Great Migration sketch for Manasseh's father Alexander Beck [GMB 1:143-45]. There we discover that when the inventory of the estate of Alexander Beck was taken on 26 October 1674, one of the appraisers was William Salter [GMB 1:144, citing SPR 5:210]. This record would eventually have been found in a thorough search of records related to Manasseh Beck, but having the Great Migration sketch allowed us to reach this point more quickly.

Additional evidence in favor of the identification has been found during further search in details of the life of William Salter. On 30 April 1672, Suffolk County court renewed the innkeeper's license of William Salter, at which time Manasseh Beck was one of his sureties [SCC 124].

We conclude, then, that "my daughter Beck" was Mary Salter, daughter of William Salter, who married by 1668 Manasseh Beck, son of Alexander Beck. We could, of course, have demonstrated this identity without the earlier published Great Migration work, but the easily accessible earlier work on immigrants Alexander Beck and Henry Beck have allowed us to solve this problem more easily than if those sketches did not already exist.

Focus on Identification

INTRODUCTION

In past issues of the *Great Migration Newsletter* we have analyzed ship passenger lists in a variety of ways, to answer several different questions. We shall now carry out a different sort of analysis, in order to examine two additional questions. First, in the current series of Great Migration volumes, for which we have relatively abundant passenger lists for 1634 and 1635, we are frequently confronted with the problem of deciding whether a particular person listed as a passenger is identical with a person of the same name who appears in New England some years later.

Second, some years in the future, as we are approaching the end of the period to be covered by the Great Migration Study Project, we will want to know whether the many men who were admitted to Massachusetts Bay freemanship in the early 1640s had or had not arrived in New England by 1640, assuming this latter date is the one we finally choose as the terminus of the Great Migration.

In order to obtain partial answers to both these questions, we shall in the present issue explore in detail two of the passenger lists for 1634, asking in each case how much time passed between the appearance of a given name on the passenger list and the first record for that name in New England. With respect to the first of the questions posed above, the results of this examination will make more explicit the criteria we use for deciding whether that passenger may be identified with a particular New England resident. With respect to the second question, the analysis undertaken here will make a small contribution to our eventual interpretation of the freemanship list of the early 1640s.

FRANCIS OF IPSWICH, 1634

The passenger list for the *Francis*, sailing from Ipswich, Suffolk, was drawn up on 30 April 1634. This passenger list, along with that of its sister ship, the *Elizabeth*, was prepared in an unusual way, with one section for the adults and another section for the children [Hotten 277-80]. In the adult section the wives were entered immediately after their husbands. In the section for children, the names were grouped by household, which sometimes included children with surnames other than that of the head of household.

In this context, those who took the Oath of Allegiance and Supremacy were listed with the adults. For these two ships departing from Ipswich, the youngest person taking the Oath was eighteen years old. All the children were fifteen years old or younger.

For the *Francis*, there were forty-four adults, comprising twenty-seven men between the ages of nineteen and sixty and seventeen women between the ages of twenty-two and forty-seven.

Five of the men have not been found in New England records: John Greene, William Haulton, Thomas King, John Mapes and Richard Wattlin [GM 2:3:141, 246, 2:4:170, 2:5:17-18]. King was nineteen and the other men were in their twenties, and none was married. With common names such as John Greene and Thomas King, these passengers might be identical with later New England settlers of the same names, but no satisfactory connections could be made.

Of the remaining twenty-two men, ten appear in New England records within a year of arrival and are easily identified with the passengers of 1634:

> **John Barnard** [GM 2:1:158-61]: Cambridge land grant, 4 August 1634 [CaTR 9]; freeman 4 March 1634/5 [MBCR 1:370].

> **Thomas Boyden** [GM 2:1:366-68]: admitted to Scituate church on 17 May 1635 [NEHGR 9:279].

> **Thurston Clarke** [GM 2:2:99-101]: daughter Faith, who was also on the *Francis*, married Edward Doty at Plymouth on 6 January 1634/5 [PCR 1:32].

> **Robert Coe** [GM 2:2:125-32]: freeman 3 September 1634 [MBCR 1:369].

> **William Freeborn** [GM 2:2:573-75]: admitted to Roxbury church in 1634 [RChR 80]; freeman 3 September 1634 [MBCR 1:369].

> **John Livermore** [GM 2:4:297-302]: freeman 6 May 1635 [MBCR 1:370].

> **Hugh Mason** [GM 2:5:74-81]: freeman 4 March 1634/5 [MBCR 1:370].

> **Abraham Newell** [GM 2:5:245-50]: admitted to Roxbury church in 1634 [RChR 80]; freeman 4 March 1634/5 [MBCR 1:370].

> **Richard Pepper** [GM 2:5:437-38]: admitted to Roxbury church in 1634 [RChR 80]; freeman 4 March 1634/5 [MBCR 1:370].

> **William Westwood**: freeman 4 March 1634/5 [MBCR 1:370].

The remaining twelve men appear in New England records between 1636 and 1642, and can be reasonably identified with the 1634 passengers on the basis of a variety of types of circumstantial evidence:

> **John Betts** [GM 2:1:273-77]: owned a houselot in Cambridge by 8 February 1635/6 [CaTR 18]; other passengers on the *Francis* also settled in Cambridge.

Edward Bugby [GM 2:1:456-59]: was granted eight acres of land at Roxbury on 1 June 1639 [RTR 1:1]; he was accompanied on the *Francis* by a daughter Sarah, aged 4, and in his will the Roxbury man made a bequest to a daughter Sarah who would be of about the same age.

Justinian Holden [GM 2:3:355-62]: granted a farm at Watertown on 10 May 1642 (implying that he had purchased the proprietary right of an earlier grantee of Watertown land) [WaBOP 13]; other passengers on the *Francis* settled in Watertown; brother of Richard Holden who was also on the *Francis*.

Richard Holden [GM 2:3:363-68]: child born at Watertown on 19 July 1642 [WaVR 1:10]; circumstantial arguments as for brother Justinian Holden.

Nicholas Jennings [GM 2:4:50-58]: served from Hartford in the Pequot War of 1637 [HaBOP 172]; other passengers on the *Francis* also settled in Hartford.

John Pease [GM 2:5:414-18]: granted land at Salem in 1636 [STR 1:24]; brother Robert Pease also on *Francis* and also settled in Salem; from Great Baddow, Essex, an area from which other passengers on the *Francis* derived.

Robert Pease [GM 2:5:418-20]: granted land in Salem in 1636 [STR 1:24]; circumstantial arguments as for brother John Pease.

Robert Rose: first seen in New England records at Wethersfield in early 1640; of the eight children in the passenger list, seven are found in New England [Christine Rose, *Descendants of Robert Rose of Wethersfield and Branford, Connecticut* (San Jose, 1983)].

Thomas Sherwood: sold land at Wethersfield on 25 March 1640 [FOOF 1:548-49]; of the four children in the passenger list, three are found in New England [TAG 80:278-82].

Rowland Stebbins: granted land at Springfield on 24 December 1640 [Springfield Hist 1:167]; of the four children in the passenger list, all four are found in New England [TAG 31:196-98].

Anthony White: granted land at Sudbury on 22 March 1639/40 [TAG 82:39-48]; moved to Watertown by 1644, where other passengers on the *Francis* had already settled.

Robert Wing: child born at Boston on 22 July 1637 [BVR 5]; on 11 November 1647, "Rob[er]t Wing, he being above 80 years of age," petitioned Massachusetts Bay General Court [MBCR 2:216], an age which agrees with the age of the 1634 passenger.

MARY & JOHN OF SOUTHAMPTON, 1634

The passenger list for the *Mary & John*, sailing from Southampton, was prepared on 24 March 1633/4 and 26 March 1634 [Drake's Founder 70-71]. Unlike the list for the *Francis*, this compilation contained only the names of males who had taken the Oath of Allegiance and Supremacy. Based on the example of the *Francis*, we can assume that all of those named were at least sixteen years old.

This passenger list contains fifty-six names, but our analysis will cover only fifty-four of them, as two of the men are explicitly noted as being left behind to sail on a later vessel: John Anthony and Matthew Hewlett [GM 2:1:67, 2:3:314].

Seventeen of these men have not been found in New England records: William Ballard, William Clarke, Thomas Cole, William Hibbens, Abraham Mussey, Joseph Myles, William Newby, John Newman, Robert Newman, Richard Reynolds, William Savery, William Spencer, Thomas Sweet, William Tracy, Henry Trask, Adrian Vincent and Thomas West [GM 2:1:151, 2:2:101, 157, 2:3:315-17, 2:5:203-4, 216-17, 242, 253-54]. Some of these passengers might be identical with later New England settlers of the same names, but no satisfactory connections could be made.

Of the remaining thirty-seven men, sixteen appear in New England records within a year of arrival and are easily identified with the passengers of 1634:

Richard Browne [GM 2:1:432-35]: freeman 6 May 1635 [MBCR 1:371].

Nicholas Easton [GM 2:2:396-403]: freeman 3 September 1634 [MBCR 1:370].

Philip Fowler [GM 2:2:560-64]: freeman 3 September 1634 [MBCR 1:369].

Richard Jacob [GM 2:4:28-32]: freeman 6 May 1635 [MBCR 1:371].

Stephen Jordan [GM 2:4:114-16]: on 20 August 1635, apparently at Ipswich, his daughter Ann married Robert Cross [NEHGR 68:201, citing SJC Births, Marriages, and Deaths, folio 85].

Richard Kent Junior [GM 2:4:142-45]: freeman 4 March 1634/5 [MBCR 1:370].

William Moody [GM 2:5:135-37]: freeman 6 May 1635 [MBCR 1:371].

John Mussey [GM 2:5:204-6]: granted land at Ipswich on 26 January 1634/5 [ITR].

John Newman [GM 2:5:251-53]: granted land at Ipswich in 1634 [ITR]. (Note that there were two men of this name on the passenger list of the *Mary & John*.)

James Noyes [GM 2:5:282-86]: freeman 3 September 1634 [MBCR 1:370].

Christopher Osgood [GM 2:5:318-22]: freeman 6 May 1635 [MBCR 1:371].

Thomas Parker [GM 2:5:367-70]: freeman 3 September 1634 [MBCR 1:370].

Robert Seaver [GMB 3:1644-46]: admitted to Roxbury church in 1634 [RChR 80].

Henry Short: freeman 3 September 1634 [MBCR 1:369].

John Spencer: freeman 3 September 1634 [MBCR 1:369].

William White: involved in a dispute at Ipswich on 29 December 1634 [ITR].

The remaining twenty-one men appear in New England records between 1636 and 1642, and can be reasonably identified with the 1634 passengers on the basis of a variety of types of circumstantial evidence:

Thomas Avery [GM 2:1:113-15]: admitted to Salem church on 30 September 1638 [SChR 7]; freeman 28 February 1642/3 [EQC 1:50]; other passengers on the *Mary & John* also settled at Salem.

John Bartlett: freeman 17 May 1637, sixth in a sequence of eight Newbury men [MBCR 1:373]; other passengers on the *Mary & John* also settled at Newbury. (This immigrant was inadvertently omitted from the appropriate Great Migration volume.)

George Browne [GM 2:1:418-20]: freeman 13 May 1640 [MBCR 1:377]; other passengers on the *Mary & John,* including his brother Richard Browne, also settled at Newbury.

Robert Coker [GM 2:2:142-44]: eldest known child born at Newbury on 6 October 1640; other passengers on the *Mary & John* also settled at Newbury; the sons of William Moody, another passenger on the *Mary & John,* were his "kinsmen" [EPR 3:403-4].

William Franklin [GM 2:2:568-73]: eldest known child born at Boston on 3 October 1638 [BVR 6]; he settled first at Ipswich, where other passengers on the *Mary & John* had also settled.

Matthew Gillett [GM 2:3:65-66]: on 30 March 1641, he completed his apprenticeship of seven years to a Salem man [EQC 1:25], which implies that his apprenticeship began at the time he left England; other passengers on the *Mary & John* also settled in Salem.

John Godfrey [GM 2:3:88-91]: first resided at Newbury, and, on 12 July 1642, he sued Richard Kent, another passenger on the *Mary & John* [EQC 1:43-44].

Richard Kent Senior [GM 2:4:140-42]: daughter married in New England by 1641 [TAG 75:181-86]; sued by John Godfrey in 1642 and 1643 [EQC 1:43, 53]; other passengers on the *Mary & John* also settled in Newbury.

Robert Kinsman [GM 2:4:188-91]: granted land at Ipswich on 2 March 1637/8 [ITR]; other passengers on the *Mary & John* also settled in Ipswich.

Daniel Ladd [GM 2:4:217-21]: eldest known child born at Salisbury on 1 November 1640; freeman 28 March 1648 [EQC 1:139]; other passengers on the *Mary & John* also settled at Ipswich.

Richard Littlehale [GM 2:4:294-96]: granted land at Newbury on 12 March 1641/2 [Newbury Hist (Currier) 54]; other passengers on the *Mary & John* also settled at Newbury.

John Luff [GM 2:4:359-61]: granted land at Salem in 1636 [STR 1:23]; other passengers on the *Mary & John* also settled at Salem.

Henry Lunt [GM 2:4:365-68]: freeman 2 May 1638 [MBCR 1:374]; other passengers on the *Mary & John* also settled at Ipswich.

John Marsh [GM 2:5:26-30]: granted land at Salem in 1636 [STR 1:23]; admitted to Salem church on 12 May 1639 [SChR 8]; freeman 26 February 1649/50 [EQC 1:184]; other passengers on the *Mary & John* also settled at Salem.

Thomas Newman [GM 2:5:254-57]: granted land at Ipswich on 4 January 1638/9 [ITR]; brother of John Newman who was also a passenger on the *Mary & John* and settled at Ipswich.

Nicholas Noyes [GM 2:5:286-93]: freeman 17 May 1637 [MBCR 1:373]; brother of James Noyes who was also a passenger on the *Mary & John* and settled at Ipswich and Newbury; Cotton Mather told the story of the two brothers coming to New England on the same vessel [Magnalia 484-85].

Joseph Pope [GM 2:5:487-91]: granted land at Salem in 1636 and admitted to Salem church before the end of that year [STR 1:24; SChR 6]; freeman 17 May 1637 [MBCR 1:373]; other passengers on the *Mary & John* also settled at Salem.

Thomas Savery: on 4 December 1638, "Thomas Savory, for his gross lying, was referred to the court at Ipswich" [MBCR 1:248]; he was again in Massachusetts Bay court on 2 June 1640 [MBCR 1:297]; other passengers on the *Mary & John* also settled at Ipswich.

Henry Travers: proprietor at Newbury in 1637 [Pope 461]; other passengers on the *Mary & John* also settled at Newbury.

John Wheeler: proprietor at Salisbury by 1639, and had perhaps resided at Hampton just prior to his residence at Salisbury [GDMNH 743; Hoyt 353-54]; removed to Newbury by 1650; this sequence of moves suggests earlier residence in Newbury, where other passengers on the *Mary & John* had also settled.

John Woodbridge: deputy for Newbury to Massachusetts Bay General Court, 18 April 1637 [MBCR 1:191]; nephew of Thomas Parker who was also a passenger on the *Mary & John* and who also settled at Newbury.

CRITERIA FOR IDENTIFICATION

The two passenger lists that we have been studying included eighty-one males aged sixteen or older. Of these, twenty-two left no records in New England, twenty-six were found in New England records within a year of being entered on the passenger list, and thirty-three have been identified as arriving in New England but not making a mark on the records for anywhere from two to eight years after the creation of the passenger lists. Each of these three categories requires separate discussion.

The twenty-two men who have been described as not leaving any records in New England fall into two groups: those with names that never appeared in early New England and those with names that did. In those cases where the name never appeared in New England, we may be quite certain of our conclusions, although it is possible that these passengers did actually arrive in New England, but left or died before leaving any record.

The second class of those who are not found in New England is more problematic. Here we must analyze many New England records for the name in question and decide whether the New England person is the same as the passenger in question. Our conclusions in these instances may not always be correct, but reasons are included in the appropriate sketches in each case. An important conclusion of the present analysis is that in all cases where we do identify the 1634 passenger with a settler, the first New England record occurs no later than 1642, a gap of eight years. In many of the cases where we do not identify the passenger with a later New England resident, the gap in years is much greater.

The twenty-six passengers who were found in New England records within one year of arrival are among the easiest to deal with, although it is not simply their appearance within a year that leads to the identification with the passenger. Other evidence is helpful and sometimes necessary, for we must always be alert for the possibility that two or more persons of the same name arrived in a given year, only one of whom is included in the surviving passenger lists, and that it will not necessarily be the one in the passenger lists who is represented in the later records.

Finally, we need to take a much closer look at those immigrants who are, we conclude, identical with the passengers of 1634, but who do not appear in the records for two years or more after arrival. Several different types of evidence will be helpful to us in examining these cases.

Perhaps the most important feature of these two lists is that each ship drew its passengers from a restricted number of English counties, and these passengers, once they were in New England, chose a limited number of towns to settle in.

The *Francis* set sail from Ipswich, gathering its passengers from a number of parishes along the Stour River valley, in southern Suffolk and northern Essex. Upon arrival in New England, most of these immigrants went to Cambridge, Watertown or Roxbury, towns that had already received many settlers from the same part of England. Furthermore, since by 1634 the movement to the Connecticut River Valley was just getting under way, some of the passengers moved on almost immediately to Hartford and Wethersfield, the towns that derived so many of their settlers from Cambridge and Watertown.

The *Mary & John*, by contrast, coming from the port of Southampton, had collected most of its passengers from Hampshire and Wiltshire. These new arrivals moved for the most part to the Essex County towns of Ipswich, Newbury and Salem.

As may be seen by examining our stated circumstantial reasons for identifying passengers with New England settlers,

this set of circumstances has been employed repeatedly to assist us in making our decisions. Of course, additional evidence is also welcome, and these patterns of migration do not apply in every case. For example, Robert Seaver, who sailed on the *Mary & John*, settled in Roxbury rather than one of the Essex County towns.

Another important consideration in making these identifications is the that the immigrant may be accompanied by other family members. Because of the different structures of the two passenger lists examined here, only the list for the *Francis* is helpful in that regard. Three families are especially instructive: Robert Rose, Thomas Sherwood and Rowland Stebbins. In 1634 these three men were 40, 48 and 40 years old respectively, and each had a wife and between four and eight children with them. Although these men may well have spent a year or so in one of the Massachusetts Bay towns, none left a record there, and all three show up in one of the Connecticut River towns by 1640. Given this gap of six years, we might be hard pressed to make the identification without the congruence between the children seen on the passenger list and those found later in New England. This type of evidence makes up in part for the relative scarcity of town records in early Connecticut.

RELEVANCE TO THE END OF THE GREAT MIGRATION

We turn now to our second question, regarding the interpretation of the post-1640 lists of freemen. Of the fifty-nine men from these two ships who did settle in New England, twenty-six appeared in the records within one year of arrival. And of these, nineteen made this first appearance in the records of admission to Massachusetts Bay freemanship.

Looked at in another way, this means that two-thirds of our sample of 1634 passengers did not become freemen of Massachusetts Bay within a year of arrival. This may have come about for a variety of reasons. Some did eventually become freemen, but not for two or more years. Some never became freemen, even though they lived out their lives in Massachusetts Bay. Some moved almost immediately to Connecticut and so never had the opportunity to become freemen of Massachusetts Bay.

Whatever the reason, when we come to study the end of the Great Migration, we should not expect that all the passengers of 1640 would have attained freemanship by 1641. Thus, many of the arrivals of the last year or two of the Great Migration will be found in the lists of freemen for 1642 or later years.

We will, therefore, need other criteria for deciding whether those in the lists of freemen of the early 1640s should or should not be accounted as having been part of the Great Migration as we define it. One way to gain more information on this point would be to study some of these lists of freemen from the early 1640s to see what other tools may be employed to answer this question. Just such an analysis will be undertaken in an upcoming issue of the *Newsletter*.

RECENT LITERATURE

Michael J. Leclerc and D. Brenton Simons, "Origin of Accused Witch Mary[1] (Williams) (King?) Hale of Boston and Her Brothers Hugh[1], John[1], and, Possibly, Nathaniel[1] Williams," *The American Genealogist* 82 (2007):161-71. The authors explore the genealogical relationships of Mary Hale of Boston, who was accused of witchcraft in 1681. They first discuss the husbands of Mary Hale and then tell the story of the later accusations of witchcraft made against Mary Hale's daughter and granddaughter, both named Winifred Benham. Then, Leclerc and Simons identify two (and possibly three) brothers for Mary Hale. The two certain brothers were Hugh Williams, who was a resident of Boston by 1641, and John Williams, who was in New England by 1664. The third possible brother was Nathaniel Williams, of Boston by 1638.

Michael J. Leclerc, "Sarah[2] (Parker) Williams, Wife of Hugh[1] Williams of Boston, Massachusetts, and Block Island, Rhode Island," *The American Genealogist* 82 (2007):172-77. Leclerc extends the work of the previous article by identifying the wife of Hugh Williams of Boston. He argues that she was Sarah Parker, born in England, the previously unidentified daughter of Parnell (Gray) (Parker) Nowell by her first husband. Her second husband was Increase Nowell, immigrant to Charlestown in 1630.

William Wyman Fiske, "The Perry Family of Sawbridgeworth, Hertfordshire: Shared Ancestry of Six Massachusetts Immigrants: John[1] Perry of Roxbury, Isaac[1] Perry of Boston, Mary[1] (Perry) Heath of Roxbury, Phebe[1] (Perry) Desborough of Roxbury, John[1] Reddington of Topsfield, and Abraham[1] Reddington of Topsfield and Boxford," *The American Genealogist* 82 (2007):187-95. Fiske continues his investigation of the Perry family of Sawbridgeworth, Hertfordshire. In this installment, he presents genealogical summaries of the families of Thomas[C] Perry, born perhaps 1480, and his eldest son, John Perry, born perhaps 1505. Future installments will cover two additional sons of Thomas[C], as well as later generations and also accounts of other related families.

Leslie Mahler, "The Parentage of Alice Tiler, First Wife of Thomas[1] Sherwood of Wethersfield, Stamford, and Fairfield, Connecticut," *The American Genealogist* 82 (2007):211-13. Having recently identified the English origin of Thomas[1] Sherwood of Connecticut, Mahler now presents evidence for the identity of his first wife. The clue appears in a will found by a systematic search of the records of the Archdeaconry of Sudbury, Suffolk. Joan Stephens, widow of Thomas Stephens of Preston, Suffolk, made a bequest to "Alice my daughter weife of Thomas Sherwoode of Kettlebarston." Further research showed that Joan had earlier been married to John Tiler, with whom she had six daughters, including Alice (Tiler) Sherwood.

John Blythe Dobson, "Chamberlaynes in the Ancestry of the Betts Family of Newtown, Long Island," *The American Genealogist* 82 (2007):227-32. Extending his earlier work on Robert Chamberlayne of Strood, Kent, Dobson sets forth evidence for the identity of Robert's father. The will of Thomas Chamberlaine, vicar of Oakley, Bedfordshire, identifies a family which matches that outlined in the later will of Robert. Additional clues suggest strongly that this Thomas was the father of Robert. Robert Chamberlayne was father of Samuel Chamberlain of Ipswich, Massachusetts, and of Joanna (Chamberlain) Betts, wife of Richard[1] Betts of Newtown, Long Island.

Priscilla Colstad Greenlees, "Identification of the Unnamed Daughter of John[1] and Elizabeth (Thomas) Cogswell Who Remained in England," *The New England Historical and Genealogical Register* 162 (2008):5-7. John[1] Cogswell had a daughter Phyllis baptized in England on 2 July 1624, a daughter for whom there is no record in New England. By examining a number of English wills, the author demonstrates that Phyllis remained in old England, or returned there, and married John Broadhurst at Chirton, Wiltshire, on 23 January 1643/4, and has with him at least seven children. John[2] Cogswell had returned to England in 1652, and in a letter back to his parents he reported that "My sister hath 2 children." This report matches what is known about the children of Phyllis (Cogswell) Broadhurst.

Michael J. Leclerc, "Mary[3] Hemenway, Wife of George[2] Lawrence of Watertown, Massachusetts," *The New England Historical and Genealogical Register* 162 (2008):15-17. George Lawrence of Watertown, son of the immigrant of the same name, married by 1698 a woman named Mary, surname unknown. In the course of research on the family of Ralph[1] Hemenway (or Hemingway), resident of Roxbury by 1633 [GMB 2:908-10], Leclerc found documents from the early eighteenth century which demonstrate that Mary was a daughter of John[2] Hemenway, son of Ralph.

Henry B. Hoff, Michael J. Leclerc, and Helen Schatvet Ullmann, "Jeremiah[1] Rogers of Dorchester and Lancaster, Massachusetts," *The New England Historical and Genealogical Register* 162 (2008):18-22. In the early 1650s Jeremiah Rogers appeared in Dorchester, where he married Abigail Pierce, daughter of John[1] Pierce, who had settled in Dorchester by 1630 [GMB 3:1469-72]. The authors have prepared standard genealogical summaries of the families of Jeremiah Rogers and his son of the same name.

Gale Ion Harris, "Wolston[1] Brockway of Lyme, Connecticut: With Further Analysis of His Associations," *The New England Historical and Genealogical Register* 162 (2008):37-46. In this first installment of a multipart article, Harris takes a detailed look at the New England career of Wolston[1] Brockway, with particular reference to his associations with various Harris families.

Ernest Hyde Helliwell III, "A Jordan-Silvester Connection Revealed," *The New England Historical and Genealogical*

Register 162 (2008):47-53. John Jordan of Milton, Massachusetts, had married by 1673 a woman whose name has not been known. Through examination of Milton town records in the early eighteenth century, Helliwell has demonstrated a connection of John Jordan with the family of Richard[1] Silvester, who had settled in Weymouth by 1630 [GMB 3:1677-81]. Further research identified the wife of John Jordan as either Esther or Naomi Silvester, daughters of Richard whose adult history had not been previously determined. This line of research also led to further information on Dinah Silvester, another daughter of Richard.

William Wyman Fiske, "Ancestry of Bennet Eliot of Nazeing, Essex, Father of Seven Great Migration Immigrants to Massachusetts (*continued*)," *The New England Historical and Genealogical Register* 162 (2008):65-72. Fiske continues his genealogical summary of the Eliot family of Hertfordshire and Essex with sketches of four more heads of family of the sixteenth century. The last of these sketches is for Simon Forbes of Much Hadham, Hertfordshire, born about 1520, father of Bennet Eliot and grandfather of the seven immigrants to Massachusetts.

[Pat Hatcher], "Peter[3] Tefft and Occam's Razor," *The New York Genealogical and Biographical Record* 139 (2008):103-8. John[1] Tefft of Warwick, Rhode Island, was brother of William[1] Tefft who had settled in Boston by 1638. John Tefft had two sons, Joshua and Samuel; older sources have claimed that only Samuel had children who survived to adulthood. Hatcher carefully analyzes all available evidence and concludes that there were two adult Peter Teffts of the third generation, one who was son of Joshua and one who was son of Samuel. The article concludes with a standard genealogical summary of the first three generations of the descendants of John Tefft.

Susan Hardman Moore, *Pilgrims: New World Settlers & the Call of Home* (New York and London: Yale University Press, 2007). Moore examines carefully the conditions in old England in the 1620s and 1630s that led to the Great Migration. She then describes the establishment of the New England Way, the organization and practices of the churches that the immigrants established upon their arrival. Finally, she looks at the motivations for returning to old England in the 1640s and the lives of those immigrants who recrossed the Atlantic to their country of birth. The author makes extensive use of the publications of the Great Migration Study Project in her work. A substantial appendix consolidates data on several hundred individuals who returned to England in the 1640s and 1650s, with information on places of residence in both old and New England and dates of migration in both directions. Of especial interest, Moore has unearthed additional information on the post-New England careers of a number of individuals already treated in Great Migration volumes, such as Edward Bendall and John Mylam.

Great Migration Newsletter

Vol. 17   July-September 2008   No. 3

GEORGE RUSSELL OF HINGHAM

A recurrent theme in the methodology of the Great Migration Study Project is the problem of sorting out records for two or more men of the same name. We present here an example of this methodological problem, drawn from research on the current Great Migration volume, that provides several striking instances of records that tie together the multiple migrations within New England of one family.

The immediate impetus for this research was the presence on the passenger list of the *Elizabeth* on 9 April 1635 of "Geo[rge] Russell," aged 19 [Hotten 54]. Both Savage and Pope identified this 1635 passenger with the man of the same name who was granted land at Hingham in 1636 [Savage 3:590; Pope 395]. Our task is to decide whether or not Savage and Pope were correct in this claim. In order to do so, we shall have to trace the full career in New England of George Russell of Hingham, which will lead us to an interesting series of interlocking land records.

On 3 July 1636, there was "given unto George Russels [*sic*] by the town of Hingham for a house lot five acres of land" [HiBOP 60]. This entry was followed immediately by a list of grants of planting lots, a great lot and a lot of salt marsh to Henry Rust, indicating that Rust had acquired Russell's houselot within a short time, perhaps a few months, after the grant to Russell. As usual in early New England towns, the houselot carried with it the full proprietary share, which explains the placement of the Russell and Rust entries as one group.

A year later, a George Russell appears a few miles to the south, in the town of Plymouth. On 2 October 1637, "seven acres of lands are granted to Georg[e] Russell, lying in the same place [from Winslowe's Walk northward towards the Cedar Swamp], to belong to his house to be built in Plymouth" [PCR 1:65]. On 17 November 1637, "Richard Wright of New Plymouth, tailor," sold to "Georg[e] Russell of the same place, yeoman, ... all that his lot of lands with the fence and labors upon the same upon Oulbery Plain containing about four or five acres (which said lot of land the said Richard Wright bought of Mr. Alexander Higgens)" [PCR 12:24]. On 4 December 1637, a "garden place is granted to George Russell in the neighborhood of Mr. John Weeks, and to have that parcel of land lying in Woberry Plain, he lately bought of Richard Wright, to be made up seven acres" [PCR 1:70]. On 2 July 1638, "George

Russell" was one of four men who entered a "request for a swamp which lyeth betwixt part of some of their lands at Willingsby Brook" [PCR 1:90]. These are the only records found for George Russell in Plymouth, and nothing connects them with the George Russell seen in 1636 in Hingham.

On 14 February 1639[/40], George Russell married "widow James" at Hingham, and they had three children baptized there: Mary, on [blank] April 1641; Elizabeth on 12 January 1642[/3]; and Martha on [1]9 October 1645 [NEHGR 121:12, 13, 15, 18]. On 2 June 1643, "Edward Foster of Scittuaat" sold to "George Russell of Hingham ... my lot of land both marsh land & upland lying in Scittuaat at the First Herring Brook ... both upland be it sixteen, eighteen or twenty acres more or less and marsh land be it ten acres more or less" [PCR 12:183-84]. Soon after the date of this deed, Russell had moved to Scituate, where he appeared in a number of records from 1643 to 1651 [PCR 2:90, 116, 138, 139, 153, 170, 172, 7:44, 8:183, 191].

Then, on 7 October 1651, "G[e]orge Russell of Scittuate" sold to "Gyles Richard Senior of the town of Plym[outh] ..., weaver, ... his house and land at Wellingslay near Plymouth aforesaid ... with two acres of land be it more or less on which the said house now standeth with seven acres of upland more or less lying at Wobery Plain" [PCR 12:213]. Comparison of this deed with the land granted to a George Russell in Plymouth shows that this is the same land, thus neatly tying together the migration of George Russell from Plymouth to Hingham to Scituate. Furthermore, the proven move from Plymouth to Hingham suggests that the 1636 Hingham land grant was made to the same man.

(continued on page 18)

EDITOR'S EFFUSIONS

Again and again in the *Great Migration Newsletter* we have emphasized the importance of the detection of patterns in the records that we analyze. In the lead article in this issue we encounter again an important pattern which we introduced in the first issue of the *Newsletter*.

In our treatment of "George Russell of Hingham," the first New England record discussed is an entry from the Hingham land inventory. On 3 July 1636, George Russell was granted "for a house lot five acres of land" [HiBOP 60]. This is the only occurrence of the name George Russell in the Hingham land inventory, and is followed immediately on the same page by four entries of the same form for parcels of land granted to Henry Rust. After these five entries is the statement that "all the abovesaid parcels of land and meadow given unto Henery Rust were given unto him and his heirs forever."

Notice that even though the first parcel had been granted to George Russell, the summary statement at the end was written as though all the parcels had been granted directly to Henry Rust. There is, then, no explicit statement of the actual sequence of events, in which George Russell sold his houselot to Henry Rust soon after the grant, and with the houselot would have come the full proprietary rights, under which Rust received the additional four parcels of land.

In the *Focus* section of the first issue of the *Newsletter*, we examined the early land records of Watertown. In the Inventory of Grants, we saw that under the heading for Thurston Rainer was a homestall (or houselot). This was followed by a separate heading for Gregory Stone, with five grants of upland and meadow. Then there was a third heading, for Thomas Boyson, with one grant of upland. In the Composite Inventory, all seven of these parcels are gathered together, implying by this arrangement the transfer of the proprietary share from Rainer to Stone to Boyson [GMN 1:4-6].

We have, then, a pattern with variations. The basic mechanics of granting proprietary lands were much the same from town to town, but each town clerk found his own way to record the transfers of land. None of the clerks, however, stated the transfers explicitly, leaving to the modern researcher the task of inferring these exchanges of land.

Robert Charles Anderson, FASG   Editor
Jean Powers, Production Assistant

The Great Migration Newsletter is published quarterly by the Great Migration Study Project, a project of the New England Historic Genealogical Society, 101 Newbury Street, Boston MA 02116
www.NewEnglandAncestors.org
www.GreatMigration.org
GreatMigration@nehgs.org

(continued from page 17)

On 6 June 1654, George Russell was made constable at Marshfield. On 8 June 1655, he was propounded for Plymouth Colony freemanship, and, on 3 June 1657, was admitted [PCR 3:78, 117]. George Russell appears in the Marshfield section of the 1658 Plymouth Colony list of freemen [PCR 8:201]. In late 1657 and early 1658 "George Russell, of Marshfeild," was engaged in a lawsuit with Abraham Sutliffe [PCR 7:84, 86-87] and, on 7 February 1660/1, George Russell served on a coroner's jury on the death of a Marshfield man [PCR 3:208].

On 22 March 1657[/8?], "Gyles Rickard Senior of Plymouth" deeded to "his son Gyles Rickard of Plymouth aforesaid planter all that his parcel of upland ground lying and being in the township of Plymouth aforesaid at a place called Woobery Plain at the eastern end thereof containing seven acres" and other land "which the said Gyles Rickard Senior bought of G[e]orge Russell of Marshfeild" [MD 12:132-33, citing PCLR 2:1:205]. Giles Rickard Senior was kind enough to take note explicitly of George Russell's move from Scituate to Marshfield between his purchase of the land in 1651 and his sale of the same land in 1657, thus securing this link in the chain of identity.

On 20 April 1658, "George Russell of Marshfeild" sold to "John Turner Junior of Scittuate ... a certain parcel of upland lying and being in Scituate aforesaid containing by estimation twenty-two acres ... and I the said George Russell do covenant, promise and grant by these presents that Jane my wife shall surrender up her right in the aforesaid land before a magistrate according to order of court in that case provided within one month after the sealing and delivery hereof" [PCLR 3:45-46]. This may be the same land that George Russell had purchased from Edward Foster in 1643. More importantly, we have here the first occurrence of the given name of George Russell's wife, which will assist us at the next stage of our journey.

By 1 March 1663/4, court proceedings arranged for a payment in settlement of a lawsuit to be made "at the house of G[e]orge Russell, of Scittuate," and, on 7 June 1665, he was made constable of that town [PCR 4:53, 91]. George Russell then appears in the Scituate sections of the Plymouth Colony lists of freemen of 29 May 1670 and 1 [blank] 1683/4 [PCR 5:275, 8:202].

On 1 August 1668, "George Russell of Scituate ..., yeoman," sold to "Thomas King Junior of Scituate aforesaid, wheelwright, ... a certain parcel of upland lying and being in Scituate aforesaid containing eight acres and three-quarters which is a part or moiety of a lot of land which the said George Russell bought of Isaac Stedman"; on 6 April 1669, "this deed was acknowledged by George Russell & Jane his wife" [PLR 3:219]. In this instance, the move from Marshfield back to Scituate, sometime between 7 February 1660/1 and 1 March 1663/4, is confirmed by the participation in two deeds by George Russell's wife Jane.

(continued on page 24)

Focus on Immigration

INTRODUCTION

In the last issue of the *Great Migration Newsletter*, we examined two short passenger lists, in part to answer the question of how much time elapsed between a person appearing on a passenger list and the same person appearing in New England records [GMN 17:11-14]. We found that many of these passengers generated New England records within a few months of arrival, but that a substantial number did not appear in the records for as many as seven years.

In this issue and the next we will ask a similar question, but looking in the reverse direction. Our basic source will be the list of those admitted as freemen of Massachusetts Bay on 2 June 1641 [MBCR 1:378-79], the opening day of the General Court of Elections. We use this date each year as the cutoff for determining that a given immigrant had arrived in New England no later than the previous year, on the assumption that very few passengers ships can have arrived in New England any earlier than this date, given the difficulty of crossing the North Atlantic during the winter.

On three previous occasions we have asked the question "When Did the Great Migration End?" [GMN 1:9, 10:1-2, 8, 14:25-26]. In the most recent of these articles, we concluded that 1639 was the last year of heavy migration to New England as part of the Great Migration. If this conclusion is correct, we should expect that relatively few of those admitted to freemanship on 2 June 1641 had actually arrived in 1640.

METHODOLOGY

The list for 2 June 1641 includes the names of 126 men, two of these names being incomplete. Our procedure will be to examine each of these names, in search of independent evidence of their presence in New England prior to that date. We will also seek out the records of admission to church, in those towns where the church records have survived, since church admission was at this time a prerequisite to freemanship.

In some cases, our entries will be very simple, when we have a passenger list entry for the immigrant, but have no record of church admission. Examples of this sort are Thomas Davis and John Emery of Newbury.

In other instances, the entries may be quite lengthy, if, for example, the person in the list had resided in more than one town before 2 June 1641, or if there were two or more men of the name in New England by that date, and we need to review and discuss a number of records to be sure we have the right freeman. Moses Payne and John Stevens fall into this category.

In the process, we will also be demonstrating the value of the analysis of these lists for determining the residences of some of these immigrants. This derives from the frequent practice of grouping the freemen from a given town together in the lists of freemen. This practice was not always followed faithfully, so some sections of the list will not be as neatly organized as others.

To assist in visualizing this aspect of the list, we will place a two-letter code after each name, designating the church to which they had been admitted, thus qualifying them for freemanship:

Bo	Boston
Br	Braintree
Ca	Cambridge
Ch	Charlestown
Co	Concord
De	Dedham
Do	Dorchester
Hi	Hingham
Ip	Ipswich
Ly	Lynn
Ne	Newbury
Rx	Roxbury
Sm	Salem
Su	Sudbury
Sy	Salisbury
Wa	Watertown
We	Weymouth

LIST OF FREEMEN, 2 JUNE 1641

Mr. Henry Dunster (Ca): He came to New England in the summer of 1640, settled at Cambridge and was elected President of Harvard College on 27 August 1640 [Morison 376-77].

Mr. Richard Russell (Ch): "Richard Russell and Maud Russell" were admitted to Charlestown church on 22 May 1641 [ChChR 10].

Mr. John Allen (Ch): "John Allen" was admitted to Charlestown church on 22 May 1641 [ChChR 10]. He had been granted land at Charlestown in 1639 [Wyman 17].

John Maies (Rx): "John Mays" was admitted to Roxbury church in 1640 [RChR 84].

Richard North (Sy): Received land at Salisbury in the "first division," 1640 [Hoyt 266]. (Settlement of Salisbury began in 1639, and the "first division" was spread over 1639 and 1640. In the absence of further evidence, we will assume 1640 as the date of the "first division" [Hoyt 7-10].)

John Seir (Ch): "John Seers" was admitted to Charlestown church on 28 March 1641 [ChChR 10]. His wife, "Susanna Seers," had been admitted on 2 February 1639/40 [ChChR 10], thus implying that the family had arrived in New England no later than 1639.

John Stevens (Sy): He received land in the "first division" at Salisbury, 1640 [Hoyt 8, 325]. (There is another John Stevens who might cause some confusion, the passenger on the *Confidence* in 1638 [Drake's Founders 59]. This 1638 passenger settled at Newbury and was admitted to freemanship on 18 May 1642 along with other Newbury men, including his brother William who had sailed with him [MBCR 2:292; Hoyt 322-24]. Our confidence in assigning the John Stevens in the present list to Salisbury is the presence of other Salisbury men close by in the list.)

Mr. Adam Winthrope (Bo). "Adam Winthrop one of the sons of our brother Mr. John Winthrop Senior" was admitted to Boston church on 4 July 1640 [BChR 29]. He was born in 1620 and had come to New England in the early 1630s [GMB 3:2038-42].

William Barnes (Sy): He received land in the "first division" at Salisbury, 1640 [Hoyt 9-10, 54]. (He is distinguished from William Barnes of Gloucester by his association here with other Salisbury men.)

John Harrison (Sy): He received land in the "first division" at Salisbury, 1640 [Hoyt 8, 195]. On 17 February 1643/4, "John Harryson, a roper, and Grace his wife, both of them dismissed members from the Church of Salsbury," were admitted to Boston church [BChR 40]. (Note that there is a second John Harrison later in this list.)

John Lowell (Ne): His son Joseph was born at Newbury on 28 November 1639. John Lowell was son of Percival Lowell, who came to New England in 1639 [Phoebe Tilton Anc 216, 221].

Thomas Davies (Ne): Thomas Davis sailed for New England in 1635 on the *James* [GM 2:2:310-16].

John Emery (Ne): John Emery sailed for New England in 1635 on the *James* [GM 2:2:446-52].

Samuel Plummer (Ne): He was born about 1619, son of FRANCIS PLUMMER, who had arrived in New England by 1633 and was among the early settlers of Newbury [GMB 3:1482-86].

Moses Payne (Br): On 14 January 1638/9, "Mr. Paine granted unto Goodman Shepard a third part of his yard" at Cambridge [CaTR 35, 40]. In the Cambridge land inventory of 6 September 1642, "Moses Payne" held "in the town one dwelling house with about half a rood of ground," but by 30 September 1646 this lot was held by Henry Adams [CaBOP 113, 125]. He died at Braintree on 21 June 1643 [NEHGR 3:247], and, based on his proximity to other Braintree men in this list, must have moved to Braintree and been admitted to church there by 2 June 1641 [TAG 21:187-89].

Daniel Weld (Br): On 24 February 1639/40, "Mr. Danyell Welles, of the same [Mount Wollaston]," was granted eighty acres there for a household of twenty [BTR 1:49]. (This grant of land was probably not for twenty persons; the calculation was probably based in part on the size of the grantee's estate.)

Samuel Bidfield (Br): On 24 February 1639/40, "Samuel Bitfield" was granted twenty acres at Mount Wollaston [Braintree] for a household of five [BTR 1:50; TAG 67:236-42].

Francis Eliot (Br): Daughter Mary Eliot was born at Braintree on 27 January 1640[/41] [NEHGR 3:127]. Francis Eliot had married Mary Saunders, daughter of Martin Saunders, who had been in New England since 1635. This implies that this child was conceived in New England no later than April 1640, which further implies that Francis Eliot was already in New England by 1639.

Abell Kelly (Sm): "Abell Kelly" was admitted to Salem church on 12 September 1640 (later annotated "removed") [SChR 10]. On 29 June 1641, "Abell Kelly" appraised the estate of John Watkins, servant of Walter Price of Salem [EQC 1:27].

Jacob Wilson (Br): On 16 April 1638, "Jacob Wilson" was granted a Great Lot at Muddy River for a household of three [BTR 1:33]. On 24 December 1638, "Jacob Willson of this town [Boston], sawyer," sold his house to "Willyam Teffe, a tailor" [BTR 1:36, 37]. On 24 February 1639/40, "Jacob Wilson" was granted sixteen acres at Mount Wollaston [Braintree] for a household of four [BTR 1:49]. Isaac, son of Jacob Wilson, was born at Braintree on 28 January 1640/1, and Sarah, daughter of Isaac Wilson, was born there on 28 January 1641/2 [NEHGR 3:248].

Nicholas Wood (Br): On 13 February 1638/9, "Nicholas Wood" was appointed cowherd at Dorchester [DTR 38]. On 25 December 1642, "Mary Wood [and] Sarah Wood, twins, daughters of [blank] Wood of the church of Braintree, who married our brother Pig's daughter" were baptized at Roxbury [RChR 114; TAG 36:110-17; GMB 3:1464-66]. Nicholas Wood was not admitted to Dorchester church, and so must have been a member of Braintree church at the time of this list. This conclusion is supported by the proximity of this entry to other Braintree names.

John Harbert (Br): On 24 February 1639/40, "John Harbar" was granted twelve acres at Mount Wollaston [Braintree] for a household of three [BTR 1:49]. (John Herbert of Salem was not admitted to church there, and so cannot have been this freeman [GM 2:3:311-13].)

Thomas Lake (Do): "Tho[mas] Leike" was admitted to Dorchester church on 20 November 1640 [DChR 5; TAG 12:18].

Andrew Pitcher (Do): He was granted land at Dorchester on 1 September 1634 [DTR 7], but was not admitted to the church there until 16 April 1641 [DChR 5; GM 2:5:468-71].

Rob[e]rt Holmes (Ca): Based on the placement of his conversion narrative in the record kept by Rev. Thomas Shepard, Robert Holmes was admitted to Cambridge church in late 1640 [Shepard 142-43]. His wife had made her conversion narrative in late 1639 or early 1640 [Shepard 76-80]. Dorcas, the daughter of "Rob[er]t Homes & Jane his wife" was born at Cambridge in August 1638 [NEHGR 4:181].

Goulden More (Ca): Based on the placement of his conversion narrative in the record kept by Rev. Thomas Shepard, "Golding Moore" was admitted to Cambridge church in late 1640 [Shepard 122-24].

Rich[a]rd Cutter (Ca): "Richard Cutter" made his conversion narrative soon after that of John Fessenden, perhaps even on the same day, and so would have been admitted to Cambridge church in early 1641 [Shepard 179-81].

John Fossenden (Ca): "Goodman Fessington" made his conversion narrative on 8 January 1640/1, and would have been admitted to Cambridge church on that date or soon after [Shepard 176-77]. In late 1638 or early 1639, "John Fishenden" purchased land from Nicholas Robbins [CaBOP 46, 58].

Will[iam] Woodberry (Sm): On 29 December 1639, "William Woodbery" was admitted to Salem church [SChR 9]. This man was son of WILLIAM WOODBURY {1636, Salem} who was granted twenty acres of land at Salem in 1636 [STR 1:25].

Will[iam] Geares (Sm): On 9 September 1640, "William Geere" was admitted to Salem church [SChR 10]. On 9 December 1639, "William Geare desireth to be an inhabitant [at Salem] and to have accommodations" [STR 1:93, 96].

Philemon Dickenson (Sm): On 7 February 1640/1, "Phillemon Dickerson" was admitted to Salem church [SChR 10]. On 10 May 1637, "Feleaman Dickerson," servant of Benjamin Cooper of Brampton, Suffolk, enrolled at Yarmouth on the *Mary Anne* for passage to Salem in New England [Drake's Founders 48]. On 11 February 1638/9, "Philemon Dickerson desireth ... accommodation" at Salem [STR 1:83].

Esdras Reade (Sm): On 10 May 1640, "Esdras Read" was admitted to Salem church [SChR 9]. On 24 December 1638, "Esdras Reade, a tailor, is this day allowed to be an inhabitant [at Boston], and to have a great lot at Muddy River for 4 heads" [BTR 1:36]. On 25 February 1638/9, "Esdras Reade is received to be an inhabitant at the town of Salem" [STR 1:84].

John Robinson (Sm): On 22 September 1639, "John Robbinson" was admitted to Salem church [SChR 8]. On 21 January 1638/9, the town of Salem granted to "John Robinson a lot of ten acres of planting ground" [STR 1:78].

Thom[as] Gardner (Sm): On 15 December 1639. "Thomas Gardener Junior" was admitted to Salem church [SChR 9].

He was born by about 1614, son of THOMAS GARDNER {1624, Cape Ann} [GMB 2:731-37].

Thom[as] Marston (Sm): On 7 September 1640, "Thomas Marstone" was admitted to Salem Church [SChR 10]. "Thomas Marston" was included in a 1636 list of Salem land grants, without any acreage indicated [STR 1:23]. On 25 December 1637, "Tho[mas] Marston" received half an acre of marsh land for a household of one [STR 1:103].

Rich[a]rd Bartelmew (Sm): On 1 September 1640, "Richard Bartholomew" was admitted to Salem church [SChR 10]. "Rich[ard] Bartholomew" requested a houselot at Salem on 25 December 1637, and on the same day was granted marshland there with a household of one [STR 1:62, 102].

Thom[as] Gould (Ch): On 7 June 1640, "Thomas Gould" and "Hannah Gould" were admitted to Charlestown church [ChChR 10]. Thomas Gould came to New England in 1639 on the *Jonathan* [NEHGR 32:409].

Thom[as] Wildar (Ch): On 30 March 1640, "Thomas Wilder" was admitted to Charlestown church [ChChR 10]. In the 1638 Charlestown Book of Possessions, "Thom[as] Wilder" held "five acres of woodland ... in Mystic Field ... he bought of Benjamin Hubbard" [ChBOP 55].

Rich[a]rd Robinson (Ch): On 24 May 1640, "Richard Robbins" and "Rebeckah "Robins" were admitted to Charlestown church [ChChR 10]. "Richard Roberts" was an inhabitant of Charlestown in 1639 [Wyman 816].

John Marston (Sm): On 6 September 1640, "John Marstone" was admitted to Salem church [SChR 10]. On 11 April 1637, "John Maston," aged 20, servant of Mary Moulton of Ormsby, Norfolk, enrolled at Yarmouth as a passenger on the *John & Dorothy* [Drake's Founders 46].

Rob[e]rt Fuller (Do): "Robert Fuller" was admitted to Dorchester church on 29 June 1640 [DChR 5]. On 19 January 1648/9, "Robe[r]t Fuller of the church of Dorchester being dismissed from thence" was admitted to Dedham church [DeChR 31]. (Another Robert Fuller was granted land at Salem on 18 November 1639 [STR 1:91] and would seem to belong here given the adjacent names on the list, but the Salem Robert Fuller was not admitted to the church there, and soon moved on to Rehoboth.)

Willi[am] Blanchard (Sm): On 14 February 1640/1, "William Blancherd" was admitted to Salem church [SChR 10]. He was in Salem by 1638 if he was the son of "widow Blancher" who was granted six acres there on 14 November 1638 [STR 1:74] and if she was the "Ann Blancherd" admitted to Salem church on 30 July 1643 [SChR 12].

Bozoun Allen (Hi): In 1638 "Mr. Bozone Allen and his wife and two servants came from Lynn, in Norfolk, and settled in New Hingham" [NEHGR 15:27]. Their daughter Priscilla was baptized at Hingham in August 1639 [NEHGR 121:12].

Miles Ward (Sm): "Miles Ward" was admitted to Salem church on 29 December 1639 [SChR 9]. On 29 June 1641, Miles Ward was co-plaintiff with other Salem men in a civil suit [EQC 1:28].

Samu[el] Corning (Sm): "Samuell Corning" and "his wife" were admitted to Salem church on 5 April 1640 [SChR 9]. On 23 April 1638, the town of Salem granted to "Samuell Corning one acre of ground" [STR 1:69]. On 25 June 1638, "Sam[uel] Cornish" was one of four persons "forgotten in the division shall have their half acres apiece of marsh land" (referring to the division of marsh and meadow on 25 December 1637) [STR 1:70].

Jonathan Porter (Sm): On 5 April 1640, "Jonathan Porter" was admitted to Salem church [SChR 9]. In 1636 "Jonathan Porter" was granted twenty acres at Salem [STR 1:24]. On 25 December 1637, "Jo: Porter" was granted three-quarters of an acre at Salem, for a household of five [STR 1:102] (which matches the known size of his family at that time [FOOF 1:490]).

Rich[a]rd Pattinggell (Sm): "Richard Pettingall" was admitted to Salem church on 21 March 1640[/1] [SChR 10], implying he had arrived in New England by 1640. Based on his age given in various depositions, Richard Pettingill was born about 1620 [Abel Lunt Anc 51-54], so he was admitted a freeman very close to his twenty-first birthday.

John Goodnow (Su): "John Goodenowe" and his family sailed for New England in 1638 on the *Confidence* [Drake's Founders 58]. "John Goodenow" was granted four acres and a half at Sudbury on 22 March 1639/40 [Sudbury TR 3].

Willi[am] Browne (Su): "William Browne" was granted one acre at Sudbury on 22 March 1639/40 [Sudbury TR 3]. Of the many William Brownes in Massachusetts Bay at this time, we identify this freeman as the Sudbury man because he follows John Goodenow in the list.

Samu[el] Chapun (Rx): "Samuel Chapin" was admitted to Roxbury church in 1638 [RChR 83; GMN 6:25]. "Japhet Chapin the son of Samuel Chapin" was baptized at Roxbury on 15 October 1642 [RChR 114].

Christo[pher] Stanley (Bo): On 23 June 1639, "Susanna Stanley the wife of one Christopher Stanley, tailor," was admitted to Boston church [BChR 24]. On 16 May 1641, "Mr. Christofer Stanley, a tailor," was admitted to Boston church [BChR 34]. On 29 April 1635, "a tailor, Christopher Stanley," aged 32, and "*uxor* Susanna," aged 31, were enrolled at London as passengers for New England on the *Elizabeth & Ann* [Hotten 72].

John Harrison (Unknown): John Harrison of Salisbury appears near the beginning of this list. The only other early records for a man of this name in Massachusetts Bay were for "Mr. John Harrison Jr." who arrived at Salem late in 1637, moved soon to Boston, and had returned to England by May or June of 1639 [MBCR 1:248, 249, 265; Lechford 127, 145, 147, 151, 158, 191, 192, 202, 203; WP 3:517,

4:87, 93, 138, 206, 193-96, 226-27]. Perhaps this second entry for a John Harrison in this list of freemen is a simple clerical error.

Thom[as] Davenish (Sm): On 21 March 1640/1, "Thomas Devinish" was admitted to Salem church [SChR 11]. On 25 July 1639, "Thomas Davenish is received to be an inhabitant within this town [Salem], & there is granted to him ten acres of land for planting ground" [STR 1:89].

Walter Harris (We): On 22 April 1637, "Walter Harris, his wife, 6 children and 3 servants" were listed as passengers on the *Speedwell* of Weymouth, Dorset, bound for New England [NGSQ 71:176]. His first known residence in New England was Weymouth [Weymouth Hist 3:255-56; NEHGR 156:145-52].

Ellis Barrone (Wa): "Sarah the daughter of Ellis & Grace Barron" was born at Watertown on 24 July 1640 [WaVR 1:8]. In the 1644 Watertown Inventory of Possessions, "Elliz Baron" held "an homestall of ten acres" [WaBOP 121; Kempton Anc 1:119-31].

Willi[am] Parker (Wa): "Ephraim the son of William & Elizabeth Parker," 6 months old, was buried at Watertown on 12 August 1640 [WaVR 1:8]. In the 1644 Watertown Book of Possessions, "William Parker" held "an homestall of six acres" and "one acre of meadow" [WaBOP 120]. He is almost certainly the William Parker who was granted one acre and a half at Sudbury on 22 March 1639/40 [Sudbury TR 3].

Philip Veren (Sm): On 3 January 1640/1, "Phillip Veren Junior" was admitted to Salem church [SChR 10]. He was baptized at Salisbury, Wiltshire, on 1 May 1619, son of PHILLIP VEREN {1635, Salem} who had sailed for New England on the *James* in 1635 [Drake's Founders 56; NEHGR 131:100-6].

John Palmer (Ch): On 23 September 1640, "John Palmer" was admitted to Charlestown church [ChChR 10]. He was born about 1615, son of WALTER PALMER {1629, Charlestown} [GMB 3:1379-83; Wyman 725].

Rich[a]rd Parker (Bo): On 23 January 1640/1, "Mr. Richard Parker a merchant" was admitted to Boston church [BChR 33]. "Joseph of Richard & Anne Parker" was born at Boston on 1 August 1638 and died there on 30 November 1638 [NEHGR 2:275].

Edw[a]rd Tinge (Bo): On 5 September 1640, "Mrs. Mary Ting the wife of one Mr. Edward Tinge merchant" was admitted to Boston church [BChR 31]. On 30 January 1640/1, "Mr. Edward Tinge merchant" was admitted to the same church [BChR 32]. Prior to 26 September 1636, "William Aspewall hath sold a houseplot and a garden unto one Mr. Tinge" [BTR 1:12]. In 1638 William Tyng followed his younger brother to New England and also settled at Boston [BTR 1:35].

(to be continued in next issue)

RECENT LITERATURE

Matthew Hovius, "Norwich Revisited: The Origin of John[1] Jenney, Plymouth Colonist," *The Genealogist* 22 (2008):3-28. Hovius first presents evidence for the presence of a John Jenney in Lakenham, Norfolk, immediately adjacent to Norwich, in the 1590s. John Jenney of Plymouth is known from Leiden records to have been from Norwich, and at Plymouth was granted lands at a place called Lakenham. The author then goes on to present records of a Jenney family of Dunwich, Suffolk, some members of which had connections with Norwich, and so may have been ancestral to John Jenney of Plymouth. Of particular importance is the presence of a widow Avis Jenney in both places, possibly the same woman, and possibly the grandmother of the immigrant.

William Wyman Fiske, "Ancestry of Arthur[1] and Frances (Warman) Gary of Roxbury, Massachusetts, Revisited," *The Genealogist* 22 (2008):78-79. Building on his earlier research on the Whipple and Gary families, Fiske presents a will which solidifies the connection, showing that Arthur Gary of Roxbury was second cousin once-removed of Matthew[1] and John[1] Whipple of Bocking, Essex, and Ipswich, Massachusetts.

Patricia St. Clair Ostwald, "Peter[1] Hackley of New London, Connecticut, and His Two Wives, Elizabeth (Waterhouse) Baker and Elizabeth (Marshal) Darrow," *The New England Historical and Genealogical Register* 162 (2008):85-90. The author demonstrates that Peter Hackley of New London had two wives named Elizabeth. The first of these wives was Elizabeth Waterhouse, daughter of Jacob Waterhouse, who had settled in Wethersfield by 1639. She had married first someone named Baker, perhaps John Baker, son of Alexander Baker who was in Boston by 1635 [GM 2:1:130-32].

Martin E. Hollick, "William Reynolds of Plymouth Colony and Cape Porpoise, Maine," *The New England Historical and Genealogical Register* 162 (2008):91-92. Hollick provides evidence that various records relating to William Reynolds at Plymouth, Duxbury and Cape Porpoise all pertain to the same man.

Patricia A. Metsch, "The Identity of Phillipa, Second Wife of Nicholas West of Drayton, Somerset, and Grandmother of Joan (West) White of Lancaster, Massachusetts," *The New England Historical and Genealogical Register* 162 (2008):93-97. John West, who had settled in Salem by 1639 and moved on to Wenham and Lancaster, had married in England Joan West. Metsch sets forth parish register and probate records which show that the maternal grandparents of Joan (West) White were John and Philippa (Hawker) Staple of Drayton, Somerset.

Robert F. Henderson and James R. Henderson, "English Origins of Lawrence[1] Leach of Salem, Massachusetts," *The New England Historical and Genealogical Register* 162 (2008):98-100. The authors present parish register entries which show that Lawrence Leach, who arrived at Salem in 1629, married Elizabeth Mileham at Hurst, Berkshire, on 2 February 1605/6 and that they had several children baptized at Hurst and, beginning in 1615, at the adjacent parish of Sonning, Berkshire.

Glade Ian Nelson, "Identifying Mercy, Wife of Thomas[4] Hinckley of Harwich, Massachusetts, as Mercy (Bangs) (Hinckley) Cole," *The New England Historical and Genealogical Register* 162 (2008):101-112. Samuel Hinckley, grandson of Samuel Hinckley who settled in Scituate in 1635 [GM 2:3:331-335], married Sarah Pope, daughter of Thomas Pope, who had arrived in Plymouth by 1632 [GMB 3:1496-99]. Nelson reveals the identity of the wife of Thomas Hinckley of the fourth generation by showing that three children of Samuel Hinckley of the third generation married three children of Jonathan Bangs, son of Edward Bangs, who arrived at Plymouth in 1623 [GMB 1:86-91].

Leslie Mahler, "Various English Wills Relating to New England Colonists: Gillett, Swaine, Cheney, and Tutty-Knight-Whitman," *The New England Historical and Genealogical Register* 162 (2008):113-17. Mahler adds to our knowledge of several Great Migration families. The 1623 will of Rev. William Tyes of Donyatt, Somerset, named Jonathan Gillett (who settled in Dorchester by 1633 [GMB 2:766-70]) and called Abia, wife of William Gillet, father of Jonathan, "my daughter-in-law." Next, Mahler transcribes the 1630 will of William Swain of Horsell, Surrey, father of Richard Swain who was an original settler of Hampton. Then, the author abstracts the will of George Lansdalle of Lawford, Essex, which further confirms the English origin of John Cheney, who was in Roxbury by 1635 [GM 2:2:60-63]. Finally, he provides a transcript of the 1621 will of Audrey Pasden of London, great-grandmother of Anne (Tutty) (Knight) Whitman, wife of Alexander Knight and then of Robert Whitman, both of Ipswich.

William Wyman Fiske, "Ancestry of Bennet Eliot of Nazeing, Essex, Father of Seven Great Migration Immigrants to New England," *The New England Historical and Genealogical Register* 162 (2008):128-39. Fiske concludes his study of the family of Bennet Eliot, finishing with the sketch for Bennet Eliot himself. There is also a sketch for Blyth (Eliot) Haynes, wife of George Haynes and mother of John Haynes, who was in turn father of John Haynes, Governor of Connecticut. The article also shows connections to a number of Virginia immigrants.

Gale Ion Harris, "Wolston[1] Brockway of Lyme, Connecticut, With Further Analysis of His Associations," *The New England Historical and Genealogical Register* 128 (2008):140-48. Harris concludes his study of Wolston Brockway with a compiled genealogical summary of the family of that immigrant. This compilation includes detailed information on each of Brockway's ten children, identifying sixty-eight grandchildren.

(continued from page 18)

Finally, on 6 September 1687, "George Russell, sometime of Scituate but now of Hingham ..., husbandman," deeded to "Thomas Palmer of Scituate ..., mariner, and Elizabeth his wife the natural child of the said George Russell, ... all that part of his marsh or meadow land lying to the westward of the causeway containing by estimation twelve acres ... and all that part of his upland and swamp land ... being by estimation twenty acres" [PLR 1:94-95]. For this last move in his life, George Russell conveniently informs us directly of his change of residence from Scituate back to Hingham, probably not long before the date of this deed. The daughter Elizabeth, wife of Thomas Palmer, would be that Elizabeth who had been baptized at Hingham on 12 January 1642[/3].

We have now traced George Russell of Hingham in 1636 to Plymouth in 1637, back to Hingham by 1639, on to Scituate in 1643, to Marshfield by 1654, back to Scituate by 1663, and finally back to Hingham by 1687. For each of these moves except the first, we have confirmatory evidence from land records. Sometimes this is an explicit statement of residence in two of these towns. Sometimes his wife Jane is involved in deeds in different towns. Sometimes we are able to match the land mentioned in two deeds when the residence for George Russell is different in the two deeds. Except for the first move, we have more to go on than just "the name's the same," and a common name at that.

That the same man made all these moves is also supported by the records of freemanship. George Russell took the oath of fidelity at Scituate on 15 January 1644/5. He was propounded for freemanship on 8 June 1655, was admitted on 3 June 1657, and appeared in the Marshfield section of the 1658 list of freemen. He then appeared in the Scituate sections of the lists of 29 May 1670 and 1 [blank] 1683/4. This sequence is consistent with the existence of one man of the name over this long period. In no instance do we have two men named George Russell appearing in the same year in any of these lists of freemen.

Now, having traced this man's many moves, we may return to the original question. Was he the passenger of 1635? George Russell died at Hingham on 26 May 1694, aged 99 years, and his wife Jane died there on 22 February 1688/9, aged about 83 years [Hingham Hist 3:141, citing Hingham gravestone inscriptions]. Taking these dates at face value, George would have been born about 1595 and Jane about 1605. Even if we assume that George's age at death has been somewhat exaggerated, as frequently happened, he would not have been born any later than 1605. But the age of the 1635 passenger was given as 19, which would give a date of birth about 1616. Based on this discrepancy, we conclude that the 1635 passenger was not identical with George Russell of Hingham and beyond. George Russell of Hingham will be treated as an immigrant of 1636 and thus will not appear in the next volume of the current series.

Great Migration Newsletter

Vol. 17   October-December 2008   No. 4

BECOMING A FREEMAN

In this issue of the *Great Migration Newsletter* and in the previous issue we have analyzed the list of Massachusetts Bay freemen admitted on 2 June 1641, at the beginning of the 1641 Court of Election. Our standard assumption is that anyone admitted a freeman at the annual spring Court of Election must have arrived in New England by the previous year, at the latest. Our main concern in carrying out this analysis has been to make an estimate of how many of those who were admitted free on 2 June 1641 might actually have arrived in 1640, and how many can be shown to have arrived earlier. As we shall see, this will tell us something about dating the end of the Great Migration, but will also throw light on other issues as well.

The 2 June 1641 list of freemen contains 126 names, but not all of these are useful for our analysis. Two of the names are incomplete and totally unidentifiable. A third name, the second occurrence of the name John Harrison, is quite legible, but cannot be connected with any early New England settler. As a result, our numerical analysis will be based on only 123 of these names.

By 1641 Massachusetts Bay had been settled for more than a decade and a half, with the result that a number of sons of early immigrants had reached maturity and were now eligible for freemanship. In the 1641 list are seven of these men, arranged here in order of arrival of the fathers: Thomas Gardner (son of Thomas Gardner [1624]), John Palmer (son of Walter Palmer [1629]), Adam Winthrop (son of John Winthrop [1630]), Samuel Plummer (son of Francis Plummer [1633]), Philip Veren (son of Philip Veren [1635]), William Woodbury (son of William Woodbury [1636]), and John Lowell (son of Percival Lowell [1639]).

With these exceptions, there remain 116 freemen who were themselves immigrant heads of family and whose dates of immigration are known or have been estimated. Our first step will be to enumerate how many we believe arrived in each year prior to 1641.

1633	1
1634	2
1635	9
1636	7
1637	14
1638	21
1639	29
1640	33

This presents a very clear pattern, with the number for each year becoming steadily smaller as one works backward from 1640. (The one exception to the pattern, in which 1635 is slightly greater than 1636, will be discussed at a later point.) Our first conclusion, then, is that slightly more than a quarter of the 1641 freemen *might* have come to New England in 1640. (Or, to state the same conclusion differently, nearly three-quarters of the 1641 freemen came *before* 1640.) This is a maximum estimate, but could the number be even smaller?

First, we note that we have no surviving passenger lists from 1640, so this category of evidence does not help us in determining who actually arrived in that year.

Second, positive evidence for a 1640 arrival exists for only two of these men, and even that evidence is not as strong as we might like. Henry Dunster, who was elected president of Harvard College on 27 August 1640, was stated by Morison to have arrived in 1640 [Morison 376-77]. Morison does not give any documentation for this claim. We would expect, though, that such a prominent man as Dunster would have left some record of his presence had he arrived prior to 1640, and, since no such evidence has survived, the claim that he came in 1640 is likely correct.

(continued on page 26)

EDITOR'S EFFUSIONS

The publication of this issue of the *Great Migration Newsletter* coincides with the twentieth anniversary of the beginning of the Great Migration Study Project. A lengthy discussion of the current status of the Project will appear in the Holiday 2008 issue of *New England Ancestors*. We wish to use this space to elaborate on one point made in that article.

Work on the Great Migration Study Project began on 15 November 1988. Aside from the basic goal of writing a series of books on the earliest immigrants to New England, the Project has also published since 1990 the *Great Migration Newsletter*. In the *NEA* article, we note that the *Newsletter* has served an unexpected purpose: "work on the lead article and *Focus* section has served as a sort of research and development division."

Some records may be analyzed as well in isolation as in the context of the surrounding records. Most deeds are entered in the deed registers in no particular order (other than the date they were brought in for registration), and so the inferences to be drawn from a deed are generally not influenced by the deeds registered just before and just after.

Many other records, though, depend for their fullest interpretation on their context with respect to other records entered in the same source. A good example is the work presented in the last issue of the *Newsletter* and in the present issue, on the list of freemen admitted on 2 June 1641. If we are studying one of the many Edward Brownes or William Brownes who came to early New England, and simply consult the index to the Massachusetts Bay court records, we would find men of that name admitted on that day, but would not know immediately whether these entries represented the men we were looking for. Only in the context of the surrounding names in the list do we discover that on this day Edward Browne of Ipswich and William Browne of Sudbury were admitted.

If our work were focussed solely on the preparation of sketches, we would not always feel that we had the time to devote to the analysis necessary to arrive at such useful conclusions. The different focus of preparing *Newsletter* articles, however, allows time for deeper investigation, resulting in the writing of more comprehensive sketches.

Robert Charles Anderson, FASG   Editor
Jean Powers, Production Assistant

The Great Migration Newsletter is published quarterly by the Great Migration Study Project, a project of the New England Historic Genealogical Society, 101 Newbury Street, Boston MA 02116
www.NewEnglandAncestors.org
www.GreatMigration.org
GreatMigration@nehgs.org

Copyright © 2008
New England Historic Genealogical Society

(continued from page 25)

The second man supposed to have arrived in 1640 was Robert Bridges of Lynn. The first record for him in New England was on 1 February 1640[/1] [EQC 1:49] and, as with Henry Dunster, he was a prominent enough man that had he been in New England any earlier than 1640 he would almost certainly have left a record. Furthermore, other records place him in England in 1639 [Lechford 367-71; EQC 1:382-86], again making him a likely 1640 arrival.

Third, of the thirty-three men we have tentatively accounted as arriving in 1640, a third came from two towns whose early records are sparse, four from Salisbury and eleven from Concord. In the case of Salisbury, the town was founded in 1639 and the earliest surviving record is a list of the first grant of lands, the dating of which is uncertain, so that we cannot be sure whether persons appearing in this list were in New England by 1639 or 1640 (see discussion under Richard North [GMN 17:19]). Conceivably, then, all those included in this list might have arrived by 1639, but, equally conceivably, all might not have arrived until 1640.

In addition, since Salisbury was founded at the very end of the heaviest period of immigration, we might be witnessing a phenomenon seen as early as 1635, at the beginning of the heaviest period of migration. A number of those arriving in 1634 on the *Mary & John* from Southampton make their first appearance on record in New England in 1635 in Newbury, while others on the same vessel had settled in 1634 in Ipswich. The likely explanation is that with Ipswich having reached its capacity for accepting new proprietors, a number of the 1634 arrivals had to await the formation of Newbury in 1635 before they could establish a permanent residence. These families would have spent the winter of 1634-5 at Ipswich, doubling up with friends and relatives, before moving on to Newbury. A similar situation might have prevailed with families arriving a few years later, perhaps in 1638, being unable to find permanent accommodations in existing towns and sojourning in some older settlement until the formation of Salisbury. In the absence of passenger lists for these later years and of well-dated early Salisbury town records, we may never be able to document such a sequence of events.

The case of Concord is different, for that town had been settled in 1635, but, with the exception of some vital records beginning in 1639, very few early records survive for this town. Here the useful comparison may be with Dedham, which was formed just a year later. For that town, we have complete survival of the earliest vital, church and town meeting records. In this same list of freemen are more than a dozen Dedham men, and with the available records we are able to determine that most of them arrived well before 1640.

So, although more than a quarter of the 2 June 1641 freemen are scored as 1640 arrivals based on our analysis, no more than two can be said with any certainty to have come

(continued on page 32)

Focus on Immigration

(continued from previous issue)

[*In the Focus section of the last issue of the* Great Migration Newsletter *we began to identify those men who were admitted to Massachusetts Bay freemanship on 2 June 1641 [GMN 17:19-22], and we conclude that process here. Analysis of this information may be found in the lead article in the present issue.*]

Nehemiah Bourne (Do): On 4 November 1639, "Mr. Nehemiah Bourne" and "Mrs. Hannah Bourne" were admitted to Dorchester church [DChR 4]. On 10 April 1638, a "pass for Nehemiah Bourne, of the parish of White Chapell, whitebaker, to travel into the parts of America" was issued at London [NEHGR 27:28]. On 22 August 1638, "Mr. Nehemiah Bourne was admitted a townsman [at Charlestown]" [ChTR 39].

Franc[is] Lawes (Sm): On 7 September 1640, "Frances Lawes" and "his wife" were admitted to Salem church [SChR 10]. On 8 April 1637, "[F]rancis Lawes born in Norw[i]ch in Norf[olk] and there living, weaver, aged [worn], and Liddea his wife aged 49 years with one child Marey" were enrolled at Norwich for passage to New England [Hotten 290]. On 8 November 1637, "Francis Laws [made a] request for a further portion of land" at Salem [STR 1:59].

Rob[e]rt Bridges (Ly): On 1 February 1640[/1], "Capt. Robert Bridg[e]s" and Edward Holyoke were assigned to audit an account [EQC 1:49]. On 25 January 1641/2, "Capt. Rob[er]t Bridges" served on the Essex grand jury from Lynn [EQC 1:33]. (Robert Bridges was apparently still in England in 1639 [Lechford 367-71; EQC 1:382-86].)

John Baker (Ch): On 31 May 1640, "John Baker" was admitted to Charlestown church [ChChR 10; GMB 1:74-75].

Rob[e]rt Cooke (Ch): According to Wyman, Robert Cooke was admitted as an inhabitant of Charlestown in 1640 [Wyman 235]. On 30 November 1643, "Sarah Cooke" was admitted to Charlestown church [ChChR 10]. On 10 August 1644, "Samuel, son of Robert & Sarah Cooke," was born at Charlestown [ChVR 1:8]. No Robert Cooke was admitted to Charlestown church in this period. However, on 30 May 1641, "Richard Cooke" was admitted to Charlestown church [ChChR 10] and records for a Richard Cooke in Charlestown begin appearing in 1649 [Wyman 235]. The likely resolution of this problem is that the church admission for Richard is correctly for Robert.

Henry Dauson (Bo): On 16 May 1641, "Henry Dawson a laborer" was admitted to Boston church [BChR 34]. On 25 January 1640/1, "Henry Dawson is also accepted for a townsman [at Boston] … for three [heads]" [BTR 1:58].

Willi[am] Tiff (Bo): On 2 August 1640, "Willyam Teffe a tailor and Anne his wife" were admitted to Boston church [BChR 30]. On 24 December 1638, "one Willyam Teffe, a tailor, is allowed to be an inhabitant, and hath this day fully agreed with Jacob Wilson of his house, and the ground under it, in this town [of Boston]" [BTR 1:36, 37].

Willi[am] Brisco (Bo): On 30 January 1640/1, "Willyam Briscoe a tailor" was admitted to Boston church [BChR 32]. On 24 February 1639/40, "William Briscoe, tailor, is allowed to be an inhabitant, and to have a Great Lot, for eight heads, at the Mount [Braintree]" [BTR 1:48].

Rich[a]rd Sanford (Bo): On 30 January 1640/1, "Richard Samford a laborer" was admitted to Boston church [BChR 32]. On 22 February 1640/1, "Richard Sandford is admitted a townsman [at Boston], who also desireth a lot when any are to be granted" [BTR 1:59].

Augustine Walker (Ch): On 23 September 1640, "Augustin Walker" was admitted to Charlestown church [ChChR 10]. In the 1638 Charlestown Book of Possessions, "Augustine Walker" held "one house plot containing half a rood of ground … at Sconce Point" [BBOP 43].

Henry Archer (Ip): On 4 June 1639, Massachusetts Bay General Court ordered that "Goodman Foster & Henry Archer are referred to Ipswich Court" [MBCR 1:266]. On 4 December 1639, Henry Archer and Elizabeth Stow were married at Roxbury. ("Goodman Foster" was Hopestill Foster; Hopestill Foster and Elizabeth (Stow) Archer were grandchildren of Rachel (Martin) Bigg [GM 2:1:284-89].) On 28 [December] 1641, Henry Archer was a member of the petit jury for Ipswich Court [EQC 1:37].

Charles Glover (Sm): On 10 May 1640, "Charles Glover" was admitted to Salem church (later annotated "removed") [SChR 9]. On 15 April 1639, "Charles Glover is admitted to be an inhabitant within this town [of Salem" [STR 1:86]. (The "Charles Glower" who sailed for New England in 1632 is almost certainly a different man [GMB 2:776].)

Rob[e]rt Paine (Ip): On 13 January 1639/40, "Ro[bert] Payne" was included in a list of those in Ipswich holding three-year-old bulls [ITR]. On 11 January 1640/1, "Mr. Robert Payne" was appointed to an Ipswich committee "for furthering trade amongst us" [ITR].

John Baker (Ip): On 8 April 1637, "John Baker, born in Norw[i]ch in Norfolk, grocer, aged 39 years, and Elizabeth his wife, aged 31 years, with 3 children, Elizabeth, John and Thomas," were enrolled at Ipswich for passage to New England [Hotten 289; GMB 1:74]. In a grant of land at Ipswich on 16 April 1638, one of the abutters was "a house lot now in the possession of John Baker" [ITR].

Micha[el] Kathericke (Ip): On 20 April 1635, the town of Ipswich granted to Philip Fowler "an houselot in High Street, having Michael Cartwright on the northwest" [ITR; GM 2:2:31-32].

John Jackson (Ip): In a grant of a homelot to William Fuller in Ipswich in 1635, "John Jackson" was an abutter on the southeast [ITR; Ipswich Hist 1:335]. On 1 March 1637/8, there was "granted to John Jackson a houselot on the side of the hill, next to Edward Browne's at six rod broad" [ITR; Ipswich Hist 1:379]. (This John Jackson has been distinguished from other men of the same name [GMN 12:17-18, 24; GM 2:4:22-28].)

John Deane (Ip): Two men named John Dane, father and son, resided at Ipswich in 1641. The son had come to New England in 1636; he settled briefly at Roxbury, but soon went to Ipswich [NEHGR 8:147-56, 132:18-19]. The father had arrived in New England and settled at Ipswich by 9 April 1639, when "John Deane the elder" was granted "an houselot one acre of ground" and two planting lots [ITR]. Either of these men could have been the freeman recorded here.

Edward Browne (Ip): On 5 February 1637/8, the town of Ipswich granted to "Edward Browne, a house lot in the High Street next under William Bartholomew on the one side of the hill, and six acres for planting on this side Muddy River" [ITR; Ipswich Hist 1:381-82].

Dani[el] Warner (Ip): On 5 July 1639, an Ipswich grant of land to John Wyatt included six acres of planting ground abutted on the north and northeast by "a planting lot in the possession of Daniell Warener" [ITR].

John Knouleton (Ip): On 15 October 1639, "William Fuller of this town [Ipswich], gunsmith," sold to "John Knowlton of this town, shoemaker, all the said land, being five roods ..., together with one small dwelling house" [ITR].

Symon Tompson (Ip): On 13 January 1637[/8], the town of Ipswich granted "to Simon Thompson, twenty acres of ground meadow and upland at the New Meadows" [ITR].

Rob[e]rt Daye (Ip): Robert Day sailed for New England in 1635 on the *Hopewell* [Hotten 46]. He arrived as a single man, settled at Ipswich, and married by 1638 [GM 2:2:329-33].

Andrewe Hodges (Ip): On 26 August 1639, "Isaack Comings of this town [Ipswich], husbandman," sold "a parcel of land about seven acres ... unto Andrew Hodges of this town, likewise husbandman" [ITR].

Jacob Leager (Bo): On 1 June 1638, Boston selectmen permitted "our brother Richard Brockett, to sell his house and garden ... unto one Jacob Legar" [BTR 1:34]. On 12 May 1639, "Elizabeth the wife of one Jacob Legar" was admitted to Boston church [BChR 24]. On 14 March 1640/1, "Jacob Legar a husbandman" was admitted to Boston church [BChR 33].

George Bullard (Wa): "Margaret the wife of Georg[e] Bullard [was] buried 8 (12) 1639 [8 February 1639(/40?)]" at Watertown [NEHGR 7:161]. "Mary the daughter of George & Bettris Bullard [was] born 12 (12) 1639 [12 February 1639(/40?)]" at Watertown [NEHGR 7:161]. (One of these records must be erroneous, assuming there was only one George Bullard.)

Henry Chick[e]ry (De): "Henery Chechery & his wife were received also the same day [29 January 1640/1] with good satisfaction to the church [at Dedham]" [DeChR 24]. On 21 January 1639/40, Salem selectmen granted to "Henry Chickering & John Yongs 50 acres of [land] apiece" [SChR 1:98]. On 16 March 1640/1, Dedham selectmen granted to "Henry Chickeringe 6 acres of plowing land on the south plain" [DeTR 1:78; NEHGR 69:229].

Michaell Powell (De): "Mr. Michaell Powell & his wife Abigaile were both admitted [to Dedham church] the same day [16 April 1641]" [DeChR 25]. On 29 November 1639, Dedham selectmen permitted "Michael Powell ... to purchase Mr. Dalton's lot" [DeTR 1:62; NEHGR 131:173-74].

Joseph Kingsberry (De): "Joseph Kingsbury of whom mention was made before that he was left out of the foundation of the church for some cause there mentioned" was admitted to Dedham church on 9 April 1641 [DeChR 24-25]. On 18 July 1637, the town of Dedham authorized "Ezechiell Holliman ... of our society to turn over his lot, as also that which he purchased of Raffe Shepheard, unto John Kingsbery & Joseph his brother" [DeTR 1:32]. On 1 September 1637, "Mary, the daughter of Joseph & Millicent Kingsbury" was born at Dedham [DeVR 1].

John Roaper (De): "[blank] Roper the wife of John Roper was received into the church [at Dedham] the 13 of the 7 month [13 September] 1639" [DeChR 21]. "Hannah the daughter of our brother John Roper & his wife our sister was baptized [at Dedham] 9th 2 month [9 April] 1642" [DeChR 26]. Sometime between these two events, John Roper himself must have been admitted to Dedham church, with his admission not being recorded. On 13 April 1637, "John Ropear of New Bucknam, carpenter, aged 26 years, and Alles his wife, aged 23 years, with 2 children, Alles and Elizabeth," were enrolled at Great Yarmouth as passengers for New England [Hotten 292]. On 11 August 1637, the town of Dedham granted that "John Bacheler & John Roper may have lots" [DeTR 1:33].

Nathani[el] Coalborne (De): "Nathaniell Colborne was received into the church after long & much inquisition into his case 29th of 11 month [29 January] 1640[/1]" [DeChR 24]. On 11 August 1637, the town of Dedham "consented that Nathaniell Colborne may have Philemon Dalton's gratification lot" [DeTR 1:34].

John Elis (De): On 17 July 1640, "John Ellice" was admitted to Dedham church [DeChR 23]. On 18 August 1636, "John Ellis" attended the founding meeting for the town of Dedham [DeTR 1:20]. (As this meeting was held at Watertown, that may have been his residence at the time.)

Edward Rich[a]rds (De): On 17 July 1640, "[Edmond] Richards" was admitted to Dedham church [DeChR 23]. On 10 September 1638, "Edward Richards & Suzan Hunting" were married at Dedham [DeVR 126]. On 23 November 1638, "Edward Richards, shoemaker," and two other men were "propounded to consideration against the next meeting" at Dedham [DeTR 1:50].

Beniamin Smyth (De): "Benjamin Smith was also received [to Dedham church] the same day [28 May 1641]" [DeChR 25]. On 10 August 1641, "Benjamin Smith & Mary Clarke" were married at Dedham [DeVR 126]. On 10 July 1642, Dedham selectmen granted to "Beniamyne Smith six acres of upland near unto the South Meadow" [DeTR 1:87].

Austen Kilham (De): "Austen Kella[m] was received into the [Dedham] church 28[d] of the 6th month [28 August] 1640" [DeChR 24]. On 7 August 1637, "Augustin Kellham is admitted for inhabitant" at Salem [STR 1:53]. On 12 January 1640/1, "Austen Kalem is chosen measurer" for the town of Dedham [DeTR 1:76].

Thom[as] Payne (De): "Thomas Paine & his wife Rebecka were received into the communion of the church [of Dedham] 23 of the 2[d] month [23 April] 1641" [DeChR 25]. On 28 November 1640, "Thomas Payne" was mentioned in a grant of land at Dedham [DeTR 1:73].

Tymo[thy] Dwight (De): "Timothy Dwite was received into the church giving good testimony of the fruit of the ordinances in his conversion to God 30th of the 6 month [30 August] 1649" [DeChR 24]. On 28 August 1638, at a Dedham town meeting, "Timothy Dwite [was] entertained unto his brother Jno. his gratification lot to have half an acre for situation of his house" [DeTR 1:47; GM 2:2:376].

Henry Wilson (De): "Henery Willson with much comfort to the church [at Dedham] was received the same day [6 March 16(39/)40]" [DeChR 23]. On 23 June 1640, Dedham selectmen granted to "Henry Wilson & Samuel Bullen" a small parcel of land [DTR 1:68].

Samu[el] Bullen (De): "Mary the daughter of our brother Samuell Bullin & his wife Mary was baptized 24th 5 month [24 July] 1642" at Dedham [DeChR 26]. "Samuell the son of our brother Samuell Bullin & his wife Mary was baptized 29 day 11 month [29 January] 1644[/5]" at Dedham [DeChR 28]. These two baptisms imply that Samuel Bullen was admitted to Dedham church prior to 24 July 1642, but that his admission was omitted from the surviving church records. On 23 June 1640, Dedham selectmen granted to "Henry Wilson & Samuel Bullen" a small parcel of land [DTR 1:68].

Willi[am] Fuller (Ip or Co): There were two men named William Fuller who might have been this freeman; unfortunately in this instance, context does not assist us in determining which one to choose. One, who came to New England in 1635 on the *Abigail*, settled first at Ipswich and then moved to Hampton in 1640 or 1641 [GM 2:2:602-6]. This William Fuller served on the grand jury at Ipswich Court on

28 December 1641 [EQC 1:37] and so might not have made the move to Hampton until after that date. The second William Fuller "which kept the mill at Concord, was [on 4 June 1639] fined £3 for gross abuse in overtolling" [MBCR 1:267]. "Hannah the daughter of William Fuller was born [at Concord] the 8° (6°) [8 August] 1641" and "Elizabeth the wife of William Fuller died [at Concord] 24° (5°) [24 July] 1642" [CoVR 2].

Willi[am] F[blank] (Unknown): There is not enough information to identify this freeman.

Mr. [blank] [blank] (Unknown): There is not enough information to identify this freeman.

Evan Thomas (Bo): On 4 April 1641, "Evan Thomas a Welshman" was admitted to Boston church [BChR 33]. On 1 September 1640, "Evan Thomas, having a wife & four children, is allowed twenty bushels of corn at harvest, & what necessary charge Goodman Button is at to be allowed them" [MBCR 1:300]. On 26 October 1640, "Evan Thomas is to be taken into consideration for becoming a townsman with us [at Boston]" [BTR 1:56].

Abell Parr (Bo): Aside from this record of admission as a freeman, there are no other records in early New England for an Abel Parr. This is a case where the inclusion of this name between two other men admitted to Boston church about the same time helps make the identification. On 23 January 1640/1, "Abell Porter a singleman" was admitted to Boston church [BChR 33]. On 19 February 1637/8, Boston selectmen granted to "Abell Porter, having served our brother Thomas Grubbe four years, a houseplot and a great lot at the Mount for two heads" [BTR 1:31].

Benia[min] Ward (Bo): On 6 June 1640, "Beniamin Warde ship carpenter and Marye his wife" were admitted to Boston church [BChR 30]. On 8 January 1637/8, pursuant to a town order of 14 December 1635, Boston selectmen granted to "Beniamyn Warde, twelve acres" at Muddy River [BTR 1:22].

Willi[am] Hunt (Co): On 12 February 1640[/41?], "Hanna the daughter of W[illia]m Hunt" was born at Concord [CoVR 2].

Willi[am] Bateman (Ch): On 30 December 1638, "William Bateman is granted planting ground [at Charlestown] when the Indians are satisfied" [ChTR 41].

Josias Firman (Bo): On 6 June 1640, "Josiah Ferman servant to our brother Mr. John Winthroppe" was admitted to Boston church [BChR 30]. In an account dated about 1636, John Winthrop was billed for clothing purchased for "Josias Firmin" [WP 3:219-20].

Willi[am] Cop (Bo): On 4 July 1640, "Willyam Copp a shoemaker" was admitted to Boston church [BChR 29]. (This freeman was not the "William Cope" who sailed for New England in 1635 on the *Blessing* [Hotten 93; GM 2:2:212].)

Natha[n] Halstedd (Co): On 15 March 1641[/2?], "Isabell the wife of Nathan Halsted" died at Concord [CoVR 2]. On 3 February 1643/4, "Nathan Halstead" died at Dedham [DeVR 127]. The inventory of "the goods and chattels of Nathan Halsted late of Concord deceased" was taken on 5 February 1643[/4] [SPR 2:19]. (Halstead was apparently visiting Dedham when he died.)

Natha[niel] Billing (Co): In January 1661[/2?], "John Billings and Elizabeth Hastings" were married at Concord [CoVR 10]. (John Billings was the son of Nathaniel. No other records for this family have been found between 1641 and 1661, although some are undoubtedly buried in town and county records. Although this is an extreme example, we have little evidence from the late 1630s and early 1640s for most of the early Concord immigrants, and so our placement of some of these freemen as Concord men in 1641 is reliant on the present context and our estimates of year of arrival for these families must be tentative.)

Benia[min] Turney (Co): On 16 February 1639[/40?], "Rebeccah the daughter of Benjamin Turney" was born at Concord [CoVR 3]. He had two more children born at Concord, in 1641 and 1643 [CoVR 3]. He was still in England as late as 8 January 1636/7 and moved to Fairfield, Connecticut, in 1644 with others from Concord [Gillespie Anc 473-75].

Rich[a]rd Rice (Co): On 1 March 1635[/6], the town of Cambridge agreed "with Richard Rice to keep 100 cows for the space of three months" [CaTR 19]. On 27 October 1641, "Elizabeth the daughter of Richard Rice" was born at Concord [CoVR 3].

James Blood (Co): On 12 July 1640, "Mary the daughter of James Bloud" was born at Concord [CoVR 1].

Thom[as] Clarke (Bo): On 18 July 1640, "Thomas Clarke, a blacksmith," was admitted to Boston church [BChR 30]. On 25 November 1639, "Thomas Clarke, a locksmith, is allowed for an inhabitant [at Boston] and to be considered for a houseplot here and a Great Lot at Mount Wollystone for six heads" [BTR 1:44].

John Viall (Bo): On 2 May 1641, "John Vyall a laborer" was admitted to Boston church [BChR 34]. On 11 July 1641, "Mary Vyall, the wife of our brother John Vyall," was admitted to Boston church [BChR 33]. On 14 August 1639, "Hopestill, daughter of John & Mary Vyall," was born at Boston [BVR 8]. On 27 January 1639/40, "John Vyall, weaver, is allowed to be an inhabitant [at Boston]" [BTR 1:47].

Thom[as] Buttolph (Bo): On 22 September 1639, "Thomas Buttall, a glover," was admitted to Boston church [BChR 26]. On 28 September 1639, "Anne the wife of the said Thomas Buttall" was admitted to Boston church [BChR 26]. On 4 May 1635, "Tho[mas] Buttolph," aged 32, and "uxor Ann Buttolph," aged 24, were enrolled at London as passengers for New England on the *Abigail* [Hotten 73; GM 2:1:517-22].

Franc[is] Douse (Bo): On 20 June 1640, "Francis Dowse, one of our brother Burdon's family," was admitted to Boston church [BChR 30]. On 30 December 1639, "Francis Dowse, servant to our brother, George Burdon, is allowed for an inhabitant [of Boston]" [BTR 1:45; TAG 29:161-69].

John Sweete (Bo): On 10 February 1638/9, "Temperance, the wife of one John Sweete, a shipcarpenter," was admitted to Boston church [BChR 23]. On 30 January 1640/1, "John Sweete a shipcarpenter" was admitted to Boston church [BChR 32]. On 22 February 1640/1, Boston selectmen noted that "Brother Sweete is to be considered for a Great Lot" [BTR 1:59].

Arthur Gill (Do): On 27 November 1642, "Arthur Gill, a shipcarpenter, and Anne his wife" were admitted to Boston church "upon letters of dismission from Dorchester" [BChR 37]. (There is no record of his admission to Dorchester church, unless the "John Gill" admitted there on 20 November 1640 was really Arthur [DChR 5].) Gill came first to Richmond Island in 1636 and left for Massachusetts Bay in 1639 [Trelawny Papers 133-34, 159, 161-62, 204-5; GDMNH 261].

Thom[as] Clipton (We): On 28 January 1640/1, Massachusetts Bay Court ordered that "Mr. James Parker is allowed to marry Thomas Clifton & Mary Butterworth within a month" [MBCR 1:313]. Thomas Clifton moved from Weymouth to Rehoboth by 1644 [Weymouth Hist 3:165].

George Merriam (Co): On 8 November 1641, "Elisabeth the daughter of Georg[e] Miriam" was born at Concord [CoVR 2]. (His brothers Robert and Joseph had come to New England in 1638 on the *Castle* and by 1639 had settled in Concord [Lechford 140, 162-68, 174; Waters 1214].)

John Heald (Co): On 22 May 1645, "Dor[c]as the daughter of John & Dorothie Held" was born at Concord [CoVR 4]. This immigrant married Dorothy Royle at Alderley, Cheshire, on 3 December 1636 and their son John was baptized at that parish the following March [Hale, House 262; TAG 10:15].

George Wheeler (Co): On 30 March 1640, "Sarah the daughter of Georg[e] Wheeler" was born at Concord [CoVR 3].

Obedi[ah] Wheeler (Co): On 27 January 1640[/1?], "John the son of Obadiah Wheeler" was born at Concord [CoVR 3].

Franc[is] Bloyce (Ca): "Francis Blosse" was buried at Cambridge on 29 September 1646. (No other records have been found for this immigrant prior to 1646, so we assume that he was of Cambridge in 1641. In this case we lack further context to assist us in this determination.)

Thom[as] Marshall (Ly): This admission to freemanship is probably for Captain Thomas Marshal of Lynn, who might be the Thomas Marshall who sailed for New England in 1635 on the *James* [Hotten 107; GM 2:5:46-47].

RECENT LITERATURE

Clifford L. Stott, "The Chaplin Family of Co. Suffolk: Ancestors of the Plumb and Parke Families of Connecticut," *The American Genealogist* 82 (2007):250-60. John Plumb settled in Wethersfield, Connecticut, by 1636. Stott has identified his wife as Dorothy Chaplin, baptized at Semer, Suffolk, on 10 June 1596. He also shows that she was sister of Clement Chaplin, who came to New England in 1635, settling first in Cambridge and then moving on to Hartford and Wethersfield [GM 2:2:46-51], and of Martha (Chaplin) Parke, wife of Robert Parke, who was in New England no later than 1639, and whose son William Parke sailed for New England in early 1631 and resided at Roxbury [GMB 3:1386-91]. The author includes genealogical summaries of the families of the father and paternal grandfather of these siblings.

Glade Ian Nelson, "Thomas[1] Sharpe and Philip[1] Watson Challis: Family Connections Continued," *The American Genealogist* 82 (2007):261-66. Nelson expands on earlier work on Philip Watson Challis, first by presenting extensive new information on the family of Thomas Sharpe, who married an aunt of Philip Watson Challis. Sharpe came to Massachusetts Bay in 1630, but returned to England the following year, settling in Sandon, Essex, where he was brought before the church court for Puritan activities. The author then sets forth additional information on the Watson family.

William Wyman Fiske, "The Perry Family of Sawbridgeworth, Hertfordshire: Shared Ancestry of Six Massachusetts Immigrants: John[1] Perry of Roxbury, Isaac[1] Perry of Boston, Mary[1] (Perry) Heath of Roxbury, Phebe[1] (Perry) Desborough of Roxbury, John[1] Reddington of Topsfield, and Abraham[1] Reddington of Topsfield and Boxford," *The American Genealogist* 82 (2007):273-89. Fiske concludes his multipart article on the Perry and related families with genealogical summaries of several members of the Perry family in England. Most important of these for the study of the Great Migration is the sketch for Abraham Perry of Sawbridgeworth, Hertfordshire, ancestor of several immigrants to New England. His daughter Hannah married Thomas Reddington, and their sons John and Thomas came to New England and resided in Essex County. Abraham's daughter married William Heath of Roxbury [GMB 2:901-4]. Abraham's sons John and Isaac Perry also came to New England, settling in Roxbury and Boston respectively.

Leslie Mahler, "The English Ancestry of John[1] Gosse of Watertown, Massachusetts, and His Niece Sarah Caly, Wife of John[1] Dillingham of Massachusetts," *The American Genealogist* 82 (2007):295-307. John Gosse sailed to New England in 1630 in the Winthrop Fleet and settled in Watertown [GMB 2:795-98]. Mahler first identifies the father and paternal grandfather of John Gosse and sets forth genealogical summaries for these two men. He then demonstrates that Thomasine Gosse, John's elder sister, married Thomas Caly and that their daughter, Sarah Caly, married John Dillingham, 1630 immigrant to Boston, on one of his return trips to

England [GMB 1:547-50]. The article concludes with sketches of four generations of agnate ancestry for Sarah Caly.

Ken Stevens, "Gowen[1] Wilson of Hingham, Exeter and Kittery," *The New England Historical and Genealogical Register* 162 (2008):174-80. In this first installment of a multipart article, the author begins by examining possible evidence for Gowen Wilson's origin in Scotland. He then surveys exhaustively the records describing Wilson's life, including evidence of landholding and officeholding. Wilson first appeared in New England in 1641, perhaps residing at Weymouth, and then moving on to Hingham, Exeter and Kittery. Finally, the author summarizes what is known about the children of this immigrant, with further information on the son Joseph to follow in a later installment.

Glade Ian Nelson, "Identifying Mercy, Wife of Thomas[4] Hinckley of Harwich, Massachusetts, as Mercy (Bangs) (Hinckley) Cole," *The New England Historical and Genealogical Register* 162 (2008):212-21. Nelson completes his argument for the identity of the wife of Thomas Hinckley as Mercy Bangs, daughter of Jonathan Bangs, based on evidence from land records and from naming patterns, and also on an argument by elimination after investigation of likely women named Mercy. The article contains a genealogical summary of the life and children of Jonathan Bangs, son of Edward Bangs, who arrived in Plymouth by 1623 [GMB 1:86-91].

Myrtle Stevens Hyde, "Augments and Adjusts to Stacie and Archer Ancestors of New England Settlers Archer and Fitch, With the Addition of Searle Ancestors," *The Genealogist* 22 (2008):175-85. Extending earlier published work by William Wyman Fiske and herself, Hyde revises the ancestry of Anne Stacie, wife of Thomas Fitch of Norwalk, Connecticut. She first corrects the Stacie lineage and provides additional information on the father and paternal grandfather of Anne Stacie. The author then provides three generations of agnate ancestry for Isabel Searle, who married William Archer. The latter couple had a daughter Isabel who married Laurence Stacie, grandfather of Anne (Stacie) Fitch.

John Blythe Dobson, "Notes on the Family of Thomas Chatfield, Great-Uncle of the Three Chatfield Brothers of Connecticut, and Probable Father-in-law of Joannes Verveelen of New Amsterdam," *The Genealogist* 22 (2008):212-20. The brothers Francis, Thomas and George Chatfield settled at Guilford, Connecticut, in 1639. Thomas Chatfield, great-uncle to these three brothers, was born about 1568 and migrated to the Netherlands where he lived for at least thirty years. With his first wife, Thomas Chatfield had five children, including a daughter Anne, who in 1637 married Joannes Verveelen at Amsterdam. In 1657 this latter coupled migrated to New Amsterdam, not far from their Chatfield cousins.

(continued from page 26)

in that year, and as many as a third of that quarter are placed as 1640 arrivals largely because of a lack of early records for some towns. From these circumstances we arrive at two conclusions. First, although there seem to have been more 1640 arrivals among the 1641 freemen than 1639 arrivals, this may well be an illusion, and the 1640 arrivals were probably less than those in 1639. Second, on the other hand, we will probably never be able to prove this first conclusion, and so in order to give full coverage of the Great Migration immigrants we will have to include those deemed here to be 1640 arrivals, without being certain that they came in that year. (We will be able to arrive at a better assessment of the first of these conclusions by carrying out a similar analysis of 1642 and 1643 freemen.)

Now let us look at the results of our analysis from a different perspective. We find that one of the freemen of 1641 had arrived as early as 1633. This was Abel Porter, and we learned this only because of a record of 19 February 1637/8, which stated that he had served for four years as a servant of Thomas Grubb [BTR 1:31]. Thomas Grubb himself arrived in Boston in 1633 [GMB 2:826-29], and so probably brought Abel Porter with him as a servant at that time. (Note also that Abel Porter's name was given incorrectly in the list of freemen as "Abel Parr," and that we were able to identify him correctly because of his placement in the list between two Boston men.)

Undoubtedly, some of the other men who appear in this list of freemen had arrived in New England as servants, without leaving a record of the sort that helped us with Abel Porter. Most of the men seen here, though, probably came as adult single men, or already married with children. We conclude, then, that it was not unusual for a man to wait, for whatever reason, for as many as six or seven years after arrival in New England before being admitted as a freeman.

Two issues ago we carried out a similar analysis, but looking in the other direction. After studying two passenger lists from 1634, we discovered that some of the male heads of family in these lists did not become freemen for as many as eight years, but beyond that span of time we were not confident in making identifications [GMN 17:11-14]. This is symmetrical with the conclusion reached here in the analysis of the 1641 passenger list. A gap of up to eight years between arrival in New England and admission to freemanship was not unusual, but anything beyond that should be considered rare.

Finally, note that some parts of the list of freemen are highly structured, such as the sequence of Dedham men, but other sections have little or no structure. This structure assisted us in showing that "Abel Parr" was really Abel Porter, but the lack of structure in another part of the list frustrated us in our attempt to identify the second John Harrison who was made a freeman on 2 June 1641. We regret that the colony clerk was not more systematic in creating this list.

Great Migration Newsletter

Vol. 18   January-March 2009   No. 1

ANNE HUTCHINSON AND JOHN WHEELWRIGHT

In an occasional Great Migration sketch, usually for a resident of Boston, we will note when there is evidence that the immigrant was a supporter of Anne Hutchinson and John Wheelwright, without describing just what that support meant and what the consequences were.

A pertinent example from the most recent Great Migration volume may be found in the treatment of Thomas Marshall, who had settled in Boston by 1634 [GM 2:5:41-46]:

> Thomas Marshall was one of the leading supporters of Anne Hutchinson and Rev. John Wheelwright [Saints and Sectaries 102, 210, 216]. On 2 November 1637, "Thomas Marshall being convented for having his hand to the said seditious writing, & justifying the same, is also disfranchised" [MBCR 1:207]. On 20 November 1637, "Thomas Marshall" was one of fifty-eight Boston men who were disarmed for their involvement in this controversy [MBCR 1:211]. There is no record that Thomas Marshall recanted, but he was not forced to leave Boston, and eventually returned to a position of respect, as evidenced by the wide range of town and church duties to which he was elected or appointed.

What does all this signify?

Our starting point is the observation that all the leaders of the migration to Massachusetts Bay, whether civil or ecclesiastical, were from the Calvinist wing of Protestantism. Their fundamental belief was that at the beginning of time God had chosen some people for salvation and some for perdition, and nothing that any person could do in the world could change that condition. Those chosen for salvation were known as the elect. The church government that grew out of this position was known as the New England Way, and eventually became the Congregational Church.

Having taken this position, the colony leaders were forced to navigate between the Scylla of Arminianism and the Charybdis of Antinomianism. The Arminians believed that anyone could be saved and that salvation was in part dependent upon one's behavior in the world. Critics of Arminianism referred to this as preaching a Covenant of Works. Strict Calvinists were expected to preach only a Covenant of Grace, arguing that one could not affect one's own election. This led to the position that if one could not change God's decision on salvation, there was no motivation for performing good works in this world. Anyone who arrived at this conclusion was naturally abhorrent to the colony leaders, and were later referred to as Antinomians, those who felt no need to conform to the moral law.

Anne (Marbury) Hutchinson, wife of William Hutchinson of Alford, Lincolnshire, came to New England in 1634 and settled at Boston [GM 2:3:477-84]. William Hutchinson's sister Mary had married Reverend John Wheelwright, rector of Bilsby, Lincolnshire, the parish just to the east of Alford; this couple came to New England in 1636 [GDMNH 743-44]. These two parishes were less than twenty miles north of Boston, Lincolnshire, where the powerful Puritan John Cotton had held sway for many years and had influenced the Hutchinsons and Wheelwrights strongly.

Once in New England, Anne Hutchinson began holding private religious meetings in her home, in which she provided her own interpretation of scripture, arguing that some New England ministers were preaching a Covenant of Works. Once Wheelwright arrived, he began giving sermons with the same message. They believed that they had Cotton's support in these efforts to focus only on the Covenant of Grace.

The authorities, and especially Governor John Winthrop and Reverend Thomas Shepard, viewed these activities as a threat, tending toward a usurpation of their authority.

(continued on page 2)

EDITOR'S EFFUSIONS

In this first issue of the New Year, we are making two experiments. First, in addition to our normal distribution to both print and electronic subscribers, we will be sending this issue, and this issue only, to all NEHGS members with electronic addresses. We believe that there are many members of the Society, and especially many new members, who are not familiar with the *Great Migration Newsletter*, and we hope in this way to broaden the circulation of this publication.

So, for the benefit of those who are not already regular readers, we state first that the purpose of this periodical is to cover topics that have no proper place in the published volumes of Great Migration sketches. Each issue has four sections. First, a lead article of about two pages usually addresses a specific topic of methodological or historical interest. This might be something like the techniques we use in documenting marriages or, as in the present case, the background for a historical event which impacted many of the Great Migration immigrants.

Half of each issue, the center four pages, is called the *Focus* section. This provides an in-depth study of an early New England town or a broad class of records. In the case of an article on a town, such matters as the settlement process, the granting of lands and the establishment of the church will be covered. In this issue, the *Focus* section begins a discussion of the records generated by the county courts.

The remaining two sections are *Recent Literature*, which summarizes recent articles and books on Great Migration immigrants or the broader history of the period, and *Editor's Effusions*, which provides us an opportunity to make comments about the progress of the Great Migration Study Project.

The second experiment is connected with the *Focus* article commenced in this issue. That article studies in depth a single session of the Middlesex County Court. To enhance the presentation, we will be posting on the Project website images of the original pages of the record book for this court session (*www.GreatMigration.org*). We hope that these images will increase your understanding of these records. If successful, we will post more such images in the future.

Robert Charles Anderson, FASG   Editor
Jean Powers, Production Assistant

The Great Migration Newsletter is published quarterly by the Great Migration Study Project, a project of the New England Historic Genealogical Society, 101 Newbury Street, Boston MA 02116
www.NewEnglandAncestors.org
www.GreatMigration.org
GreatMigration@nehgs.org

Copyright © 2009
New England Historic Genealogical Society

(continued from page 1)

Winthrop began to take note of the activities of Hutchinson and Wheelwright in October of 1636 [WJ 1:239-43]. Attempts to bring Hutchinson and Wheelwright back to orthodoxy continued for a year, but eventually failed. The two heretics were summoned before the General Court of 2 November 1637 and, after much wrangling, Wheelwright, and then Hutchinson, were banished [MBCR 1:205-7].

The General Court continued to meet throughout most of the month of November. On the 15th a number of men who had signed a petition in support of Wheelwright were disfranchised (that is, were stripped of their freemanship). On the 20th a larger number, mostly from Boston but some from a handful of other Massachusetts Bay towns, were disarmed as well [MBCR 1:207-8, 211-12].

Within a few days, many of those named in the court records on the 15th and the 20th signed a petition in which they submitted to authority, stating that, "having joined in preferring to the Court a writing called a Remonstrance, or Petition, I acknowledge it was ill done, ... and therefore I desire my name may be put out of it" [WP 3:513-16].

Not everyone did so, however. On 22 March 1637/8, Anne Hutchinson was excommunicated by the Boston church and went with many of her followers to the northern end of Aquidneck Island in Narragansett Bay and founded the town of Portsmouth [BChR 21-22].

Wheelwright led a group of his supporters north to found the town of Exeter (at that time outside the bounds of Massachusetts Bay, and now in New Hampshire). On 6 January 1638/9, Boston church dismissed several men "unto the Church of Christ at the Falls of Paschataqua" and, on 3 March 1638/9, several women were dismissed to "the forenamed Church at the Falls now called Exeter" [BChR 23].

These two categories of men and women (those who recanted almost immediately, and those who left with Hutchinson and Wheelwright) do not encompass all those who were punished by the court in November 1637. As noted above in our extract from the sketch of Thomas Marshall of Boston, no record could be found of his renouncement of his Antinomian activities, and yet he had clearly been rehabilitated at some later date.

Recent research in the collection of colonial Massachusetts documents known as the Massachusetts Archives serendipitously resolved the puzzle. While searching for material on immigrants to be covered in the next Great Migration volume, the following petition was found [MA Arch 38B:213].

To the Honored Court

May it please this Honored Court that whereas some years since I put my hand to a petition which concerned Mr. Whelewright wherein were some things offensive and upon mature consideration I do acknowledge they might

(continued on page 8)

Focus on County Courts

INTRODUCTION

Of the many original sources exploited in the preparation of Great Migration sketches, none provides a wider range of information than the records of the county courts. Furthermore, aside from such sources as private letters and diaries, court records frequently provide the greatest insights into the individual personalities of the immigrants. To better understand this class of records, we will examine the early county courts of Massachusetts Bay.

For the first six years of its existence, Massachusetts Bay was served by a single court, presided over by the Governor, Deputy Governor and Assistants, meeting usually at Boston or Cambridge. With the great growth in the population of the colony in the middle years of the 1630s, the General Court decided on 3 March 1635/6 to institute another layer of courts, to be held on a quarterly basis [MBCR 1:168]:

> Further, it is ordered, that there shall be four Courts kept every quarter, 1, at Ipswich, to which Newberry shall belong; 2, at Salem, to which Saugus shall belong; 3, at Newe Towne [Cambridge], to which Charlton, Concord, Meadford, & Waterton shall belong; 4th, at Boston, to which Rocksbury, Dorchester, Weymothe, & Hingham shall belong.

These courts were tasked with both civil and criminal jurisdiction, but, as we shall see, this did not limit the varieties of business that would be transacted at these venues. The Quarter Court to be held at Boston was considered superior to the other three. On 25 May 1636, the succeeding General Court appointed the first groups of magistrates to preside over each of the four courts [MBCR 1:175]. On this occasion, the Quarter Courts were also referred to as Particular Courts, a designation more frequently seen in some of the other New England colonies.

With the continued growth in population over the next few years, and the concomitant increase in the number of new towns, the General Court on 10 May 1643 divided the colony into four counties: Norfolk, Essex, Middlesex and Suffolk [MBCR 2:38]. (Norfolk County as originally created was not the same as the modern Norfolk County. As defined in 1643, Norfolk encompassed the towns north of the Merrimack River: Salisbury, Haverhill, Exeter, Hampton, Dover and Strawberry Bank [later Portsmouth].) The Quarter Courts then became associated with the counties.

NORFOLK: Norfolk court sat at both Salisbury and Hampton. Surviving records for these courts have been published in the same volumes with the Essex records, as described in the next paragraph. Although included in Norfolk County, Dover and Portsmouth already had a functioning court prior to 1643, with its own records [NHPP 40]. This court at

times had independent status as a separate county. In 1679, with the establishment of the Province of New Hampshire, Norfolk County was dissolved, with the first tier of towns north of the Merrimack being absorbed in Essex County.

ESSEX: As created in 1643, Essex County included all the towns comprised in the two Quarter Courts erected in 1636 at Ipswich and Salem. These courts continued to sit separately. The records from 1636 through 1686 have been published in nine volumes, in the set we refer to as EQC.

MIDDLESEX: Although erected in 1643 along with the other three counties, Middlesex did not take on a separate existence until 1649. Prior to that time all Middlesex court business, included probate matters and registration of deeds, may be found in Suffolk records. None of the surviving Middlesex court records have yet been published *in extenso*. We refer to the manuscript volumes containing the minutes of this court as MCR.

SUFFOLK: For a brief period after the establishment of the Quarter Courts, the records for the Boston court were recorded in the same volume with the records of the General Court and the Court of Assistants (e.g., 7 June 1636, 6 July 1636, 4 December 1638, 7 September 1641 [MBCR 1:176-77, 245-48, 334-36]). Eventually, the records for this Quarter Court were maintained in separate volumes. The records of the Suffolk County Court from 1671 through 1680 were edited and published in 1933 (*Records of the Suffolk County Court, 1671-1680*, 2 vols., in *Publications of the Colonial Society of Massachusetts*, vols. 29 and 30 [Boston, 1933], cited herein as SCC).

For the remainder of this article, we will examine in detail a single session of the Middlesex County Court [MCR 1:246-257]. We will make occasional reference to single sessions of Dover, Ipswich and Suffolk courts, for purposes of comparison, and to describe transactions not seen in the Middlesex session. Dover: 29 June 1675 [NHPP 40:314-22]. Ipswich: 26 September 1654 [EQC 1:362-68]. Suffolk: 30 January 1671/2 [SCC 31-96].

PERSONNEL

All properly recorded Quarter Court sessions begin in a formulaic way. First comes a heading defining the session then being held:

> At a County Court held at Cambridge
> October 6th, 1663

The heading is followed by lists of the court personnel for that sitting, first the magistrates, then the grand jury, and finally the trial jury.

On the Bench
Ri[chard Bellingham, Deputy Governor
Mr. Francis Willoughby
Capt. Daniel Gookin
Major Simon Willard
Mr. Richard Russell
Thomas Danforth, Recorder

At this period in the colony's history, the county magistrates were generally also men who held high colony office. In this instance, Richard Bellingham had been elected Deputy Governor in the Court of Elections on 27 May 1663, and all the other magistrates in this list, including Danforth, but excepting Willoughby, were elected Assistants at the same court [MBCR 4:2:71]. Willoughby had been an Assistant in the past, and would be elected to that office again on 18 May 1664 [MBCR 1:99].

The Grand Jury that
was impannelled in April
was summoned and
attended this Court

Looking back to the session of 2 April 1663, we find a list of fourteen names of men on the Grand Jury [MCR 1:233]. In the margin of the April session is the annotation "6.8.63, Thom[a]s Fuller, Jno. Blanchard added." In other words, the October Grand Jury consisted of the fourteen men who had been impannelled in April, with two more men added, but the information on the men added for the October session is found only in the record of the April session.

On the Jury of
Trials
Impannelled & Sworn

This last heading for personnel is followed by a list of twelve names: John Parker, William Hailstone, Anthony Peirce, Zachariah Hickes, Walter Hastings, John Smedley, George Fowle, John Smith, John Call, Thomas Peirce, Samuel Stratton and Abraham Hill. While not all of these men can be placed in a particular Middlesex town at this date, we may tentatively allocate them as follows: Cambridge (Hastings and Hicks), Charlestown (Call and Fowle), Watertown (Stratton and Anthony Peirce), Woburn (Parker and Thomas Peirce), Chelmsford (Hailstone), Malden (Hill) and Concord (Smedley), with John Smith unallocated. In general, the towns which were the oldest in the county or the closest to Cambridge, or both, had two trial jurymen apiece, while the towns that were most recently settled or the farthest from Cambridge, or both, were not represented at all (Billerica, Groton, Marlborough, Reading, Sudbury).

Each town was apparently allocated a specific number of trial jurymen per session, and the town meetings made the appointments. This is clearly seen in the Salem and Essex records. On 18 November 1657, for example, a "general town meeting" at Salem chose "Mr. Conant, Mr. Price, Samuel Gardner, Robert Lemon, John Putnam, William Dodge" for the jury of trials, and these are the men seen actually serving at the court of 24 November 1657 [STR 1:206; EQC 2:58-59].

CIVIL

In most of the county courts, the first business taken up were the new civil suits. We will look closely at two cases from the Middlesex session under consideration, and then make a few comments about the selected Suffolk session.

> Moses Eyres plaintiff against Theod[o]re Adkinson defendant in an action of the case, for not fulfilling his covenant with him by indenture of apprenticeship, to learn him his art of a feltmaker. Both parties appeared & joined issue in the case.
>
> The jury having heard & considered their respective pleas brought in, their verdict finding for the plaintiff damages twenty shillings, & costs of court sixteen shillings, and the plaintiff to give the defendant a release of his covenant by indenture for the learning him the art of a feltmaker.

This case poses some interesting problems. When these courts were first established, one of the procedural conditions was that "All actions shall be tried at that Court to which the defendant belongs" [MBCR 1:169]. Theodore Atkinson came to New England in 1634 as a servant, settled at Boston where he became a feltmaker and prominent merchant, and resided there without interruption until his death in 1701 [GM 2:1:95-103].

Much less is known about the plaintiff. "Moses Eyres was married unto Bethiah Millet" at Dorchester on 3 August 1666 [DVR 21], and he lived there and in Boston, both Suffolk County towns [NEHGR 15:56]. His parentage is not known, and so he also has no known connection with Middlesex County. Based on this court record alone, there seems no reason for bringing this action in this county.

> Mr. Jno. Shearman, attorney of Mr. Edmund Shearman of Dedham in Essex, old England, plaintiff, against John Shearman & John Livermore, executors of the last will & testament of Thomas Hammond of Watertowne, deceased, in an action of the case for an account of two broadcloths, committed to his custody about 13 years since, on attachment September [blank] 1663.
>
> The jury having heard the pleas & evidences of both parties which are on file with the records of this court brought in their verdict finding for the plaintiff damages of forty pounds to be paid in money or goods at money price, & costs of Court one pound, three shillings and six pence.

This case raises a different set of interesting issues. We see that both principals in the original business transaction, Edmund Sherman and Thomas Hammond, are represented in court by other men. Edmund Sherman was the son of an earlier Edmund Sherman, who had settled briefly at Watertown in 1635, then moved on to Wethersfield and New Haven, where he died in late 1640 or early 1641. The younger Edmund, plaintiff in this case, probably never came to New England. His attorney was his younger brother, who was also the minister at Watertown. At this early date, there were very few men with legal training in the colony, and Rev. John Sherman was undoubtedly acting on the authority of a letter of attorney issued for this particular occasion.

The statement of the action taken by the court refers to the "evidences of both parties which are on file with the records of this court." At least one document pertaining to this case does survive in the loose court papers for the county, a contract dated 14 April 1648 for the delivery of two broadclothes to Thomas Hammond by Edmund Sherman, witnessed by John Livermore [MCF Folio #34]. When this instrument was presented in court, Thomas Danforth, court recorder, added this note:

> Jno. Livermore, executor to the last will of Thomas Hammond, appearing in Court 6.8.63, acknowledged this to be a true bill & just debt & signed by Th[omas] Hammond deceased.

Extensive files of such supporting documents survive for many of the early courts. We obtain a better feel for this phenomenon by looking at the Suffolk Court session for 30 January 1671/2. In editing this set of court minutes, Samuel Eliot Morison scoured the Suffolk files for all relevant documents and included many of them in the published volume. These records may be found in the files of the Supreme Judicial Court, which we refer to as SJC.

The first case in this Suffolk session was Peck v. Bonner et al., involving the hire of "the ketch called the *Recovery*." Morison comments that "Several hundred documents in the Suffolk Files ... relating to this case, and the subsequent litigation between Lawton, Bonner, and Ashton, enable one to reconstruct the story of the ketch *Recovery*'s voyage" [SCC 31]. Not all cases are as voluminous as this, but we are reminded that behind each of these cases is a complicated personal story, and we are fortunate when even a few of the supporting documents survive to help us understand the lives of these immigrants.

OLD BUSINESS

After concluding work on the new civil cases, Middlesex Court turned to some matters still pending from previous court sessions.

> Mercy Rice, relict widow of Edm[und] Rice, deceased, appearing in Court, presented her request, that the order of the last Court, for the division of her husband's estate, so far as it refers to Benjamin Rice, may be suspended until there may be a clearing up & right understanding of what he received of his father as a part of his portion or is otherwise justly indebted to that estate, pleading that otherwise both herself, & her children by the said Rice, deceased, would be inevitably injured.

> The Court on hearing of her complaint ordered that the order of the last Court for the division of the said estate, so far as it refers to Benjamin Rice his proportion thereby granted, be suspended until there may be a full hearing of the case from both parties therein concerned.

Edmund Rice of Marlborough had died intestate in early 1663 and the widow and children had signed a petition for division on 16 June 1663, which was presented at Middle-

sex Court on the same day. That court appointed the widow administratrix and approved the petition for division, and we see here in the October session her request for an adjustment in that order. In a later section of this article we will look more closely at the probate jurisdiction of the county courts in the seventeenth century.

> Marmaduke Johnson, being formerly sentenced to depart home to his wife & not observing the order of the Court therein, is fined twenty pounds, unless he give security to depart home to his wife by the first opportunity & that he stands convicted until he perform this order of Court.

> Marmaduke Johnson, Samuel Goffe and John Barnard appearing in Court do acknowledge themselves jointly & severally to stand bound to the Treasurer of this County in the penal sum of forty pounds sterling on condition that the said Marmaduke Johnson shall depart this jurisdiction, according to the order of the Court, within six weeks time next ensuing, or by Christopher Clark's ship now bound for England.

Marmaduke Johnson had first arrived in New England at the end of July 1660, having been sent by Society for the Propagation of the Gospel to work at Cambridge with Samuel Green in printing the Indian Bible. (The biographical detail given here is taken from George Parker Winship, *The Cambridge Press, 1638-1692* [Philadelphia, 1945].) By the fall of the following year, he was courting Elizabeth Green, daughter of Samuel Green, without her father's permission. By October of 1661 Johnson was before the Middlesex Court for his misbehavior, and by the time of the court of 1 April 1662, the court had learned that he already had a wife in old England and ordered him to return to her.

The above court record shows that he had still not left New England as of October 1663, and in fact he would not do so until 1664. By 1665, however, he had returned to New England, apparently having satisfied the authorities that his wife in England had died. On 28 April 1670 he married at Cambridge Ruth Cane, daughter of Christopher Cane [GM 2:2:5]. He soon moved to Boston where he died in 1675. His widow died a year later, naming no children of her own in her will, but bequeathing to "my brother Jonathan Cane that house and land at Cambridge in case that my husband's son (whom I never saw) come not to demand it" [SPR 6:180].

CRIMINAL

After completing these odds and ends of old business, the court then turned to its second major category of business, the trial of criminal cases, of which there were half a dozen at this session of Middlesex Court. In most instances, these cases would have come before the county court pursuant to presentments by the Grand Jury.

> Robert Parris inhabitant at a farm near Chelmsford bounds, appearing in Court, and being by his own confession convicted of fornication committed with his wife before marriage is sentenced to be whipped 20 stripes.

Robert Parris, W[illia]m Bachelder & W[illia]m Attwood appearing in Court, do jointly & severally acknowledge themselves, their executors & administrators to stand bound to the Treasurer of this County in the penal sum of £20 sterling on condition that the wife of the said Robert Parris shall make her appearance at the next session of this Court, by adjournment to the 16th of this instant, then & there to answer for fornication committed before marriage, & that she shall abide the order of this Court & not depart without license.

At the adjourned session on 16 October 1663, the only recorded business was the appearance of the wife of Robert Parris.

Seaborne the wife of Robert Parris being by her own confession convicted of fornication before marriage and being a second offense of this kind, the Court sentenced her to be openly whipped 15 stripes on her naked body.

"Roberd Paris and Seaborne Cromwell" were married at Chelmsford on 22 May 1663 and their son Thomas was born there on 23 July 1663, thus providing evidence for the charge of "fornication before marriage." The wife of Robert Parris (or Parish) was daughter of William Bachelor, who had settled at Charlestown by 1634 [GM 2:1:122-26].

The evidence for the first offense of fornication comes from colony records six years earlier. On 6 May 1657, the General Court ordered in "the case of Seaborne Batchiler, now Cromwell, bound over by the Court of Assistants for committing folly with Ezekiell Everell, being with child by him & marrying with Jno. Cromwell, & not discovering the same to him, which she confessed, the whole Court, having heard the case, sentenced her to be whipped with twenty stripes" [MBCR 4:1:295].

On 12 May 1657 a group of midwives examined "Seaborn Cromwell" and determined that "it is more probable by what we find she is with child than other.... We are jointly doubtful in our spirits that if Seaborn have any bodily correction at present it may prove dangerous and hurtful to her." "The magistrates know no time fitter to whip her than what is appointed & therefore see no cause on this motion to alter their judgment." The deputies thought otherwise [MA Arch 38B:240], but we don't know the outcome.

Seaborn (Bachilor) (Cromwell) Parish died at Chelmsford on 28 September 1664, less than a year after her appearance at Middlesex Court, and not yet thirty years old. Robert Parish moved to Groton and married twice more [Sarah Hildreth Anc 49-51].

Ezekiel Everill, the father of Seaborn's first child, was himself no stranger to scandal. He had been baptized at Boston on 15 May 1636, son of James Everill [GM 2:2:469-76]. On 3 April 1653, "Ezekiell Everill son of our brother James Everill of the age of 16 years born and baptized into the fellowship of the Covenant for his choosing evil company and frequenting a house of ill report and that at unseasonable times with bad persons was called before the church and admonished" [BChR 54]. On 28 June 1657, "Ezekiel

Everill being of the age of 21 years born and baptized in the fellowship of this church, for his committing the sin of fornication and his contempt of the church that would not come to hear them was in the name of the Lord Jesus and with the consent of the church excommunicate" [BChR 56]. No further record has been found for Ezekiel. No reference to him or any issue was made in James Everill's will of 11 December 1682.

Ursilla the wife of John Cole of Charlstowne being convicted of reviling the Reverend Mr. Simes & Mr. Shepard, ministers of God's word at Charlstowne, saying she had as lief hear a cat meow, as them preach, is fined five pounds, or to be openly whipped, and she being also convicted of meeting with sundry Quakers at Ben[anue]ll Bowers house, was admonished of her evil & sin therein, & warned to attend the worship of God on the Lord's Days in the public assembly, with more frequency & delight. Costs three shillings to the witnesses. John Coale her husband appearing in Court engaged to pay her fine of five pounds.

John Cole was son of Rice Cole who had come to New England in 1630 and settled at Charlestown [GMB 1:426-29; TAG 78:183-84]. John had married Ursula by 23 November 1655 [MLR 2:35]; her parentage remains unknown.

Much of the attention of this court was taken up by concerns about the Quakers and Benanuel Bowers.

Sarah the wife of W[illia]m Osburne of Charlstowne being convicted of meeting with some Quakers at Ben[anue]ll Bowers, was admonished in Court to beware of the cursed tenets & practices of those heretics, & to return herself to the fellowship of God's people, and attendance on his ordinances. Costs three shillings to the witnesses.

Thomas Danforth seems to have gone astray in entering this case, for there was no early William Osburne in early Charlestown [Wyman 716-17]. There was, however, a Thomas Osburne with wife Sarah, and this must be the couple intended.

Shortly after the court session the Charlestown church took action. On 18 November 1663, "Brother Thomas Osburn being leavened with principles of Anabaptism was ... admonished for frequent irregular withdrawing himself from the public worship of God.... On the same day also, it was consented to by the brethren, that his wife, leavened with principles of Anabaptism, & Quakerism, should receive an admonition, for her notorious neglect of the public worship of God, denying our churches to be true churches, & denying her membership with us, & also the churches power over her, & continuing impenitent in her sin" [NEHGR 24:10].

On 30 July 1665, after repeated attempts to bring this couple back into the fold, "nothing of repentance intervening, brother Thomas Gool, brother Thomas Osburn, & his wife our sister Osburn, were ... excommunicated, for their impenitency in their schismatical withdrawing from the church, neglecting to hear the church" [NEHGR 24:133].

(to be continued)

RECENT LITERATURE

Leslie Mahler, "The English Origin of Nathaniel[1] Ward of Hartford, Connecticut, and Hadley, Massachusetts, Mary[1] (Ward) Cutting of Newbury, Massachusetts, Rebecca[1] (Ward) Allen of Newbury, and Their Nephew William[1] Markham of Hadley: A Previously Unknown Kinship Group," *The American Genealogist* 83 (2008-9):13-18. Using the 1664 will of Nathaniel Ward of Hadley as a springboard, Mahler presents records from old and New England which demonstrate that Nathaniel was son of Edward Ward of Little Wratting, Suffolk, and that he was joined in New England by two sisters, Mary (Ward) Cutting, wife of John Cutting of Newbury, and Rebecca (Ward) Allen, wife of Walter Allen of Newbury, and by a nephew, William Markham of Hadley, son of his sister Lydia (Ward) Markham.

David Curtis Dearborn, "Mary Tilman, Wife of Thomas[1] Frost of Arrowsic, Maine," *The American Genealogist* 83 (2008-9):46-49. Dearborn presents a 1734 deed and two associated depositions which trace a line of descent over three generations and nearly a century, back to a Great Migration immigrant. These documents show that Mary, wife successively of Thomas Frost and Joseph Soper, was a daughter of John Tilman and his wife Magdalen, and that the latter was a daughter of Robert Gutch, who had settled in Salem by 1637 and then moved to the Kennebec.

Jane Fletcher Fiske, "New Light on the English Background of the Osgoods of Essex County, Massachusetts," *The American Genealogist* 83 (2008-9):51-58. In this first installment of a two-part article, Fiske expands our knowledge of Christopher Osgood, who sailed for New England in 1634 and settled at Ipswich [GM 2:5:318-22]. Although it had been known for some time that his last residence in England was Marlborough, Wiltshire, we now learn that he was baptized at Newton Tony, Wiltshire, on 17 April 1606. The author identifies three generations of his agnate ancestry, providing genealogical summaries of the families of each of these men.

Martin E. Hollick, "Mary[2] Lester, Wife of Thomas[2] Clark(e) of Hartford, Connecticut," *The American Genealogist* 83 (2008-9):69-74. Taking note of a pertinent Hartford court case of 1669, Hollick shows that the given name of the daughter of Andrew Lester who married Thomas Clark was Mary. (Thomas Clark was son of Nicholas Clark, who had settled at Cambridge in 1632 and then moved to Hartford in 1635 [GMB 1:373-75]). The author then adds a genealogical summary of Thomas Clark and his children, listing all known grandchildren.

Jane Fletcher Fiske, "The English Background of Richard Kent Sr. and Stephen Kent of Newbury, Massachusetts, and Mary, Wife of Nicholas Easton of Newport, Rhode Island," *The New England Historical and Genealogical Register* 162 (2008):245-54. In this first installment of a multipart article, building on a will discovered by Leslie Mahler, the author clarifies a number of connections in the Kent family, with

relations to other Great Migration families. Richard Kent Sr., who came to New England in 1634 and settled soon at Newbury [GM 2:4:140-42], and his brother Stephen, who came to New England in 1638, were sons of Thomas Kent of Upper Wallop, Hampshire, who made his will in 1605. Furthermore, Fiske has identified Mary Kent, a daughter of this Thomas, as the first wife of Nicholas Easton, who sailed for New England in 1634 in the same vessel with Richard Kent Sr. [GM 2:2:396-403].

Robert Wayne Hart, "Genealogical Material on the Willet and Saffin Families From the Notebook of John Saffin," *The New England Historical and Genealogical Register* 162 (2008):264-68. The author has recovered the source for the birth records of the children of Thomas Willett, who had settled at Plymouth by 1630 [GMB 3:1997-2002]. The records of these vital events were preserved by John Saffin, who married one of Willett's daughters. The notebook kept by Saffin was published in 1928 and Hart has extracted the material of genealogical significance, including material pertaining to Saffin's own family.

Sarah Vowell, *The Wordy Shipmates* (New York, 2008). The "shipmates" discussed by Vowell were John Winthrop, John Cotton, Roger Williams, Anne Hutchinson, and a number of other early immigrants to New England. In the aftermath of 9/11, Vowell felt the need to re-examine the roots of American exceptionalism, and devoted herself to an intensive exploration of Puritan literature and how it has reverberated through American history.

Her point of entry is "God's Promise to His Plantation," the sermon preached by John Cotton at Southampton in 1630 as the Winthrop Fleet was preparing to depart from England. She then looks at the sermon prepared by Winthrop himself for the same occasion, "A Model of Christian Charity." This latter document contains the enduring trope of the "city upon a hill," later used by many others, including especially Ronald Reagan during his Presidency.

Vowell enlivens her presentation and makes it more accessible to modern readers by explaining the seventeenth-century concepts in modern terms and by relating these Puritan ideas, both political and religious, to later and more familiar events in American history. For example, in describing the temperamental difference between John Winthrop and Roger Williams, she states that "At his city-on-a-hill best, Winthrop is Pete Seeger, gathering around the campfire to sing their shared folk songs. Williams is Bob Dylan plugging in at Newport, making his own noise."

Vowell has done her research very well, providing an excellent introduction to early New England Puritan thought for the non-specialist, while also connecting this thinking with current history. If you have avoided dipping into Puritan religious writings for fear that they would be too dry, try this volume. Imagine Molly Ivins channelling Perry Miller.

(continued from page 2)

justly so be taken, viz: such passages as wherein both magistrates and magistracy were not only slighted but affronted and not that due honor put upon them which became a people possessing peace and Godliness. I do therefore beseech this Honored Court to remit this my offense whereby I may enjoy your former favor and my former liberty and I shall rest

> Your humble petitioner
> Thomas Marshall
> 3 of the 9th 1643

Recommended Reading

David D. Hall, ed., *The Antinomian Controversy, 1636-1638: A Documentary History* (Middletown, Connecticut, 1968; second edition, 1990). Hall has collected and annotated a dozen contemporary documents relating to the crisis, including tracts and other items written by John Cotton, a sermon by John Wheelwright, John Winthrop's history of the events, and the proceedings of both the civil and the ecclesiastical trials of Anne Hutchinson.

Emery Battis, *Saints and Sectaries: Anne Hutchinson and the Antinomian Controversy in the Massachusetts Bay Colony* (Chapel Hill, North Carolina, 1962). Battis has carried out a sociological and psychological history of the Antinomian Controversy and Anne Hutchinson's part in it. He looks back into the English background and the family history leading up to the events in Massachusetts Bay, and then provides a detailed narrative of the crucial years in the mid-1630s. Several important appendices provide prosopographical data on all known adherents of Hutchinson and Wheelwright.

Amy Schrager Lang, *Prophetic Woman: Anne Hutchinson and the Problem of Dissent in the Literature of New England* (Berkeley, California, 1987).

Jane Kamensky, *Governing the Tongue: The Politics of Speech in Early New England* (New York, 1997), especially Chapter Three, "The Misgovernment of Woman's Tongue," and Chapter Five, "Saying and Unsaying."

Eve LaPlante, *American Jezebel: The Uncommon Life of Anne Hutchinson, the Woman Who Defied the Puritans* (San Francisco, 2004).

Three different treatments of Anne Hutchinson herself, with special emphasis on her influence on discourse in early New England.

Michael P. Winship, *Making Heretics: Militant Protestantism and Free Grace in Massachusetts, 1636-1641* (Princeton, 2002). Winship provides a new narrative of the controversy, covering the years from 1636 to 1641. He objects to the term "Antinomian Controversy" and proposes instead referring to the "Free Grace Controversy." He also emphasizes the role of Thomas Shepard both in opposing John Cotton and in forcing the issues in the synod and in court.

Great Migration Newsletter

Vol. 18   April-June 2009   No. 2

BOSTON VITAL RECORDS: 1651-1657

In 2003 we analyzed the earliest Boston vital records, from 1630 to 1650 [GMN 12:19-22]. These earliest records survive only in a copy made for the Suffolk county records. They were submitted to the county at three times, each section covering a number of years: 1630-1644; 1643-1646; and 1646-1650. We now extend this analysis by examining the next group of Boston vital records, from 1651 to 1657.

We note first that this set of Boston vital records is arranged differently than the earlier submissions. Whereas the 1646 to 1650 grouping of records was for the most part presented as a single alphabetic sequence, without regard for the type of event or the date of the event, for the years from 1651 to 1657 there are separate sections for births, deaths and marriages, and within each section the entries are listed in something approaching chronological sequence with most of the records for 1651 appearing together, followed by the events for 1652, and so on. Within each year the records are not in order and, as we shall see, some of the entries are not placed under the expected year.

Unlike the submissions for the earlier time periods, there is a sort of letter of transmission included at the end of each section:

[Births]: This above written & in the several pages under the title of births, was brought in by Mr. Jonathan Negus, Clerk of the Writs in Boston, as a true transcript since what he brought in to the time he begins them, as he affirmed this 28:8mo:1657 [NEHGR 10:70].

[Deaths]: This above written was brought in by Mr. Jonathan Negus as a true transcript of the several deaths in Boston since what he brought in before to the beginning of this time as he affirmed [NEHGR 10:221].

[Marriages]: This book I received from Mr. Negus being a true transcript of the Births, Deaths & Marriages since his last, brought in as he affirmed 28 December 1657 [NEHGR 11:205].

These three endorsements do not agree completely with one another, especially in the date of submission. They also imply that, in addition to sending this group of records to the county, Negus had also been responsible for sending the entries for the years from 1646 to 1650. Before examining more closely each of the three categories of records, we will attempt to determine more accurately the range of dates covered on this occasion.

On 14 October 1651, Massachusetts Bay General Court ordered that "upon the request of the inhabitants of Boston, Jonathan Negus shall be approved of as clerk of the writs for that town, in the room of Mr. Aspinwall, who is hereby ordered to deliver him the records of deaths, births, & marriages, as belonging to that office" [MBCR 3:258, 4:1:68; GM 2:5:233-35]. This record, in conjunction with the three endorsements quoted above, implies that Negus had taken the records he had inherited from Aspinwall in October 1651 and prepared them for submission to the county.

When we look more closely at the records for the period from 1646 to 1650, we find that most of the entries comprise a single alphabetic sequence of more than 150 vital events for 1646, 1647 and 1648 (with a few early records interspersed, including a substantial number for 1644 and 1645). Of these, sixty-six were for 1646, fifteen for 1647 and twelve for 1648. Following this is another brief alphabetic sequence with only seventeen entries for 1649 and 1650, including three birth records and one death in early 1651, the last of which occurred on 23 April 1651 [NEHGR 8:349-50, 9:165-67].

Turning to the records submitted by Jonathan Negus in 1657, we find relatively few entries for the part of the year

(continued on page 10)

EDITOR'S EFFUSIONS

The *Recent Literature* section of this issue of the *Newsletter* discusses the conversion narrative of William Adams. That document contains a single sentence that demonstrates concisely and powerfully the overarching principle of genealogical methodology that guides all work on Great Migration sketches.

This principle states that we must be able to state a reason for claiming that any two records pertain to the same individual. Some years ago we were confronted with a situation in which we had a number of records for the name William Adams in the year 1635, including a passenger list entry for a 15-year old William Adams and a Cambridge land record implying a William Adams held land there. Since the landholder must have been at least 21 years old, we concluded that these must be two different men. Furthermore, nothing about these two men could be connected with further records for the name William Adams in Ipswich a few years later (although nothing disproved that possibility either) [GM 2:1:13-14].

The maker of the conversion narrative is William Adams of Ipswich. Near the beginning of this account he states that "[w]hen I was between 14 & 15 years of age, I came over to New England & here [lived] first under the ministry of Master Hooker" [NEQ 82:144]. In one stroke this statement ties all the records together. This William Adams of Ipswich was the same age when he came to New England as the passenger of 1635. This William Adams of Ipswich had first lived at Cambridge, where "Master Hooker" was preaching in 1635, and where an older William Adams held land. When this evidence is combined with what we already know of the family in Ipswich, we may conclude that the maker of the conversion narrative was the passenger of 1635 and that he was the son of the 1635 Cambridge landholder.

We must also keep in mind the reason for the original caution in not linking all these records. We can imagine that William Adams might have told a different story in his conversion narrative which would have reinforced our original conservatism. We are always on guard against an undiscovered record which might destroy a possible but poorly supported connection between two or more other records.

Robert Charles Anderson, FASG   Editor
Jean Powers, Production Assistant

The Great Migration Newsletter is published quarterly by the Great Migration Study Project, a project of the New England Historic Genealogical Society, 101 Newbury Street, Boston MA 02116
www.NewEnglandAncestors.org
www.GreatMigration.org
GreatMigration@nehgs.org

(continued from page 9)

preceding the date that he assumed the job of the clerk of the writs. For the six months from April through September 1651, there are only twelve births recorded. In October there are four births, all dated after Negus assumed the post. Then, from 1 November 1651 to 24 March 1651/2, we find forty-four births.

The deaths and marriages are even more deficient for the portion of 1651 prior to 14 October. There are records of seventeen deaths from 7 November 1651 to 20 March 1651/2, with only one for an earlier date, 27 September 1651. Of the thirteen marriages recorded for the year, eleven fall between 3 December 1651 and 10 March 1651/2. The two earlier items are dated 20 July and 23 September.

William Aspinwall had been appointed town clerk on 7 September 1643 [MBCR 2:45; GMB 1:55-60]. For a few years he performed his duties well, compiling the Boston Book of Possessions and recording the vital records. By the evidence of the preceding three paragraphs, though, he began to neglect his work in 1647, and by 1651 was gathering records for only a small fraction of the vital events occurring in Boston.

As for the terminal date for this set of records, the evidence is clearer and simpler. The endorsement for the birth section claims a submission date of 28 October 1657, but there are thirteen birth records from 30 October to 25 December 1657. The death and marriage sections also include several entries from the closing months of 1657, and a few at the end for the eleventh month of 1657, which, if intended for January 1657/8, means that entries later than the stated submission date of 28 December 1657 were included.

In summary, the overwhelming majority of the records in this section are dated from 14 October 1651 to 28 December 1657, with a handful from an earlier date and perhaps a few from January 1657/8.

We turn now to the three individual sections. As noted above, in all three sections the records for any one year are more or less together, but within each year are not in chronological order. As ever, this causes problems for resolving the double-dating for those events which occurred between 1 January and 24 March in any given year.

For example, the births section begins with forty-three entries all given as for 1651, with no indication of double-dating [NEHGR 9:172, 249]. The next entry is for 26 March 1651, which causes no problems in interpretation, but a few entries further on we find births on "28.12.1651," "17.12.1651" and "14.2.1651." We would probably be correct in resolving the first two of these dates as 28 February 1651/2 and 17 February 1651/2, as they come so close to the crossover from the 1651 to the 1652 grouping of records. But the third of these dates we interpret as 14 April 1651. Is this an error for "14.12.1651," or is the entry just grossly out of place?

(continued on page 16)

Focus on County Courts

CRIMINAL (*continued from GMN 18:6*)

We turn now to a few criminal cases from Dover, Ipswich and Suffolk courts.

The 29 June 1675 session of the Dover court conducted relatively little criminal business. Reconsideration was given to a previous case involving William Penney, who would not conform to the expectations of society [NHPP 40:321; GDMNH 540]:

> This court see meet to continue W[illia]m Penney in prison till this court or authority take further order, & if he do not behave himself well & work for his living that Major Waldren shall cause him to be whipped as he in his discretion shall see cause.

The other piece of criminal business at this session of Dover court related to the intersection of liquor regulation and relations with the Native Americans [NHPP 40:322]:

> W[illia]m Furbush being brought before the court for giving the Indians strong liquor owned that he had half a pint & drank one dram himself & gave Richard the Indian one dram & Mr. Harry the Indian being then in his company said he drank a dram of it also. Sentence to pay a fine of 10s. money & fees.

So far as the published court minutes for 26 September 1654 show, Ipswich court disposed of its criminal business very efficiently [EQC 1:365];

> Joseph Mussye fined for drunkenness and admonished for breach of Sabbath.
> Tho[mas] Moore, being presented, was admonished, having been corrected by his master.
> Sherborne Willson confessed that he spoke some ribaldry speech, and was admonished; also ordered to sit half an hour in the stocks the next day before lecture.
> Thomas Rowell fined for taking tobacco out of doors and near a house. His wife was admonished for cruelty.

The Suffolk court of 30 January 1671/2 dealt with a wide range of criminal business. The first of these was for fornication, a very common type of case for this time and place, generally brought when a couple's first child was born only a few months after marriage [SCC 80]:

> Christopher Wheaton of Hull with Martha his wife presented for fornication. He owned the presentment and preferred a humble petition, she being not well appeared not, but the humble desire of many of that town on her behalf was received. The court sentences that they both make an acknowledgement in public at Hull to the satisfaction of the congregation, & pay twenty shillings fine to the county & the party failing to be whipped with ten stripes by the constable, & pay fees of court this to be done within a month.

This case had been initiated at the court of 31 October 1671 [SCC 23]:

> Christopher Wheaton & Martha his wife presented for fornication. The court being informed that the man was at sea respited his presentment till the next court.

Martha was the daughter of JOHN PRINCE {1634, Cambridge} [GM 2:5:527-32], and had been baptized at Hingham on 10 August 1645 [NEHGR 121:18]. Secondary sources state that this couple married in 1674 and name only one child, a son Christopher, born about 1676 [Hingham Hist 3:284; NEHGR 143:251]. These court records demonstrate that the marriage would have taken place sometime in 1671, assuming that the untimely child had appeared not long before the October court session.

Another case which had also been initiated at the October 1671 court occupied much of the time at this session. In October, "Jeffrey Richardson" and "William Read Junior" were presented for "suspicion of breaking open Jno. Pincheon Junior his warehouse which not being proved but only being a night walker" the court bound them over to appear at the next court [SCC 23-24].

By the session of 30 January 1671/2, the case had broadened. Richardson and Read were now accused of other crimes, including stealing goods from vessels in the harbor and "breaking open Thomas Grubb's cellar," being accompanied by additional accomplices, John Hurd Junior in the latter escapade and Robert Belton in "breaking open the warehouse of Capt. Jno. Hull" [SCC 82].

In the end, Richardson and Read were sentenced for stealing from nine men and were ordered to make restitution, to be whipped and to "be kept as a prisoner & kept in hard servitude during this court's pleasure" [SCC 84-85]. Hurd and Belton received lighter sentences [SCC 87].

This was not the end of the crime spree, however, for these men had been visited while in prison by relatives, who attempted in their different ways to subvert justice [SCC 88, 89]:

> Isaac Read, convicted for conveying a file & gimlet to the prisoners (after he was admonished to the contrary by Mr. Ting) whereby to practice their escape whereby the prison was broken & Jeffery Richardson ran away. The court sentenced the said Read to be whipped with fifteen stripes, or pay ten pounds in money fine to the county.

> Benjamine Hurd, convicted for advising W[illia]m Read in prison not to confess to the burning of the barn & nothing else could hurt him with several such like expressions tending to encourage him in denying his crimes, he confessed what was alleged, & the court sentenced him to be admonished & pay fees of court.

Richardson and Reade were apparently unable to pay all the restitution ordered by the magistrates, as we learn from a further order at the court of 30 April 1672 [SCC 117]:

> In answer to the petition of Jeffery Richardson & William Reade, the court orders that the petitioners be sent to the quarries at Charles Towne & what they earn above their maintenance is to pay their creditors proportionably.

PROBATE

Separate probate courts were not established in the counties until late in the seventeenth century, so the point of entry for all probate business in the early decades was at the county court. Separate registers were maintained for the probate documents themselves, however.

The amount of probate business at the Middlesex court session of 6 October 1663 was not unusual. We have already pointed out in the first installment of this article that in a section dealing with old business, the court made an order relating to the estate of Edmund Rice of Sudbury [GMN 18:5].

One simple form of entry was used for those persons who had died leaving a will.

> The last will & testament of Edward Convarss, & an inventory of his estate, were attested on oath.

> The last will of Sarah Stone, wife of Simon Stone of Water-Towne, with an inventory of her estate, were exhibited in court & attested on oath.

When the decedent did not leave a will, there were additional complications, as the court had to apply the law regarding division of intestate estates.

> An inventory of the estate of Mr. Jno. Miller lately deceased at Grotton was exhibited in court by his son John Miller & administrator of the said estate & by him attested on oath to be the full of that whereof he died seized. The court ordered the estate be divided to the said Jno. Miller being his eldest son a double portion & to the rest of the children equal shares.

This was Rev. John Miller, who had resided at Roxbury, Rowley and Yarmouth before settling at Groton, where he died on 12 June 1663 [Wyman 673; Rowley Families 242; GM 2:5:117-19].

> An inventory of the estate of Henry Prentice was exhibited in court & attested on oath by Jno. Gipson & Joanna his wife the relict of the said Henry, to whom the court granted power of administration of the said estate.
> Also the court ordered the division of the said estate to be made in manner following, viz: to the said Joanna £20 and the remainder to his children, the eldest son having a double portion, & the rest equally shares to be paid them by the widow as they come of age or at their marriage and in the meantime the whole estate to remain in the custody & to the use of the said Joanna & the land to remain security

for the children's portions & Deacon Grigory Stone & Gilbert Cracbone are empowered to set out the widow her portion of £20.

Henry Prentice died at Cambridge on 9 April 1654, yet his widow waited until 24 July 1662 to marry JOHN GIBSON {1634, Cambridge} [GM 2:3:49-52]. There is no obvious explanation for the gap of nine years between Prentice's death and the probate of his estate.

One more item of probate business, of an unusual nature, was conducted at this court session.

> On the request of Water-Towne selectmen, the court ordered that the estate left by Mr. Robert Feaks be disposed by them in part of satisfaction for their great disbursements for his supply during the time of his long infirmity.

The New England career of ROBERT FEAKE {1630, Watertown} [GMB 1:656-60] was eventful and, in the end, tragic. He had been a goldsmith in London and came to New England in 1630 with the Winthrop Fleet, settling in Watertown. Given his wealth and social standing, he was granted extensive lands and he represented the town at the General Court on a number of occasions.

In late 1631 he married Elizabeth (Fones) Winthrop, widow of Henry Winthrop, who was son of Governor John Winthrop. In 1640 Feakes, his wife and three small children went to Greenwich. After having two more children, his wife left him and moved in with William Hallett. Feakes became distracted, returned to Watertown and died there.

In addition to proving wills, granting administrations and receiving inventories, an important part of the probate business of the county courts was the appointment of guardians for minors. There are several examples of this from the Suffolk court session of 30 January 1671/2. An especially informative example concerns the children of Thomas Robinson of Boston, who had died in 1665 [SCC 78]:

> Thomas Robinson appeared in court & made choice of Mr. Anthony Stoddard to be his guardian which the court allowed & he accepted.
> James Robinson appeared in court & made choice of Mr. W[illia]m Bartholameu for his guardian which he accepted & the court allowed.
> The court appoints Deacon William Parks to be guardian to Joseph Robinson which said Parks accepted of.
> The court appoints Mr. Joseph Rock to be guardian to Mary Robinson which he accepted.

In colonial New England a minor between the ages of fourteen and twenty-one could choose his or her own guardian, whereas younger children would have a guardian appointed by the court. On the basis of this court entry, we conclude that the first two children, Thomas and James, were born between about 1651 and 1658, and the other two children, Joseph and Mary, were born after 1658.

Another example from a different family provides somewhat more information about the children [SCC 80]:

Moses Peirce appeared in court & made choice of Capt. Roger Clap commander of Castle Island in the County of Suffolk (said Pierce being the 3d son of William Peirce late of Boston deceased) to be his guardian which the court allowed.

Easther Peirce chose Phineas Upham of Malden in the County of Middlesex to be her guardian which the court allowed & he accepted.

The court appointed Joseph Web to be guardian to Ebenezer Peirce which he accepted of.

The father of these children was William Pierce, the son of WILLIAM PIERCE {1632, Boston} [GMB 3:1472-78]. "Ebenezer of William & Esther Pearse" was born at Boston on 16 March 1661[/2?] [BVR 79], and so was about ten years old when the court appointed his guardian.

CORONER'S INQUESTS

When someone died under unusual circumstances, a coroner's inquest was called, and these proceedings often created business for the county courts. An example from the Dover court of 29 June 1675 demonstrates the further actions which might arise from such an inquest.

The jury of inquest brought in their verdict concerning the untimely death of Robert Williams brought into court & is put upon file together with an account of his charge laid out upon his burial allowed of & the court orders that it be paid him by Elias Stileman which is £1 17s. & do further order that the estate secured by him as a public officer (which they approve of) he keep in his hand & make the best improvement by selling any part thereof to pay such emergent charge out for the deceased & secure the rest until this court or the Court of Associates take further order thereabout [NHPP 40:318].

Robert Williams resided at Great Island, Portsmouth, and was murdered by his servants at Spruce Creek [GDMNH 757]. The inquest on the death of "Robing Williams,... found dead in the cellar of John Fabing's house in Spruce Creek," was taken on 23 February 1674/5 [GDMNH 33 (List 286)]. On 27 June 1676, Elias Stileman was granted administration on the estate and, on 31 October 1677, he brought in an inventory of the estate [NHPP 40:329, 337-38].

Although the above records do not include the actual findings of the jury of inquest, an early New Hampshire case provides an example of this fascinating category of records [NHPP 40:468-69]:

We whose name are underwritten being called together & panelled a jury by Phillop Chesley, constable of Dovor, to view & take notice of the sudden death of Thomas Canyda, do find & declare as followeth:
That the said Thomas Canyda according to our understandings was killed by a tree near to the house of Thomas Humfres, the tree being found upon him, & was forced to be cut before he could be got from under it, & this we judge was the cause of his death, witness our hands 26:10:60 [26 December 1660].

John Bickford	Charles Adams
John Davis	Thomas Willy
Mathias Gyles	Willyam Smith
Will[ia]m Willyams	Pattericke Ginison
John Meader	James Middleton
Thomas Stevenson	Joe Field
	Steven Joanes

ADMINISTRATIVE

The county courts in these early years also had jurisdiction over a wide variety of matters which might be described as administrative in nature. Many of these items would now be attended to by the county commissioners.

The county courts oversaw the workings of the town trainbands, the local militias, as we see from the 6 October 1663 session of the Middlesex court.

Mr. Edward Jackson is released from all ordinary trainings, paying eight shillings per annum to the military company of the place where he lives.
Thomas Wiswall is released from all ordinary trainings, paying 5s. per annum to the military company of the place where he lives.
Richard Parks is released from all ordinary trainings, paying six shillings per annum to the military company of the place where he lives.
John White of Lanchaster is released from all ordinary trainings, paying six shillings per annum to the military company of the place where he lives.

The reason for the differing sums these men were required to pay is not apparent, although the one man accorded a title of respect paid the most, indicating that perhaps the annual payment was related to ability to pay.

Able-bodied adult males were expected to participate actively in training from the ages of sixteen to sixty. We should not, however, always assume that exemption from training meant that the individual so excused had reached the age of sixty on or about the date of the court record, as some men were freed from duty at a younger age because of some disability, and others served beyond the age of sixty.

The county courts also approved the trainband officers.

Woburne presenting their election of military officers for the acceptance & approbation of this court, viz: Ensign John Carter their Lieutenant, William Johnson [for] Ensign, Thomas Peirce [and] Mathew Johnson [for] Sergeant, testimony being given of their good conversation & that they are freemen of this commonwealth, the court declared their approbation thereof.

John Nutting is allowed to be a corporal of the military company at Grotton.

The county treasurer had duties as well:

The treasurer of this county is ordered to pay unto David Fiske for the heads of 7 whelps conceived to be wolves, the one half of which the law provideth for wolves heads, viz: 10s. a head.

The county courts also had to deal with cases that would in modern times be taken care of by a social services officer.

> John Cutler of Woburne appearing before the court, & complaint made against him, for idleness & neglect of his family, on examination of the matter, it appeared that the said Cutler had sundry times been legally convicted of the like misdemeanor & that he is somewhat distempered in his head. The court on hearing & serious consideration of his condition, ordered the said Cutler to be committed to the care & government of James Parker of Grotton for one year next ensuing, & by him to be provided all his meet necessaries of diet, apparel &c. and by him to be improved in labor & that his wife take care of his family & estate at home, & order & dispose of the same by the advice & direction of Woburne selectmen. Also that on condition their lands in Maulden do remain as security for her children's portions, it be propounded to the executors of Edward Convars deceased that the bond made between the said Cutler & his wife on marriage be given in & made null, which is hopeful may have a tendency to compose the distemper of his mind. To this order & proposal of the court, Jno. Cutler & his wife manifested their full & free concurrence, also James Parker manifested his willingness to accept & discharge the trust by the court reposed in him.

This item poses an interesting genealogical challenge. According to secondary sources, John Cutler of Woburn married first Olive Thompson, daughter of JAMES THOMSON {1633, Charlestown} [GMB 3:1809-11], and second Mary (Brown) Lewis, daughter of ABRAHAM BROWN {1631, Watertown} [GMB 1:244-46]. The wife referred to above is almost certainly the second of these wives.

The relevance of the executors of the will of EDWARD CONVERSE {1630, Charlestown} [GMB 1:459-63] is hard to understand. Edward Converse had died on 10 August 1663 and his will was entered at this same court. Simon Thomson, brother of Olive, had married Mary Converse, daughter of Edward, but this does not seem relevant. Was his name entered by error in the Cutler entry because the clerk had just encountered it, or is there some unknown connection between the Cutler and the Converse families?

At the Dover court for 29 June 1675, administrative business was dispersed throughout the proceedings [NHPP 40:317, 318, 320, 322]:

> George Lewis & Jos[eph] Morss took oath for constables of Portsmouth
> James Nute & Nicholas Harris took the constable's oath for the town of Dover.
>
> Sam[ue]ll Keaies came into court & took the freemen's oath.
>
> Granted license unto Jno. Johnson of Greenland to keep an ordinary there to entertain strangers.
> Granted to Edw[ard] West of Great Island the renewal of his license to keep a house of entertainment he paying his duty according to order of General Court to the Collector.
>
> This court grants Lt. Pomfrey the renewal of his license to retail strong waters.

> Granted unto James Waymouth of Isles of Sholes the renewal of his license.
> Upon the motion & request of Jno. Fabes to this court that he might have liberty to supply his fishermen with liquor as their occasions should call for it in greater or lesser quantity he not selling to any out of doors or to any other less than the law allows all persons is granted to him.
> Granted unto W[illia]m Cotton & Jno. Pickerin the renewal of their license they paying their entry to the Collector is granted them.
> Granted unto Sam[ue]ll Wintworth of Great Island the renewal of his license.

Suffolk court, having jurisdiction over the cosmopolitan Boston, had occasion to issue licenses of a more exotic sort [SCC 85]:

> Mrs. Dorothy Jones had her license continued to sell coffee & chocolate for the year ensuing.

CONCLUSION

Having considered these various categories of court business, we observe that from time to time the county courts were required to attend to matters that were not so easy to classify. An interesting example of this sort from the Dover court of 29 June 1675 also demonstrates the added complication of interactions with the local Native Americans [NHPP 40:318-19]:

> It appearing unto this court that there were two Indians taken upon suspicion (on two horses riding over the river of Piscattaq[ua]) that they might have stolen them from some of the English the like not having been known before, & being contrary to law that the English should sell horses or horse kind to the Indians, & thereupon brought before authority here were examined & committed to prison till the matter might be clear which said Indians having made an escape, & upon information given by the worshipful Major Willard thereabouts, the court orders that the whole case may be drawn out by the clerk of this court & sent to the worshipful Capt. Googin, & inform that the Indians may have their horses again when they send or come for them, paying thirty shillings for their keeping & charge thereabout.
> Ephra[im] Crockett for taking away the Indian's horse upon suspicion as he owned & not informing of authority nor yet securing the Indian as well as his horse or mare sentence of court that he pay a fine of 20s. & fees.

In summary, the exploration of county court records improves our Great Migration sketches in two different ways. First, we frequently find pieces of evidence which help in the strictly genealogical work of constructing the family connections. The examples of the Wheaton fornication case and the William Pierce guardianships demonstrate this beneficial aspect of these records, not to mention the challenge arising from the Cutler entry. Second, from almost every item in the court records we gain a deeper insight into the daily lives of our seventeenth-century ancestors, into their behavior, both normal and deviant, an insight not provided by most of the other standard genealogical sources we regularly use in our research.

RECENT LITERATURE

Doris Schreiber Wilcox, "Massachusetts Descendants of the Rev. Thomas Wilson, Author of the Pilgrims' *Christian Dictionarie*: Theophilus Wilson, Martha (Wilson) Bachelor, Mary (Wilson) Treadwell, and Their Nephew Samuel Taylor," *The New England Historical and Genealogical Register* 163 (2009):5-15. Wilcox has discovered the 20 December 1601 baptism of Theophilus Wilson, settler at Ipswich by 1636, at St. George the Martyr, Canterbury, Kent, son of Rev. Thomas Wilson, rector of that parish. His younger sisters Martha and Mary married Henry Bachelor and Thomas Treadwell, also early immigrants to Ipswich. And his elder sister, Jane, who married Robert Taylor, was mother of Samuel Taylor, who sailed to New England in 1637 with Henry Bachelor.

Ernest H. Helliwell III, "Was Elizabeth[2] Kilbourne the First Wife of Hugh[1] Gunnison of Boston and Kittery?" *The New England Historical and Genealogical Register* 163 (2009):16-18. The author argues that the "grandchild Elizabeth Geneson" named in the 1650 will of Frances Kilbourn, the wife of Thomas Kilbourn {1635, Wethersfield} [GM 2:4:148-51], was the first wife of Hugh Gunnison {1635, Boston} [GM 2:3:173-80].

John Wardlow, "Revisiting the Family of Gershom[2] Flagg of Woburn, Massachusetts," *The New England Historical and Genealogical Register* 163 (2009):19-26. The author has identified a number of errors and omissions among the immediate descendants of Gershom[2] Flagg, son of Thomas[1] Flagg, who settled at Watertown in 1637. This first installment of a multipart article presents genealogical summaries for Gershom[2] and his three eldest sons.

James R. Henderson, "English Origins of John Lovejoy of Andover, Massachusetts," *The New England Historical and Genealogical Register* 163 (2009):27-32. Henderson publishes English records which demonstrate that John Lovejoy of Andover, who came to New England in 1638, and his sister Grace, were baptized in the adjacent Oxfordshire parishes of Caversham and Sonning. The author also presents circumstantial evidence suggesting that Grace married William Ballard of Andover.

Gail Blankenau, "Some Descendants of Nathaniel[3] Mead of Greenwich, Connecticut, Through His Son Josiah[4] Mead," *The New England Historical and Genealogical Register* 163 (2009):33-38. In this first part of a multipart article, Blankenau begins the presentation of genealogical summaries for the families of Nathaniel[3] Mead (son of John[2] Mead and grandson of William[1] Mead, who had settled at Stamford by 1641) and of his children.

Deborah Kimball Nowers, "George[1] Standley of Beverly, Massachusetts, and His Children," *The New England Historical and Genealogical Register* 163 (2009):39-50. George Standley, who was born about 1635, married Bethia[2] Lovett, daughter of John[1] Lovett, who settled at Salem in 1639. The author provides genealogical summaries for George Standley and for his four sons who had children.

Jane Fletcher Fiske, "The English Background of Richard Kent Sr. and Stephen Kent of Newbury, Massachusetts, and Mary, Wife of Nicholas Easton of Newport, Rhode Island," *The New England Historical and Genealogical Register* 163 (2009):51-65. In this conclusion of a two-part article, Fiske provides four generations of agnate ancestry for Richard Kent Senior, who came to New England in 1634, settling briefly in Ipswich and then moving on to Newbury [GM 2:4:140-42], his brother Stephen Kent, who came to New England in 1638, and their sister Mary (Kent) Easton, wife of Nicholas Easton, who followed the same migration pathway as Richard Kent Senior [GM 2:2:396-403].

Robert M. Gerrity, "Mary (Bulkeley) Clarke's Birth Year Corrected," *The New England Historical and Genealogical Register* 163 (2009):66. Gerrity presents a tombstone inscription which determines the year of birth of Mary Bulkeley, daughter of Edward Bulkeley and granddaughter of Peter Bulkeley {1635, Concord} [GM 2:1:459-65].

Robert Strong, ed., "Two Seventeenth-Century Conversion Narratives from Ipswich, Massachusetts Bay Colony," *The New England Quarterly* 82 (2009):136-69. Strong transcribes two conversion narratives, for William Adams of Ipswich and his wife Elizabeth (Stacy) Adams. A conversion narrative was an account of one's path to a conviction of saving grace, a necessary step leading to one's admission to church in the early decades of New England history.

The two documents presented here are unusual in that they are longer and more detailed than most other surviving conversion narratives, which were the copies kept by the ministers of the churches involved. These were probably prepared for private consumption, and not only as part of the process of seeking church admission.

Most conversion narratives may be viewed as spiritual autobiographies, and so have little substantive detail about the quotidian lives of the narrators. The present narratives do, however, have a few nuggets which have a significant effect on two Great Migration sketches already published. William Adams tells us that "[w]hen I was between 14 & 15 years of age, I came over to New England & here [lived] first under the ministry of Master Hooker," and then goes on to describe his move to Ipswich a few years later.

In the first volume of the second series of Great Migration volumes, we included two sketches for men named William Adams, one for a 1635 passenger aged 15 years and the other for a man who held land at Cambridge in 1635 and 1637 [GM 2:1:13-14]. Despite statements in the secondary literature, we were at the time unwilling to connect these records with the William Adams family of Ipswich.

We can now say that the second of these sketches pertains to the immigrant head of family, living first in Cambridge and then in Ipswich, but with no surviving passenger list entry, and that the first of these sketches is for his son.

(continued from page 10)

The answer to this last question is somewhat disconcerting. The birth record is for "Armitage, Samuel, son of Godfrey and Mary" [NEHGR 9:249]. When we consult the records of the First Church at Boston, we find a baptism for "Samuell Armitage son of our brother Godfry Armitage," dated 18 April 1652 [BChR 322]. So, the month is correct, but the year is wrong in the birth records.

We conclude, then, that as with the earlier Boston vital records, we must exercise great caution in resolving the double-dates, and look for supporting evidence in other places, such as the baptismal records, and again the church records should be considered more accurate than the town records.

Another phenomenon we encountered in the 1643-1646 and 1646-1650 groupings of Boston vital records was the late entry of events that had actually taken place at a date earlier than the range of years covered by that grouping. This practice continued into the 1651-1657 period.

One example is the family of Christopher and Anne Holland, where we find four births grouped together: John, born 1 February 1647; Bridget, born 14 March 1649; Johannah, born 1 February 1652; and Johannah born 13 October 1653 [NEHGR 9:253]. In the deaths section, we find "Johanna daughter of Christopher & Ann Holland died 1:3:52 [1 May 1652]" and "Johannah daughter of Christopher & Ann Holland died 2:1:53-54" [2 March 1653/4]" [NEHGR 10:217].

Thus, the correct date of birth for the first Johannah would have been 1 February 1651/2. Holland resided at Woburn in 1645. In an undated deed, acknowledged on 16 February 1652[/3?], Francis Smith of Boston sold land there to "Christopher Hollon of the same, lighterman" [SLR 1:325]. Thus, we cannot be certain when Holland moved from Woburn to Boston, and so cannot be certain whether all these children were born in Boston, suggesting that, as with earlier groupings, we must be careful in these cases in ascribing Boston as the place of birth for late-recorded entries.

William B. Trask, the transcriber of these records for the *Register*, omitted more than a year's worth of records in moving from one installment of the publication to another. The July 1855 portion ends in the middle of a sequence of 1654 births, while the January 1856 portion begins with 1656 births [NEHGR 9:254, 10:67]. Thus, all 1655 births, along with some from 1654 and 1656, were not printed in this series, although they were included in the Record Commissioners volume [BVR 50-51]. Recourse to the manuscript (at the Boston Municipal Archives) would be needed to determine just what was missed.

The death and marriage sections share some of these problems, but not to the same extent. An interesting feature of these sections is that they demonstrate the growing importance of Boston as the leading city of New England, with many death records, and some marriage records, for residents of England and of other colonies.

Great Migration Newsletter

Vol. 18   July-September 2009   No. 3

DORCHESTER CATECHISTS, 1676

The published records of Dorchester church include a list of names described in 1891 by the compiler as "a list found on two loose leaves of a book larger than the Church Book, but folded and kept in the latter, time out of mind." [DChR 183-85]. The list itself carries the title

The names of Persons to be Catechized in the Town of Dorchester Anno 1676

The document first gives the boys and young men, and then the girls and young women, ordered approximately by age. There are eighty-eight males and eighty-five females in the list. The oldest of the young men was 28, while the oldest of the young women was 31. The youngest children in both parts of the list were aged seven. The list of males has a division between those aged 13 and older and those aged twelve and younger, with the interpolated heading "Children from 12 *et infra*." The list of females has a break at the same point, but without any comment. At the end of both parts of the list are four boys and three girls, without ages given, with the surnames Leadbetter, Lyon and Thomas.

When compared against other knowledge we have of Dorchester families, this record can assist us greatly in reconstructing the families of that town. Although we will limit our explorations to this list only, we note that there is another list in the Dorchester church records of about the same time that may be related. On 5 March 1676/7, "they were appointed to come together both the church & the children of the church," in order to exhort "the children of the church" to subscribe to the Halfway Covenant. About 75 men and women subscribed that day, and a few dozen more shortly thereafter [DChR 72-75].

The first question we will ask of the list of catechists is the status of those who were adults. There were twelve men and six women aged 21 or older. Were any of these catechists married? If not, we would be inclined to conclude that every unmarried person in town, aged seven and older, had to participate in this process.

The twelve adult males were Nehemiah Clap (28), Hopestill Humphrey (26), Samuel Hall (25), "Ebenezer Hill's ser-vant" (25), John Trescott (24), Isaac Humphrey (23), James Blake (22), Elisha Foster (22), Richard Mather (22), Charles Davenport (22), James Baker (21) and John Mason (21).

For eight of these men we have dates of marriage:

Nehemiah Clap, 17 April 1678, to Sarah Leavitt [NEHGR 121:201].
Hopestill Humphrey, 21 November 1677, to Elizabeth Baker [DVR 23].
Samuel Hall, 6 June 1681, to Bathshua Hinckley [DVR 24].
Isaac Humphrey, 7 July 1685, to Patience Atherton [DVR 101].
James Blake, 6 February 1682[/3?], to Hannah Macy [DVR 25].
Elisha Foster, 10 April 1678, to Sarah Payson [DVR 24].
Richard Mather, 1 July 1680, to Katherine Wise [DVR 24].
John Mason, 15 October 1679, to Content Wales [DVR 24].

Two more of these men did marry. The eldest known child of John Trescott was born on 1 February 1678[/9?] and the eldest known child of Charles Davenport was born on 20 June 1679 [DVR 17]. No evidence has been found that James Baker ever married, and "Ebenezer Hill's servant," whatever his name was, would not have been married while still in servitude.

(continued on page 18)

EDITOR'S EFFUSIONS

As this issue of the *Great Migration Newsletter* goes to press, the next Great Migration volume of sketches is also at the printer. This volume is the sixth in the second series, covering the letters R and S for the years 1634 and 1635. (No immigrant whose surname begins with the letter Q arrived in New England during this time period.)

More than two hundred sketches are contained in this volume, including about twenty just for the surname Smith. Among this latter group is the sketch of Quartermaster John Smith of Dorchester, the longest single entry we have ever created. In general, the average length of each sketch is increasing slightly; possible reasons for this development will be addressed in the next issue of the *Newsletter*.

Work has already begun on the next volume of sketches, the last in this second series. This volume will also have about two hundred sketches, mostly for the letters T and W, but also with a few surnames beginning with U, V and Y.

For this issue of the *Newsletter*, and for the next issue, we have a guest contributor for the *Focus* section. Patricia Law Hatcher FASG, editor of *The New York Genealogical and Biographical Record* and of *The Pennsylvania Genealogical Magazine*, has undertaken a detailed examination of the earliest settlers of Rowley, Massachusetts.

Regular readers of this column will be aware of the importance we attach to the process known as "list analysis," in which we examine a document which provides information of a defined type about a cohort of individuals. The goal is to gain new understanding which is not available just from examining single entries in the list.

In 1997 Pat Hatcher undertook such an analysis of the list of the earliest admissions to Roxbury church, which we published here [GMN 6:179-85]. In the present issue and the next, Pat begins with a statement by Governor John Winthrop about the size of the group that migrated to New England in 1638 with Rev. Ezekiel Rogers and soon founded the town of Rowley. Then, working from an early list of Rowley landholders, she develops a synthetic list of those families and individuals likely to have accompanied Rogers, paying special attention to their English origins.

Robert Charles Anderson, FASG   Editor
Jean Powers, Production Assistant

The Great Migration Newsletter is published quarterly by the Great Migration Study Project, a project of the New England Historic Genealogical Society, 101 Newbury Street, Boston MA 02116
www.NewEnglandAncestors.org
www.GreatMigration.org
GreatMigration@nehgs.org

(continued from page 17)

The six adult females were Sarah Davenport (31), Anna Davenport (24), Thankful Baker (24), Elizabeth Hall (22), Patience Atherton (22) and Sarah Blackman (21).

Only one of these women has a recorded marriage. On 7 July 1685, Patience Atherton and Isaac Humphrey were married at Dorchester [DVR 101]. Three more of these women are known to have married: Anna Davenport to Samuel Jones (eldest known child born at Dorchester 14 November 1680 [DVR 18]); Thankful Baker to William Griggs (eldest known child born at Boston 30 May 1682 [BVR 157]); and Elizabeth Hall probably to John Wood (eldest known child born at Dorchester 27 March 1690 [DVR 35]). No evidence has been found that Sarah Davenport or Sarah Blackman ever married. (The fate of the Davenport sisters will be examined more closely below.)

Our first conclusion, then, is that all the catechists, regardless of age, were unmarried. Note that almost all the men who were not married by the age of twenty were married by the customary age of twenty-five or thereabouts, whereas all the women who had not married by age twenty had still not married until they were about thirty, or never married at all.

To examine this list from a different perspective, we will look at all the children from one family, that of Thomas Davenport, who had arrived in Dorchester by 20 November 1640, when he was admitted to the church there [DChR 5]. By 1643 he had wife Mary, who was admitted to Dorchester church on 8 March 1644[/5] [DChR 6]. This couple had ten recorded children: Sarah, b. 28 December 1643; Thomas, bp. 2 March 1644/5; Mary, bp. 21 January 1648/9; Anna, bp. 29 December 1650; Charles, bp. 7 November 1652; Abigail, bp. 8 July 1655; Mehitable, b. 14 February 1656/7; Jonathan, b. 6 March 1658/9; Ebenezer, b. 26 April 1661; and John, b. 20 October 1664 [DVR 2, 5, 6, 7, 9; DChR 157, 159, 160, 162, 167].

Five of these children appear in the list of catechists: Charles (22); Jonathan (16); John (8); Sarah (31); and Anna (24). Why do the other five not appear in the list, and what was the later fate of the five who were in the list?

The deaths of two of the children are on record before 1676. "Mehitophel the daughter of Thomas Damfort died 18 of (8 month [October]) 1663" [DVR 26]. (Despite the orthographic oddities, this was the death record for daughter Mehitable.)

The son Thomas served in King Philip's War and was killed in action in December 1675 [Bodge 162-63, 432]. He made a will, proved on 28 January 1675/6, in which he made his brother Charles his principal legatee and left "one room of my dwelling namely the parlor ... to my sister Sarah as long as she lives," which suggests that she was not expected ever to marry. He also bequeathed forty shillings to each of his brothers and sisters, who were unnamed [SPR 6:112].

(continued on page 24)

Focus on Rowley and Ezekiel Rogers' Company

By Patricia Law Hatcher FASG

ROWLEY, MASSACHUSETTS

(For discussion on the settlement and records of Rowley, Massachusetts, see "Focus on Rowley," GMN 10:27–30.)

On 2 December 1638, Gov. John Winthrop noted "Ezekiel Rogers, son of Richard Rogers of Weathersfield in Essex, a worthy son of so worthy a father, lying at Boston with some who came out of Yorkshire with him, where he had been a painful [painstaking] preacher many years" [WJ 1:334–35]. The land for what became Rowley, wedged between Ipswich and Newbury, was granted 13 March 1638/9, and the settlement begun by April 1639, at which time Winthrop wrote in his journal "there came over one Mr. Ezekiel Rogers . . . and with him some twenty families, godly men, and most of them of good estate" [WJ 1:354–55]. The church at Rowley was established on 3 December 1639.

The first relatively comprehensive list of Rowley settlers was a survey of land holdings taken 10 January 1643/4, almost five years after the initial settlement. It lists fifty-eight lot-holders, as well as Ezekiel Rogers. Thomas Sumner, who is on the list, had died by 31 8m [October] 1643, which suggests the lot-holders list was not "as of" 10 January 1643/4 but, like many such lists in New England, was created over time. For many of the names on the list, both historians and genealogists often claim they were "of" Rowley, Yorkshire, and they came "with" Ezekiel Rogers in 1638. This article examines those claims.

Nine additional families or individuals, derived from other sources, will also be analyzed. The vital records of Rowley note four marriages and the births of children to thirty-three couples between 1639 and 1643/4, revealing the presence of five couples and one individual not among the lot-holders: James and Lydia Bailey, Richard and Alice Clark, John and Dorcas Pearson, William and Katherine Tenney, and Joseph and Miriam Wormwool, and Mary Bradley (who married Thomas Leaver). Finally, three more names not on the lot-holders list and not in the vital records bring the total to sixty-seven: servant Jeremiah Northend, widow Katherine (Elithorp) Constable, and widow Margaret (Cliffe) Cross.

The analysis below suggests that of those sixty-seven individuals or families, six came from Rowley, Yorkshire; twenty were from within Rogers' sphere of influence in Yorkshire (within about fifteen miles of Rowley church); and four who sailed from Hull, Yorkshire, and settled at Rowley were probably part of Rogers' original company. Thus, the "some twenty families" mentioned by Winthrop in 1638 seem to have been amply accounted for. Seventeen of the sixty-seven came to Rowley having been elsewhere in New England before Rogers' arrival.

Soon after Rogers' arrival, on successive Sundays, 30 10th month [December] 1638 and 6 11m [January] 1638[/9], eight persons joined the church at Boston: Henry and Sybil Sandys; Margery Shove; William and Elizabeth Stickney; Margaret Crosse; Michael Hopkinson, servant of Jacob Elyott; and Richard Swanne, a husbandman [BChR 22–23]. On 24 9th month [November] 1639, Mr. Henry Sandys, Willyam Stickney, Richard Swanne, and Michaell Hopkinson were dismissed to the gathering of a church at Rowley [BChR 25]. Unfortunately, the Rowley church records prior to 1664 do not survive.

Between the arrival of Rogers' ministerial company and the lot-holders list, thirty had become freeman, a prerequisite for which was church membership [MBCR 1:375-78, 2:291]: on 22 May 1639 (John Rimington, John Miller, Mathewe Boyse, Joseph Jewett [names not together]); 23 May 1639 (Mr. Ezechi. Rogers, Mr. Thom. Nelson [names not together]); 13 May 1640 (Thoma. Barker, Thoma. Mighill, Maxami. Jewet, Franc. Parrat, Richrd Swan, Robrt Haseldine, John Haseldene, Franc. Lambert, Willi. Scales, John Burbanke, Willi. Bointon, John Jarrat, Micha. Hopkinson, Geo. Kilborne [names together] and John Trumbell [name separate]); 7 October 1640 (James Barcker, Henry Sands, Robrt Hunter, and Willi. Stickney [names together]); 12 October 1640 (Mr. Willi. Bellingham); 18 May 1642 (Edward Carleton, Humphrey Reyn'r, Hugh Smith, Hugh Chapline [names together]).

ROWLEY, YORKSHIRE

The living of the parish church of Rowley was preferred to Ezekiel Rogers in 1621 by Sir Francis Barrington; he held it until departing for New England in the fall of 1638. It has been said, incorrectly, that the population of the village of Rowley was decimated when they left, possibly because all that was visible at the beginning of the twentieth century was the church and rectory. However, Rowley never existed as a village and was always only the church and rectory with possibly a house or two. Rowley parish contained the villages of Bentley, Hunsley, Ripplingham, Risby, and Weeton, which are named regularly in the surviving church records; Rowley appears only once. Contemporaneous confirmation appears in Cotton Mather's discussion of Ezekiel Rogers in *Magnalia Christi Americana*, which, in reference to Rowley in Yorkshire, mentions "the Church there, standing in the center of many Villages" [Magnalia 1:409].

The early parish register for Rowley is not extant, but a few Bishops' Transcripts survive. Those for 1622, 1623, 1624, 1630, 1631, and 1632 have been published [EIHC 44:305–12]. Those for 1604 [through April 1605], 1607, 1620, 1621, and 1633–1640 also survive, resuming with 1663 [FHL #919,436, item 2]; they are dark and difficult to read.

Rowley, although endowed with a generous living, had relatively few parishioners. In the eighteen years of extant Bishops' Transcripts between 1604 and 1640, the annual average is seven or eight christenings, seven or eight burials, and one or two marriages.

There are two other useful sources for the area. Both include all of the East Riding of Yorkshire except Hull, Kirk Ella, and some nearby parishes. They are organized village by village. In 1629 a subsidy was assessed on those with £3 in moveable goods or 20 shillings annual income from land [Christopher J. Watson, *A Lay Subsidy of the East Riding of Yorkshire, 1629* (Chorley, Lancashire: the author, 2003)]. In 1636 a muster was taken to inventory arms (actually, only muskets and corselets), with designation of whether the arms were held for personal use or in common (for community use) [Christopher J. Watson, *A Muster Roll of the East Riding of Yorkshire (1636)* (Chorley, Lancashire: the author, 2002)]. The 1629 subsidy has entries for the Rowley villages of Weeton et Ripplingham (Robert Northend, John Northen), Risby, and Bentley. The 1636 muster has entries for Hunsley-Weeton et Riplingham (Robert Northen, "clergie Ezekiel: Rogers"), Risby, and Bentley. (Neither of these sources mentions Rowley itself, only its villages.)

EARLY SETTLERS OF ROWLEY

The sketches below focus on emigration and records immediately before and after and are not complete family sketches. No attempt is made herein to document the numerous incorrect statements about origins or times of emigration found in secondary sources.

FROM ELSEWHERE IN NEW ENGLAND

Many Rowley settlers were already in New England when Rogers arrived. Those who became freemen before 23 May 1639 (when Ezekiel Rogers and Thomas Nelson became freemen) or whose names are isolated in the freemen lists almost surely were already in New England. Several Rowley settlers were members of the Roxbury [GMN 6:25 and author's notes] or Dorchester churches. Rogers had preached at York Minster [Magnalia 2:410], so Boyse, the Jewetts, and Reyner may have heard him in England.

James Bailey was born about 1612 or 1615 [EQC 3:30, 6:15, 275], the brother of Richard Bailey [EPR 1:92], who had immigrated in 1638 on the *Bevis* out of Southampton as a servant of Richard Dummer, who was returning to New England [GMB 1:588]; James may have come at the same time. The 1677 will of James Bayley names children Lidia, Damaris, John, and James [EPR 3:162–64], all born in Rowley from 1642 to 1650, children of James and Lydiah [RowVR 1:15–17].

Mathew Boyse and unnamed wife joined the Roxbury church in early 1638 (#176, 177) [GMN 6:25]. A 14 January 1661 deposition after his return to England calls him: "Mathew Boyes of Leeds, Yorkshire, aged about fifty years" [EQC 3:235]. This is compatible with the baptism 15

December 1611 at St. Peter, Leeds, Yorkshire, of Mathew son of Jo. Boyes, the townend; John Boyes married at Leeds 5 December 1603 Grace Moxom [Registers of the Parish Church of Leeds, *Publications of the Thoresby Society*, 1:262, 282; also NEHGR 60:385]. [This corrects the erroneous origin given by me in GMN 6:25.] A marriage license was issued in 1638 to Matthew Boyes, clothier of Leeds, and Mary Gleadston, spinster, 22, of All Saints, Pavement, to be married there [Paver's, 127]; Mathew Boyes and Mary Gleadston married at All Saints, Pavement, York, 15 September 1638 [YPRS 100:91]. It is not clear how, but Mathew was a cousin of Rev. Elkanah Wales of Pudsey (near Leeds), not son-in-law as stated in Moore, 84–85 (Elkanah had no children [Wales' 1669 will, transcribed in *John Redington of Topsfield* (1909), 43–47]).

Edmund Bridges, 23, was listed for the *James* out of London in 1635; on 7 September 1639, he was residing at Lynn [GM 2:1:389–92]. A daughter of Edmund and Alice Bridges was born in 1641 in Rowley [RowVR 1:32].

John Harris, **Thomas Harris**, and **William Harris** were sons of Thomas Harris who emigrated in 1630 from Hatherup, Gloucestershire, settling first at Winnissimmett [GMB 2:864–65].

Michael Hopkinson, servant of Jacob Elyott, was admitted to the Boston church 6 January 1638/9, along with others who soon moved to Rowley. There is no definitive evidence to show if he arrived with Rogers' group or had come with Eliot in 1631.

Maximilian Jewett and **Joseph Jewett** were sons of Edward Jowett and Mary Tayler, who married 1 October 1604 in Bradford, West Riding, Yorkshire. The 2 February 1614/5 will of Edward Jowet of Bradford names children William, Maximilian, Joseph, and Sara; wife Mary; and father-in-law William Taylor [Hazen, NEHGR 94:101–4]. Maximilian, son of Edward Jowett of Eckilshill (a village near Bradford, Yorkshire), was baptized 4 October 1607 (compatible with his deposition that he was born about 1606 [EQC 5:393]). Joseph, son of Edward Jewett of Bradford, was baptized 31 December 1609 (making him a reasonable 25 at marriage). The 1684 will of Maximilian names children Ezekiel (eldest son), Joseph, Elizabeth, Anna, Mary, Sarah, and Faith [Jewett, 11–12], all born in Rowley beginning in 1643 [RowVR 1:106–15]. Joseph married in Bradford 1 October 1634 Mary Mallinson; children of Joseph Jewette of Bradford were Sarah (3 January 1635/6) and Jeremie (26 December 1637) [Hazen, NEHGR 94:99–107]. Joseph and Mary Jewett were admitted to the Dorchester church 4 9m [November] 1639 [DChR 4]. The 15 February 1660[/1] will of Joseph Jewett mentions brother Maximilian, seven unnamed children (including two by his last wife), and eldest son Jeremiah. Estate papers mention youngest son Joseph and Faith, Nehemiah, and Patience [EPR 1:327–30].

George Kilborne, a manservant, joined the Roxbury church in late 1638 (#197) [GMN 6:25]. Donald Lines Jacobus argues that he was not the George Kilborne baptized 12

February 1611/2 at Wood Ditton, Cambridge, son of Thomas [Hale, House 653; Sarah Stone Anc 95].

Thomas Mihill and unnamed wife joined the Roxbury church in early 1638 (#174, 175) [GMN 6:25]. The 1654 will of Thomas Mighill names wife Ann; children Samuel, John, Thomas, Ezekiel, Nathaniel, Stephen, and Mary (under twenty-one); sister Ann Tenny; estate papers indicate that Ann was the second wife and mother of the last three children; Ellen, his first wife, was mother of the first three, of whom Samuel was the eldest [EPR 1:206–10]. Two sons were born in England: Samuel (about 1630 [EQC 8:98]) and John (about 1634–1636 [EQC 3:187, 7:157, 318; Harris, NEHGR 158:256]). The surname is in Welton in 1629 and 1636, and in Hessle, where there was a Thomas (Samuel and John were not found, but the register is extremely poor).

John Miller and wife Lidea joined the Roxbury church in early 1638 (#180, 181) [GMN 6:25]. John Miller was baptized 21 October 1604 at Ashford, Kent, son of Martin Miller. He was at Caius College, Cambridge, where he received his BA in 1627/8 [Venn 3:189]. He was a freeman from Roxbury 22 May 1639, but at Rowley by 28 8m [October] 1639, where, as clerk, he recorded the town's first birth.

John Newmarch was of Ipswich before settling in Rowley and later returned there [Savage, 3:276]. He was born about 1614, 1615, or 1622 [EQC 6:67, 8:270, 9:220]. The surname was in Welton in 1629 and 1636 and in the Kirk Ella and Hessle registers.

John Remington was first of Newbury, where he was a freeman. A son of John and Elizabeth was born in 1639/40 in Rowley [RowVR 1:182]. The surname is in Lund (Richard, armigerous; twenty miles east of Rowley) and Lockington ("clergie" Henry Remington; nine miles north of Rowley) in 1629 and 1636.

The 1660 will of **Humphrey Reyner** names wife Mary, brother John Reynor, pastor at Dover, son[-in-law] Wigglesworth, and daughters Whipple and Hobson [EPR 1:320–22]. Humphrey Reyner was born say 1606, son of John and Ellen Reyner of Gildersome (southeast of Leeds), Batley parish, West Riding, Yorkshire, and grandson of another Humphrey, whose 1628/9 will mentions his grandson Humfrey, Mary, wife of said Humfrey, and their daughters Mary and Martha [NEHGR 109:9]. Stansell [NEHGR 156:309–26] corrects errors and fills in blanks in Whitmore [NEHGR 11:102–12] and Coddington [NEHGR 109:5–11]. It is likely Humphrey and his family accompanied his sister Elizabeth to Plymouth where their brother John was then minister.

John Trumbell joined the Roxbury church in early 1639 (#204) [RChR 84]. An, widow of John, was appointed his administratrix in 1657; eleven children of three marriages (his, hers, theirs) are identified, including John, Hannah, Judah, Ruth, and Joseph (children of John and Ellen) [EPR 1:259–60]. The last four were born in Rowley between 1641 and 1647 [RowVR 1:225–26]. John, the eldest child, would have been born in England or in Roxbury.

William Wilde/Wildes had arrived in 1635 from London, age 30 (with Alice, 40, and John, 17), settling first in Ipswich, then returning there in 1655 [Dudley Wildes Anc 313]. The 1662 will of William Wild of Ipswich names wife Elizabeth, his kinsman John Wild of Topsfield, and his son John [EPR 1:397–99].

1638: FROM ROWLEY, YORKSHIRE

Only a small portion of those sailing with Rogers in 1638 had known Rowley, Yorkshire, connections. William Jackson (with wife and daughter) and William Scales (with wife Anne) were the only lot-holders truly "of" the parish of Rowley. Widowers William Bellingham (with teenage servant Jeremiah Northend) and Thomas Nelson (with two sons) were nonresident gentry drawn to Rogers' preaching.

William Bellingham was the son of William Bellingham, Esq., and Francis Amcotte of Bromby Woode, Lincolnshire (now Bromby, in Frodingham parish; eighteen miles southwest of Hull) [Townshend, NEHGR 36:381–82]. His eldest brother, governor Richard Bellingham, and sister Susannah, wife of Philemon Pormort, emigrated earlier [GMB 1:243–47; GM 2:5:491–93]. Susannah's baptism (1 September 1601) and her marriage (11 October 1627) were in Alford, Lincolnshire (which is far from Frodingham) [Lincoln Records Society 5:23, 68; Harleian 52:70], but the family held land in South Cave, Yorkshire, the parish southwest of Rowley, which may explain William's presence in the area. William Bellingham and Elizabeth Winill were married 29 May 1634 in Rowley, Yorkshire; Elizabeth, wife of Mr. William Bellingham, was buried there 9 May 1636.

Margaret (Cliffe) Cross. Leonard Crosse of Ripplingham and Margaret Cliffe, servant to Mr Pickerd of Rowley, married 6 June 1620 in Rowley, Yorkshire. Alice, daughter of Leonard Crosse of Ripplingham, was baptized there March 17 1622/3, and Mary, daughter of Leonard Crosse of Bentley, was baptized 20 February 1624/5. Margaret joined the Boston church, but was not dismissed to Rowley. She is named in the undated will (proved 24 September 1650) of William Bellingham, at which time she was probably living at Rowley.

William Jackson of Hunsley married Joane Collin 12 May 1636 in Rowley, Yorkshire; Elizabeth, daughter of William Jackson of Hunsley, was baptized there 14 May 1637 (she married James How of Ipswich and was executed in Salem for witchcraft in 1692). Daughter Mary was born on 8 February 1639/40 in Rowley [RowVR 1:106], so son John was born later in New England, not England [as in Blodgett and Jewett, 166].

Thomas Nelson was baptized 17 June 1601 at Drax, Yorkshire, son of Thomas. He relocated to Cottingham (five miles east of Rowley) when his widowed mother married a man from there [from a genealogy of the brothers Philip and Thomas Nelson by Christopher Child, in preparation]. Thomas Nelson of Cottingham and Dorothy Stapleton of All Saints, North Street, York, were married at All Saints 17 January 1626/7 [FHL #1,068,422]. Children of Thomas

Nelson (usually styled *gentleman*) were baptized and buried at Cottingham between 1628 and 1636, three surviving: Katherine (18 May 1630), Philip (22 January 1634/5), and Thomas (14 July 1636) [FHL #919,478]. Dorothie, the wife of Mr Thomas Nelson, was buried at Rowley, Yorkshire, 27 September 1637.

"Mr. **Jeremiah Northend**, dyed April 12, 1702, he went with Mr. Rogers in to America, bout 12 years old, and staid there about 9 years. The enclosure at Rowley was made in his absence" [Rowley Parish Registers, but in a noncontemporaneous entry related to the history of the parish, quoted in NEHGR 66:352]. Jeremiah, son of Robert Northend of Weeton, was baptized 26 September 1624. Ezekiel Northend, aged 40, deposed in 1662 that his cousin Jeremiah Northend lived with William Bellingham when he died [EQC 2:361, 397; EPR 1:120]. Bellingham's undated will, proved 24 September 1650, mentions his servant Jeremy Northende, whose term was not completed [EPR 1:120-21].

Three of Jeremiah's cousins later came to New England. John Northend and Elizabeth Coole married 13 April 1605 in Rowley. Children of Mr John Northend of Rippingham baptized there: Margaret (30 March 1620), Ezekiel (10 February 1622/3), and Joan (6 June 1624). The 1625 will of John Northend, lord of the manor of Hunsley, names wife Elizabeth; Rev. Ezekiel Rogers and brother Robert Northend were to hold twenty acres in trust for the "younger children" Anthonie, Ezechiell, Elizabeth, Margaret, and Joane (under primogeniture, eldest son John need not have been mentioned) [EIHC 12:85-86]. Apparently, although Rogers was an excellent minister, he left something to be desired as guardian of an estate, as on 5 April 1638 Rev. Ezekiell Rogers released to Robert Northend property for which they were trustees for sale under the will. The document states Rev. Ezekiell Rogers "is not fitt for such business" [DDHB/42/5, Harrison-Broadley Family of Hull and Welton, East Riding of Yorkshire Archives and Records Services, catalogue entry at www.a2a.org.uk].

Ezekiel Northend's baptism is compatible with his depositions in Massachusetts as to his age [EQC 2:397, 3:30, 426, 5:17]. He had emigrated by 1648 when he married Edna [*blank*] in Rowley [RowVR 1:356], widow of Richard Bayley (brother of James Bayley), apparently born Edna Halstead, as her son Joseph refers to money from his "unckle" William Halsted [EPR 1:93–94]. A 1678 letter from Anthony Northend to "Brother" Ezekiel states (emphasis added) [EIHC 12:86-87]:

> yo[u]r letter came to my sister [Joan] Stoute hande which was very welcome news to us both to hear that you and your wife *my sisters and their husbands* were alive with all your children, . . . my Unckle [Robert] Northend and his [oldest] sonnes are all dead, . . . my cousen Jeremiah hath now gotten my uncle Northends whole estate.

The sisters of Anthony and Ezekiel Northend as yet unplaced would be Elizabeth and Margaret. It has been said, without evidence, that Elizabeth Northend was the wife of

Francis Parrat [Blodgett and Jewett, 256, 266]. Blodgett and Jewett claimed that Margaret Northend was the widow Cross and that she married again to John Palmer [93, 262], but, as shown above, the maiden name of the widow Cross was Cliffe. On 14 July 1650, John Palmer married a woman named Margaret, surname unknown [RowVR 359].

William Skales married Anne Smyth 17 October 1636 in Rowley, Yorkshire. The surname is found in Kirk Ella.

1638: SPHERE OF INFLUENCE

The charismatic Rogers probably drew much of his company from those with Puritan sympathies who were within walking distance of Rowley, about a fifteen-mile radius, and able to attend his sermons. Solid evidence has been found in several parishes for immigrants who were recruited in this way. In other cases, the proposed link is made through the presence of the surname in the area. The parishes from which the immigrants came may include Holme-upon-Spalding-Moor [Holme] (a sprawling parish twelve miles northwest of Rowley, with no records for the key period 1601–1622 when most of the emigrants would have been baptized), Hessle (between Kirk Ella and the Humber), Howden (on the Humber River about fifteen miles from Rowley), Kirk Ella (about five miles from Rowley), and Welton (on the Humber, three miles south of Rowley).

William Acy was from Kirk Ella. The registers of Kirk Ella were published in 1897, but were not consulted by Hazen and Jacobus [TAG 24:19–21], who omitted many entries pertinent to the Acy ancestry, including the marriage of the immigrant's parents Willemus Acye and Jana Skales 22 October 1593. The immigrant Willelmus, son of Willelmi Acey, was baptized 18 March 1596/7 ("about ninety" in 1682, slightly exaggerated [EQC 8:269]). Willmus Asie and Mergretta Haiton were married 25 January 1620/1. Their daughter Ruth was baptized 14 March 1621. The immigrant is said also to have had Mary (born say 1626), Elizabeth (born say 1630), and John (born about 1638) in England [Blodgett and Jewett, 2], but their baptisms, which are chronologically reasonable, were not found in Kirk Ella.

The will of **Thomas Barker** names wife Mary and "deare sister Jane Lambert," but no children, makes bequests to many residents of Rowley, and leaves half of his real property to Thomas Lambert (under twenty-one), residually to Thomas' siblings with double portion to Jonathan [undated, inventory 11 10m (December) 1650; EPR 1:128–30]. These were children of Francis and Jane (Barker) Lambert, who married in Holme (see below). The 1647 will of Francis Lambert mentions Brother Thomas Barcker. Thomas Barker was in Holme in 1629 and 1636. There is no record in Holme of a marriage for Thomas in the 1630s, so it must have occurred either in a nearby parish or in New England.

Mary Bradley married Thomas Leaver in 1643 in Rowley [RowVR 1:340]. The surname is in Holme, Howden, and Aughton. She likely came as a servant to a family in 1638.

(to be continued)

RECENT LITERATURE

Leslie Mahler, "The Maternal Ancestry of Mary Rowning, Wife of Simon[1] Ray and Peter[1] George of Braintree, Massachusetts," *The American Genealogist* 83 (2008):108-15. Utilizing English wills and parish register entries, Mahler has identified the parentage of the mother and maternal grandmother of Mary Rowning, wife of two Great Migration immigrants.

Iris M. Gray, "Enigmas #25: Was Experience[3] Howland the Wife of James[2] Bearse/Bierce of Barnstable, Massachusetts?" *The American Genealogist* 83 (2008):122-26. The author presents the evidence that the wife of James Bierce, son of Austin Bierce, who arrived in New England in 1638, was Experience Howland, granddaughter of John Howland of the *Mayflower* [GMB 2:1020-24].

Jane Fletcher Fiske, "New Light on the English Background of the Osgoods of Essex County, Massachusetts (*concluded*)," *The American Genealogist* 83 (2008):141-55. Fiske concludes her investigation of the Osgood immigrants of Essex County with a discussion of the descendants of Richard Osgood of Over Wallop, Hampshire. In light of all this new evidence, she also explores the possible ancestry of John Osgood, who sailed for New England in 1638, and of William Osgood, who came to New England about the same time.

Clifford L. Stott, "Humphrey Blake (1494?-1558) and His Descendants in New England and South Carolina: Blake, Richards, Selleck, Torrey, and Wolcott," *The New England Historical and Genealogical Register* 163 (2009):85-97. In this first installment of a multipart article, which ties together more than half a dozen immigrants to New England and South Carolina, Stott first details the life of the ancestor of this group of immigrants, Humphrey Blake, who died at Over Stowey, Somerset, in 1558. Next, he presents sketches of Humphrey's two eldest sons, John Blake, born perhaps in 1522, and Robert Blake, born perhaps in 1530. Stott concludes this first installment with a treatment of John Blake's daughter Alice, who married in 1569 James Richards. Future segments of this article will trace these lines down to the colonial immigrants.

Leslie Mahler, "The Paternal Ancestry of Abigail (Salter) Hammond of Watertown and Hannah (Salter) (Phillips) Ruggles of Boston," *The New England Historical and Genealogical Register* 163 (2009):113-16. Mahler publishes an abstract of the will of Thomas Salter of Rattlesden, Suffolk, which demonstrates that Thomas was the grandfather of Abigail Salter, who married John Hammond of Watertown, and of Hannah Salter, who married Nicholas Phillips of Boston and then John Ruggles of Boston.

Edward J. Harrison, "Ann Neave, Wife of Stephen Gates, 1638 Immigrant to Massachusetts," *The New England Historical and Genealogical Register* 163 (2009):134-36. Harrison argues that previous readings of the Hingham, Norfolk, marriage of Stephen Gates have produced the wrong surname for his bride. He then discusses the possible placement of Ann Neave in the Neave family of Norfolk.

William Wyman Fiske, "The Two Wives of Lionel Chute, Schoolmaster of Ipswich, Massachusetts," *The New England Historical and Genealogical Register* 163 (2009):137-38. The author demonstrates that Lionel Chute, who had settled in Ipswich by 1638, had two wives. The first of these was Thomasine Barker and the second was Rose ____. Fiske also presents evidence that the second wife may have been Rose Clarke, sister of the wives of John[1] Whipple and Simon[1] Stacy of Ipswich.

Jon Wardlow, "Revisiting the Family of Gershom[2] Flagg of Woburn, Massachusetts (*concluded*)," *The New England Historical and Genealogical Register* 163 (2009):139-46. The author concludes his study of the family of Gershom[2] Flagg with sketches for his younger children, daughters Hannah and Abigail and sons Ebenezer and Thomas.

Gail Blankenau, "Some Descendants of Nathaniel[3] Mead of Greenwich, Connecticut, Through His Son Josiah[4] Mead (*continued*)," *The New England Historical and Genealogical Register* 163 (2009):147-55. Blankenau continues her examination of this branch of the Mead family of Greenwich with sketches of Josiah Mead's son Nathaniel and of Josiah's grandson John Mead, son of his daughter Abigail.

Terri Bradshaw O'Neill, "New York City Huguenot Families: Barberie, Brinquemand, Lambert, and Minvielle," *The New York Genealogical and Biographical Record* 140 (2009):163-72. This study of four Huguenot families revolves around Gabriel Minvielle, mayor of New York in 1684 and testator of 1698. Gabriel married as his second wife Susanna Lawrence, daughter of JOHN LAWRENCE {1635, Ipswich} [GM 2:4:254-58].

Louise Walsh Throop, "Pilgrim George Soule: Update on His Possible Ancestry," *The Mayflower Quarterly* 74 (2008):140-43. The author explores a number of Leiden records which might have some connection with George Soule of the *Mayflower.*

George J. Hill, "Pilgrim Contemporaries: Was James Prescott of Hampton, New Hampshire (in 1665), the Son of Sir William and Margaret (Babington) Prescott (bp. 1637/8), For Whom an Arrest Warrant Was Issued in 1659/60?" *The Mayflower Quarterly* 74 (2008):245-68. James Prescott had settled by the mid-1660s in Hampton, where he married Mary Boulter, a granddaughter of RICHARD SWAIN {1635, Newbury} [GM 2:6:609-17]. After presenting a genealogical summary of the children and grandchildren of James Prescott, the author presents his argument for the identification of Sir William Prescott as the father of James. There is no known connection to JOHN PRESCOTT {1641, Watertown}.

(continued from page 18)

The father of all these children, the elder Thomas Davenport, died on 19 November 1685 and left a will, dated 24 July 1683, in which he left bequests to "Mary well beloved wife"; "son John Davenport"; "my son Samuel Jones … and unto his child that he had by [my] daughter"; "Charles Davenport and John Davenport my sons"; "their brother Jonathan Davenport & their brother Ebenezer Davenport & their sister Mary"; "my daughter Mary the wife of Sam[ue]ll Maxfield" [SPR 6:519-21]. (Since the two daughters mentioned had been or were married, there were almost certainly no other surviving daughters in 1683.)

Mary Davenport had married Samuel Maxfield by 13 August 1671, when their eldest known child was born at Dorchester [DVR 12], and so would not have been subject to catechism. This leaves two children whose absence from the list must be explained: Abigail and Ebenezer. No record for Abigail has been found after her baptism. Ebenezer certainly was living in 1676, for he was named in his father's will, and married and had several children [GDMNH 183]. There would seem to be two explanations for his absence from the list: either the list is defective; or Ebenezer, who would have been fifteen years old at the time of the list, was residing in some other town. This would not have been unusual, as boys and girls of this age were frequently put out to service in other households. Ebenezer was known to be Down East at Falmouth by 1680, before he married, so per-

haps he was already residing there in 1676. Whatever the answer may be, we may not take the absence of an unmarried child from the list of catechists as evidence that that child was deceased by that date, although that was probably the case for Abigail.

And what of the five children who were named in the list? Later records show that the sons Charles, Jonathan and John married and had sizable families [NEHGR 33:25-28]. This leaves the daughters Sarah and Anna to be accounted for. One of them must have been the daughter who married Samuel Jones and had one child with him. In the Dorchester vital records, we find that "Ann the daughter of Samuel Joanes [was] born November 14th, [16]80, & then the mother died" [DVR 18]. Secondary sources state that daughter Sarah married Samuel Jones, but since the only child of this marriage was named Ann, this may be doubted, as such a child would more likely be named for the mother. We note the marriage in Roxbury on 5 September 1679 of Samuel Jones and "Ann Danford." Since Samuel Danforth, minister at Roxbury at this time, had no sister or daughter named Ann, we believe this marriage was for Anna Davenport [GM 2:2:281-85; Sibley 1:88-92; Savage 2:8]. Thus, daughter Sarah Davenport must have died without issue, and probably unmarried, between 1676 and 1683.

This article merely skims the surface of the uses to which this list may be put in our understanding of Dorchester families in the middle of the seventeenth century.

Great Migration Newsletter

Vol. 18   October-December 2009   No. 4

CHILDREN'S INHERITANCE PORTIONS

A prime consideration for every head of household in colonial New England was to provide for the economic security of his children. Depending on the circumstances within each family, this process might be accomplished in one step during the life of the head of household, or it might take place in several steps for each child (sometimes completed during the lifetime of the head of household and sometimes not), or the entire process might await the death of the head of household. During the course of the preparation of the most recent Great Migration volume, a number of illustrative examples of this aspect of family life have emerged. We will examine both a case in which the child's portion was transferred at the time of marriage and some other instances in which the transfer of the child's portion was incomplete at the time of the death of the head of household.

An excellent example of a marriage portion may be seen in the agreement between JAMES ROGERS {1635, Saybrook} and THOMAS STANTON {1635, Cambridge} at the marriage of their children Samuel Rogers and Mary Stanton in 1662 [GM 2:6:72-84, 467-79]:

> On 1 May 1662, "an agreement between James Rogers of New London on the one part and Tho[mas] Stanton of Poccatuck of the other part, witnesseth that upon a contract of marriage engaged and upon the consummation thereof between Samuell Rogers the son of the said James Rogers and Mary Stanton the daughter of the said Thomas, the said Thomas doth hereby engage to give with his said daughter Mary as her portion in marriage the full sum of one hundred pounds sterling ... to be delivered to the said Samuell as also one hundred pounds before or at his decease ... and upon the same condition of marriage promised the said James Rogers did hereby engage himself formally and doth hereby settle and confirm upon his said son Samuell the now dwelling house of the said James Rogers in New London to him and his heirs of him the said James and his now present wife the natural mother of the said Samuell Rogers"; witnessed by Richard Lord Senior, Elizabeth Rogers and Anna Stanton [NLLR 4:1r, 5:23r].

Unfortunately, not many such documents as this survive. When they do, they are generally found among the recorded deeds, while on occasion they may be found attached to court proceedings arising from later disputes.

We will now look at three records, each of which shows a snapshot of the distribution process still in progress at the time of the father's death. Jared Spencer was baptized at Stotfold, Bedfordshire, on 25 April 1614, one of four sons of Gerard Spencer to migrate to New England [GM 2:6:419-28]. He resided at Cambridge, Lynn, Hartford and Haddam, and died at the latter town by 29 June 1685 (the date of his probate inventory), and so would have been just past his 71st birthday at the time of his death. He had twelve known children born between about 1638 and 1660, all alive and married at the time of his death.

In his will, dated 17 September 1683, he opened by stating his plan for distributing his estate, ordering that "my sons have after the rate of twenty & my daughters fifteen," intending that each son would receive £20 of his estate and each daughter would receive £15, for a total of £210. In the will, and in an undated codicil, he then proceeded to make specific bequests to several of his children, among which were the following:

> my son Nathaniel ... an acre of swamp lying at the end of my meadow lot and joining to his brother William's formerly given
>
> my son Thomas forty acres on Matchamodus side being part of that lot whereof his brother Nathaniel hath a share
>
> my son Timothy Spencer the remainder of that six score acre lot whereof his two brothers had their share before which six score acres are those my sons shall choose

(continued on page 26)

EDITOR'S EFFUSIONS

Although the basic structure of a Great Migration sketch has remained unchanged over the twenty years of the project, a number of adjustments have been made. For some time now, we have been including more material in the *EDUCATION* section, such as references to books in probate inventories. We have also been adding to the *OFFICEHOLDING* section references to arms and ammunition, also from probate inventories, on the grounds that these references reflect the militia activities of the deceased.

Some changes have been more subtle and spontaneous, however. With the completion of the most recent Great Migration volume, we became aware that over the years the average length of a sketch has been steadily increasing. In *The Great Migration Begins*, the average sketch was 2.23 pages long. In all six volumes in the second series, the average length of a sketch has been longer than that, growing from 2.40 pages in the A-B volume, to 2.60 in the M-P volume, and now to 3.17 pages in the just-released R-S volume. How did this growth come about?

At least three causes for this secular growth in sketch length come to mind. First, as we just noted above, additional material has been included in some parts of the biographical sections of sketches. This is probably the least of the causes for the growth in sketch length.

Second, we have gradually switched from abbreviated abstracts of some documents, especially trial depositions, to lengthier verbatim transcripts. Such documents are often the closest we will ever get to hearing the voices of the immigrants directly. Also, reading these longer passages provides the opportunity to appreciate, understand and savor the language of the time, so close to that of Shakespeare and the King James Bible.

Third, we have in many instances chosen to commit to print more detailed presentations of the logical trail we have followed in arriving at some of our conclusions. In the volume just completed, two examples of this process may be seen in the sketches of Quartermaster John Smith of Dorchester [GM 2:6:373-87] (at fourteen pages the longest Great Migration sketch to date) and of Thomas Stanton of New London and Stonington, the Indian interpreter [GM 2:6:467-79].

Robert Charles Anderson, FASG   Editor
Jean Powers, Production Assistant

The Great Migration Newsletter is published quarterly by the Great Migration Study Project, a project of the New England Historic Genealogical Society, 101 Newbury Street, Boston MA 02116
www.NewEnglandAncestors.org
www.GreatMigration.org
GreatMigration@nehgs.org

Copyright © 2009
New England Historic Genealogical Society

(continued from page 25)

however my estate falls out for portions to my children that my daughter Ruth Clarke's portion shall be fifteen pounds which was my covenant with her father[in-law] at her marriage which fifteen pounds she hath received some part of it as my book will testify

Aside from these direct statements, there are other indications that he had distributed portions of his estate prior to his death. First, although his will and codicil include bequests to several grandchildren, three of the daughters received no bequests, indicating they had already received their portions. Second, although he wished his children to receive a total of £210, his inventory only amounted to £124 12s. There would be no conflict between these numbers if we assume that some of his children had already received parts of their portions.

Our second example will be the estate of Quartermaster John Smith of Dorchester, who was born about 1606 and died at Dorchester in 1678, about 72 years old [GM 2:6:373-87]. With his first wife he had a daughter Mary and with his second wife he had eight children (including another daughter Mary), most of whom were unmarried at the time of his death.

In his will of 28 December 1676, he ordered that "when my children come to change their condition and marry, my wife may supply them with something to begin withal, and keep an exact account of what she letteth any of them have … that it may be discounted as part of their portion, when a final division is made," and also noted that "my daughter Mary hath received something already, and my will is it should be accounted onward of her part."

Two days later John Smith made a codicil to his will, in which he included this clarification:

> Whereas it is said my daughter Mary hath received part of her portion, it is to be understood of Mary Pelton, who hath received about £20 or more as by my book page 166 will appear. Lastly as for my daughter Mrs. Mary Hinckley she is paid what I promised her upon her marriage to Mr. Nathaniel Glover as will appear by a writing under her hand & seal bearing date the 18th 9:1660 [18 November 1660].

The first of these Marys was his eldest child with his second wife, while the second Mary was his only child with his first wife. (There are several dozen cases of early New England families with two surviving siblings of the same name; in all known cases they are half-siblings. In this instance, about twenty-four years separate the half-sisters.) Only the younger of these daughters had been named in the will.

Our final example is John Strong of Hingham, Taunton, Windsor and Northampton, born about 1606 and died at the latter town on 14 April 1699 [GM 2:6:581-88]. He had one son with his first wife and, with his second wife, fifteen

(continued on page 32)

Focus on Rowley and Ezekiel Rogers' Company

By Patricia Law Hatcher FASG

1638: SPHERE OF INFLUENCE (continued)
Sebastian Brigham and Mary had four children born in Rowley between 1640 and 1648 [RowVR 1:33]. Sebastian Brigam of Holme married Marie Favcett [Fawcett] of Lathom 20 June 1633 at Aughton [YPRS 86:14]. Sebastian had two children baptized in Holme: Timothy (24 August 1635) and Mary (30 October 1637) [FHL #98,534, item 3].

Jane Brocklebank either came as a widow or was widowed soon after arrival. Samuel Brocklebank, born about 1628 or 1629 [EQC 2:397, 3:29], and John Brocklebank, born say 1632, were almost surely her sons. No records for them in England have been located, but the surname is in Welton in 1629, and in Hessle, Howden, and Kirk Ella (including the burial of William 3 December 1635).

Katherine (Elithorp) Constable, possibly a sister of Thomas Elithorp, was the widow of Marmaduke Constable, a member of a wealthy Catholic family, but a Puritan minister at Everingham (twelve miles northwest of Rowley), where they had three sons baptized: William (3 June 1633), Marmaduke (28 August 1634), and George (23 December 1635). George was buried there 18 August 1638. She may have briefly settled at Rowley, but soon was in New Haven and later married there [Coddington, TAG 31:24–29].

Constance (Brigham) Crosby was the widow of Robert Crosby of Holme, where their children were baptized: John (25 January 1623/4), Jane (22 April 1627), Mary (4 December 1629), Robert (22 July 1632), and Hannah (31 October 1634). There is no record of Robert's burial [FHL #98,534, item 3; Prindle NEHGR 119:248].

A 1654 petition about the estate of **Thomas Elithorp** mentions wife Abigail, eldest son, and three youngest children [EPR 1:174–75]. Children of Thomas (obviously at least two men of that name) baptized in Holme: William (12 February 1628/9, buried 20 January 1632/3), William (12 April 1633, buried 27 January 1634/5), Mary (4 May 1633), Sebastian (4 April 1634, buried 11 April 1634), Nathaniel (1 December 1634), Mathew (20 September 1635, buried 17 October 1635), Elizabeth (4 February 1635/6, buried 6 July 1636), David (November 1636). Coddington identifies Mary and Nathaniel as immigrants (although working from erroneous dates on both). It is possible the Margarett wife of Thomas buried 25 May 1635 was their mother; it is also possible she was the wife of the other Thomas and that David is Thomas's son, so Thomas's wife and David could have been on the ship [FHL #98,534, item 3; also Coddington, TAG 31:20–21].

Jane (Haburne) Grant, who held a Rowley lot, was the widow of Thomas Grant. A 1698 deposition by Samuel[2]

Stickney states: "I Sam'll Stickney Sr of Bradford do testifie & say that I came over from England to New-England in the same ship w[i]th Thomas Grant & Jane Grant his wife, who brought over w[i]th them foure children, by name John, Hannah, Frances, & Ann" [EPR Case #11510, quoted in Blodgette and Jewett, 125]. Thomas Grant married Jana Haburne 21 September 1624 in Cottingham; surviving children of Thomas Grant baptized there: John (5 March 1627/8), Hannah (16 October 1631), Francis (12 June 1634), and Anne (21 December 1637) [FHL #919,478, #1,565,741].

John Haseltine, Sr., died in 1690, aged about 70 years, in Haverhill [HVR 2:415], suggesting he was unmarried when he arrived, aged about 18. John and wife Joan had children in Rowley between 1645 and 1648 [RowVR 1:90–91].

Robert Haselton married Ann [*blank*] 23 December 1639 in Rowley [RowVR 1:309]. The 1673 will of Robert Haseltine of Bradford names wife Anne and children David, Abraham, Anna, Robert, Gershom, Dilliverence, and Mercy [EPR 2:413–16]; all but David recorded in Rowley beginning in 1641 [RowVR 1:90]; David was possibly by a first wife.

The surname is in Horton; Knedlington, Howden; Hunmanby (twenty-nine miles northeast of Rowley); and Stillingfleet (south of York) in the 1629 and 1636 lists and in the Holme registers. John in Aslaby cum Nedlington [Knedlington] in 1636 is identified as recusant [Catholic]. Robert (2 January 1609/10) and John (23 August 1612), sons of Robert Hessltine of Knedlington, Howden, who was buried 5 January 1619/20 are the best possibilities found for the immigrants [YPRS 21:202, 209, 24:165].

The 1647 will of **Francis Lambert** names wife Jane; children John, Ann, Jonathan, Gershom, and Thomas; and brother Thomas Barker [EPR 1:94]. The 1659 will of Jane Lambert names eldest son John, children Jonathan, Gershom, Thomas, and Ann [EPR 1:300]. Francis Lambert married 30 June 1630 in Holme Jane Barker; children of Francis baptized there: Thomas (28 July 1633) and Ann ([blank] May 1636) [FHL #98,534, item 3]; the others were born in Rowley [RowVR 1:126–26].

Thomas Leaver was born about 1615 [EQC 8:268]. Thomas, son of Bernard Leaver of Howden, was baptized 9 October 1614 [YPRS 21:215]. He married Mary Bradley in 1643 in Rowley [RowVR 1:340].

Administration of the estate of **Thomas Lilforth** of Haverhill was granted in 1673 to wife Elizabeth; a 1695 petition says he left only daughters Elizabeth (eldest) and Mary [EPR 1:340–42]. Elizabeth, Mary, and Martha, children of Thomas and Elizabeth (Emerson) Linfurth, were born in

Haverhill in 1648, 1649/50, and 1654/5 [HVR 1:207]. The surname is in Kirk Ella and Hessle.

Henry Sands/Sandys and wife Sybil were admitted to the Boston church 20 December 1638. Samuell, son of Henery and Sybbill Sandys, was born in 1640 in Rowley [RowVR 1:187]. Sibbella Sands was born about 1617 [Sanborn, *Ages from Court Records*, 1:183]. All known children were born in New England. The surname is in Kirk Ella and Howden.

John Spofford was born about 1612 [EQC 2:362]. The 1678 will of John Spofford mentions wife [unnamed; Elizabeth in the inventory] and children, all born in Rowley [EPR 3:257–59]. The surname is in Kirk Ella and South Cave.

William Stickney and wife Elizabeth joined the Boston church 6 January 1638/9. The 1664/5 will of William Stickney names wife Elizabeth and children Samuell, Amos, John, Andrew, Thomas, Mary, Faith, and Mercy [EPR 2:5–8]. William Stickney married Elizabeth Dawson 29 November 1628 in Cottingham, Yorkshire. Surviving children of William Stickney baptized there: John (30 August 1629), Samuel (6 March 1630/1), Mary (28 December 1633), and Amos (11 February 1637/8) [FHL #919,478; Nichols, NEHGR 139:319].

Thomas Sumner is on the lot list, but he had died by 1643 when his goods were appraised for his widow Abigail [NEHGR 3:80; witnesses were Joseph Jewet and William Boynton, so the appraisal was surely done in Rowley]. The surname is in Rowley, Yorkshire. Abigail Sumner married second Thomas Elithorp; she married third in Boston Thomas Jones [Blodgett and Jewett, 112, 370].

The 1678 will of **Richard Swan** names wife Ann, children Robert, Sarah, Jane, Frances, Dorothy, and Mercy. The 1678 will of Ann Swan names daughters Abigail and Mary [EPR 3:225–30, 253–54]. Mercy, daughter of Richard and Ann, was born in 1640 in Rowley [RowVR 1:212]. Richard Swan married Anna Spofford 24 February 1622 at South Cave, Yorkshire [FHL #98,550]. Children of Richard baptized at Dicke [Gilberdike], Eastrington: Robert (26 February 1625/6), William (25 November 1627), Frances (7 November 1630), and Dorothy (23 October 1634) [FHL #1,702,848, item 13].

Richard Thorley and wife Jane had a son in 1644 in Rowley. Lidea Thorly, parents not named, was born there in 1640 [RowVR 1:217]. Son Francis was born about 1630, 1632, or 1634, and son Thomas was born about 1631 or 1635 [EQC 4:261; 6:344; 7:156–57; 9:238]. This is compatible with the baptisms in Holme of the children of Richard Thorley/Thorwell: John (21 August 1628, buried 6 June 1636), Francis (7 February 1630), Thomas (1 January 1632/3), Lidia (25 January 1635/6, buried 29 July 1636), and Mary (28 May 1637) [FHL #98,534, item 3].

1638: SAILING FROM HULL

Ships sailing from Hull to New England would not have been frequent. For the following families, their places of residence in the East Riding or Lincolnshire and the dates of known events suggest that they were passengers on the ship departing from Hull that carried Rogers' company. It is not possible to determine when their decision was made to settle with Rogers in Massachusetts—before, during, or after the voyage—but one suspects that the word was out in the East Riding and northern Lincolnshire of Rogers' planned departure, and this was a welcome opportunity for Puritans wanting to go to New England.

Edward Carlton was baptized 20 October 1610 at Beeford (three miles in from the North Sea and fifteen miles north of Hull), son of Walter Carlton [and Jane Gibbon]. His father was of Hornsea, on the North Sea, when he died in 1623. Edward married 3 November 1636 at St. Martin (Micklegate), York, Ellen Newton. No reason for the location of the marriage has been uncovered, as she was from Hedon, a parish near the Humber, east of Hull. The English baptism for their son John has not been found, but they sold land in England in April 1638 [Hazen, NEHGR 93:22; 94:17–18]. Children of Edward and Ellen Carlton were born in Rowley between 1639 and 1644 [RowVR 1:41]. He was "out of the country" when he died in 1678; his only heirs were by his [second] wife Hannah [EPR 3:277–78].

Widow **Margery (—) Shove** joined the Boston church 30 December 1638. The 1647 will of Robert Hunter left 40 shillings to Mrs. Shove "for helping her sonne when he is to Cambridg." Her son George did become a minister, but did not attend Cambridge. Her husband, Edward Shove, "matric. pens. from Kings, Cambridge, Easter 1622; B.A. 1625/6; M.A. 1629" [Venn 4:70]. Edward was vicar from at least April 1632 through March 1636/7 (but not in March 1638/9) at Elsham, Lincolnshire (eight miles south of Hull, across the Humber), where he had children baptized: Nathaniel (3 July 1632, buried same day), Elizabeth (25 September 1633), George (20 May 1634, mother Margerie), and Sarah (21 September 1636, mother Margerie); no marriage or burial was found for him [FHL #435,992, item 2]. It is said he was to be Rogers' assistant in New England, even that he was Rogers' assistant in Yorkshire and died on the ship [Moore, 197], but the curate at Rowley in March 1637/8 was Samuel [*illegible*] [FHL #919,436, item 2]. Widow Margery Shove married Richard Peacock in 1654 [BVR 48]. At Taunton "Mistris Margery Peacocke the mother of mr Gorge Shove buried the 17 Day of Aprill in the yeare 1680" [MD 22:114].

Thomas Tenney and **William Tenney** were from Great Limber, Lincolnshire (ten miles south of Hull), sons of John Tenney and Ursula Mumber. Thomas was baptized 25 June 1615, compatible with his statement of age in New England [EQC 5:277], and William was baptized 23 December 1616 [Richardson, NEHGR 151:337].

ORIGINS KNOWN, ELSEWHERE

The 1678 will of **James Barker**, "born at Stragewell in Low Suffolk in Old England," names wife Mary, children Burzilai (eldest child), Grace, James, Nathaniel, and Unice [EPR 3:246–50]. Grace, Nathaniel, and Unice were born in

Rowley [RowVR 1:19–20]. Stragewell is local vernacular for Stradishall [*Proceedings of the Suffolk Institute of Archaeology* 11(1903):253], but there is no marriage there for them [FHL #991,991, item 13].

ORIGINS UNCERTAIN
It is possible that some of these settlers were in New England prior to 1638 but left no record.

George Abbott died prior to 30 March 1647 [EQC 1:111]. The account of his estate, which mentions no wife, names his brothers Thomas and Nehemiah, and children Thomas Sr., George, Nehemiah, and Thomas Jr., who had guardians. The 1659 will of Thomas[2] names brothers George, Nehemiah, and Thomas, hence George appears to have had two sons named Thomas [EPR 1:84–86, 301–3]. His first four sons were born in England: Thomas (born say 1628), George (born say 1633), Nehemyah (born say 1634), and Thomas (born about 1637 [EQC 3:132]). He was not the George Abbott baptized 22 May 1617 in Bishop's Stortford, Hertfordshire, who came to Roxbury [Moriarty, NEHGR 85:84–85]. The surname was in Settrington (twenty-five miles north of Rowley) in 1629 and 1636, where it is common in the parish register, but does not include George's marriage or the baptisms of his sons.

John Boynton was born about 1614 [EQC 2:362.] He married Ellen/Helen Pell between 1 8th month [October] 1643 and 21 2nd month [April] 1644 [BChR 33, 39, 41]. The 1670/1 will of John Boynton names wife Ellen, brother William, and seven children [EPR 2:214–16].

William Boynton was born about 1605 or 1606 [EQC 2:397, 5:188]. The surname is in Sledmeer cum Crome (twenty miles north of Rowley) and Knapton (twenty-eight miles north of Rowley) in 1636.

John Burbank and An had a son in 1641 in Rowley [RowVR 1:38].

The 1654 will of **Hugh Chaplin** names wife Elesabeth, eldest son John, "all my children" (estate division refers to "the other three children") [EPR 1:250–52]. John, son of Hugh and Elizabeth, was born in 1643 in Rowley [RowVR 1:43]. The surname is in Market Weighton in 1636.

Richard Clark married Alice [*blank*] in 1643 in Rowley [RowVR 1:270].

The 1667/8 will of **Peter Cooper** names wife Emm and children Samuel, Mary, Deborah, and Sarah [EPR 2:120–22], all born in Rowley [RowVR 1:51–52]. He was not the 1635 emigrant [GM 2:2:205].

The 1661/2 will of **Thomas Dickinson** names wife Jennett and children, all born in Rowley [EPR 1:372–73].

John Dresser was born about 1607 [EQC 4:71]. His 1671/2 will names wife Mary and eldest son John [EPR 1:262–65], who may have been born in England.

The 1647 will of **Robert Hunter** names wife Mary, but no children [EPR 1:80–81]. The surname is in Welton in 1629 and in Howden registers.

The 1647 will of **John Jarrat** names wife Susannah and daughter Elizabeth [EPR 1:98]. Elizabeth, daughter of John, died in Rowley in 1660, unmarried [RowVR 1:478]. The surname is in Spauldington and Howden registers.

Thomas Miller and wife Isabel are mentioned in Lechford's notebook in 1640: Thomas Taylor bound to Thomas Miller for 42 shillings to be paid to his wife Isabell Miller, 24 August 1640 [Lechford, 289]. Thomas Miller was born about 1610 [Middletown, Connecticut, will, quoted in Blodgette and Jewett, 242].

Thomas Palmer married Ann [*blank*] in 1643 in Rowley [RowVR 1:360]. The 1669 will of Thomas Palmer names wife Ann and sons [EPR 2:169–70], all born in Rowley [RowVR 1:150]. The surname is in Howden.

The 1655 will of **Francis Parrat**, "intending to take a journey to England," mentions wife Elizabeth and six unnamed daughters [EPR 1:244–45]. The lengthy 17 April 1660 will of Ezekiel Rogers mentions "my sumtimes servant Elizebeth Tenney ells [*alias*] Parrat" [EPR 1:331–36]. Thomas Tenney had married widow Elizabeth Parrat 24 February 1657 [RVR 1:413]. The births of seven daughters of Francis and Elisabeth and the death of one are in the Rowley records [RowVR 1:151]. Francis is said to have had sisters (who likely came with him): Ann, who married Thomas Mihill (not recorded), and Faith Sr., who married John Smith in 1657 in Rowley [RowVR 1:361]. The surname is in Driffeilds Ambo (sixteen miles north of Rowley) in the 1636 muster roll.

John Pearson and wife Dorcas had a child in 1643 in Rowley [RowVR 1:156]. The surname is in Driffeilds Ambo, Holden, Leppington, and Beverly in 1629. It is common in Howden.

The 1655 will of **Hugh Smith** mentions wife Mary and unnamed children; estate papers identify them as Samwell, Mary, Sara, Hannah, Marthay, and Edward [EPR 1:235–37], all but Samuel born in Rowley beginning in 1642 [RowVR 1:197–205].

Margaret Stanton was buried in 1646 in Rowley [RowVR 1:524]. There is no indication if she was a widow, and no children have been found.

Richard Wicam [Wickham] and wife (Ann by 1661) had sons Daniel (born between about 1641 and 1644 [ECR 4:347; 8:128, 214; 9:258, 584]), Thomas, and John (born say 1648) [Blodgette and Jewett, 408–9]. This is not a Yorkshire surname.

The 1661 will of **Joseph Wormall** of Scituate names wife Miriam, and children Josias, Sarah, and Hester [NEHGR 6:94]. Josiah was born in 1642 in Rowley [RowVR 1:236].

EZEKIEL ROGERS' COMPANY

This reconstructed list is based primarily on likely English origins within Ezekiel Rogers' sphere of influence, excluding common surnames present elsewhere in England and keeping in mind Winthrop's "some twenty families." It may include some who died on, shortly before, or shortly after the voyage.

William & Margaret (Haiton) Acy; Ruth
Thomas Barker
William Bellingham; Jeremiah Northend
Mary Bradley
Sebastian & Mary (Fawcett) Brigham; Timothy, Mary
Jane (—) Brocklebank; Samuel, John
Edward & Ellen (Newton) Carleton; John
Katherine (Elithorp) Constable; William, Marmaduke, George
Robert & Constance (Brigham) Crosby; John, Jane, Mary, Robert, Hannah
Leonard & Margaret (Cliffe) Cross; Alice, Mary
Thomas & — (—) Elithorp; Mary, Nathaniel, David
Thomas & Jane (Haburne) Grant; John, Hannah, Francis, Ann
John Haseltine and Robert Haseltine
William & Joane (Collin) Jackson; Elizabeth
Francis & Jane (Barker) Lambert; Thomas, Ann
Thomas Leaver
Thomas Lilforth
Thomas Nelson; Katherine, Philip, Thomas
Henry & Sybil (—) Sands/Sandys
William & Ann (Smith) Scales
Edward & Margery (—) Shove; Elizabeth, George, Sarah
John Spofford
William & Elizabeth (Dawson) Stickney; John, Samuel, Mary, Amos
Thomas Sumner
Richard & Ann (—) Swan; Robert, Frances, Dorothy
Thomas Tenney and William Tenney
Richard & Jane (—) Thorley; Francis, Thomas, Mary

SOURCES

George Brainard Blodgette and Amos Everett Jewett, *Early Settlers of Rowley, Massachusetts: A Genealogical Record* (Rowley: A. E. Jewett, 1933).

John Insley Coddington, "The Elithorp Family of Yorkshire, England, and New England," TAG 31(1955):16–23. There are at least five errors in the register extracts as published in the article.

John Insley Coddington, "Katherine (Elithorp) (Constable) Miles, Ancestress of Certain Miles and Street Families," TAG 31 (1955):24–29.

John Insley Coddington, "The Rayner Family of Batley, Co. York, England, and of New England," NEHGR 109(1955):5–11.

A. N. Cooper, "How Rowley in Yorkshire Lost Its Population in the 17th Century, and How Rowley in Massachusetts Was Founded," *Transactions of the East Riding Antiquarian Society* 15 (1909):85–100.

James Foord, *The Register of Kirk Ella, Co. York: Baptisms, 1558–1837; Burials, 1558–1837; Marriages, 1558–1841*, volume 11 in Parish Register Society (London: Parish Register Society, 1897).

Thomas Gage and James Bradford, *History of Rowley . . .* (Boston: F. Andrews, 1840). Includes text of grants, but incorrectly names sixty lot-holders in their summation, adding William Tenney.

Gale Ion Harris, "John[2] Mighill of Massachusetts, New Hampshire, and Connecticut," NEHGR 158(2004):254–79.

Tracy Elliot Hazen, "The Ancestry of Edward Carlton of Rowley, Mass.," NEHGR 93(1939):3–46.

Tracy Elliot Hazen, "The Ancestry of Ellen Newton, Wife of Edward Carlton of Rowley, Mass.," NEHGR 94(1940):3–18.

Tracy Elliot Hazen, "Two Founders of Rowley, Mass.," NEHGR 94(1940):99–112 [Jewett and Mallinson].

[Tracy E. Hazen and Donald Lines Jacobus], "The English Ancestry of William Acye of Rowley, Massachusetts," TAG 24(1948): 15–22.

Jay Holbrook, microfiche of original Rowley town records, includes 1883 transcript of vital records and original pages of the 1643/4 lot list. Citations above to the vital records are to the published version, but the original was consulted.

J. Henry Lea, "Transcript of the Lost Register of Rowley, Co. York, England," EIHC 44(1908):305–12. Modernization of spelling and rearranging of text was done.

Susan Hardman Moore, *Pilgrims: New World Settlers and the Call of Home* (New Haven: Yale University Press, 2007).

G. Andrews Moriarty, "Ancestry of George Abbott of Andover, Massachusetts," NEHGR 85(1931):79–86.

Elaine C. Nichols, "Notes on English Origins: Elizabeth, Wife of William Stickney of Rowley, Mass.," NEHGR 139(1985):319–21.

Paul W. Prindle, "The Yorkshire Ancestry of the Three Crosby Sisters of Rowley, Mass.," NEHGR 119(1965):243–48.

Douglas Richardson, "The Ancestry of Dorothy Stapleton, First Wife of Thomas Nelson of Rowley, Massachusetts, with a Provisional Royal Line," NEHGR 148(1994):130–40.

Douglas Richardson, "The Tenney Family of Lincolnshire and Rowley, Massachusetts," NEHGR 151(1997):329–41.

Walter Lee Shepard, "Ancestral Clues: Some Early Settlers of Rowley, Mass.," NGSQ 68(1980):9–14. Includes notes on Hazleton, Leaver, Bradley, Lambert, and Barker. The article is published with an editorial warning that much therein are just clues.

Maxine Stansell, "The Middlebrook Sisters: Mother and Mother-in-Law of Michael Wigglesworth," NEHGR 156(2002):309–21; "More on the Reyners," 156:322–26.

Charles Hervey Townshend, "Bellingham Sketch," NEHGR 36 (1882):381–86.

W. H. Whitemore, "Lane Family Papers," NEHGR 11(1857):102–12.

RECENT LITERATURE

Myrtle Stevens Hyde, "Revised Ancestry for William Moulton of Hampton, New Hampshire, Including Some Revisions of the Early Ancestry of His New England Cousins," *The New England Historical and Genealogical Register* 163 (2009):165-73. In this first installment of a multipart article, the author first presents a full transcript of the English copy of a power of attorney made by WILLIAM MOULTON {1637, Salem}, which states explicitly that William was the son of Benjamin Moulton. She then proceeds to compile a genealogical summary of four generations of William Moulton's agnate ancestry, and in the process corrects earlier misreadings of English wills.

John C. Brandon, "The 1638 Emigration of William[1] Sargent and George[1] Curwen," *The New England Historical and Genealogical Register* 163 (2009):192-93. Brandon presents a diary entry from 31 March 1638 which states that "Mr. Sargent, Mr. Curwyn, and their wives" were about to leave for New England, thus establishing an approximate emigration date for these families.

John C. Brandon, "Nicholas and Agnes (Master) (Colwell) Gifford, Ancestors of William[1] Sargent," *The New England Historical and Genealogical Register* 163 (2009):194-98. The author demonstrates that the parents of William Sargent's paternal grandmother, Margaret (Gifford) Sargent, were Nicholas and Agnes (Master) (Colwell) Gifford. He resolves longstanding confusion by providing evidence that Agnes Master had married Thomas Colwell before marrying Nicholas Gifford.

Clifford L. Stott, "Humphrey Blake (1494?-1558) and His Descendants in New England and South Carolina: Blake, Richards, Selleck, Torrey, and Wolcott (*continued*)," *The New England Historical and Genealogical Register* 163 (2009):199-211. In this second installment of his study on this network of immigrants descended from Humphrey Blake, Stott first discusses two daughters and a son of John Blake, son of Humphrey. Elizabeth (or Isabel) Blake married Robert Selleck, and they were grandparents of DAVID SELLECK {1639, Dorchester}. Ann Blake married Thomas Saunders, and they were parents of Elizabeth Saunders who was the wife of HENRY WOLCOTT {1630, Dorchester} [GMB 3:2049-52]. The third of these children of John Blake was William Blake, who was father of WILLIAM BLAKE {1635, Dorchester}. The article then provides a genealogical summary of Humphrey Blake, grandson of Humphrey Blake through his son Robert, and father of Benjamin Blake of South Carolina. The article concludes by moving on a generation to treat Humphrey Blake's probable great-grandson Thomas Richards, who was in turn father of THOMAS RICHARDS {1633, Dorchester} [GMB 3:1575-79].

Grover V. Johnson and Marian Lewis Johnson, "Sarah Medbury of Swansea, Massachusetts, Daughter of Benjamin and Hannah Albee," *The New England Historical and Genealogical Register* 163 (2009):212. The authors provide evidence demonstrating that Sarah, the wife of John Medbury of Swansea, was daughter of BENJAMIN ALBEE {1639, Boston}, who later lived in Braintree.

Gail Blankenau, "Some Descendants of Nathaniel[3] Mead of Greenwich, Connecticut, Through His Son Josiah[4] Mead (*concluded*)," *The New England Historical and Genealogical Register* 163 (2009):213-19. The author concludes the third and final installment of her Mead study with an account of Smith Mead, grandson of Josiah Mead.

Caleb Johnson, "Two Letters Written by *Mayflower* Passenger Bartholomew Allerton," *The Mayflower Quarterly* 75 (2009):46-48. Johnson presents here the full text of two letters written in June 1645 from Bamfield, Suffolk, by Bartholomew Allerton, son of ISAAC[1] ALLERTON {1620, Plymouth} [GMB 1:35-39].

Caleb Johnson, "Hanged for Adultery: The Untold Story of *Mayflower* Passenger William Latham's Wife Mary," *The Mayflower Quarterly* 75 (2009):49-53. The author points to records that demonstrate that WILLIAM LATHAM {1620, Plymouth} [GMB 2:1160] did have a wife, named Mary, who was hanged for adultery in 1644.

Leslie Mahler, "A Clue to the Parentage of Isaac[1] Allerton," *The Mayflower Quarterly* 75 (2009):54-56. Mahler publishes here a brief record from Ipswich, Suffolk, which shows the presence there in 1609 of an apprentice named Isaac Allerton, son of a Bartholomew Allerton. He shows that the surname is extremely rare in Suffolk, but this record may be an important clue to discovering the correct ancestry for this *Mayflower* passenger.

Caleb Johnson, "The Correct Baptism Dates for Mary Chilton and Edward Winslow," *The Mayflower Quarterly* 75 (2009):137-38.
Caleb Johnson, "A New Record Relating to James Chilton," *The Mayflower Quarterly* 75 (2009):139-40.
Caleb Johnson, "Taxing Time for the Pilgrims and Their Ancestors in England, *The Mayflower Quarterly* 75 (2009):140-42.
In these three brief articles, Johnson publishes a number of newly discovered English records adding to our knowledge of the early lives of several *Mayflower* passengers before their arrival in New England.

Hannah Farber, "The Rise and Fall of the Province of Lygonia, 1643-1658," *The New England Quarterly* 82 (2009):490-513. Farber provides a clear narrative of the history of the Province of Lygonia, a jurisdiction of uncertain legitimacy which covered much of what is now coastal Maine from 1643 to 1658. Much of her story revolves around the activities and the characters of two of the more interesting of the early settlers of New England, THOMAS MORTON {1622, Merrymount} [GMB 1:1299-1300] and GEORGE CLEEVE {1630, Spurwink} [GMB 1:383-389].

(continued from page 26)

more children, all but one of whom survived to marry and have children.

In his will, dated 14 February 1696[/7?], John Strong stated

> my seven daughters Abigaile, Elizabeth, Mary, Sarah, Hannah, Hester & Thankfull my will is that with what they have already received they shall have each of them forty pounds their remainder of what is still behind that they have not received … and whereas my daughter Hannah is already dead my will is that what is behind of her portion be equally divided among her children.

Like Jared Spencer and John Smith, John Strong also felt the need to add a codicil, dated 9 February 1697/8, in which he stated the precise amounts of their portions that he had already given to each of his daughters:

> to Abigail thirty-eight pounds and thirteen shillings, to Elizabeth thirty-six pounds & seven shillings, to Mary thirty-six pounds & eighteen shillings, to Sarah twenty-eight pounds & one shilling, to Hannah twenty-eight pounds & twelve shillings, to Hester twenty-three pounds & fifteen shillings, to Thankfull sixteen pounds & seventeen shillings.

In referring to the portion of his daughter Ruth, Jared Spencer stated that what "she hath received … my book will testify." John Smith said that his daughter Mary Pelton "hath received about £20 or more as my book page 166 will appear." John Strong did not mention such a "book" explicitly, but the careful details related in the codicil to his will imply that he also maintained such a record.

Most adult males in colonial New England maintained an account book, the bulk of which usually recorded their economic transactions with other individuals, sometimes just a record of sharing agricultural produce with others, but also their dealings with tradesmen. These account books were also used, as the examples here show, to keep track of estate distributions made to children during the lifetime of the keeper of the book.

In a recent study of the local economy of early New England, James E. McWilliams notes that "[c]ommon farmers, local traders, and artisans kept account books as a matter of course. Few—perhaps about twenty-five—have survived from the seventeenth century" [*Building the Bay Colony: Local Economy and Culture in Early Massachusetts* (Charlottesville, Virginia, 2007), 5]. And most of these few are from the latter part of the century, kept by the sons or grandsons of the immigrants.

At one time hundreds of these account books must have existed, created by the immigrant heads of household; now we have only a small handful. These lost records could have solved many genealogical problems.

Great Migration Newsletter

| Vol. 19 | January-March 2010 | No. 1 |

THE AGE OF DISCRETION

Some principles of genealogical analysis are universal and apply to all cultures, while other such principles are variable and tied to a particular time and place. Among the former are various inescapable logical and biological constraints. No one can be born before their parents were born. No one can become a parent at age two.

Among the analytical principles of a variable nature are a number that can be gathered under the heading of the "age of discretion." How old did one have to be to buy and sell land? How old to marry without parental consent? How old to witness a legal document? How old to give testimony in court?

These questions have different answers in different times and places. Some of the answers derive from statutory law and others from local custom. In addressing these questions in the context of the first generation of New England settlers, we will rely on a compilation of early statutes, prepared in 1890 by William H. Whitmore:

The Colonial Laws of Massachusetts. Reprinted from the Edition of 1672, With the Supplements Through 1686. Containing Also, A Bibliographic Preface and Introduction, Treating of all the Printed Laws From 1649 to 1686. Together With The Body of Liberties of 1641*, and the Records of the Court of Assistants, 1641-1644 (*Boston 1890*).*

The Body of Liberties of 1641 consists of a series of numbered statutes, two of which relate to our concerns here:

11. All persons which are of the age of 21 years, and of right understanding and memories, whether excommunicate or condemned shall have full power and liberty to make their wills and testaments, and other lawful alienations of their lands and estates.

53. The age of discretion for passing away of lands or such kind of hereditaments, or for giving of votes, verdict or sentence in any civil courts or causes, shall be one and twenty years.

These two stated liberties pertain for the most part to matters of estates and conveyances, and would appear to be quite definite. We must, however, always guard against taking a too legalistic approach in our interpretation of the records. Sometimes liberties were taken with the dates and ages involved.

Jared Spencer was baptized at Stotfold, Bedfordshire, on 25 April 1614, son of Gerald and Alice (Whitbread) Spencer [TAG 27:84, 164; GM 2:6:419-28]. By 1634 he had settled in Cambridge. Our evidence for this is that on 1 September 1634 "Garrad Spencer" was granted four acres "on the west side of the river" in Cambridge [CaTR 10].

At the time of Jared's baptism, English ecclesiastical law required that a child be baptized within a week of birth, and this requirement was adhered to in most cases. Thus, at the time he was granted land in Cambridge, Jared Spencer was about eight months short of his twenty-first birthday. Perhaps Jared did not know his own age accurately; perhaps the Cambridge town fathers were content with knowing that he was in his twenty-first year. In any case, strictly speaking, Jared should not yet have been eligible for a grant of land. On the other hand, we should not expect to find examples where even greater liberties are taken with the age at which one could be granted land.

Some other activities are associated with the age sixteen. Most drastic, among the capital laws, are two infractions based on Biblical precedent (henceforth, all citations to statutes are to the 1672 edition noted above):

(continued on page 2)

EDITOR'S EFFUSIONS

On a regular basis we devote large portions of the *Great Migration Newsletter* to the consideration of very narrow issues, such as the meaning of a single technical term or the importance of one particular type of record. There is also importance in moving to the opposite extreme and looking at our subject matter from the broadest perspective.

From the viewpoint of placing the Great Migration in a broad historical context, nothing is more important than the English Puritan movement of the sixteenth and seventeenth centuries, a topic which we do not often consider here.

To make up for that deficiency, we strongly recommend a small new book by Francis J. Bremer, who was earlier the author of a biography of Governor John Winthrop [GMN 12:32]. This volume, published in 2009, is titled simply *Puritanism*, one entry in an interesting series published by Oxford University Press under the rubric "A Very Short Introduction."

Bremer begins with the English Reformation under Henry VIII, and continues with the development of the movement under Edward VI, Mary and Elizabeth. He describes the changing meanings of the term "Puritanism," which has become a very slippery category for modern scholars.

All of this, of course, provides the background for the Great Migration and, as Bremer moves into the seventeenth century and the reigns of James I and Charles I, we begin to see the events that led to the migration to New England. The author points out where and when the Puritan activities in the New World began to diverge from what had begun in old England.

The volume also covers such topics as the effects of Puritanism on the daily life of those who chose this form of religious practice, and follows the influence of Puritan concepts and practices in later centuries. Bremer includes a useful bibliography at the end of the book.

After the passage of more than three centuries, the convolutions of Puritan theology can be difficult to understand, but Bremer makes this world comprehensible to us, and so assists in our understanding of the Great Migration.

Robert Charles Anderson, FASG   Editor
Jean Powers, Production Assistant

The Great Migration Newsletter is published quarterly by the Great Migration Study Project, a project of the New England Historic Genealogical Society,
101 Newbury Street, Boston MA 02116
www.NewEnglandAncestors.org
www.GreatMigration.org
GreatMigration@nehgs.org

(continued from page 1)

> If any child or children above sixteen years old, and of sufficient understanding, shall CURSE or SMITE their natural FATHER or MOTHER, he or they shall be put to death …

> If a Man have a STUBBORN or REBELLIOUS SON of sufficient years of understanding (viz:) sixteen years of age, which will not obey the voice of his Father, or the voice of his Mother, … such a son shall be put to death [page 15].

In his compilation of executions in New England, historian Daniel Hearn found no instance in which either of these laws was enforced [Daniel Allen Hearn, *Legal Executions in New England: 1623-1960* (Jefferson, North Carolina, 1999)].

Sixteen years was also the age at which women could marry without consent:

> No Orphan, during their minority, which was not committed to tuition or service by their Parents in their lifetime, shall afterwards be absolutely disposed of by any, without the consent of some Court, wherein two Assistants (at least) shall be present, except in case of marriage, in which the approbation of the major part of the Selectmen of that Town, or any one of the next Assistants shall be sufficient, and the minority of women in case of marriage, shall be sixteen years [page 28].

On 20 January 1640/1, Emmanuel Downing wrote to John Winthrop that

> I have here in Salem a desire to match my son James to a maid that lives in Mr. Endicott's house. Her sister is married here who says the maid was left to her dispose by her parents, but they dying intestate, the administration and tuition of the maid was by the court committed to Mr. Hathorne, Mr. Batter and Goodman Scruggs…. Mr. Endicott said to my good friend Mr. Hathorne that he had the whole dispose of the maid and would provide a better match for her, Mr. Hathorne answered him that they the Feoffees were trusted with the person and the estate until the maid should be of years to dispose of herself, which said he, that she now was of full years to dispose of herself, being past 16, for she is about 17 years of age [WP 4:305].

The young maid was Rebecca Cooper. For whatever reason, the marriage did not take place [GMB 1:578-79].

Young men and women of sixteen were also subject to charges of heresy:

> [W]hat person or persons soever, professing the Christian Religion, above the age of sixteen years, that shall within this Jurisdiction, wittingly and willingly, at any time after the publication of this Order, deny either by Word or Writing, any of the Books of the Old Testament … Or New [shall be fined or whipped] [page 59].

(continued on page 8)

Focus on Immigration

INTRODUCTION

Two years ago we continued our examination of the question of when the Great Migration ended by studying the list of those admitted as freemen of Massachusetts Bay on 2 June 1641 [MBCR 1:378-79; GMN 17:19-22, 27-30]. This date was the opening day of the General Court of Elections. We use this date each year as the cutoff for determining that a given immigrant had arrived in New England no later than the previous year, on the assumption that very few passengers ships can have arrived in New England any earlier than this date, given the difficulty of crossing the North Atlantic during the winter.

On three previous occasions we have asked the question "When Did the Great Migration End?" [GMN 1:9, 10:1-2, 8, 14:25-26]. In the most recent of these articles, we concluded that 1639 was the last year of heavy migration to New England as part of the Great Migration. Based on this conclusion, we expected that relatively few of those admitted to freemanship on 2 June 1641 had actually arrived in 1640. We discovered that at most about a quarter of those in the 1641 list could have arrived in 1640 (33 of 126) and that there were good reasons for believing that many of those had arrived earlier [GMN 17:25-26, 32]. In addition, we learned that a few of those admitted as freemen in May of 1641 had arrived as early as 1633 and 1634 and that seven of the 126 were of the second generation, sons of men who had arrived at an earlier stage of the Great Migration.

Toward the end of our analysis of the 1641 list, we noted that "We will be able to arrive at a better assessment [of the date of the end of the Great Migration] by carrying out a similar analysis of 1642 and 1643 freemen." In this issue and the next, we redeem the first half of this offer by examining the list of freemen for 18 and 19 May 1642.

METHODOLOGY

The list for 18 and 19 May 1642 includes the names of 114 men [MBCR 2:291-92]. The General Court of Elections for 1642 gathered on 18 May, but conducted relatively little business on that day, mainly the election of colony officers [MBCR 2:1-2]. The court then recessed and regathered on 20 May, when many more actions were taken [MBCR 2:2-6]. At the end of the day on 20 May, the court adjourned again, reconvening on 14 June for an even longer session [MBCR 2:6-22].

The main body of the freemen for this year were admitted on 18 May. Then, on 19 May, while the court was in recess, five more men were admitted. Interestingly, two of these men were William Hilton and William Waldron, the deputies to the court sent from the town of Dover. Perhaps, since they were coming from a great distance, they were delayed

and the court did not wish to proceed further in their absence. Another of the five men added to the list of freemen on 19 May was John Sadler, who had on 18 May been sworn to head the train band at Gloucester, which he should not have been were he not a freeman.

Through this analysis, we will be demonstrating the value of examining of these lists to determine the residences of some of these immigrants. This derives from the frequent practice of grouping the freemen from a given town together in the lists of freemen. This practice was not always followed faithfully, so some sections of the list will not be as neatly organized as others.

To assist in visualizing this aspect of the list, we will place a two-letter code after each name, designating the church to which they had been admitted, thus qualifying them for freemanship:

Bo	Boston
Br	Braintree
Ca	Cambridge
Ch	Charlestown
Co	Concord
De	Dedham
Do	Dorchester
Dv	Dover
Gl	Gloucester
Ha	Hampton
Hi	Hingham
Ip	Ipswich
Ne	Newbury
Rw	Rowley
Rx	Roxbury
Sm	Salem
Wa	Watertown
We	Weymouth

LIST OF FREEMEN, 18 AND 19 MAY 1642

Mr. Francis Norton (Ch): "Francis Norton" was admitted to Charlestown church on 10 April 1642 [ChChR 10]. On 1 August 1637, "Mr. Fra[ncis] Norton is admitted a townsman [at Charlestown] if he please" [ChTR 31]. In the 1638 Charlestown land inventory, he held six parcels [ChBOP 55]. He also had interests on the Piscataqua [GDMNH 513].

John Withman (Ch): "John Weightman" was admitted to Charlestown church on 31 July 1641 [ChChR 10]. On 18 February 1639[/40?}, "Isaack Coale of Charlton granted unto John Whitheman his dwelling house, yard, and garden, situate in Charlton" [SLR 1:16]. He was probably closely related to Mary (Wightman) Nash, wife of WILLIAM NASH {1634, Charlestown} [GM 2:5:229-31].

Gawdye James (Ch): "Gardy James" was admitted to Charlestown church on 15 May 1642 [ChChR 10]. In the 1638 Charlestown Book of Possessions, "Gauddy James" held three parcels of land, including "two acres of land ... with a dwelling house upon it," which he had bought of William Dady [ChBOP 65].

John March (Ch): "John March" was admitted to Charlestown church on 15 May 1642 [ChChR 10]. In the 1638 Charlestown Book of Possessions, "John March" held seven parcels of land, including "one dwelling house with a garden plot bought of "Rob[ert] Haukines" [ChBOP 64]. On 30 December 1638, "John March" held two cow commons in the stinted common at Charlestown [ChTR 42].

Rob[e]rt Button (Sm): On 27 February 1641/2, "Robert Button" was admitted to Salem church [SChR 11]. On 27 March 1642, "Samuel, son of Robert Button," was baptized at Salem [SChR 18]. Robert Button's wife was Abigail Vermais, sister of the next man named in this list [Dudley Wildes Anc 124].

Benia[min] Vermaes (Sm): On 6 March 1641/2, "Benjamin Fermaies" was admitted to Salem church [SChR 11]. On 29 October 1638, "Marke Vermais is admitted to be an inhabitant amongst us at Salem & doth desire to be accommodated amongst us with land. Ellis [Alice] Vermais widow desireth accommodation of land at Salem" [STR 1:72-73]. Benjamin was son of Alice Vermais [Dudley Wildes Anc 121-25].

Thom[as] Antrum (Sm): "Thomas Antram, weaver," sailed for New England in 1635 from Southampton in the *James* [Drake's Founders 56]. He settled in Salem and was admitted to church there on 24 March 1638/9 [SChR 8; GM 2:1:69-71].

Michaell Shaflin (Sm): On 30 September 1638, "Michaell Shaflin" was admitted to Salem church [SChR 7]. He had sailed to New England in 1635 on the *James* from Southampton, settled first at Charlestown and in the following year moved to Salem [GM 2:6:250-55].

Thom[as] Putnam (Sm): On 3 April 1642, "Thomas Putnam" was admitted to Salem church [SChR 11]. On 20 January 1640/1, the town of Salem granted "fifty acres of land unto Thomas [Putnam] and five acres of meadow both to be laid out by the town" [STR 1:109]. Thomas Putnam was baptized at Aston Abbots, Buckinghamshire, on 7 March 1614/5, son of John Putnam, who also first appeared in Salem in 1640 [Perley 2:109; TAG 15:8].

John Cooke (Sm): On 21 March 1640/1, "John Cooke" was admitted to Salem church [SChR 10]. In the 1636 Salem land grant, "Jno. Cook" received twenty acres, not in the freeman's land [STR 1:22]. This entry may be a late addition to the 1636 list of grants, for on 30 July 1637, "John Cooke desireth to be an inhabitant & is referred to the next meeting"; at the next meeting, on 7 August 1637, "John Cooke is admitted for inhabitant & granted 5 acres" [STR 1:53].

Phineas Fiske (Sm): On 21 March 1640/1, "Phineas Fiske" was admitted to Salem church [SChR 10]. On 3 December 1641, the town of Salem granted "to Phyneas Fiske 20 acres more at the village near the pond" [STR 1:112].

Willia[m] Fiske (Sm): On 2 July 1641, "William Fiske" was admitted to Salem church [SChR 11]. In the 25 December 1637 division of marsh and meadow at Salem, "Will [iam] Fisk was granted half an acre for a household of one [STR 1:103]. On 16 July 1638, "W[illia]m Fisk desireth a ten-acre lot [at Salem]" [STR 1:72]. William was brother of Rev. John Fiske of Salem, Wenham and Chelmsford, and was first-cousin once-removed of Phineas Fiske [NEHGR 88:270-73].

James Fiske (Sm): On 2 July 1641, "James Fiske" was admitted to Salem church [SChR 11]. He was born about 1620, son of Phineas Fiske [NEHGR 88:271-72].

George Byam (Sm): On 7 September 1640, "George Byam" was admitted to Salem church [SChR 10]. On 14 April 1644, "Abraham, son of Brother Byam," was baptized at Salem [SChR 20]. The family soon moved to Wenham.

Rich[a]rd Bishope (Sm): On 25 August 1639, "Richard Bishop" was admitted to Salem church [SChR 8]. Richard Bishop had arrived in Salem by June 1635, by which time he had married the widow Dulsabel King [MBCR 1:151; GM 2:1:307-10].

Allen Kenniston (Sm): On 24 March 1638/9, "Dorithy Kenestone" was admitted to Salem church [SChR 8]. On 16 January 1641/2, "Mr. Kenniston" was admitted to Salem church [SChR 11]. On 26 December 1636, "Mrs. Keniston is received for [an] inhabitant but not to have land but what she purchaseth, & so hath purchased Lieut. Davenport's house" [STR 1:29]. On 4 February 1638/9, the town of Salem "granted to Mr. Keniston a ten-acre lot lying between Mr. Downing's farm & Mr. Endecott's" [STR 1:81]. The clear implication of these records is that Dorothy Kenniston preceded her husband to New England by two years. (See the sketch of JOHN CROW {1634, Charlestown} [GM 2:2:245-48] for another example of a wife coming to New England before her husband.)

Elias Stileman (Sm): On 18 August 1639, "Elias Stileman Junior" was admitted to Salem church [SChR 8]. He was baptized at Wantage, Berkshire, on 17 June 1615, son of ELIAS STILEMAN {1629, Salem} [GMB 3:1759-62], who had himself been admitted as a freeman on 3 July 1632 [MBCR 1:367].

John Tomkins, qu. (Sm): On 10 February 1638/9, "Hanna, daughter of John Tomkins," was baptized at Salem [SChR 17]. On 20 March 1636/7, "Jno. Tompkins is promised to be received for inhabitant in case he procure free dismission" [STR 1:41]. On 12 July 1637, "Jno. Tomkins is received a[n] inhabitant and have granted five acres of land" [STR 1:51]. The absence of John Tompkins from the published list of admissions to Salem church indicates that that record is defective in this instance. John Tompkins was the son of RALPH TOMPKINS {1635, Dorchester} and the town of Salem was asking for a "free dismission" from the town of Dorchester. (The abbreviation "qu." stands for "quaere," the Latin for "query," indicating that the clerk was questioning this entry, because there was another entry for the same name later in the list. As we shall see, both entries are legitimate. Interestingly, the clerk did not question another instance in this list of duplicate names, that of Richard Taylor.)

Ananias Conkling (Sm): On 29 December 1639, "Annanias Concklyne" was admitted to Salem church [SChR 9]. On 25 June 1638, the town of Salem "ordered that Ananas Conkclin and William Osborne shall have an acre of land apiece for a houselot" [STR 1:70].

John Neale (Sm): On 22 May 1642, "Jo[h]n, son of John Neale," was baptized at Salem [SChR 19]. This baptism occurred only four days after John Neale was made a freeman. Both of these events imply admission to Salem church, but his name is not to be found in the Salem church records, which must be defective in this instance. (On 3 September 1639, "John Neale, for running away & stealing, was censured to be severely whipped, & committed to his master to be kept chained" [MBCR 1:268]. On 25 January 1641/2, "John Neal of Marblehead, servant to Mr. W[illia]m Cokraine [was ordered] to be whipped for burglary" [EQC 1:35]. Walter Goodwin Davis has pointed out that, given the chronology and circumstances of these latter two events, these records do not pertain to the 1642 freeman [Sarah Stone Anc 57].)

John Bulfinch (Sm): On 9 September 1640, "Goodman Bulfinch" was admitted to Salem church [SChR 10]. On 30 June 1640, John Luff sued "Jno. Bullfinch" for debt [EQC 1:19]. On 4 April 1641, "Goodman Bulfinch" was appointed fenceviewer at Salem [STR 1:110].

Joseph Boyse (Sm): On 7 February 1640/1, "Joseph Boyer [*sic*]" was admitted to Salem church [SChR 10]. On 21 February 1640/1, "Hester, daughter of Joseph Boyce," was baptized at Salem [SChR 18]. On 9 December 1639, "Joseph Boys desireth to be an inhabitant and to have accommodations" [STR 1:93]. On 15 July 1640, the town of Salem granted "to Joseph Boys, 10 acres of land to be laid out at Cape Anne's side" [STR 1:105].

Samu[el] Grimes (Bo): On 26 March 1642, "Samuel Grame a pewterer" was admitted to Boston church [BChR 35]. On 17 September 1638, Boston selectmen allowed to "Samuell Gryne towards his losses in his corn 40s." [BTR 1:35]. On 27 April 1639, "Mary Greames daughter of Samuel Greames & Francis his wife" was born at Boston [NEHGR 2:189]. On 29 April 1639, "Samuell Grame is allowed for an inhabitant [at Boston]" [BTR 1:40]. On 27 January 1639/40, "Samuell Grame hath a great lot granted unto him for 4 heads at the Mount" [BTR 1:46].

Theodo[re] Atkinson (Bo): On 11 January 1634/5, "Theodorus Atkinson servant to our brother John Newgate" was admitted to Boston church [BChR 19]. Theodore Atkin-

son had arrived in New England by 1634 and was about twenty years old when admitted to church [GMB 2:1:95-103]. He received his first land grant in 1640 and married at about the same time or soon after., and so had finished his term of service by 1640 He would not have been made a freeman while still a servant, thus explaining in part the seven-year gap between his admission to church and to freemanship.

Rob[e]rt Bradford (Bo): On 4 July 1640, "Robert Bradford a tailor" was admitted to Boston church [BChR 29]. On 27 January 1639/40, "Robert Bradford, tailor, [is] allowed to be an inhabitant [of Boston]" [BTR 1:46].

Hugh Williams (Bo): On 1 January 1641/2, "Hugh Williams a singleman and an hatter" was admitted to Boston church [BChR 35]. On 27 November 1643, "Nathaniel Newgate, apprentice to … Hugh Williams," was hired as town drummer at Boston [BTR 1:76].

Rich[a]rd Crithley (Bo): On 24 April 1642, "Richard Crichley a blacksmith" was admitted to Boston church [BChR 36]. On 15 August 1639, "Richard Crutchly of Boston" and "Al[i]ce Dynely widow late the wife of William Dyneley barber deceased" entered into a marriage contract [SLR 2:105; GM 2:2:353]. On 27 January 1639/40, Boston selectmen "granted to Richard Critchley a great lot for 5 heads at the Mount" [BTR 1:46]. On 25 December 1640, "Samuel Croycley, son of Richard Croychley & Alice his wife" was born at Boston [NEHGR 2:79]. On 29 November 1645, "Alice Critchley the wife of our brother Richard Critchley" was admitted to Boston church [BChR 44].

John Guttering (Bo): On 29 January 1641/2, "John Guttridge a tailor" was admitted to Boston church" [BChR 35]. On 31 January 1641/2, "John Gutteridge is admitted to be a townsman [at Boston]" [BTR 1:66]. On 1 October 1642, "Joseph Guttridg the son of John Guttridge & Prudence his wife" was born at Boston [NEHGR 2:189].

John Ingoldsbey (Bo): On 6 November 1641, "John Ingolsby a singleman" was admitted to Boston church [BChR 35]. "John of John & Ruth Ingolsby" died at Boston on 3 August 1649 [BVR 29].

Robert Howen (Bo): On 13 June 1641, "Robert Howen a cutler" was admitted to Boston church [BChR 34]. On 29 June 1640, "Robert Howen is granted a great lot upon the land near Braintree for four heads" [BTR 1:54]. On [blank] June 1640, "John the son of Robert Howen & Elizabeth his wife" was born at Boston [NEHGR 2:190]. On 27 January 1644/5, Boston selectmen ordered "ten shillings allowed to be paid by the town unto widow Howin towards her relief, in consideration of her shop now standing in the market place speedily to be removed" [BTR 1:83].

Thoma[s] Snowe (Bo): On 5 September 1641, "Thomas Snow a barber" was admitted to Boston church [BChR 35]. On 11 January 1637/8, pursuant to a town order of 14 December 1635, "Thomas Snow" was granted ten acres at Muddy River in Boston [BTR 1:14, 26; GM 2:6:413-17].

Thoma[s] Foster (Bo): On 26 March 1642, "Thomas Foster the gunner" was admitted to Boston church [BChR 35]. On 30 September 1639, Boston selectmen "granted to Thomas Foster, the gunner at Castle Island, a great lot at the Mount, for six heads" [BTR 1:42]. (Savage and Pope thought he was the Thomas Foster who sailed for New England on the *Hercules* in 1634, but this is far from certain [Drake's Founders 71; GM 2:2:555-56].)

Dani[el] Briskoe (Bo): On 17 April 1642, "Daniell Briscoe the son of our brother Willyam Briscoe" was admitted to Boston church [BChR 36]. On 28 March 1642, "Daniel Briskoe" was one of several men "admitted to be townsmen [at Boston]" [BTR 1:68]. On 24 February 1639/40, "William Briscoe, tailor, is allowed to be an inhabitant, and to have a great lot, for eight heads, at the Mount" [BTR 1:48]. On 30 January 1640/1, "Willyam Briscoe a tailor" was admitted to Boston church [BChR 32].

John Search (Bo): On 19 September 1641, "John Search a weaver" was admitted to Boston church [BChR 35]. On 31 May 1641, "John Serch is admitted a townsman [at Boston], he behaving himself inoffensively" [BTR 1:61]. On 27 September 1641, "there is an houselot granted to John Search near unto the homelot of Richard Walker" [BTR 1:63]. Given the date of his admission as a townsman, this man was probably already in New England by 1640.

John Baker (Bo): On 26 March 1642, "John Baker a husbandman" was admitted to Boston church [BChR 35]. On 28 March 1642, "John Baker" was one of several men "admitted to be townsmen [at Boston]" [BTR 1:68]. There were several John Bakers in early New England, more than one of whom resided at Boston. For the possibility that the John Baker who was a freeman in 1642 had an interesting later career in York, Wells and finally London, where he was hanged in 1663, see the sketch of JOHN BAKER {1630, Charlestown} [GMB 1:72-78].

Rich[a]rd Knight (Bo): On 26 March 1642, "Richard Knight a slater" was admitted to Boston church [BChR 35]. On 31 January 1641/2, "Richard Knight is admitted to be a townsman [at Boston]" [BTR 1:66]. On 15 May 1642, "Dinah Knight the wife of our brother Richard Knight" was admitted to Boston church [BChR 36]. On 18 [*sic*] February 1642/3, "Samuel the son of Richard Knight & Dinah his wife" was born at Boston [NEHGR 2:191] and, on 12 February 1642/3, he was baptized there [BChR 291].

Rich[a]rd Tayler (Bo): On 1 January 1641/2, "Richard Taylor a singleman and tailor" was admitted to Boston church [BChR 35]. On 31 January 1641/2, "Richard Taylor is admitted to be a townsman [at Boston]" [BTR 1:66]. On 2 February 1646 [*sic*], "John son of Richard & Mary" Taylor was born at Boston [NEHGR 9:166] and, on 6 February 1647/8, "John Taylor the son of our brother Richard Taylor being about 4 days old" was baptized there [BChR 310].

Philip Tayler (Unknown): This is one of those instances where we are hindered in identifying a town of residence because the name falls into one of the seams of the list, be-

ing at the end of a Boston grouping and the beginning of a Cambridge grouping. In his Taylor section, Savage included an entry for "PHILIP, Freeman of Massachusetts 18 May 1642 may have been brother of Richard, who in the list stands next before him, but I am not able to say more, than that he was of another church than that of Boston" [Savage 4:262]. No other record for a Philip Taylor has been found in early New England records. (There is a slim possibility that this entry is an error for "Philip Ryse a tailor" who was admitted to Boston church on 21 November 1641 [BChR 35].)

John Bulkeley (Ca): John Bulkeley was baptized at Odell, Bedfordshire, on 6 February 1619/20, son of PETER BULKELEY {1635, Cambridge} [GM 2:1:459-65]. As such, one would expect him to have joined the church at Concord, where his father was minister in 1642. However, he appears in this list immediately before two Cambridge men, and some distance from other Concord men. The explanation is that in 1642 he was residing at Harvard College, where he was nearing the end of his studies as a member of the first graduating class there [Sibley 1:52-54].

Edward Okes (Ca): Urian Oakes, eldest son of Edward Oakes, was "about 10 years old when his father joined here [Cambridge church]" [CaChR 6]. Urian was born about 1631, so Edward Oakes was admitted to Cambridge church about 1641 [Sibley 1:173]. On 8 November 1642, "Edward Oakes" was elected constable at Cambridge [CaTR 46].

Thom[as] Okes (Ca): Thomas Oakes was brother of Edward Oakes. On 3 November 1646, Elizabeth Oakes, daughter of Thomas and Elizabeth, was born at Cambridge.

Edward Gooding (Bo): On 26 March 1642, "Edward Goodden a laborer" was admitted to Boston church [BChR 35]. On 27 April 1640, "Ed[ward] Goodwine is allowed a lot at the Mount for two heads" and "is granted a lot next to Willia[m] Briscowe, provided he build on it within six months" [BTR 1:53].

Sampson Shore (Bo): On 29 January 1641/2, "Samson Shore a tailor" was admitted to Boston church [BChR 35]. On 29 November 1641, "Samson Shore is admitted to be a townsman [at Boston]" [BTR 1:63]. On 31 May 1646, "Abigall Shore the wife of our brother Samson Shore" was admitted to Boston church [BChR 46]. On 12 June 1643, "Jonathan the son of Sampson Shoreborne [*sic*] & Abigail his wife" was born at Boston [NEHGR 2:401] and, on 18 June 1643, "Jonathan the son of our brother Samson Shore being about 7 days old" was baptized there [BChR 292].

Willi[am] Torry (We): On 3 December 1641, Naomi, daughter of William Torrey, was born at Weymouth. On 27 April 1639, Jane (Haviland) Torrey, the second wife of William Torrey, was buried at Combe St. Nicholas, Somerset [Weymouth Hist 4:677]. Naomi was the first child William Torrey had with his third wife, whom he apparently married in New England and whose name is not known with certainty [NEHGR forthcoming].

(to be continued in next issue)

RECENT LITERATURE

John E. D'Anieri, "Notes on John[1] Lyford of Plymouth Colony and Virginia, His Child Ann, and His Widow's Second Husband," *The American Genealogist* 83 (2009):174-78. The author analyzes the will of JOHN LYFORD {1624, Plymouth} [GMB 2:1214-17], proposes a possible identity for the second husband of the widow, identifies an additional child (a daughter Ann), and adds further information on some of Lyford's other children.

Patricia Donaldson-Mills, "The English Origins of John[1] Mygatt and His Servant John[1] Colt of Hartford, Connecticut," *The American Genealogist* 83 (2009):195-98. Based on the English marriage of John Colt and Anne Mygatt in Coggeshall, Essex, in 1633, Donaldson-Mills demonstrates that JOSEPH MYGATE {1634, Cambridge} [GM 2:5:209-12] and his servant John Colt derived from that parish.

Leslie Mahler, "Medieval Ancestors of Edward[1] Rawson of Newbury, Massachusetts," *The American Genealogist* 83 (2009):207-16. Mahler presents information on Bridget Ward, paternal grandmother of EDWARD RAWSON {1637, Newbury}, and on her mother, Winifred Hawtrey, and on the ancestry of each of these women.

Kent Randell, "William[1] Burnell of Boston: Eight Generations of Male-Line Descendants in Boston and Nantucket, Massachusetts," *The American Genealogist* 83 (2009):223-31. The author has compiled eight generations of the agnate descendants of WILLIAM BURNELL {1640, Boston} and presents here genealogical summaries of the immigrant and of his two sons. Randell includes detailed discussions of the impact on the family of the Quaker religion and of the contested estate of Samuel Burnell, son of the immigrant.

Martin E. Hollick, "The English Ancestry of William[1] Dudley of Guilford, Connecticut," *The American Genealogist* 83 (2009):232-33. Hollick corrects his earlier article on the ancestry of William Dudley, noting that the immigrant's mother was Eleanor Hooker (and not Eleanor Gooder). He then adds information from the will of John Hooker, Eleanor's father.

Jan Porter and Daniel F. Stramara Jr., "The Origin of Gabriel[1] Whelden of Yarmouth and Malden, Massachusetts," *The New England Historical and Genealogical Register* 163 (2009):253-61. The authors demonstrate that Gabriel Whelden, who had arrived in New England by 1639, derived from Basford, Nottinghamshire. They include a full transcript of an unusual document, an inventory of Whelden's English property compiled in early 1638, in preparation for his departure for New England.

Myrtle Stevens Hyde, "Revised Ancestry for William Moulton of Hampton, New Hampshire, Including Some Revisions of the Early Ancestry of His New England Cousins," *The New England Historical and Genealogical Register* 163 (2009):273-77. The author concludes her study of the English ancestry of William Moulton with genealogical summaries of the Watts, Grene and Taylor families, ancestral to three of the spouses of Moulton men.

Clifford L. Stott, "Humphrey Blake (1494?-1558) and His Descendants in New England and South Carolina: Blake, Richards, Selleck, Torrey, and Wolcott (*continued*)," *The New England Historical and Genealogical Register* 163 (2009):278-95. Stott continues his examination of the Blake family with compilations of the families of Philip Torrey of Combe St. Nicholas, Somerset (five of whose children came to New England), Robert Selleck of Over Stowey, Somerset (whose son David came to New England), Elizabeth Saunders (who married HENRY WOLCOTT {1630, Dorchester} [GMB 3:2049-52]), WILLIAM BLAKE {1635, Dorchester} and Benjamin Blake (who settled in South Carolina).

Patricia Law Hatcher, "The Staten Island Census—A List Analysis," *The New York Genealogical and Biographical Record* 140 (2009):261-71. Although the families discussed in this article do not have any immediate relevance to the Great Migration, the methodology employed by the author is of great importance to our work. Regular readers of this *Newsletter* are familiar with the practice of list analysis. Pat Hatcher has produced here an outstanding example of this form of analysis. She takes as her text a colonial New York census, the date and place of which are not explicitly stated. Other genealogists have attempted to identify the date and place, with varying results. Unlike previous investigators, Hatcher tackles the problem systematically, studying all the names in the list (not just a sample) and comparing these names against all available sources. She concludes that the census was for Staten Island, and was compiled in the middle months of 1707. As is always the case with successful list analysis, this result may now be used to learn more about many of the families covered by the census. The technique employed here is worthy of emulation.

Robert Charles Anderson and Alvy Ray Smith, "The Genealogy of Edward[1] Riggs of Roxbury, Massachusetts, Revisited," *The Genealogist* 23 (2009):131-73. Both authors of this article had, for quite different reasons, undertaken earlier investigations of EDWARD RIGGS {1633, Roxbury} [GMB 3:1583-85] and both authors had found problems with earlier accounts of this immigrant and his descendants. They now present a complete reanalysis of the agnate descendants of this immigrant, to the fourth generation. In the process, they point out remaining problems in the study of this family, especially in the branches which settled in New Jersey late in the seventeenth century.

Caleb Johnson, "The Hunt for the English Origins of George Soule," *The Mayflower Quarterly* 75 (2009):245-661. The author presents English records for a number of men named George Soule, arguing that most of them could not have been the *Mayflower* passenger and providing several avenues for future research.

(continued from page 2)

Although not in the statutes, sixteen was apparently also the age at which one could join a church in full communion.

Another important milestone was the age of fourteen. In 1647 the law quoted earlier from *The Body of Liberties of 1641*, regarding the "passing away of lands," was amended by the addition of the provision that "in choosing guardians, [the age shall be] fourteen years" [page 1]. By this provision, the court would choose guardians for children under fourteen years of age, but children between the ages of fourteen and twenty-one could make choice of whomever they wished as a guardian. Thus, in the case of an estate that remained open for several years, a child might first appear in court to have a guardian chosen for him or her, then make another appearance some years later to choose a guardian.

In the case of gathering evidence in court proceedings, the law stated that

> any one magistrate or commissioner authorized thereunto by the General Court may take testimony of any person of fourteen years of age or above [page 158].

Although not so stated in the statute, this may be the provision which permits persons aged fourteen and above to be witnesses to deeds and wills. Many researchers in the past have reached incorrect conclusions while under the misap-

prehension that one had to be twenty-one to witness legal documents.

This provision that testimony in a court case could be taken from persons age fourteen and above seems to have been ignored more frequently than some other laws regarding the age of discretion. With the age for engaging in land transactions, we presented an example in which a man was granted land a few months earlier than the law allowed. For court testimony, there are examples of children well under fourteen testifying.

On 7 December 1648, a coroner's inquest at Newbury, investigating the case of a child who died on the way to school, took a statement from "Benjamin Morse, a child of six years old" [ILR 1:53-54; GM 2:6:405]. On 2 July 1650, in a case of sexual assault, the court at Gorgeana [York] took the "relation of the child Henry Simpson about the age of 6 years" [MPCR 1:141]. In both these cases, the legal authorities may have been adhering to the principle of obtaining "best evidence," despite the youth of the witnesses.

We have barely scratched the surface of this topic, pointing out a few of the legal milestones in a person's life in early New England, and also noting cases where these milestones were occasionally ignored. In the absence of birth and baptismal records, evidence such as that considered here may be the best we have for a person's age.

Great Migration Newsletter

Vol. 19   April-June 2010   No. 2

BECOMING A FREEMAN

In this issue of the *Great Migration Newsletter* and in the previous issue we have analyzed the list of Massachusetts Bay freemen admitted on 18 and 19 May 1642, at the beginning of the 1642 Court of Elections. This study parallels and complements our early investigation of the list of freemen for 2 June 1641 [GMN 17:19-22, 27-30] and in a broader sense continues our attempt to determine when the Great Migration ended.

Our immediate concern has been to make an estimate of how many of those who were admitted free on 18 and 19 May 1642 might actually have arrived in 1641, and how many can be shown to have arrived earlier. Then, by comparing these results with our earlier study of the 1641 list, we will examine the differences between the two years. In the future we shall similarly analyze the lists for 1640 and 1643 to further extend our understanding.

The 18 and 19 May 1642 list of freemen contains 114 names, but not all of these are useful for our analysis. Two of the names in the list (Philip Taylor and the second of the two Richard Taylors) cannot be identified with any known immigrant to New England. As a result, our numerical analysis will be based on only 112 of these names.

Organized migration to Massachusetts Bay began in 1628 with the arrival of John Endecott and his party at Salem, with the result that by 1642 a number of sons of early immigrants had reached maturity and were now eligible for freemanship. In the 1642 list are fourteen of these men, arranged here in order of arrival of the parents: Elias Stileman (son of Elias Stileman [1629]), John Green (son of John Green [1632]), John Coggan (son of John Coggan [1633]), John Bulkeley (son of Peter Bulkeley [1635]), John Tompkins (son of Ralph Tompkins [1635]), John Cooper (stepson of Gregory Stone [1635]), Michael Metcalfe (son of Michael Metcalfe [1637]), Thomas Bateman (son of William Bateman [1638]), John Brock (son of Henry Brock [1638]), Benjamin Vermayes (son of Alice Vermayes [1638]), Daniel Briscoe (son of William Briscoe [1640]), James Fiske (son of Phineas Fiske [1640]), Thomas Putnam (son of John Putnam [1640]), and Thomas Wheeler (son of Thomas Wheeler [1640]).

With these exceptions, there remain 98 freemen who were themselves immigrant heads of family and whose dates are known or have been estimated. Our first step will be to enumerate how many we believe arrived in each year prior to 1642.

1621	1
1634	1
1635	7
1636	3
1637	7
1638	13
1639	21
1640	20
1641	25

This pattern is similar to that for the 1641 analysis, with the highest number being in the most recent year, and then diminishing as one goes back in time. As with the 1641 list, there is a slight anomaly in the 1636 number, again probably related to the nearly complete survival of ship passenger lists for 1635, thus pushing up the number for that year.

(continued on page 10)

EDITOR'S EFFUSIONS

As this issue of the *Newsletter* goes to press, we are approaching the halfway point in the preparation of the final installment in the second series of Great Migration volumes. In the past we have spoken and written on the subject of "Building a Sketch," but not on "Building a Book." How do we go about the business of creating a Great Migration volume?

Many years ago, in the early days of work on the second series, we created a master database for all those individuals believed to have arrived in New England in 1634 or 1635. At the beginning of each volume we do two things with this database. First, we take each name in this checklist and create a new word processing file, using a template which has each of the categories of the sketch format already entered. Into that template we enter the specific record or records that place that person or family in New England by 1634 or 1635. To this we add the data collected by Savage and Pope, since one of our main tasks is to confirm or contradict that information. In some cases, where only one or two records are found for that individual, the sketch may be completed at this stage.

Second, as we create these nascent sketches, we are also checking the soundness of the database itself. We may find in some cases that the person did not arrive in the appropriate time period, or that we need to combine data on two people of the same name into one sketch (or perhaps the opposite). At the beginning of this process, the database contained 211 names for the letters T through Y.

These first two stages are now complete, with an embryonic file begun for each sketch, and with the checklist carefully updated. There are now 201 names in the list, mostly for the letters T (60) and W (129). With the completion of a number of very brief and easy sketches, and also of several longer sketches to be published on the Great Migration website, about a quarter of the sketches are now done.

We move now to the second half of the work on the book, in which we tackle each of the remaining 150 or so sketches and bring them to completion. Some will take a few hours and some will take a few days, but in 2011 the final volume of this series will be ready for the presses.

Robert Charles Anderson, FASG   Editor
Jean Powers, Production Assistant

The Great Migration Newsletter is published quarterly by the Great Migration Study Project, a project of the New England Historic Genealogical Society, 101 Newbury Street, Boston MA 02116
www.NewEnglandAncestors.org
www.GreatMigration.org
GreatMigration@nehgs.org

Copyright © 2010
New England Historic Genealogical Society

(continued from page 9)

The one outlier, for the year 1621, deserves separate comment. This was William Hilton of Dover [GMB 2:951-57]. He had arrived at Plymouth in 1621 and after a few years removed to the Piscataqua, where he joined his brother Edward. Their settlement grew into the town of Dover, which for several years remained outside Massachusetts Bay jurisdiction. In 1641 Dover became a part of Massachusetts Bay and was then eligible to send a deputy to the General Court. The town chose William Hilton, but before he could take his place at court he needed to become a freeman, and so achieved that status at this late date.

Leaving aside William Hilton, we find that an immigrant arriving in New England in the mid-1630s might wait six or seven years before becoming a freeman, but not any longer. This result again meshes with what we saw in 1641. And, as with the 1641 list, the earliest of these, Theodore Atkinson, came as a servant.

Before moving to more detailed analysis of these numbers, a few points need to be made about the overall arrangement of the list. Compared to some other lists of freemen, the 1642 list was arranged in highly orderly fashion, with most of the freemen from one town being carefully grouped together. For Boston and to a lesser extent Cambridge, Dorchester and Charlestown, men from those towns appeared in two or more places in the list, but still in groups of two or more in most instances.

There are a few puzzling exceptions, such as Hugh Prichard, who for some reason appears embedded in a group of Hingham men, rather than with the others from Roxbury. Prichard had only recently moved from Cape Ann [Gloucester] to Roxbury, so it would not have been surprising to find him clustered with others from either town, but there is no evidence that he ever had any connection with Hingham, nor does there seem to have been time for him to have done so.

On a related point, the two men who could not be identified—Philip Taylor and the second Richard Taylor—attained that status in part because they appear in the seams of the list, at the end of the grouping from one town and at the beginning of those from another town.

And this leads to a further point, the unusual use of the word "quaere" [Latin for "query"] with respect to the two instances of the name John Tomkins. In that case there really were two men by that name in early New England, for whom there is evidence that would place them both in this list. But the assumption would be that the clerk entered this query because he was not certain of that fact, which leads to the question of why he did not also question the two appearances of the name Richard Taylor. Perhaps he knew two men with this name and was not hesitant in listing both. On the other hand, this may have been a clerical error, and perhaps the second Richard Taylor in this list did not exist.

(continued on page 16)

Focus on Immigration

(continued from previous issue)

[*In the Focus section of the last issue of the* Great Migration Newsletter *we began to identify those men who were admitted to Massachusetts Bay freemanship on 18 and 19 May 1642 [GMN 19:3-6], and we conclude that process here. Analysis of this information may be found in the lead article in this issue.*]

John Coggan Junior (Bo): On 8 May 1642, "John Cogan the son of Mr. John Cogan" was admitted to Boston church [BChR 36]. "Mr. John Cogan" had arrived in New England by 1633, settling first in Dorchester and then moving to Boston in 1634 [GMB 1:401-5]. "John Coggan Junior" was born about 1621, and so had just attained his majority when admitted as a freeman.

John Clough (Wa): On 10 May 1642, "John Clough" was granted a Farm of ninety-one acres at Watertown [WaBOP 13]. (Pope assigned this freemanship record to two men named John Clough, one of Watertown and one of Salisbury. The proximity to two other Watertown men argues in favor of the former assignment [GM 2:2:107-14].)

John Witherell (Wa): On 22 February 1639/40, "Goodman Witherill" was granted land at Sudbury [Sudbury TR]. Given the close connection between Watertown and Sudbury at this time, this is almost certainly the man who appeared at Watertown a few years later.

Samu[el] Thatcher (Wa): "Hannah Thatcher the daughter of Samuell and Hannah Thatcher [was] born the 9th day of the 8th month [October]" 1645 at Watertown [WaVR 1:12].

John Hill (Bo): On 25 July 1641, "John Hill a blacksmith" was admitted to Boston church [BChR 34].

Rich[a]rd Wody (Rx): "Richard Woddy" and "[blank] Woddy the wife of Richard Woddy" were admitted to Roxbury church in 1640 [RChR 85].

John Mathis (Rx): "John Mathews" and "[blank] Mathews the wife of [blank] Mathews" were admitted to Roxbury church in 1640 [RChR 84-85]. On 25 July 1641, "Gersham, son of John Mathew," was born at Roxbury.

Willi[am] Lewes (Rx): "William Lewis" and "[blank] Lewis the wife of William Lewis" were admitted to Roxbury church in 1640 or 1641 [RChR 85]. On 25 December 1640, "Lidea, daughter of William Lewis," was born at Roxbury.

Richard Taylor (Unknown): This is the second entry for a man of this name as a freeman on this date, the earlier one easily identified as a resident of Boston [GMN 19:6]. Since the present entry comes at the end of a sequence of Roxbury men and at the beginning of a sequence of Rowley men, we might expect that this Richard Taylor would be from one of those towns, but no record for this name has been found in either town, nor has any likely candidate been found in any other town.

Edward Carleton (Rw): On 28 October 1639, Edward, son of Edward and Ellen Carleton, was born at Rowley. In the Rowley land inventory of 1643, Edward Carleton held a houselot and other parcels of land.

Humphrey Reyn[e]r (Rw): Humphrey Reyner may have accompanied his brother Rev. John Reyner when the latter left England and settled at Plymouth in 1636 [NEHGR 109:5-11; GMN 18:21]. Humphrey Reyner may have been named ruling elder of Rowley church at its founding on 3 December 1639 [Rowley Fam 321]. In the Rowley land inventory of 1643 he held a houselot and other parcels of land.

Hugh Smith (Rw): On 17 March 1642, Mary, daughter of Hugh and Mary Smith, was born at Rowley. In the Rowley land inventory of 1643, Hugh Smith held a houselot and other parcels of land.

Hugh Chapline (Rw): On 26 August 1643, John, son of Hugh and Elizabeth Chaplin, was born at Rowley. In the Rowley land inventory of 1643 Hugh Chaplin held a houselot and other parcels of land.

Rich[a]rd Lowder (Ch): On 15 January 1641/2, "Richard Lowden" was admitted to Charlestown church [ChChR 10]. On 27 August 1638, "Rich[ar]d Lowden is admitted a townsman & granted a houseplot [at Charlestown] by Goodman Tomson" [ChTR 40].

John Burrage (Ch): On 10 April 1642, "John Burrage" was admitted to Charlestown church [ChChR 10]. On 11 September 1637, "John Burrage hath liberty to take Jno. Charles's houseplot by Goodman Blott's [in Charlestown]" [ChTR 31]. In the 1638 Charlestown Book of Possessions, "John Beridge" held six parcels, including "one dwelling house with a garden plot situate in the East Field" [ChBOP 13-14].

Solomon Phips (Ch): On 15 January 1641/2, "Sollomon Phips" was admitted to Charlestown church [ChChR 10]. He died at Charlestown on 25 July 1671, aged 52, and so was born about 1619 [Wyman 749, citing gravestone].

John Greene (Ch): On 17 April 1642, "John Green" was admitted to Charlestown church [ChChR 10]. John Green was born perhaps about 1620, son of JOHN GREEN {1632, Charlestown} [GMB 2:811-13].

Isaack Comins (Ip): On 22 February 1634/5, the fourth child of Isaac Cummings was baptized at Mistley, Essex [NEHGR 145:239-40]. On 25 July 1636, "Isaac Cummins" was granted thirty-five acres in the Great Dividend at Watertown [WaBOP 5]. By 9 April 1639, "Isaack Comings" owned land at Ipswich [ITR]. Inasmuch as he did not participate in the grants of land in Watertown in 1637, Isaac Cummings was probably already in Ipswich by 1637.

Allen Pearley (Ip): "Husbandman Allin Perley," aged 27, sailed for New England in 1635 on the *Planter* and settled at Ipswich [GM 2:5:438-41].

Thom[as] Thackster (Hi): Thomas Thaxter was granted land at Hingham in 1638 [Hingham Hist 2:229]. On 19 May 1641, "Samuell Thaxter," son of Thomas, was born at Hingham [NEHGR 121:13].

Willi[am] Ripley (Hi): In 1638 "William Riply and his wife and 2 sons and two daughters came from Old Hingham, and settled in New Hingham" [NEHGR 15:27]. He was granted land at Hingham in 1638 [Hingham Hist 2:131].

Mathewe Hawkes (Hi): In 1638 "Mathew Hawk and his wife, and his servant John Ferring, came from Cambridge, in Old England, and settled in New Hingham" [NEHGR 15:27]. In July 1639 "Elezebeth Hawkes," daughter of Mathew, was baptized at Hingham [NEHGR 121:11].

Hugh Prichard (Rx): "Mr. Hugh Prichard recommended from the church at Cape Ann" and "Mrs. Elnor Prichard the wife of Mr. Hugh Prichard" were admitted to Roxbury church in 1641 [RChR 85]. On 26 December 1641, "Abiel Prichard the son of Mr. Hugh Prichard" was baptized at Roxbury [RChR 114]. On 2 March 1640/1, "Mr. Heugh Prychard" was propounded for freemanship of Plymouth Colony (along with other members of the Blinman party) [PCR 2:8]. In 1641 Prichard followed Blinman and his group to Gloucester, and then soon moved on to Roxbury.

Thom[as] Lincolne (Hi): There were four adult men named Thomas Lincoln residing in Hingham by 1638, distinguished by their occupations of cooper, miller, husbandman and weaver [Hingham Hist 3:3-21]. Any one of these men might have been the freeman of 1642, as all were early members of Hingham church. In February 1637/8 Thomas Lincoln, miller, had sons Samuel and Thomas baptized at Hingham [NEHGR 121:10; Hingham Hist 3:20]. On 6 May 1638, Thomas Lincoln, son of Thomas Lincoln, cooper, was baptized at Hingham [NEHGR 121:10; Hingham Hist 3:3]. In March 1641, "Sussanna the wife of Thomas Lincoln weaver died," her death being entered in the church record [NEHGR 121:13; Hingham Hist 3:21]. On 8 October 1643, "Caleb Lincoln," son of Thomas Lincoln, husbandman, was baptized at Hingham [NEHGR 121:16; Hingham Hist 3:16]. (One other Thomas Lincoln of Hingham was made free, on [blank] March 1637/8 [MBCR 1:374]. At least three of the Thomas Lincolns were in Hingham early enough to have been this freeman: the cooper, the miller and the weaver. Thomas Lincoln, weaver, had arrived by 1633 [GMB 2:1187-88].)

John Stoder (Hi): John Stodder was granted Hingham land in 1638 [Hingham Hist 3:191]. On 14 June 1640, "Samuel Stodder," son of John, was baptized at Hingham [NEHGR 121:13]. On 20 May 1642, "John Stodder" was one of those planning to settle at Nantasket [Hull] [MBCR 2:5].

Willi[am] Robinson (Do): "William Robinson" was admitted to Dorchester church by early 1638 [DChR 3]. On 30 September 1639, "Thomas Hawkins of Dorchester in New England, shipwright," leased land in Dorchester to "William Robinson of the same, husbandman" [Lechford 210-14].

Robert Peirce (Do): On 19 June 1640, "Robert Peerce" was admitted to Dorchester church [DChR 5]. On [blank] January 1639/40, it is "ordered that Robert Pierce shall be a commoner" of Dorchester [DTR 40].

Thom[as] Davenport (Do): On 20 November 1640, "Thomas Davenport" was admitted to Dorchester church [DChR 5]. "Sarah the daughter of Thomas Davenport & Mary his wife was born 28 (10 [December]) 1643" at Dorchester [NEHGR 5:98].

Rich[a]rd Baker (Do): On 4 November 1639, "Richard Baker" was admitted to Dorchester church [DChR 4]. "Mary the daughter of Richard Baker & Faith his wife was born the 27 (2 [April]) 1643" at Dorchester [NEHGR 5:97].

Robert Pond (Do): No Robert Pond was admitted to Dorchester church in 1642 or earlier. There was a Robert Pond of Dorchester who died by 27 December 1637, when his inventory was taken [SPR NS 1:417]. "William Pond" and his wife "Goody Pond" were admitted to Dorchester church on 28 February 1641/2 [DChR 6], so this freemanship record may have been intended for William rather than Robert. Whether William was son of the Robert who died in 1637 is unknown, but some kinship relation is likely.

John Rigbey (Do): "John Rigbie" was admitted to Dorchester church by early 1638 [DChR 3]. On 18 March 1637/8, "John Rigby" was granted land at Dorchester [DTR 313]. On 3 March 1638/9, "Elizabeth Rigby" was baptized at Dorchester [DChR 151].

George Right (Br): On 29 January 1639/40, "George Wright hath a [Great Lot] granted to him [at the Mount] for eight heads, 32 acres" [BTR 1:45].

Thom[as] Blisse (Br): On 24 February 1639/40, Boston selectmen granted to "Thomas Blyss, of [Mount Wollaston], for 9 heads, 36 acres there" [BTR 1:50].

Benia[min] Albey (Br): On 24 February 1639/40, Boston selectmen granted to "Beniamyn Albye, of [Mount Wollaston], for 3 heads, 12 acres there" [BTR 1:49]. "Hanna the daughter of Benjamin Albie was born 16 (6 [August]) 1641" at Braintree [NEHGR 3:126].

Roger Bancroft (Ca): By 1639 "Roger Bankcrafte" had purchased a dwelling house at Cambridge from Nathaniel Sparrowhawk [CaTR 70].

Rich[a]rd Eckels (Ca): "Our brother Jackson's man Richard Eagle" made his conversion narrative in late 1639 or early 1640 [Shepard 114-16]. Having made this conversion narrative, he would soon have been admitted to Cambridge church.

John Cooper (Ca): John Cooper presumably came to New England in 1635 with stepfather GREGORY STONE {1635, Watertown} [GMB 2:6:546-52]. By 1637 Gregory Stone had moved to Cambridge. On 16 November 1643, "Annah the daughter of John Cooper & Anna his wife" was born at Cambridge [NEHGR 4:55].

John Tomkins, qu: (Co): "Ruth the daughter of John Tompkins was born 1 (4 [June]) 1640" at Concord [CoVR 2]. In 1644 he joined the migration from Concord to Fairfield [FOOF 1:612-13]. (The "qu." stands for "quaere," the Latin for "query," indicating that the clerk was questioning this entry, because there was another entry for the same name earlier in the list, John Tomkins of Salem [GMN 19:4-5].)

Willi[am] Dickson (Ca): In the Cambridge land inventory of 6 September 1642, "William Dixon" owned a dwelling house in town [CaBOP 114].

Moses Wheat (Co): "Samuel the son of Moses Wheat was born the 25 (8 [October]) 1640" at Concord [CoVR 3].

Rob[e]rt Edwards (Co): Robert Edwards sailed for New England in 1635 on the *Hopewell* [GM 2:2:411-12]. On 4 June 1639, "William Fuller, which kept the mill at Concord, was fined 3 pounds for gross abuse in overtolling; the town of Concord was discharged the lot to Robert Edwards, being but reserved for him" [MBCR 1:267]. "Sarah the daughter of Robert Edwards was born the 12 (7 [September]) 1640 & buried 26 (7) 1640" at Concord [CoVR 2].

Thomas Bateman (Co): Thomas Bateman was son of William Bateman of Fairfield [FOOF 1:38], who was almost certainly the man of that name who had a land grant at Charlestown in 1638 and was admitted to freemanship on 2 June 1641 [GMN 17:29; Wyman 67].

Willi[am] Aline (Co): A William Allen died at Concord in 1659, when his estate was administered [Rodgers 1:402-4]. Earlier records for a William Allen at Concord have not been found, and some documents in the probate file indicate that he may not have been in New England as early as 1642. The only other early William Allen not otherwise accounted for was of Salisbury, but previous researchers have not claimed this freemanship for him [Hoyt 31], and he would be out of place in this list. (William Allen of Salem was made free on 18 May 1631 [GMB 1:31-35].)

Thom[as] Wheller (Co): "Allice the daughter of Thomas Wheeler died 17 (1 [March]) 1640" [CoVR 3]. (There is extensive literature on the many confusing Thomas Wheelers at Concord and Fairfield. Donald Lines Jacobus thought that this Thomas Wheeler was son of another Thomas Wheeler who resided briefly in Concord and then moved on

to Fairfield, while this Thomas remained in Concord [FOOF 1:662-65].)

Willi[am] Hartwell (Co): "John the son of Will[ia]m Hartwell was born the 23 (12 [February]) 1640" at Concord [CoVR 2].

John Stevens (Ne): "John Stephens of Caversham, Oxon, 31," husbandman, sailed for New England in 1638 on the *Confidence* and settled at Newbury [Drake's Founders 59; NEHGR 85:399]. On 20 June 1639, "John, son of John Steevens, husbandman," was born at Newbury.

Willi[am] Stevens (Ne): "William Stephens of Caversham, Oxon, 21," husbandman, sailed for New England in 1638 on the *Confidence* and settled at Newbury [Drake's Founders 59; NEHGR 85:400].

Antho[ny] Somersbey (Ne): Based on a deposition given in 1652, Anthony Somerby was a passenger to New England on the *Jonathan* in 1639 [EQC 1:268; NEHGR 32:407].

Henry Somersbey (Ne): Henry Somerby may have come to New England with his brother Anthony in 1639. On 29 March 1642, "Henry Somersby" was defendant in two civil cases in Ipswich court [EQC 1:40, 41].

Willi[am] Berry (Ne): On 7 December 1642, "William Berry" was a freeholder at Newbury [Newbury Hist 292].

Samu[el] Guil (Ne): On 7 December 1642, "Samuel Gile" was a freeholder at Newbury [Newbury Hist 292]. Samuel Guile moved soon to Haverhill, where, on 1 September 1647, he married Judith Davis [Hoyt 189].

Abell Hews (Ne): On 7 December 1642, "Abel Huse" was a freeholder at Newbury [Newbury Hist 292].

John Swett (Ne): On 7 December 1642, "John Swett" was a freeholder at Newbury [Newbury Hist 292]. On 13 January 1651[/2], "old John Swett" died at Newbury.

Peter Woodward (De): On 7 January 1641/2, "Peter Woodward was received into the [Dedham] church" [DeChR 26]. On 28 September 1640, "license [was] granted to Peeter Woodward to purchase in our town & so become a townsman" [DTR 1:71].

John Brock (De): On 3 April 1640, "John Brock … was received [to Dedham church] giving good satisfaction" [DeChR 23]. John Brock was son of Henry Brock, who was, on 28 August 1638, "entertained to purchase Joseph Shawe his lot" at Dedham [DeTR 1:48].

Natha[niel] Whiteing (De): On 30 July 1641, "Nathaniell Whiting was admitted into the [Dedham] church" [DeChR 25]. On 2 January 1642/3, "Nathaniell Whiteinge" made his first appearance in Dedham town records when he attended a town meeting [DeTR 1:92]. On 4 November 1643, "Nathaniell Whiteing & Hanah Dwight" were married at Dedham [DeVR 126].

Micha[el] Metcalfe (De): On 6 March 1639/40, "Michaell the son of our brother Mettcalfe was received [to Dedham church] giving good satisfaction" [DeChR 23]. On 24 August 1639, "Michaell Mettcalfe the elder was received into the [Dedham] church with good satisfaction" [DeChR 21] and was admitted as a freeman on 13 May 1640 [MBCR 1:377]. The family had sailed to New England in 1637 [Hotten 289].

Rob[e]rt Page (Ha): In 1637 "Robertt Page of Ormsby in Norfolk, husbandman, aged 33," with his wife, three children and two servants, sailed for New England from Yarmouth [Hotten 291]. On 25 December 1637, Robert Page, with a household of six, was granted an acre of marsh at Salem [STR 1:103]. "Goodman Page" was included in the list of men who were in Hampton "the second summer" [1640] [GDMNH 55]. On 30 June 1640, the town of Hampton granted "Robert Page 10 acres for an houselot" [HampTR 1:43].

Franc[is] Pebody (Ha): Francis Peabody sailed for New England on 2 April 1635 on the *Planter* and settled first at Ipswich [GM 2:5:400-10]. "Francis Pebody" was included in the list of "the families in Hampton the first summer Mr. Batcheller came to Hampton," which was in 1639 [GDMNH 55]. On 30 August 1640, "Lydia the daughter of Francis Pebody & Lydia his wife" was baptized at Hampton [HampVR 1:3].

Isaack Perkins (Ha): "Isak Perkins" was included in the list of "the families in Hampton the first summer Mr. Batcheller came to Hampton," which was in 1639 [GDMNH 55]. On 8 December 1639, "Isaac the son of Isaac Perkins & Susana his wife" was baptized at Hampton [HampVR 1:3].

Thom[as] Worde (Ha): On 23 November 1638, the town of Dedham "granted unto Giles Fuller & Thomas Ward to have each of them 3 acres" [DeTR 1:50]. "Tho[mas] Ward" was included in the list of "Young men that had lots" at Hampton in 1639 [GDMNH 55]. On 30 June 1640, the town of Hampton granted "Thomas Ward 5 acres for an houselot" [HampTR 1:43].

Henry Ambros (Ha): "Goodman Ambros" was included in the list of men who were in Hampton "the second summer" [1640] [GDMNH 55]. On 30 October 1640, the town of Hampton granted a houselot to "Henry Ambrose" [HampTR 1:48]. On 25 July 1641, "Samuele, the son of Henry & [blank] Ambrose," was baptized at Hampton [HampVR 1:4].

Walter Ropper (Ha): "Goodman Rooper" was included in the list of men who were in Hampton "the second summer" [1640] [GDMNH 55]. On 22 August 1641, "Mary, the daughter of Walter & [blank] Roper," was baptized at Hampton [HampVR 1:4].

Henry Kibbey (Do): On 4 November 1639, "Henry Kebby" was admitted to Dorchester church [DChR 4]. On 22 October 1639, Nicholas Butler sold to "Henery Kibbie of Dorchester ... his house and about an acre of upland on the north side, and about an acre of upland and meadow on the south side" [DTR 39-40].

David Zullesh (Do): On 20 November 1640, "David Seleeke" was admitted to Dorchester church [DChR 5]. On 24 June 1639, William Hutchinson and Edward Hutchinson sold to "David Sellecke of Dorchester ..., soapboiler," land in Dorchester [Lechford 101-6]. On 1 October 1636, at St. Mary Magdalen, Taunton, Somerset, David Selleck married Susanna Kibby, daughter of Henry Kibby [TG 19:3-40].

[On 19 May 1642, five more men were admitted to freemanship, and should be considered part of the larger group admitted the previous day.]

John Sadler (Gl): On 2 March 1640/1, "John Sadler" was propounded for freemanship of Plymouth Colony (along with other members of the Blinman party) [PCR 2:8]. In 1641 Sadler followed Blinman to Gloucester.

Walter Tybbot (Gl): On 2 March 1640/1, "Walter Tibbott" was propounded for freemanship of Plymouth Colony (along with other members of the Blinman party) [PCR 2:8]. In 1641 Tibbott followed Blinman to Gloucester.

Obedi[ah] Brewen (Gl): On 2 March 1640/1, "Mr. Obadiah Brewen" was propounded for freemanship of Plymouth Colony (along with other members of the Blinman party) [PCR 2:8]. In 1641 Bruen followed Blinman to Gloucester.

Willi[am] Hilton (Dv): William Hilton came to Plymouth in 1621 on the *Fortune*. By 1628 he had moved to the Piscataqua where he joined his brother Edward and became one of the leaders of Dover [GMB 2:951-57].

Willi[am] Walderne (Dv): On 18 August 1640, "John Jorden, citizen & grocer of London," made a power of attorney to "Will[ia]m Waldern and Richard Waldern of Pascattaway in New England" [Lechford 290; GDMNH 712].

TRICKS OF THE TRADE

One of the purposes of the *Great Migration Newsletter* is to inform readers of the methodology employed in writing sketches. Not all of these techniques merit full article-length treatment. From time to time, as space allows, we will publish some of these procedures under the heading just above.

An example: In England at the time of the Great Migration, ecclesiastical law required that children were to be baptized within one week of birth. Thus, we can accept English baptismal dates as a reliable substitute for birth dates. (At the same time, attempts to relieve chronological difficulties in identification of English origins based on claims of baptism long after birth should be rejected.)

In early New England, on the other hand, there was no such requirement of baptism so soon after birth, so early New England baptismal dates may be far removed from birth dates.

RECENT LITERATURE

Marian S. Henry, "Hannah Partridge, Wife of Edward[2] Gove of Hampton, New Hampshire," *The New England Historical and Genealogical Register* 164 (2010):15-22. The author demonstrates that the wife of Edward Gove, son of John Gove of Charlestown and Hampton, was Hannah Partridge, daughter of WILLIAM PARTRIDGE {1638, Lynn}. She also shows that Hannah Titcomb, born 8 January 1641/2, daughter of WILLIAM TITCOMB {1640, Newbury}, who has in the past been suggested as the wife of Edward Gove, had died between 1647 and 1676, and includes genealogical summaries of the families of William Partridge and Edward Gove.

Eugene Cole Zubrinsky, "The Immigration and Marriage of William[1] Carpenter of Amesbury, Wiltshire, and Providence, Rhode Island," *The New England Historical and Genealogical Register* 164 (2010):36-40. Following up on his earlier work on this immigrant, Zubrinsky argues that William Carpenter of Providence was actually the "Thomas Carpenter, of Am[e]sbury, carpenter," who appears in the passenger list of the *James* of London, sailing from Southampton in April 1635, and that the given name in the passenger list is a clerical error. Through close examination of early Providence records, the author then proposes that William Carpenter, upon his arrival in New England, resided in some other town for two years, and then came to Providence in 1637, where he married Elizabeth Arnold, daughter of William Arnold.

Clifford L. Stott, "Humphrey Blake (1494?-1558) and His Descendants in New England and South Carolina: Blake, Richards, Selleck, Torrey, and Wolcott (*concluded*)," *The New England Historical and Genealogical Register* 164 (2010):63-74. Stott concludes his study of the Blake family with genealogical summaries of the families of William Torrey of Weymouth, James Torrey of Scituate, Philip Torrey of Roxbury, Joseph Torrey of Weymouth and David Selleck of Dorchester. The author appends to his article some thoughts on the ancestry of Humphrey Blake.

Gale Ion Harris, "Enigmas #26: Early Harrises of Wethersfield, Connecticut: Analysis of a Tradition," *The American Genealogist* 83 (2009):249-57. The author presents another installment in his ongoing survey of the early Harris families of New England, in which he shows that a John Harris who first appeared in Boston in the 1650s and a Thomas Harris who first appeared in Connecticut in the 1660s were brothers. He estimates that both men were born in the 1630s, and that they might be sons of an otherwise unrecorded and unidentified early Harris immigrant.

Eugene Cole Zubrinsky, "More About Mary[2] (Cole) (Almy) Pocock and John[2] Cole, Children of James[1] Cole of Plymouth," *The American Genealogist* 83 (2009):258. Zubrinsky supplements his earlier work on the family of JAMES COLE {1633, Plymouth} [GMB 1:420-24] by taking note of a deposition made by Mary (Cole) Almy, daughter of the immigrant, in which she gave her age, thus permitting a more accurate estimate of her date of birth. The author also comments on the estimated age of Mary's brother John.

Leslie Mahler, "The Roberts Family of Brenchley, Kent: Ancestral to Margaret (Sheafe) Kitchell of Guilford, Connecticut, and Newark, New Jersey; Elizabeth Sheafe, Wife of Moses[1] Payne of Braintree, Massachusetts; and Samuel[1] Greenhill of Cambridge, Massachusetts, and Hartford, Connecticut," *The American Genealogist* 83 (2009):267-77. Mahler presents sketches for Thomas Roberts, his son George Roberts, and George's son John Roberts, all of Brenchley, Kent, in the fifteenth and sixteenth centuries. Anne Roberts, daughter of George, was ancestral to the immigrants Henry Whitfield of Guilford, Connecticut, and Edmond Hawes of Yarmouth, Massachusetts. John Roberts had two daughters, Margery and Anne, who gave birth to New England immigrants. Margery married Richard Sheafe, and they were the parents of Elizabeth Sheafe, wife of Moses Payne of Braintree, and of Margaret Sheafe, wife of Robert Kitchell of Guilford. Anne married John Greenhill, and they were the parents of Samuel Greenhill of Cambridge and Hartford.

Kent Randell, "William[1] Burnell of Boston: Eight Generations of Male-Line Descendants in Boston and Nantucket, Massachusetts (*concluded*)," *The American Genealogist* 83 (2009):302-16. Randell concludes his two-part study of eight generations of the agnate descendants of WILLIAM BURNELL {1640, Boston} by first completing the genealogical summary of the family of Samuel Burnell, son of the immigrant. In each succeeding generation, down to the eighth, only one or two sons married and had surviving offspring, and Randell presents a genealogical summary for each of these agnate descendants.

C.S. Manegold, *Ten Hills Farm: The Forgotten History of Slavery in the North* (Princeton: Princeton University Press, 2010). Manegold follows the history of Ten Hills Farm, a six-hundred acre tract of land, now in the city of Medford, Massachusetts, from its acquisition by Governor John Winthrop soon after his arrival in New England in 1630, through three generations of his family, and then into the hands of first the Usher family and then the Royalls. She then intertwines with this the history of slavery in colonial New England, pointing out that Winthrop himself almost certainly acquired a few Pequot slaves in 1637 or soon after. The enslavement of Africans grew slowly in seventeenth-century New England, but increased in the latter part of that century and into the next. Both the Ushers and the Royalls were deeply involved in the slave trade. The Royalls, both Isaac the father and Isaac the son, operated a large plantation on Antigua, which was heavily dependent on African slave labor, and many of these slaves were brought to Ten Hills Farm in the middle of the eighteenth century. The world of the Royalls came crashing down in 1775 when the younger Isaac sided with the Loyalists.

(continued from page 10)

Almost half of the immigrant heads of family in the 1642 list (45 of 98) fall into the years 1640 and 1641. In our attempts to nail down the end of the Great Migration, we have been torn between identifying 1639 or 1640 as the last summer of heavy migration. If the last year of the Great Migration were 1639, then we would have to explain the seemingly large numbers for both 1640 and 1641. If, however, the last year were 1640, we would have to explain only the large number for 1641.

First, as with 1640, we have an almost complete absence of passenger lists for 1641, and receive no assistance from that category of records.

Second, for those we have tentatively assigned as 1641 arrivals, there is no direct evidence that any of them did arrive in that year, so many of them may well have arrived earlier, perhaps as servants, perhaps as single young men, and thus escaped being entered into the surviving records for a few years.

For 1640 we can identify a coherent group of four men who did come to New England in that year, the four members of Rev. Richard Blinman's party, who appeared at Plymouth on 2 March 1640/1 and soon moved on to Gloucester. This counts as evidence for the continuation of the Great Migration into 1640, inasmuch as such ministerial parties were highly characteristic of the Great Migration from 1634 on, when such groups of families clustered around a charismatic preacher constituted the predominant element in the migratory process.

Third, again as in the 1641 analysis, a number of those assigned to the 1640 and 1641 arrival groups were from towns with few early surviving records, in this case Concord and Newbury.

Having now completed the examination of freemen's lists from two consecutive years, 1641 and 1642, what have we learned about the end date of the Great Migration? The evidence at hand is mixed.

Based on this small sample, we observe first that the overall numbers are going down, with 126 names in the 1641 list and 114 names in the 1642 list. But the difference is even greater than this, for the 1641 list included seven second-generation men, while the 1642 list included fourteen. The number of immigrant heads of households in the two years was 116 in 1640 and 98 in 1641, a decrease of about fifteen percent.

On the other hand, the arrival in 1640 of the ministerial group headed by Richard Blinman indicates that the Great Migration had not come to a complete halt in 1639. Despite all our work to date, further research will be needed to answer this question.

Great Migration Newsletter

| Vol. 19 | July-September 2010 | No. 3 |

NEW IDEAS ON THE PILGRIMS

In a massive volume published last year, Jeremy Bangs brought together in one place his decades of research and thinking on the *Mayflower* Pilgrims, and especially on their years in Leiden: *Strangers and Pilgrims, Travellers and Sojourners: Leiden and the Foundations of Plymouth Plantation* (Plymouth, Massachusetts: General Society of Mayflower Descendants, 2009). Many of the chapters in this volume could stand alone as definitive studies of one or another of the aspects of Pilgrim history, and as such will be exceedingly helpful to anyone interested in Plymouth Colony and its founders.

The historiographical Preface discusses most of the modern treatments of Plymouth Colony, and in the process Bangs points out shortcomings in some of these studies, and in doing so sets the stage for many later moments in the book when he will take his own position on some of these issues, frequently in opposition to earlier authors. At the opposite end of the volume is a Bibliography of more than a hundred pages, which both demonstrates the breadth of the author's research and provides ready access for the reader to the vast literature on this subject.

In the first chapter, Bangs looks at the Pilgrims before they departed for Leiden, when they were living at Scrooby, Nottinghamshire, and vicinity. Important to his approach here is the detailed use of the records of the local ecclesiastical courts. He finds that in the last decade of the sixteenth century and the first decade of the seventeenth, many residents of Scrooby and other parishes close by were presented at the ecclesiastical courts for infractions that were associated with Puritan leanings, such as attending services in parishes other than their own, in order to hear the sermons of a favored minister.

By examining these records, Bangs demonstrates that the persecution of Puritans by the Church of England reached the lowest level of each congregation, and was not limited to the most outspoken of the ministers. In this way, he strengthens the position of those who have emphasized the importance of religious motivations in the removal to Leiden (and in the Great Migration as a whole), in opposition to those who have held, for example, that economic motiva-

tions were more important than religious in driving these migrations. (We have attempted to use this same category of records in our Great Migration sketches as well. See, for example, SIMON HUNTINGTON {1633, Roxbury} [GMB 2:1045].)

The next twelve chapters examine the lives of the Pilgrims at Leiden from many perspectives, including social, economic, military and religious. In these chapters we see the value of the author's deep knowledge of religious history and of art and architectural history for this time and place.

We learn, for example, of the finely divided varieties of the Reformed religion being discussed in the opening decades of the seventeenth century. Of especial value are the lengthy presentations of the positions of Jacobus Arminius and his disciples, known after his death as the Remonstrants. There were many public disputations between adherents of the Arminian position and their principal opponents, those who held to a strictly Calvinist predestinarian credo. Among the latter was Reverend John Robinson, the minister of the Pilgrim church.

In another chapter and an appendix, and in the absence of surviving records from the Robinson church, Bangs attempts to extract from a wide range of Leiden municipal documents as full as possible a list of members of that church, whether or not they eventually made the voyage from Leiden to New Plymouth.

(continued on page 18)

EDITOR'S EFFUSIONS

As we noted in the last issue of this *Newsletter*, the completion of the current Great Migration volume, finishing all sketches for the years 1634 and 1635, will also mean the completion of about one-half of the sketches to be compiled for the entire Great Migration Study Project. Even as we finish the current volume, we begin to look ahead to the next phase of our work.

Our first step in moving to the next segment of the project will be to compile, as accurately, as possible a checklist of the immigrants who arrived in New England in the years immediately after 1635. This is done by exhaustively mining all records created during the years to be covered in the next series of volumes, and also by combing the secondary sources for claims of arrivals in 1636 and thereafter.

Although nothing will change in the methodology that we have had in place for two decades now, there is one difference in the records that will have an effect on the way we work. With the survival of the London Port Book for 1635, and several other passengers lists for a number of the outports in both 1634 and 1635, the percentage of immigrants who are represented in the passenger lists for those years has been far higher than in any other time during the Great Migration era.

Because of this circumstance, a substantial portion of our research and writing time has been devoted to determining whether a given passenger is the same as a settler who appears in the New England records a year or two after the passenger list, or perhaps five or ten years after that. In many instances, the results have been inconclusive. For example, in the volume currently in the works, a George Taylor sailed on the *Truelove* in 1635. There was a man of that name in Saco by 1636 and another of the same name in Lynn by 1638. Was one of these two men the 1635 passenger, or neither?

In 1636 and the years immediately following, there are very few surviving passenger lists, so we will not be confronting these same problems. There will be far fewer sketches consisting only of the line "No records for this passenger have been found in New England." At the same time, there may be less certainty as to when a given immigrant arrived.

Robert Charles Anderson, FASG   Editor
Jean Powers, Production Assistant

The Great Migration Newsletter is published quarterly by the Great Migration Study Project, a project of the New England Historic Genealogical Society, 101 Newbury Street, Boston MA 02116
www.NewEnglandAncestors.org
www.GreatMigration.org
GreatMigration@nehgs.org

(continued from page 17)

With his discussions of the theology and the membership of the Robinson church as a foundation, the author then proceeds to examine the way in which Myles Standish was integrated into this congregation, and so eventually became one of the leaders of the settlement in the New World.

Standish was not one of those who had been recruited in Scrooby and vicinity and made the voyage from there to Leiden. Bangs finds evidence that he had come to the Low Countries several years before the arrival of the Scrooby pilgrims, as a soldier in the English forces that were fighting in the Protestant cause on the Continent. He then shows how the military experiences of Standish allowed him to accumulate knowledge of Dutch techniques in fortification, which translated directly into the design and construction of the earliest defensive works at New Plymouth, features of which are now portrayed in the living museum of Plimoth Plantation.

In the tenth chapter, Bangs looks closely at family life among the Pilgrims of Leiden. Here he takes issue with a number of modern historians who identified some features of family life as specifically Puritan, whereas Bangs argues that they were representative of a wider range of European practice of the time. In the same chapter, the author also disagrees with psychohistorians, such as Erik Erikson and John Putnam Demos, in their attempts to impose Freudian categories of analysis on their descriptions of the rearing of children in Pilgrim families.

In the final two chapters, Bangs looks into the processes of decision and planning that went into the move from Leiden to New Plymouth, and then examines the first years in the New World and how the development of the new colony was affected by the experiences of the Pilgrims at Leiden. He devotes substantial space to a discussion of the "Mayflower Compact" and its importance in American constitutional development.

Throughout the volume, but most importantly in these closing chapters, Bangs argues against the old paradigm of the division between Saints and Strangers, a concept most closely associated with the work of George Willison, but assumed by many more recent writers. Bangs notes that the cumulative work of the last few decades has demonstrated that far more of the *Mayflower* passengers, and of those who came to New Plymouth in the early 1620s, were associated with the Leiden church than had previously been thought. He sees the balance between Saints and Strangers as tilted far more in favor of the former than has been thought by many other historians.

These few paragraphs only scratch the surface in relating how Bangs has digested and reimagined every aspect of the Pilgrim experience in the first decades of the seventeenth century. Anyone with an interest in Plymouth Colony (and with the Great Migration in general) will benefit immensely from an immersion in the evidence and arguments set forth here by Jeremy Bangs.

Focus on the James *of London, 1635*

INTRODUCTION

When we complete the Second Series of Great Migration volumes, about a year from now, we will be in a position to summarize the data we have compiled for the first fifteen years of the Great Migration, from 1620 to 1635. As a first small step in that direction, we present here an analysis of what we have learned about the passengers of a single vessel, the *James* of London, which in April of 1635 took on passengers at the port of Southampton before sailing for New England [Drake's Founders 55-57].

In his ongoing study of William Carpenter, early immigrant to Providence, Eugene Cole Zubrinsky examined this passenger list closely and we are thankful to him for providing a clear photographic copy of the original of the list, which is the basis for the reading of the entries given below. (Zubrinsky noted two significant misreadings made by Samuel Gardner Drake more than a century ago: the date of the gathering of the ship's passengers was 6 April and not 5 April; and the grouping of nine passengers headed by Edmund Batter were "late of New Saru[m] [Salisbury]" and not "late of New England" [NEHGR 164:36-40].)

In the upper left corner of the document is the single word "South[amp]ton," followed by this heading:

> A list of the names of such passengers as shipped themselves at the town of Hampton in the James of London of iiiC [300] tons William Coop[er] Master versus New=England in & about the vj[th] of Aprill 1635.

This heading is followed by the list of passengers in two columns. At the end of the second column is this summation:

> The total number of these men, youths & boys are liii [53] persons—besides the wives & children of diverse of these.

This closing statement points up a difference between this passenger list and those created by the port of London. In 1635 the London Port Book lists the name of every passenger, regardless of gender and age, so we have a direct count of the number of passengers who sailed on each vessel departing from London [Hotten 35-144]. In the present list, from the same year, we have only the names of the "men, youths & boys."

On 3 June 1635, Governor John Winthrop reported that

> Here arrived also ... the *James*, a ship of three hundred tons, with cattle and passengers, which came all safe from Southampton within the same time [five weeks, three days]. Mr. Graves was master, who had come every year for these seven years [WJ 1:192; see also NEHGR 164:36-37].

If the stated time of passage was correct, the *James* departed Southampton on or about 26 April, more than three weeks after the date on the passenger list itself.

We will begin by reproducing each of the fifty-three names in the order they appear on the list, with a brief accounting of what we know about the migration and family of each one. (The number in parentheses at the end of each entry represents our best assessment of the number of family members who sailed for New England in 1635.) Finally, we will assess what we have learned in aggregate about the size of each of the families, the kinship connections among them, and the patterns of their origins in England and their settlement in New England.

THE PASSENGERS

Augustine Clem[en]t sometime of Reading painter (3): Augustine Clement was born by about 1603 and married Elizabeth, whose surname was not given in the parish register, at Wokingham, Berkshire, on 3 July 1628. Their daughter Elizabeth was baptized at St. Lawrence, Reading, Berkshire, on 2 March 1633/4. Augustine's wife was pregnant at the time they sailed, as their son Samuel was born at Dorchester on 29 September 1635 [GM 2:2:101-6].

Thomas Whealer his servant (1): There were several early New England settlers of this name, but none has been connected with this passenger.

Thomas Browne of Malford weav[e]r (3): Thomas Browne was born about 1606 and married at Christian Malford, Wiltshire, on 20 August 1632, Mary Healy. The first child of this couple was baptized at Christian Malford on 1 January 1632/3, and the family settled at Newbury upon arrival in New England [GM 2:1:435-38].

Hercules Woodman of the same mercer (1): Hercules (or Archelaus) Woodman was baptized at Corsham, Wiltshire, on 23 January 1613/4 [NEHGR 97:284]. He settled at Newbury, where he had joined the church in time to be admitted a freeman on 17 May 1637 [MBCR 1:373] and married for the first time by about 1638 [NEHGR 97:286-87].

The next seven names are bracketed and described as "of Marlbrough laborers or husbandmen":

John & Stephen Ev[er]ed al[ias] Webb (2): John Evered *alias* Webb was born about 1613 and was apparently single at the time he came to New England, as his first known marriage took place at Boston in the summer of 1639 [GM 2:2:459-68]. No records have been found in New England for Stephen Evered *alias* Webb, who was almost certainly closely related to John, perhaps a brother [GM 2:2:469].

Gyles Butler (1): There is no evidence that this man arrived in New England, nor has any attempt been made to find records for him in Marlborough, Wiltshire.

George Coussens (1): There is no evidence that this man arrived in New England, nor has any attempt been made to find records for him in Marlborough, Wiltshire.

Thomas Colman (5): Thomas Coleman was born about 1602 and married at Wootton Rivers, Wiltshire, on 24 November 1623, as his first of three wives, Susan Raulines, who died at Newbury on 17 November 1650. This couple had daughter Dorothy baptized at St Mary, Marlborough, on 19 December 1624 and buried at St. Peter & St. Paul, Marlborough, on 17 May 1625. Their second child, Dorcas, was baptized at the latter church on 23 July 1626 and came with her parents to New England, along with two other children who were probably born in England, but whose baptisms have not been found [GM 2:2:157-62].

Thomas Goddard (1): There is no evidence that this man arrived in New England, nor has any attempt been made to find records for him in Marlborough, Wiltshire.

John Pithouse (1): John Pithouse (or Pittice) settled at Ipswich, but records for him are scarce. He did marry, apparently in New England, and had five daughters, not all of whom have been identified [GM 2:5:471-72].

The next two names are bracketed and described as "of Marlborough shoomakers":

Anthoney Morse (5): Anthony was born about 1607 and married Ann Cox at St. Mary, Marlborough, Wiltshire, on 2 May 1629. This couple had three children baptized at Marlborough, in 1629, 1632 and 1634. Upon arrival, this family of five settled at Newbury [GM 2:5:159-67].

Will[ia]m Morse (1): William Morse, brother of Anthony, was baptized at St. Peter and St. Paul, Marlborough, Wiltshire, on 17 May 1614. He settled at Newbury and married there about 1640 [GM 2:5:178-80].

The next five names are bracketed and described as "late of Marlbrough":

John Hide tailor (1): There is no evidence that this man arrived in New England, nor has any attempt been made to find records for him in Marlborough, Wiltshire.

John Parker carpenter (6): John Parker was baptized at St. Mary, Marlborough, on 21 February 1603/4 and married there for the first time on 12 August 1627. This couple had a daughter baptized on 13 July 1628, and the mother must have died soon after, although no record has been found of her burial. John Parker married secondly, again at St. Mary, Marlborough, on 29 September 1628, Jane Kember, with whom he had four additional children before departing for New England. Of these five children born in England to his two wives, four survived to make the voyage to New England. The family settled at Boston [GM 2:5:364-67].

Richard Walker shoemaker (1): There is no evidence that this man arrived in New England, nor has any attempt been made to find records for him in Marlborough, Wiltshire. (Two men by this name appeared briefly, one in Boston and one in Salem, in 1636 and a few years thereafter, but nothing connects either one with this passenger.)

Maudit Ingles fuller (1): "Mawdith the son of Robert Ingles" was baptized on 16 November 1608 at St. Mary, Marlborough, Wiltshire. He settled in Boston upon his arrival and married about 1638 [GM 2:4:2-4].

Thomas Davyes sawyer (4): Thomas Davis was born about 1603 and married at Chipping Sodbury, Gloucestershire, on 14 November 1622 Christian Bellsire. They had three known children before 1635, of whom two certainly came to New England with their parents. The family settled at Newbury [GM 2:2:310-16].

Thomas Carpenter of Amsbury carpenter (1): Eugene Cole Zubrinsky has recently argued convincingly that a scribal error was made in this entry and that this actually represents William Carpenter who eventually settled at Providence [NEHGR 159:64-68, 164:36-40 (correcting GM 2:2:10)]. William Carpenter was born perhaps about 1610, probably in Amesbury, Wiltshire. He had settled in Providence by about 1637, and probably about the same time married Elizabeth, daughter of WILLIAM ARNOLD {1635, Hingham} [GM 2:1:84-91; NEHGR 164:38-40]. (In an article to be published later this year, Zubrinsky proposes that Carpenter resided at Salem for about two years, from his arrival in New England to his removal to Providence [NEHGR forthcoming].)

The next two names are bracketed and described as "late of London":

Will[ia]m Paddey skinner (1): William Paddy was born about 1600 (according to his tombstone, which stated that he was "aged 58 years" at his death on 24 August 1658 [BVR 66; HAHAC 1:174]). He was residing at Plymouth by 14 March 1635/6 and he married there (or at Sandwich) on 24 November 1639 Alice Freeman [PCR 1:40, 134; GM 2:5:327-36].

Edmund Hawes cutler (1): Edmund Hawes was baptized at Solihull, Warwickshire, on 15 October 1612. He was apprenticed to the Company of Cutlers in London in 1626 and was made free of that company on 9 December 1634 [GM 2:3:247-50]. He settled at Duxbury where he soon married a woman whose name is unknown.

The next nine names are bracketed and described as "late of New Saru[m] [Salisbury, Wiltshire]"

Edmund Batter malter (3): Edmund Batter was born about 1609 and married about 1630 Sarah Verin, daughter of Philip Verin (who would also sail on the *James*). This couple had a son named Edmund, born soon after their marriage, who came to New England with his parents, the family settling at Salem [GM 2:1:204-13].

John Smale his servant (1): On 16 March 1684/5, John Small deposed that he was "aged about sixty-eight years" [EQC 9:439], implying that he was born about 1616, and so was about nineteen years old at the time of his migration. The first record for John Small in New England was on 12 July 1642, when he was sued in Salem court [EQC 1:42], but he had presumably lived in that town since 1635, residing in the household of his master, Edmund Batter. John Small married by about 1639 Ann, whose surname has not been discovered [GM 2:6:345-47].

Michael Shafflin tailor (3): Michael Shaflin was born about 1605 and married at St. Edmund, Salisbury, on 22 April 1628 Elizabeth [Bancks?] [GM 2:6:250-55]. Their daughter Katharine was baptized at St. Thomas, Salisbury, on 15 March 1628/9. Their only other known child was perhaps born about 1635, so may have been born in old or New England. The family resided briefly at Charlestown, but had moved to Salem by 1636.

Josuah Verren roper (1): Joshua Veren, son of Philip Veren, who also sailed on the *James*, was born about 1612, settled in Salem upon his arrival in New England, and married about 1637 [NEHGR 131:103-4].

Thomas Antram weaver (2): This passenger was probably the Thomas Antrum baptized at St. Edmund, Salisbury, Wiltshire, on 31 December 1601, and he was certainly the man of that name who married in the same parish on 24 May 1630 Jane Batter, sister of Edmund Batter, who also sailed on the *James*. The couple's first known child, for whom there is no further record, was baptized at St. Edmund on 6 April 1634. Another four children were baptized at Salem between 1638 and 1646 [GM 2:1:69-71].

Thomas Browne his servant (1): There is no evidence that this man arrived in New England, nor has any attempt been made to find records for him in Salisbury, Wiltshire [GM 2:1:438-39].

George Smythe tailor (3): Based on his estimated date of marriage, George Smith was born about 1602. He had one known child, a son John born about 1627. Upon arrival in New England, the family settled at Salem [Sarah Johnson Anc 47; GM 2:6:359-60].

Phillip Verren roper (5): Philip Veren was born about 1581 and married by 1606 Dorcas, whose surname has not been discovered [NEHGR 131:100-12]. This couple had at least nine children born in old England, eight of whom were baptized at St. Edmund, Salisbury, or at St. Thomas, Salisbury. The two eldest children married in old England prior to 1635 and may never have come to New England. The third child, daughter Sarah, married Edmund Batter, who was also on the *James*. Son Joshua, born perhaps in 1612, sailed on the *James* and had his own entry, as seen above. One child was buried in England soon after birth and another has not been found in any record after baptism. The three remaining children (Philip, Hilliard and Nathaniel) survived to come to New England and presumably accompanied their parents, who settled at Salem.

John Greene surgeon (8): John Greene was born about 1594 and married on 4 November 1619 at St. Thomas, Salisbury, Joane Tatarsole. This couple had seven children baptized in the same parish from 1620 to 1633, six of whom survived to come to New England [GM 2:3:141-48]. The family resided first at Boston, but were in Providence by 1636, with a brief stay in Salem in between. (In an article to be published later this year, Zubrinsky shows that Greene resided at Salem before his arrival in Providence [NEHGR forthcoming].)

Zacheus Courtis of Downton laborer (1): On 20 March 1671/2, Zaccheus Curtis deposed that he was "aged about fifty-three years" [EQC 5:28], meaning that he was born about 1619, and so was about sixteen when he sailed for New England in 1635. He settled at Salem, where he first appeared in the records in late 1643 [EQC 1:56] and where his first child was born about 1646 [GM 2:2:261-64].

Henry Rose of Platford laborer (1): There is no evidence that this man arrived in New England, nor has any attempt been made to find records for him in Plaitford, Wiltshire [GM 2:6:100].

Nicholas Batt of the Devy[z]es linen weaver (3): Nicholas Batt was born about 1608 and married by about 1633 Lucy, whose surname has not been determined. They had three children, the eldest of whom, Ann, was born about 1633, and therefore born in England. The family settled in Newbury [GM 2:1:200-4].

Thomas Scoates of Saru[m] laborer (1): There is no evidence that this man arrived in New England, nor has any attempt been made to find records for him in Salisbury, Wiltshire [GM 2:6:201].

The next two names are bracketed and described as "of Langford laborers":

John Pike (7): John Pike was born about 1587 and married at Whiteparish, Wiltshire, on 17 January 1612/3 Dorothy Day. The first child of this couple was a son John, baptized at Whiteparish on 8 November 1613. He was followed by three more children born in old England, whose place of baptism has not been discovered. Two more children were baptized at Landford, Wiltshire, in 1623 and 1628. Five of these six children are found in New England records. Upon arrival John Pike resided briefly at Ipswich but soon moved to Newbury [GM 2:5:463-66].

John Musselwhite (1): John Musselwhite settled at Newbury and died there in early 1670, apparently never married [GM 2:5:201-3]. No records have been found for him in old England. Under these circumstances, there is no basis for estimating his age. His origin in Landford, Wiltshire, as stated in the passenger list, is supported by his interactions in New England with John Pike [MBCR 1:153; EQC 1:125]. In his will of 30 August 1669, Musselwhite included a bequest to "John Muslwhit of Baverstoc in Wiltsheer in old England the grandson of David Muslwhit my brother" [EPR 2:185-86], suggesting that this immigrant was not a young man at the time of his migration, and may have been a contemporary of John Pike, although no genealogical connection has been found between the two men.

Sampson Salter of Caversham fisherman (1): The first record for Sampson Salter in New England was on 20 May 1638, when he was admitted a townsman at Newport, Rhode Island [RICR 1:92]. There is no record that he married, and no solid evidence for estimating his age [GM 2:6:148-50].

Henry Kinge of Brenchley laborer (1): There is no evidence that this man arrived in New England [GM 2:4:167].

William Andrewes of Hampsworth carpenter (1): There is no evidence that this man arrived in New England. "Hampsworth" may be an alternate spelling for Hamptworth, a locality in the parish of Landford, Wiltshire.

The next two names are bracketed and described as "of Romsey tailors":

John Knight (4): John Knight was baptized at Romsey, Hampshire, on 30 January 1594/5, son of William Knight [Phoebe Tilton Anc 235]. He married there on 29 March 1624 Elizabeth Vincent. They had five children baptized at Romsey, two of whom sailed with the family to New England, where they settled at Newbury [GM 2:4:208-12].

Richard Knight (3): Richard Knight was baptized at Romsey, Hampshire, on 14 January 1602/3, son of William Knight [Phoebe Tilton Anc 235-37]. He married by 1626 Agnes, whose surname has not been discovered. They had five children baptized at Romsey, only one of whom survived to make the passage to New England. Like his brother John, Richard Knight settled at Newbury [GM 2:4:212-14].

Thomas Smith of the same weaver (1): The eldest known child of Thomas Smith was born about 1636, so his marriage could have taken place just before departure from old England or just after arrival in New England [GM 2:6:402-5]. He settled in Newbury.

Nicholas Holt thereof tanner (2): On 11 April 1671, Nicholas Holt deposed that he was "aged about sixty-three years" [EQC 4:370], meaning that he was born about 1608, and so was about twenty-seven years old when he sailed for New England. His first known child was born at Newbury on 30 March 1636, so there was just barely time for him to have married in New England within a few days after his arrival. More likely, he married in old England not long before his migration.

Robert Field of Yealing laborer (1): This passenger may be the Robert Field who appeared at Newport, Rhode Island, in 1638, along with a number of other residents of Newbury (but not including any other passengers on the *James*) [RICR 1:59; GM 2:2:522].

Anthoney Thetcher of Saru[m] tailor (6): According to his own narrative, Anthony Thatcher first settled at New-

bury, but within a few weeks chose to accompany his cousin Joseph Avery to reside in Marblehead. In the passage from Newbury to Marblehead, their vessel was shipwrecked on rocks near Cape Ann, and all four of Thatcher's children drowned, along with most of the other passengers on the vessel [Young's First Planters 485-95]. Thatcher and his wife survived, and they eventually settled at Yarmouth, where they began a new family.

Peter Higdon his servant (1): If Peter Higdon did arrive in New England, he presumably accompanied his master on the disastrous coastal voyage of 11 August 1635, which ended in a shipwreck off Cape Ann, and so he would probably have drowned on that day [Young's First Planters 489-90; GM 2:3:317].

The next two names are bracketed and described as "youths of Hampton of about 17 years old":

James Browne (1): There is no evidence that this man arrived in New England, nor has any attempt been made to find records for him in Southampton [GM 2:1:420].

Laurence Seag[e]r (1): There is no evidence that this man arrived in New England, nor has any attempt been made to find records for him in Southampton [GM 2:6:226].

The next two names are bracketed and described as "of Sarum tailors":

Henry Lev[er]age (1): There is no evidence that this man arrived in New England, nor has any attempt been made to find records for him in Salisbury, Wiltshire [GM 2:4:278].

William Parson (1): There is no evidence that this passenger arrived in New England, nor has any effort been made to find records for him in Salisbury, Wiltshire [GM 2:5:372].

The next three names are bracketed and described as "of Romsey carpenters:"

John Emery (6): John Emery was baptized at Romsey, Hampshire, on 29 March 1599, son of John Emery [NEHGR 89:376]. He married first at Whiteparish, Wiltshire, on 26 June 1620 Alice Grantham. Their first child, Alice, was born about 1622 and the next three children were baptized at Romsey in 1624, 1629 and 1633 [GM 2:2:446-52]. The family settled first at Newbury.

Anthoney Emery (4): Anthony Emery was baptized at Romsey, Hampshire, on 29 August 1601, son of John Emery [NEHGR 89:376; Phoebe Tilton Anc 185]. He married by 1631 Frances, whose surname is unknown; they had a son James baptized at Romsey on 18 September 1631 and a daughter Rebecca born about 1633 [GM 2:2:441-46]. The family settled first at Newbury.

Will[ia]m Kemp servant (1): There is no evidence that this man arrived in New England, nor has any attempt been made to find him in Romsey, Hampshire [GM 2:4:134-35]

RECENT LITERATURE

Alvy Ray Smith, "The Probable Genetic Signature of Thomas[1] Riggs, Immigrant to Gloucester, Massachusetts, by 1658," *The New England Historical and Genealogical Register* 164 (2010):85-94.

Alvy Ray Smith, "The Probable Genetic Signature of Edward[1] Riggs, Immigrant to Roxbury, Massachusetts, in 1633," *The New England Historical and Genealogical Register* 164 (2010):95-103. In these two articles Smith rigorously combines historical and genetic genealogy for two closely related early immigrants to New England. Having obtained Y-chromosome DNA sequences from a number of male-line descendants of EDWARD RIGGS {1633, Roxbury} [GMB 3:1583-85] and of Thomas Riggs, who migrated to Gloucester, Massachusetts, by 1658, and having in an earlier article argued that these two immigrants share a close, common ancestry in the Riggs family of Hawkshead, Lancashire [TAG 82:120-29], Smith now proceeds to a definitive presentation of the documentary evidence for the agnate lineages of the men who provided the DNA samples. With all this in place, Smith then establishes a set of rules by which he works backward from the modern DNA sequences to establish the highly probable DNA signatures of each of the immigrants, concluding that these signatures are identical for 65 out of 67 markers. (It must be emphasized that the precision of this conclusion still does not allow a statement of the precise degree of kinship between Edward and Thomas Riggs.)

Richard L. Bush, "English Ancestry of Bennett Hodsoll, First Wife of Edmond[1] Freeman," *The New England Historical and Genealogical Register* 164 (2010):104-11. Using English parish registers and probate records to reconstruct the list of her siblings, the author identifies the parents of Bennett Hodsoll, first wife of EDMOND FREEMAN {1635, Lynn} [GM 2:2:576-82].

Eldon Wilson Gay and Christopher Challender Child, "Joanna Hooker, Wife of John[1] Borden and John[1] Gay," *The New England Historical and Genealogical Register* 164 (2010):114-20. The authors present evidence from English parish registers which identifies Joanna, the wife of JOHN BORDEN {1635, Watertown} [GM 2:1:350-51] and of JOHN GAY {1635, Watertown} [GM 2:3:36-42], as Joanna Hooker, daughter of Robert Hooker of Lenham, Kent. They also provide the baptismal records for Joanna's first two children with John Borden.

Leslie Mahler, "William[A] Dwight, Father of John[1] and Timothy[1] Dwight of Dedham, Massachusetts," *The New England Historical and Genealogical Register* 164 (2010):135-38. Mahler found the wills of William Dwight and his brother Nicholas Dwight, the former of whom was from Woolverstone, Suffolk, and was the father of JOHN DWIGHT {1635, Watertown} [GM 2:2:371-78} and of TIMOTHY DWIGHT {1638, Dedham}. The author added entries from various Suffolk parish registers and prepared a genealogical summary of the family of William Dwight.

David A. Whittredge, "The English Origins of William[1] Whitredge of Ipswich, Massachusetts," *The New England Historical and Genealogical Register* 164 (2010):139-44. William Whitredge sailed for New England in 1635 and settled at Ipswich. By searching for this immigrant under a variety of spellings of the surname, the author has discovered records for this immigrant and his family in the parishes of Oxwich and Colkirk in central Norfolk. He presents a transcription of the will of the immigrant's father and genealogical summaries of the families of the immigrant and his father.

Michael W. Kearney, "Notes on the Children of John[1] and Mary (Woods) Bellows of Concord and Marlborough, Massachusetts," *The New England Historical and Genealogical Register* 164 (2010):153-60. Kearney extends our knowledge of three of the children of JOHN BELLOWS {1635, Concord} [GM 2:1:250-53] through a close examination of the probate records of James Woods, a brother of the wife of John Bellows, who died without issue. By tracing the distribution of his estate, the author has found marriages and children for Mary Bellows and for Nathaniel Bellows and demonstrates that Thomas Bellows died without issue.

Derrick Watson, "The English Origin of Robert[1] Kinsman of Ipswich, Massachusetts," *The American Genealogist* 84 (2010):18-25. Watson surveys a number of possible candidates in England as the 1634 immigrant to Ipswich, Massachusetts, and makes a strong case for a Robert Kinsman baptized in 1589 in Highworth, Wiltshire.

Nathan J. Rogers, "Mary[3] Kinsman, Proposed Wife of James[2] Burnham of Ipswich, Massachusetts," *The American Genealogist* 84 (2010):26-28. Rogers first demonstrates that the wife of James Burnham, son of the immigrant Thomas Burnham of Ipswich, cannot have been a Mary Cogswell. He then presents strong circumstantial evidence that the wife of James Burnham was Mary Kinsman, daughter of Robert[2] Kinsman and granddaughter of the immigrant ROBERT KINSMAN {1634, Ipswich} [GM 2:4:188-91].

John C. Brandon and Leslie Mahler, "A Royal Descent for Penelope Spencer, Wife of John[2] Treworgy of Kittery, Maine," *The American Genealogist* 84 (2010):46-49. The authors present a documented line of descent from Edward I, King of England, to Penelope Spencer, wife of John[2] Treworgy of Kittery, Maine, and niece of JOHN SPENCER {1634, Ipswich} [GM 2:6:428-36].

Eugene Cole Zubrinsky, "Townsmen and Selectmen: Variations of Title and Function in Plymouth Colony," *The American Genealogist* 84 (2010):50-51. Zubrinsky presents evidence showing that in some towns in Plymouth Colony the offices of townsman and selectman were not identical, and that the term selectman might also encompass the office of town magistrate, or what was known in Massachusetts Bay as commissioner to end small causes.

William B. Saxbe Jr., "New Old Information About the Family of Richard[1] Bowen of Rehoboth, Massachusetts," *The American Genealogist* 84 (2010):65-67. The author addresses and debunks a number of persistent myths surrounding the family of Richard Bowen, who had arrived in New England by 1640.

Ralph F. Young, "Breathing the 'Free Aire of the New World': The Influence of the New England Way on the Gathering of Congregational Churches in Old England, 1640-1660," *The New England Quarterly* 83 (2010):5-46. Young explores the extent of influence of the churches founded in New England in the 1630s on the growth of Congregational churches in old England in the 1640s and 1650s. He shows that the churches gathered in old England adopted New England practices in matters such as church officers and church discipline. The officers included a pastor, a teacher, ruling elders and deacons. Not all churches, in either old or New England, had all of these officers, but this was the ideal arrangement. Church discipline, including excommunication, was meted out by the entire congregation, usually guided by the ruling elders. Most importantly, the Congregational churches in old England adopted the crucial innovation of the New England churches, the confessions of saving grace, known also as conversion narratives. These confessions, which attempted to detail the path of a person's growing assurance of being among the elect, were the fundamental requirement for admission to church membership. When the Westminster Assembly met in England from 1643 to 1649 in an effort to resolve the differences between the Presbyterian and Independent (or Congregational) modes of church organization, the Independent side drew most of its support from the writings of New England ministers such as John Cotton.

Nick Bunker, *Making Haste from Babylon, The Mayflower Pilgrims and Their World: A New History* (New York 2010). Bunker presents a narrative history of the *Mayflower* Pilgrims from their origins in Scrooby, Nottinghamshire, and vicinity, through their time at Leiden, and then to the first few decades of their settlement in the New World. His treatment is heavily weighted towards the early years in England, with only a few pages on the Leiden sojourn. In many sections, such as the discussion of the importance to the Pilgrims of Robert Browne, a sixteenth-century Separatist, Bunker claims to be plowing new ground when this is not the case. He has found some documents which have apparently not previously been found by researchers, such as some depositions relating to the departure of the Pilgrims for Leiden in 1608. These documents do not, however, always bear the full weight of the interpretation he places on them. Bunker stresses the importance of the beaver trade to the survival of Plymouth Colony, providing much detail on the hunting of beavers and the manufacture of beaver hats. He also adverts frequently to events in Ireland, the relevance of which to the Pilgrim story is not always evident.

Great Migration Newsletter

Vol. 19   October–December 2010   No. 4

ESTABLISHING BIRTH ORDER

One of the most important steps in the construction of a Great Migration sketch is the establishment of the birth order of the children of the subject of the sketch. In the *Methods* section at the front of each Great Migration volume is a subsection titled *Ordering Families*, which discusses this process in broad outline. In the present article, we will look at this procedure in greater detail, making use of inferences based on two specific sources of information: the sequence of bequests in wills; and the baptism of several children of a couple in a group on one date.

A simple example may be seen in the will of Nicholas Robbins of Duxbury, dated 7 February 1650[/1?], in which he makes bequests to "Ann my beloved wife," to "my three daughters Katheren, Mary and Hannah," and to "my son John" [GM 2:6:65-67; MD 10:22; PCPR 1:92]. In this case, we are assisted by the corroborating data of the ages of some of these children in a 1635 passenger list, where Katherine was 12, Mary was 7, John was 5 and Sarah was 1½ [Hotten 93-94]. (Either Sarah of the passenger list was the same as Hannah of the will, or Sarah died before 1650 and Hannah was born after the family arrived in New England. In either case, the sequence of the daughters given in the will matches the birth order on display in the passenger list, and to that extent this technique is validated.)

Testators frequently made bequests first to all their sons and then to all their daughters. In her will of 5 June 1677, "Sarah Clarke the wife of Robert Clarke of Stratford," whose first husband had been FRANCIS STILES {1635, Windsor} [GM 2:6:513-21], made bequests to the following (along with some more distant kinsmen) [Fairfield PR 3:93]:

> my son Samuell Stiles
> my son Epraim Stiles
> my son Benia[min] Stiles
> my son Tho[mas] Stiles
> the children of my daughter Hannah Hinman deceased
> my grandchild Sarah Blakeman
> my grandchild Hanna Blakeman
> the children of my daughter Mary Washburne

Francis Stiles was apparently unmarried when he sailed for New England, but found a wife soon after arrival. (There are some hints that the eldest of the children of this wife was by an earlier husband, although this is not certain [GM 2:6:518-19].)

Based mostly on marriage records, but also on the age given for son Benjamin at his death, we arranged six of these seven children in the following birth order, with suggested years of birth running from 1636 to 1651: Hannah (married by 1653 Edward Hinman); daughter of unknown given name (married by 1658 James Blakeman); Samuel (married 31 December 1664 Elizabeth Sherwood); Mary (married by 1661 Hope Washburn); Ephraim (married first on 8 July 1669 Ruth Wheeler); and Benjamin ("aged about 60 years" on 13 April 1711).

At this point, we observed that "the birth order presented above, based for the most part on estimated dates of marriage, matches the order in which the mother of these children named first her sons then her daughters in the will" [GM 2:6:518]. This conclusion encouraged us to place Thomas at the end of the list of children, and to make a rough estimation of his year of birth.

This example demonstrates that the analytic sequence frequently has a dialectic form, in which we begin by estimating ages for some of the children from various life events. We then compare these results with the evidence from the will and note the consistencies between the two sequences.

(continued on page 26)

EDITOR'S EFFUSIONS

In 2004 we took a detour from the normal sequence of Great Migration volumes to produce a related book, which we titled *The Pilgrim Migration: Immigrants to Plymouth Colony, 1620-1633*. This volume was prepared by taking all those sketches, about two hundred, that had appeared nearly a decade earlier in the three volumes of *The Great Migration Begins: Immigrants to New England, 1620-1633,* and that covered immigrants who had first settled in Plymouth Colony.

The compilation of *The Pilgrim Migration* volume allowed us to improve the presentation of these sketches in at least three ways. First, the revised sketches were able to take into account newly published research on these immigrants that had been published in the intervening decade. Second, we were able to correct a number of errors that had been made in the original publication. Third, we were also able to upgrade the sketches to take into account ongoing improvements in the way we produced sketches.

About the middle of 2011, soon after work has concluded on the final volume in the Second Series of Great Migration volumes, we will begin to compile a companion volume to *The Pilgrim Migration*, to be called *The Winthrop Fleet*. The concept will be similar, in this instance selecting those sketches from *The Great Migration Begins* that cover families and individuals, mostly from East Anglia and the London area (and some from Lincolnshire), who were recruited by Governor John Winthrop to sail for New England in 1630, in order to take the settlement of Massachusetts Bay to a new level. More than fifteen years have now passed since the publication of *The Great Migration Begins*, so there is much new scholarship on these passengers to be incorporated in the new volume.

Like *The Pilgrim Migration, The Winthrop Fleet,* tentatively scheduled for publication in the summer of 2012, will encompass slightly more than two hundred sketches. Between them, the two volumes will comprise nearly one-half of the sketches originally included in *The Great Migration Begins*. The remaining half of the sketches from the earlier three-volume set consist mainly of immigrants from the West Country who arrived between 1620 and 1633 and of immigrants from East Anglia who came after the Winthrop Fleet.

Robert Charles Anderson, FASG   Editor
Jean Powers, Production Assistant

The Great Migration Newsletter is published quarterly by the Great Migration Study Project, a project of the New England Historic Genealogical Society,
101 Newbury Street, Boston MA 02116
www.AmericanAncestors.org
www.GreatMigration.org
GreatMigration@nehgs.org

(continued from page 25)

Having noted these consistencies, we then return to the job of estimating dates of birth for the remaining children, even without the benefit of clues derived from dates of marriages or ages given in depositions.

As a final example of evidence from wills, we will look at the messier and more intricate case of THOMAS STANTON {1635, Unknown} [GM 2:6:467-79]. Stanton came to prominence as an Indian interpreter during the Pequot War, and served in that capacity for decades, residing at Hartford, New London and Stonington.

Thomas Stanton and his wife Ann Lord had at least ten children. No birth records survive for any of these children, and only one baptism, for son Joseph on 21 March 1646[/7?] [HaVR 578]. The first attempts to arrange these children in birth order, based mostly on vital events, had the curious result of having four children bunched together around 1640, then Joseph, then another five bunched around 1654. Clearly, additional evidence was needed.

The lengthy will of Thomas Stanton, dated 24 October 1677, provides many clues to assist us in creating a birth order [GM 2:6:471-73]. His first two bequests, of substantial tracts of land, were to "my eldest son Thomas Stanton Junior" and to "my youngest son Daniel." (Eugene Zubrinsky has observed that "the secondary literature invariably lists Daniel[2] Stanton as the 6th of 10 children, ahead of brothers Robert and Samuel" [TAG 81:264]. These earlier investigators must not have seen the will, which is not found with the usual series of probate documents.)

Two other clues in the will are important for determining the birth order of the sons. First, on two occasions, when making bequests of parts of his moveable estate, Thomas Stanton named "Robert, Samuel and Daniel," in both cases in that order. Second, Thomas stated that "the barn is half Robert's and half Samuell's when Samuel is of age," suggesting in addition that on the date of the will Robert was of age. From these clues we conclude that these were the three youngest sons, born in the order stated in the will, with Samuel born no earlier than 1656.

For the remaining son, John, the will does not provide any helpful information for our analysis. However, we know he must be younger than Thomas, the eldest son, and, since he was married by about 1665, he was almost certainly older than Joseph. Thus, we arrive at the following sequence for the six sons of Thomas Stanton: Thomas, John, Joseph, Robert, Samuel and Daniel.

There were also four daughters, with dates of first marriage available for all four and ages at death for two. Although one or two of the sequencing choices for the daughters are arbitrary, the combination of clues from the will with other more conventional evidence allowed us to reach a reasonable sequence for the children of Thomas Stanton.

(continued on page 32)

Focus on the James of London, 1635

(continued from page 22)

[*In the Focus section of the last issue of the* Great Migration Newsletter *we listed and provided information on each of the fifty-three named passengers of the* James *[GMN 19:19-22]. We conclude our examination of the passenger list with an analysis of that data.*]

NUMBER OF PASSENGERS

The London Port Book for 1635 lists the names of all passengers, so in order to know the number of passengers on each vessel, we need merely count. For example, the *Planter*, Nicholas Trerice master, took on passengers on seven dates between 22 March 1634/5 and 11 April 1635 [Hotten 43, 45, 47-49, 50, 53, 55-56]. Each passenger is named, with an age stated, and usually an occupation for the male heads of household. There were 128 passengers on this vessel, ranging in age from 65 years to three months.

Some passenger lists, like that of the *James* under consideration here, were organized differently, with only males of a certain age included. In his account of Anthony Thatcher, Savage observed that he

> embarked on 6 April at Southampton in the James ..., and arrived at Boston 3 June, in the ship's clearance called a tayler for deception *not* of the inferiors at the custom house who certified that the total number of men, youths, and boys, was 53, when we are sure there were many more perhaps, a hundred and fifty per cent. He brought a second wife and four children William, born of first wife as may have been some of the rest, Mary, Edith, and Peter, a babe, and probably was accompanied by his cousin Rev. Joseph Avery, with wife and six children and his nephew Thomas.... Such was the mode of evasion of the petty tyranny of the Lords of the Council. The ship was of 300 tons, and might well have brought 150 passengers when so many were eager to come, yet the names of 53 alone are given. Most of these went to Ipswich, and a large part of them settled the same and following year at Newbury [Savage 4:270].

Based on the information provided in the last issue of the *Newsletter* for each of the 53 "men, youths & boys" who enrolled for passage to New England on the *James*, we may begin our analysis by calculating a minimum number of passengers on this ship. Of the 53 named passengers, at least 20 of them brought wives to New England and in these families were at least 46 children, for a minimum of 119 passengers.

Without assuming that the passenger complement included any unnamed heads of household, as have been proposed by some, we may increase this number slightly. Just as there were named manservants included in the passenger list, there would have been at least as many maidservants as

well. Also, since the wives and children of the heads of family are not named in the passenger list, there were probably a few of each who did sail for New England, but who died unrecorded after arrival and so are not included in our summary. Finally, by analogy with those passenger lists of the same year which named all those on board, some heads of household would have been accompanied by an elderly widowed mother or a young unmarried sister. These hypothetical but probable additional passengers could bring the total to something on the order of 130, very close to the number we know to have sailed on the *Planter*, and perhaps even approaching the 150 posited by Savage.

With this estimate in hand, we may state that there would not have been room on the *James* for many unrecorded families. (Many years ago, we arrived at the same conclusion for the *Mary & John* of 1630, for which the records give us only a total number of passengers on the vessel, and the names of a handful [NEHGR 147:148-61].) As a consequence, we are not justified in adding other families, just because they apparently arrived in 1635 and were in some way associated with known passengers. Specifically, we must be very cautious in following Savage in his suggestion that Joseph Avery, cousin of Anthony Thatcher, was also on the *James*. (This point will be discussed further below.)

DEMOGRAPHICS OF PASSENGERS

In 1991, Virginia DeJohn Anderson published a study of seven passenger lists for New England-bound ships, three in 1635, three in 1637, and one in 1638 [*New England's Generation: The Great Migration and the Formation of Society and Culture in the Seventeenth Century* (Cambridge, England, 1991)]. One of those seven ships was the same vessel we are examining here. Anderson compiled tables on most of the demographic categories that we will be discussing in this section [Appendix, pp. 222-27]. These tables, which provide a useful point of comparison with our conclusions, include her data for the *James*, aggregated with the data for the other six ships.

Ages

The distribution of ages for emigrants to New England was different from that of emigrants to the other English colonies. In the volume discussed just above, Virginia DeJohn Anderson made the point that

> Groups of emigrants to the Chesapeake in the seventeenth century ... consistently included a majority of people in their twenties. But among the New England settlers, young adults were far less predominant.... In fact, the age structure of New England's emigrant population closely resembled that of the home country, with both infancy and old age represented [pp. 19-20].

Aside from the ages given for the two youths from Southampton, the passenger list of the *James* provides no direct evidence for the ages of the passengers. We will limit ourselves here to an assessment of the range of ages we are able to discover from other sources for the named passengers on the list.

Three types of evidence are available to us: dates of baptism for some of those whose English origin has been discovered; ages given later in life in depositions and similar documents; and estimated ages for some others, usually based on date of first marriage. From these sources we have approximate years of birth for thirty-three of the men named in the passenger list, for whom the age distribution is as follows:

16-20	4
21-30	14
31-40	12
41-50	2
Over 50	1

This distribution is comparable to that discovered by Virginia DeJohn Anderson [p. 222], with the caveat that we have not included the young sons who presumably accompanied their parents, but are not named in the passenger list. The important distinction to note again is the difference between this age distribution and that found among the immigrants to Virginia and the Caribbean of the same year.

Of the remaining twenty named passengers, no indisputable records have been found in New England for seventeen. Of these four were servants, and so were perhaps in their late teens, while thirteen had stated occupations, suggesting that they were at least in their twenties, if not older.

This leaves a residue of three men who did have a recorded career of some years in New England, but whose ages we are unable to estimate, other than that they were adults in 1635: John Pithouse (laborer or husbandman); John Musselwhite (laborer); and Sampson Salter (fisherman).

Family structure

As noted above, at least twenty of the adult males on this vessel were accompanied by wives. (As always, we make the assumption that, unless there is evidence to the contrary, a male immigrant was accompanied by his wife and children. We do not assume that he was accompanied by any more distant kin, such as sisters or brothers, nieces or nephews, or by servants.) For these twenty couples, the number of children in each family has the following distribution:

# children	# families
6	1
5	1
4	3
3	4
2	2
1	7
0	2

These were not, for the most part, what demographers call "completed families," that is, these were mostly younger couples in which the wife had several remaining years in which she might give birth. Note again the difference between these families and the almost total lack of such families in the passenger lists for those ships bound for Virginia and the Caribbean.

Men, youths, boys

An unusual feature of this passenger list is the summary statement at the end:

> The total number of these men, youths & boys are liii persons

This would seem to divide the named passengers into three groups by age, with youths being intermediate between men and boys. "Men" would probably have been those aged twenty-one and older, but how to distinguish between "youths" and boys"? Our only direct clue in the list itself is the entry for the two "youths of Hampton of about 17 years old." What, then, was the dividing line between youths and boys?

Among its many definitions for "youth," the Oxford English Dictionary includes the following:

> The time when one is young; the early part or period of life; more specifically, the period from puberty till the attainment of full growth, between childhood and adult age

"Full growth" and "adult age" would define the "men," but what of "puberty" and "childhood"? The OED definitions for "child" and "childhood" both delimit that stage of life with reference to puberty, and the definition for puberty speaks of the biological changes during that life transition, but not a specific age. A likely solution to the problem would be that the dividing line between "youths" and "boys" came at age fourteen, the legal age for being allowed to choose one's own guardian or to witness a legal document.

Who among the fifty-three named passengers might be "boys"? As stated above, one would expect all those with a designated occupation to be twenty-one or older. Two of the passengers are specifically called "youths," without an occupation attached. This leaves only the five servants: Thomas Wheeler, Thomas Browne, Peter Higdon, William Kemp and John Small. Of these, only one, John Small has been identified in New England. From an age given in a deposition, we know that he would have been about nineteen in 1635, and so would have been included among the "youths." This leaves only four passengers who might have been "boys" in 1635. Both boys and girls under the age of fourteen were at that time taken on as servants, so any one of these four might have been "boys."

We return now to the question of whether there might have been some unnamed male passengers on the *James*, looking at the cases of Thomas Thatcher and Edward Woodman.

In our earlier discussion of the number of passengers on the *James*, we observed Savage's claim that Anthony Thatcher was accompanied by "his cousin Rev. Joseph Avery, with wife and six children and his nephew Thomas Thatcher," and then proceeded to cast some doubt on the presence on that vessel of the Avery family, based on our count of likely passengers. But what of "his nephew Thomas Thatcher"?

Thomas Thatcher was born on 1 May 1620, son of Peter Thatcher [NYGBR 41:236]. He would have been just short of his fifteenth birthday when the passenger list of the *James* was compiled, and so would have qualified as a "youth." Since he was not a son of Anthony Thatcher, we might expect that he would have been listed separately, although we cannot be certain of this.

Thomas Thatcher does not appear in New England records until the early 1640s, which, for a man born in 1620, does not preclude the possibility that he might have come on the *James* in 1635. However, we note that in Anthony Thatcher's account of the shipwreck of 1635, when we might expect Thomas to be travelling with his uncle Anthony, no mention is made of Thomas as a survivor. For this reason, we do not believe that Thomas Thatcher sailed on the *James*.

Under the surname Woodman, Savage included an entry for

> ARCHELAUS, Newbury, named Hercules in the report to government of passengers from Southampton in the James of London, embarked 6 April, arrived 3 June 1635, and called mercer of Malford. Perhaps the custom-house officers knew more of Hercules than of the other name, though both are equally heathenish, but probably the sound was not unlike. He was born 1618, but how entitled mercer, when only a minor, provokes inquiry. My conjecture is, that his elder brother Edward deserved that description and came in that ship, but it was undesirable to give his name and excite suspicion that he was not authorized under the odious orders of the council to come to our country [Savage 4:640].

Since the great majority of the heads of household on the *James* would have been of Puritan inclination, we should not expect Edward Woodman to have been singled out for this deceptive practice, and thus omitted from the list.

More pertinently, the source for Savage's statement that Archelaus was born about 1618 (which would put him in the category of "youth") is not given. More recent scholarship, published in 1943, shows that Archelaus Woodman was baptized on 23 January 1613/4 [NEHGR 97:284-85], and so would have been twenty-one when he boarded the *James*, and thus old enough, just barely, to be occupied as a mercer. None of this evidence supports Savage's claim that Edward Woodman sailed on the same vessel.

Occupations

We may divide the occupations of the named passengers on the *James* into three categories: servants, tradesmen and agriculturalists. Seven men were explicitly called servants,

and the two "youths … of about 17 years" were probably servants as well. Only one of these seven men has been identified in New England, John Small, and he became a husbandman once he had completed his servitude [GM 2:6:345].

Thirty-two of the men were tradesmen or artisans of some sort, which is not surprising, since most of them came from large towns such as Salisbury, Marlborough and Romsey. There were eight tailors, five carpenters, four weavers, three shoemakers and a scattering of others. Nineteen of these were engaged in the making or selling of clothing.

Only fourteen of the passengers could be classified as agriculturalists, seven husbandmen and seven laborers. There were, interestingly, none who were called yeomen, who were usually more affluent than husbandmen, and who made up a substantial part of the early immigrants to New England. This may reflect careless usage on the part of the clerk who compiled the passenger list, or it may indicate that this group of passengers was somewhat less wealthy than many of the other immigrants.

GEOGRAPHY OF PASSENGERS

The passenger list of the *James* is unusual in that it states explicitly the parish of origin of each of the named passengers. Many passenger lists from the 1630s provide no information on English origin, and others only occasionally provide that information. The great majority of the passengers on the *James* were from Wiltshire, with most of the remaining passengers being from the adjacent county of Hampshire.

Wiltshire

Thirty-seven of the named passengers (more than two-thirds) gave their county of origin as Wiltshire. Of these, twenty-eight were from just two towns, fourteen each from Marlborough and Salisbury. The remaining nine passengers were from six other parishes. Of these nine, six were from parishes close to Salisbury: Amesbury (1), Downton (1), Landford (3) and Plaitford (1). Only three of the passengers were from parishes at any substantial distance from either Marlborough or Salisbury, both toward the northwest quadrant of the county: Christian Malford (2) and The Devizes (1).

Hampshire

Ten of the named passengers were from Hampshire, seven from Romsey, two from Southampton and one, Robert Field, from "Yealing," which was probably Eling, adjacent to Romsey on the south. The two from Southampton were James Browne and Laurence Seag[e]r, listed together and described as "youths of Hampton of about 17 years old." No connections with other passengers on the *James* have been found for these two youths, and no records for either have been found in New England. They were probably recruited in Southampton as potential servants just before sailing.

London

The two passengers from London present an interesting puzzle. As they had no known connection with Wiltshire or Hampshire, or with any of their fellow passengers, why did they travel from London to Southampton to take ship, when there were several ships preparing at the same time to sail for New England directly from London?

Other

The remaining four passengers were from a scattering of parishes in a broad band between London and Southampton: Augustine Clement and his servant Thomas Wheeler from Berkshire, Reading; Henry King from Brenchley, Kent; and Sampson Salter from Caversham, Oxford.

In summary, we see that most of the passengers were drawn from just two small regions of south-central England. First, we note that Romsey was about eight miles northwest of Southampton, and Salisbury was another twelve miles beyond Romsey in the same direction. Taking into account the passengers from the other parishes near Salisbury, we find that thirty were from this one area. Second, as noted above, fourteen were from Marlborough. Altogether, these two clusters of origins account for all but nine of the passengers on this vessel

SETTLEMENT OF NEWBURY

We have seen that most of the passengers on the *James* were from a small region in Wiltshire and adjacent parts of Hampshire. Where did they settle once they had arrived in New England? The simple answer is Newbury—we know the residences of thirty-four of the fifty-three named passengers, and by 1635 sixteen of them had settled in Newbury.

Before looking more closely at the early settlement of Newbury, we shall account for the known residences of the remaining eighteen passengers. Ten of them were in Salem by the end of 1635: William Carpenter, Zaccheus Curtis, George Smith, Edmund Batter, Joshua Verren, Thomas Antrum, Phillip Verren, John Small, John Greene and Michael Shaflin. (Two of these men had sojourned briefly in other towns before going to Salem: John Greene at Boston and Michael Shaflin at Charlestown.) Two further points are of interest. First, eight of them were from Salisbury, Wiltshire, and the other two were from parishes close to Salisbury (Amesbury and Downton). And these Salem settlers included eight of the nine Salisbury passengers whose New England residence has been established. Second, several of them constituted a single kinship network at the time of migration. Joshua Verren was son of Phillip (and John Small was servant to Phillip). Edmund Batter had married Sarah Verren, daughter of Phillip, and Thomas Antrum married Jane Batter, sister of Edmund [GM 2:1:69-71, 204-13].

The rest of the passengers were more scattered. Three of the men from Marlborough settled in Boston and remained

there for many years: John Evered *alias* Webb, Maudit Ingles and John Parker. Two men went to Plymouth Colony, but these were the two London men whom we have already identified as outliers: Edmund Hawes to Duxbury and William Paddy to Plymouth. Finally, Augustine Clement went to Dorchester, John Pithouse to Ipswich and Robert Field possibly to Newport (although where he might have lived before 1639 remains unknown).

We return now to the sixteen passengers who were residing in Newbury by the end of 1635. Since Newbury was first settled in 1635, this makes these *James* passengers founding settlers and a substantial part of that town in its earliest years. This group of sixteen included six from Romsey, Hampshire, and four from Marlborough, Wiltshire.

Prior to 1635 there had been very few immigrants to New England from Hampshire and Wiltshire, perhaps no more than eight. Three Wiltshire men had by 1630 attached themselves to the Dorchester, Dorset, group that sailed to New England on the *Mary & John* and established the New England town of Dorchester: Stephen Terry [GMB 3:1804-6] and George and Roger Ludlow [GMB 2:1208-13].

Three others of this small group are, however, relevant to our story of the settling of Newbury by passengers of the *James* in 1635. Two of them sailed for New England on the *James* in 1632 (we have no way of knowing whether this was the same vessel as the *James* of 1635). Richard Dummer was of South or North Stoneham in Hampshire, just a few miles to the east of Romsey [GMB 1:588-95]. Dummer resided at Roxbury from 1632 to 1635, at which time he joined in the settlement of Newbury, where he was joined a few years later by a number of his siblings and where he died in 1679.

Henry Sherborn sailed on the same ship with Richard Dummer [GMB 3:1666-69]. He was from Odiham, Hampshire, in the northeast corner of the county, about thirty miles from the Stonehams. Although he settled on the Piscataqua, he and his family had connections in Newbury.

Last but far from least was the peripatetic Reverend Stephen Bachiler, who resided as early as 1606 at Wherwell, Hampshire, and in the 1620s in the nearby parishes of Abbots Ann and Barton Stacey [GMB 1:61-69]. These three locations were about twelve miles north of the Stonehams. In 1631, less than a year before sailing for New England, Bachiler lived briefly at South Stoneham, where he likely would have become acquainted with the Dummers [GMB 1:65]. And, indeed, Richard Dummer was associated with the so-called Plough Company or Company of Husbandmen, which was led by Bachiler [GMB 1:592-93]. Bachiler was just as footloose in New England as in Old, and resided briefly in Newbury before founding the town of Hampton.

No direct connections between these three men who came to New England in 1632 and the arrivals of 1635 have been found, but the proximity of Romsey to South Stoneham suggests interesting paths for future research in English records.

RECENT LITERATURE

Gale Ion Harris, "The Brothers William[2] and Daniel[2] Harris of Middletown, Connecticut," *The New England Historical and Genealogical Register* 164 (2010):165-74. In this first part of a two-part article, Harris treats the family of William Harris, son of THOMAS HARRIS {1630, Winnissimmett} [GMB 2:864-66]. William Harris had no sons, but the genealogical summary of his family includes detailed accounts of the marriages and children of his five daughters. The second installment will cover William's brother Daniel and his children.

Doris Schreiber Willcox, "Edward[1] Breck's Baptismal Record and Identification of His 'Daughter Blake,'" *The New England Historical and Genealogical Register* 164 (2010):175-83. The author demonstrates that Edward Breck, who had settled in Dorchester by 1638, was baptized at Wigan, Lancashire, in August 1596 (although all his siblings were baptized in the neighboring parish of Prescot). Willcox has compiled a genealogical summary of the immigrant, his father, and paternal grandfather. She also argues that Edward's daughter Anna married William Blake, son of the immigrant William Blake of Dorchester.

Caleb H. Johnson, "The Manorial Records of Henlow Grey: New Information on the Tilleys, Coopers, and Hursts," *The Mayflower Quarterly* 76 (2010):125-34. Based on work published by Robert Leigh Ward a quarter of a century ago, the *Mayflower* passengers Humility Cooper, Henry Samson, Edward Tilley and John Tilley have been known to have originated from the parish of Henlow, Bedfordshire. Johnson has carried out a detailed examination of the manorial records of Henlow Grey, a manor located in Henlow, the result of which is a substantial harvest of biographical details on the parents and grandparents of these immigrants to New England. Based on what he has discovered, Johnson observes that "Unlike most *Mayflower* passengers, these families had significant lands, social status, and inheritances. One has to wonder exactly how they managed to hook up with the Leiden separatists."

Karyn Valerius, "'So Manifest a Signe from Heaven': Monstrosity and Heresy in the Antinomian Controversy," *The New England Quarterly* 83 (2010):179-99. At the height of the Antinomian crisis in Massachusetts Bay, in 1637 and 1638, two of the leading figures in the controversy, Mary Dyer and Anne Hutchinson, suffered miscarriages, in each case delivering severely malformed fetuses. Valerius argues that the forces of orthodoxy, including John Winthrop and Thomas Weld, were able to employ these monstrous births metaphorically, as emblems of what they considered the monstrous shapes of the religious views espoused by Hutchinson and her followers. By setting forth these parallel biological and theological arguments, they hoped to restore order to their troubled commonwealth. (For those not familiar with the Antinomian Controversy, Valerius provides, in less than three pages, a concise summary of the issues in contention and a chronology of the crisis [pp. 182-84].)

Walter W. Woodward, *Prospero's America: John Winthrop, Jr., Alchemy, and the Creation of New England Culture, 1606-1676* (Chapel Hill, North Carolina, 2010). At one stroke Woodward both updates our biographical understanding of John Winthrop Jr. (eldest son of Governor John Winthrop of Massachusetts Bay) and also introduces us to the importance of the pursuit of alchemical knowledge in some sectors of the emerging New England culture. Woodward paints a broad picture of the alchemical enterprise, not limited to the attempts to transform base metals into gold and silver, but including also the search for the alkahest (the all-curing elixir) and, even more importantly, the acquisition of pansophia, "which would contain the essence of knowledge and reveal the unifying divine principles ordering reality."

In his early adulthood, John Winthrop Jr. had traveled to Europe and the eastern Mediterranean, in part to make contact with prominent scholars of an alchemical bent. With this knowledge in hand, he joined a select circle of the New England elite with similar proclivities, both in the very practical pursuits of medicine and mining and in the more abstract pansophic studies.

One of the corollaries of the pansophic approach was a more tolerant position at the time of outbreaks of witchcraft scares, and Winthrop certainly sidetracked a number of such scares that might in his absence have led to executions. And these positions on witchcraft connected with a nuanced understanding of the place of magic in contemporary affairs. Winthrop and his colleagues distinguished between diabolic magic, such as that associated with witches, and natural magic, such as might be associated with their alchemical pursuits. These distinctions were often lost on those not already initiated in the mysteries of alchemy.

Aside from being an important contribution to colonial New England historiography, Woodward's volume will force readers to rethink and reimagine their understanding of the seventeenth century.

Caleb H. Johnson, "Christopher Martin: A New *Mayflower* Signature Discovered," *The Mayflower Quarterly* 76 (2010):209.
Caleb H. Johnson, "Solomon Prower: New Information on a Little-Known *Mayflower* Passenger," *The Mayflower Quarterly* 76 (2010):242-43.
Caleb H. Johnson, "Mary (Prower) Martin: A New *Mayflower* Ancestor," *The Mayflower Quarterly* 76 (2010):244-46. Johnson has scoured the records of Billericay, Essex, for further information on three *Mayflower* passengers: Christopher Martin, his wife Mary (_____) (Prower) Martin, and her son Solomon Prower. He has found Christopher Martin's signature on the will of a neighbor, and a number of appearances of Solomon Prower in the church courts, indicating his Puritan leanings, and also suggesting that he was at least twenty-one years old by 1619. Finally, Johnson has tentatively reconstructed the family of Edward Prower, probable father of Solomon, and pointed to the possibility of previously unknown descents in this line.

(continued from page 26)

Turning now to the value of batch baptisms in establishing birth order, we examine first the family of HENRY LYNN {1630, Boston} [GMB 2:1220-22]. On 23 May 1647, "The children of our sister Sarah Gunnison late wife to Henry Lynne deceased" were all presented for baptism at Boston church [BChR 308]:

> Sarah Lynn being about ten years and a half old
> Elizabeth Lynn being 9 years and about 2 months old
> Ephraim Lynn being 7 years and about 4 months old
> Rebeka Lynn being about 5 years and about 3 months old

The church records do not, unfortunately, always give the ages of a group of siblings when they are brought in together for baptism. We see in this case, though, that the children were recorded in birth order, giving us some confidence that this will usually be the case when ages are not given.

We note in passing that birth records for these children were also entered at Boston, but not until 1650, when they appeared as a group [NEHGR 9:165], with some errors in dates by comparison with the baptismal record. Most of these children were born at York or Piscataqua and recorded at Boston when their mother, now remarried to HUGH GUNNISON {1635, Boston} [GM 2:3:173-80], was residing at Boston [GMN 12:29].

A different example may be found in Salem church records, on 14 October 1638 [SChR 17]:

> Ruth and Anna and John, 3 children of [*John*] Pickworth

JOHN PICKWORTH {1631, Massachusetts Bay} [GMB 3:1462-64] moved around often during his first few years in New England, going from somewhere in Massachusetts Bay to Plymouth Colony in 1631, then to Salem by 1632, where he eventually settled in that section of town which became Manchester.

"Anne Pickworth," wife of John, was admitted to Salem church on 30 September 1638 [SChR 17] and exactly two weeks later her three children were baptized. On 25 December 1637, the Pickworth household comprised five persons [STR 1:102], so presumably all three of these children had been born by that date. On this basis alone, we estimated that Ruth, Anna and John were born about 1633, 1635 and 1637. Ruth had married Nathaniel Masters by 1654 [GMB 3:1463], which would make her an appropriate twenty-one years old in that year according to our estimate. Anna had married John Killam by 1660, which is not so neat a fit, but is at least consistent with the estimated year of birth.

In this article we have discussed two of the many tools employed in establishing birth order, tools which are among the most powerful available to us.

Great Migration Newsletter

Vol. 20   January-March 2011   No. 1

TWO WILLIAM WHITES

We have from time to time published articles describing the process of discriminating among two or more immigrants of the same name. Two examples are John Carman/Kirman and John Jackson [GMN 2:9-10, 16, 12:17-18, 24]. During the preparation of the current Great Migration volume a fascinating and perhaps more complex example has arisen, the William Whites of Essex County.

The single record that determined that a sketch for a William White would be in the current volume, and that therefore triggered the research described here, was the passenger list of the *Mary & John*, preparing on 24 March 1633/4 to set sail from Southampton for New England. In that list is the name "William White," without any additional identifying information [Drake's Founders 70].

As is our usual practice, we turn first to Savage as a point of reference. His entry for this passenger begins as follows [Savage 4:515]:

> WILLIAM, Newbury, freeman 22 June 1642, had come from London in the Mary and John 1634, and first sat down at Ipswich, thence removed probably in 1635 or 6, with many of his fellow-passengers to Newbury, had John and James, the latter born says Coffin, about 1649; removed to Haverhill, there died 1690, aged 80.

Savage included two other entries with which we will also have to contend, given here in their entirety [Savage 4:515-16]:

> WILLIAM, Ipswich, had wife Catharine, who died 2 June 1671, and perhaps daughter Ruth, aged 30 in 1663, and he died 25 August 1684, aged 74.

> WILLIAM, Ipswich, the freeman 1671, may have been that youth, in 1635, aged 14, who came from London in the Increase, under protection of Philemon Dalton, and perhaps his servant. His wife Mary, by whom he had children unknown to me by name, died 22 February 1682, and he married 21 September following Sarah Foster, widow perhaps of Renold.

According to Savage, then, there were three men named William White who resided at Ipswich, apparently unrelated to one another. One of these men moved on to Newbury and then Haverhill and had sons John and James.

We turn next to Pope, who included in his compilation only one entry for a William White who resided at Ipswich [Pope 493]:

> William, husbandman, came in the Mary and John in March, 1633-4. Settled at Ipswich; proprietor 1634; freeman June 22, 1642. Removed to Haverhill about 1642. Proprietor, town officer. Wife Mary died February 22, 1681; he married September 21, 1682, Sarah Foster. She returned to Ipswich after his death and died there. His son John's will was probated 13 (2) 1669. He died September 28, 1690, aetatis about 80 years.

Pope's compilation combines elements of the first and third of Savage's entries, but nothing from the second. Pope also does not mention the move to Newbury or the son James. How do we resolve these discrepancies? How many William Whites were there, and which one, if any, was the passenger on the *Mary & John*?

Our next step is to collect all occurrences of the name William White in Essex County sources, including the Quarter Court records, Ipswich Deeds, and Ipswich and Newbury town records. To this mass of data we apply the Fundamental Law of genealogical research: *We must have a sound, explicit reason for claiming that any two records pertain to the same individual.*

(continued on page 2)

EDITOR'S EFFUSIONS

We are faced with a variety of problems in attempting to incorporate into Great Migration sketches the information contained in town records, which, for our purposes, fall into three categories. First, for some towns most of the early records survive and have been carefully edited and published. Examples in this category would be Watertown, Cambridge and Dedham [GMN 1:3-6, 4:3-6, 7:11-13].

At the other extreme are those towns whose earliest records have been lost. The most striking example of this sort is the town of Lynn (established in 1631), whose surviving town records begin in 1691. We are forced, therefore, to build our understanding of the early history of Lynn from surviving scraps of evidence, mostly found in the county and colony records [GMN 1:19-22]. Other towns that fall into this category are Concord, Saybrook and Newport. As annoying as the problem may be for these towns, there is nothing much to be done, as presumably the records are gone forever.

The third category is the most frustrating. For many towns, a substantial portion of the earliest records survive, but have not yet been published. In many of these cases the records are poorly organized and are usually not indexed. Thus, in preparing sketches for residents of these towns, obtaining the pertinent information from the town records becomes very difficult, and the results are not always complete and satisfactory.

Over two decades, the principal purpose of the *Focus* section of the *Great Migration Newsletter* has been to examine the records of early New England towns in order to assist our research. In 2005 we undertook a survey of all those towns founded by 1643, coming up with a list of fifty-nine settlements. We have now published *Focus* sections on thirty-three of these towns [GMN 14:19-22, 27-30]. These accounts are, of course, no substitute for full publication of the early records, but they are a small step in that direction.

In the twentieth volume of the *Newsletter*, we will examine at least two more of the remaining twenty-six towns. In this issue we will look at Newbury, both the land records and the town meeting records. Later in the year we will explore the church, land and town meeting records of Milford.

Robert Charles Anderson, FASG   Editor
Jean Powers, Production Assistant

The Great Migration Newsletter is published quarterly by the Great Migration Study Project, a project of the New England Historic Genealogical Society, 99-101 Newbury Street, Boston MA 02116
www.AmericanAncestors.org
www.GreatMigration.org
GreatMigration@nehgs.org

(continued from page 1)

Our starting point will be the Ipswich town records, where we find that on 26 January 1634/5, the town of Ipswich "granted unto William White twenty acres of land on the south side of this river at the west end of Mr. Spencer his land" [ITR]. Then, on 20 April 1635, the town granted to him "an houselot ..., a place to set a house ..., twenty acres of land part meadow, part upland lying on the east side of the town, ... also ... two hundred acres of land lying at the further Chebacco, bounded on the southeast by a creek that lies between it and Mr. Coggswell's land" [ITR].

We note first that both of these grants were made less than a year after the arrival of the *Mary & John*, and before the arrival of vessels carrying passengers in 1635. We note also that most of the passengers on the *Mary & John*, including those who were among the earliest settlers of Newbury, settled first at Ipswich, even if only for one winter. Thus, these grants of land could well have been made to the 1634 passenger on the *Mary & John*.

On 27 June 1638, "whereas William White of Ipswich, husbandman, had granted to him ... twenty acres of land, lying at the east end of the town, ... being part meadow and part upland now the said William White hath sold unto Thomas Treadwell of Ipswich all the said twenty acres of meadow and upland" [ITR]. According to Savage, the 1634 passenger, after a brief sojourn in Ipswich, had already removed to Newbury by 1635 or 1636, and yet here we see the 1634 Ipswich grantee still in that town in 1638.

Furthermore, on 2 October 1647, "William White of Ipswich" mortgaged to "Ralfe Dix of the same town, fisherman, ... my farm lying and being in Ipswich aforesaid at Chebaco, containing by estimation 200 acres" [ILR 1:37]. That this farm was the same as that granted to William White on 20 April 1635 is demonstrated by a deed of 6 April 1691, in which "James White of Ipswich ..., yeoman, and Martha my wife, in consideration that my father William White having sold unto Deacon Thomas Knowlton, John Knowlton & John Baker, in the year [1685] ... fourscore and two acres ... bounded in form following, viz: on the southeast by a creek, next Mr. Cogswell's farm" [ILR 5:405].

Based on these few records we have explicit evidence of a single William White in Ipswich from 1634 to 1647 and implicit evidence, in the deed of 1691, of his presence in that town for a much longer period. Broadening our field of vision to the full range of records collected in this study, we find none of the clues that would lead us to believe that the grantee of 1634 had moved away from Ipswich and that some other man of the same name had moved into town. There are no instances of the usual markers such as Senior and Junior that would indicate the presence of two men of the same name, whether related or not. There are no deeds in which a William White sells Ipswich land while calling himself a resident of another town.

(continued on page 8)

Focus on Newbury

SETTLEMENT OF NEWBURY

The town of Newbury came into existence, without recorded preliminaries, at the General Court of Elections on 6 May 1635 [MBCR 1:146]:

Wessacu[n]con is allowed by the court to be a plantation, & it is referred to Mr. Humfry, Mr. Endicott, Capt. Turner, & Capt. Traske, or any three of them, to set the bounds of Ipswich and Wessacu[n]con, or so much thereof as they can, & the name of the said plantation is changed, & hereafter to be called Neweberry.

Further, it is ordered, that it shall be in the power of the court to take order that the said plantation shall receive a sufficient company of people to make a competent town.

In his journal, summarizing the work of this court, John Winthrop reported on this event [WJ 1:191]:

At this general court, some of the chief of Ipswich desired leave to remove to Quascacunquen, to begin a town there, which was granted them, and it was named Neweberry.

There are a number of unusual features in the founding of Newbury which invite discussion. First, while it was the usual practice to assign an Algonkian name to a new town, and then order that name to be replaced by an English one at a later date, when the settlement was more stable, in this instance the lifetime of the Algonkian name was counted in seconds, encompassed in a single paragraph of the colony records. For most other towns, these two naming events were separated by one or more courts, and therefore by several months.

Second, there is a tension between the second paragraph of the court order and the brief report made by Winthrop. The court order speaks of the need to find "a sufficient company of people to make a competent town," whereas Winthrop notes it was "some of the chief of Ipswich" who petitioned for the creation of the new town.

Third, new towns usually had to wait for some time before the court would permit them to send deputies to represent the town at the General Court. In this case, Newbury seems to have been represented by deputies at the court which created the town. The last two names in the list of deputies for the 6 May 1635 court are "Mr. John Spencer" and "Tho [mas] Smyth" [MBCR 1:145]. (These two names come at the end of the list of deputies for this court, immediately after those from Ipswich. Perhaps they were added to the list during the sitting of the court, at the time Newbury was officially founded. John Spencer had been deputy from Ipswich just two months before, on 4 March 1634/5 [MBCR 1:135; GM 2:6:428-36]. In our account of Thomas Smith, we failed to take notice of his service as deputy [GM 2:6:402-5].)

The observation that explains these unusual circumstances is that the first group of settlers of Newbury, who must have been the petitioners referred to by Winthrop, were among the most affluent and influential men who had arrived in 1634 and just before. In 1634 and 1635 two vessels, the *Mary & John* and the *James*, had brought about one hundred families from Hampshire and Wiltshire. Those on the *Mary & John*, who upon landing had no place to live, spent the winter of 1634-35 residing in Ipswich, doubling up with residents of that town who had themselves only settled that town a year or so before. The crowded conditions undoubtedly encouraged these men and women, many of them of above-average socioeconomic status, to devote many long winter evenings to planning their new town, visiting the site of the future Newbury when they could, and preparing the petition and taking the other political steps necessary for the success of their plan. With the easy access they must have had to the governor and other high colony officials, the path had been cleared before the May Court of Elections, and their petition sailed through the legislature.

Not all of the Newbury settlers of 1635 had arrived just the year before. Richard Dummer, perhaps the wealthiest and most prominent of these men, had arrived in 1632, as a passenger on the *Whale*, and settled first at Roxbury. Dummer had resided in various parishes in Hampshire, and this along with his presence on the *Whale*, marks him as an associate of Rev. Stephen Bachiler, whom we will meet later. These two men were leaders in the so-called Company of Husbandmen or Plough Company [GMN 1:20, 2:16, 4:22].

On 6 May 1635, at the court which brought Newbury into existence,

It is referred to Mr. Humfry, Mr. Endicott, Capt. Turner, & Capt. Traske to set out a farm for Mr. Dumer, about the falls of Neweberry, not exceeding the quantity of 500 acres, provided also it be not prejudicial to Neweberry.

Then, on 8 July 1635,

There is liberty granted to Mr. Dumer & Mr. Spencer to build a mill & a weir at the falls of Neweberry, to enjoy the said mill & weir, with such privileges of ground & timber as is expressed in an agreement betwixt them & the town, to enjoy to them & their heirs forever.

Perhaps another distinction enjoyed by the founders of Newbury, in this instance not so welcome, was that they were immediately subject to colony taxation, being assessed on 8 July 1635 for £8 in a colony rate of £200 [MBCR 1:149]. Most other newly founded towns were allowed a grace period of a year or two before being assessed for colony taxes, with the understanding that the community would be experiencing extraordinary expenses in carving a new settlement from the wilderness.

NEWBURY TOWN RECORDS

The first volume of town meeting records for Newbury is now available as what appears to be a nineteenth-century copy [Family History Library Film #886194, item 4]:

First Book of Newbury Records

Copied from the Old Book written by Woodbridge, Rawson & Somerby. What is left commences 10 5 Month 1637

Apparently, then, a few leaves were missing from the beginning of this volume when it was transcribed, for by 10 July 1637 the town had already been in existence for a little over two years.

On the same reel of microfilm is the original of some, if not all, of the record volume on which this transcript was based [item 5]. Unfortunately, these original pages are not always legible. Enough can be read, however, to determine that the pages in this original volume were not in their original order when the microfilming was done. Also, the transcriber did not copy the pages in the order in which they are now bound. A spot check indicates that the transcript is generally reliable, with a few minor errors. A massive effort at collation and retranscription would be necessary in order to learn just where the transcriber went astray. Accordingly, the present article is based on the transcript, with the caveat that more detailed paleographic work might produce slightly different results.

Also, the transcriber was not fully familiar with the pre-1752 calendar. Despite the date given in the heading reproduced above, the first entry in the transcript is dated 10 June 1637, although a later entry will show that this date should have been 10 July 1637, as promised. In order to get a flavor of the volume, we reproduce the full transcribed record of this earliest surviving meeting:

> The town taking into consideration the diverse inconveniencies likely to ensue that those who have their accommodations on the south side of the river should have their house lots on the north side of the same & further considering how beneficial the land may be to those on that side of the river & are ready to improve the same it is therefore on due consideration agreed that the neck on the south side of the great river not yet broken up & formerly reserved for the waining of the calves shall be divided into house lots & the residue into planting lots as shall be judged & thought fit upon due consideration.
> It is agreed that Edward Woodman shall have an house lot and a planting lot both which shall amount to the __ __
> ___
> There is likewise granted a farm of 200 acres to Edward Woodman beginning at the little river beyond the great hill to enjoy to him & his heirs forever.

We observe the usual mixing of broad subjects, in this case the repurposing of a major section of land in the town, with very particular subjects, such as grants of land to an individual. Since two years' worth of records are missing, we must assume that many grants of land had already been made.

And, since Edward Woodman was one of the first settlers of Newbury, and one of its wealthiest and most prominent inhabitants, we must also assume that he had received earlier grants of land. In such a case, we would normally expect that he would be asked to relinquish any earlier grants in return for a new house lot.

The next recorded meeting was held on 4 October 1637, at which small grants of land were made to four men. In addition, at this meeting "John Blumfield hath rightly & lawfully purchased a house lot of Mr. Thomas Parker." As brief as this entry is, it constitutes a deed for this transfer of land, which is probably recorded nowhere else. We are reminded with these few words that the early New England settlers were still in the process of inventing an entirely new system of land conveyancing and recording, for which no equivalent existed in old England. And throughout New England in these earliest years, recording of land transfers was done at the town level, as counties in Massachusetts Bay did not come into existence until 1643, and even after that date many sales of land continued to be recorded in the towns rather than the counties.

Not long after, the town confronted a problem which every early New England town faced, although not every town recorded their actions in dealing with the problem:

> It was ordained in a lawful meeting November 5 [1637] that whosoever is admitted unto the town of Newbury shall have the consent and approbation of the body of freemen of said town.

The town of Newbury itself had been founded as the rate of immigration to New England reached its highest levels, of about three thousand persons per year from 1634 to 1640. The colony and the towns were struggling with the problem of finding the right size for a coherent agricultural town, and trying to keep out those who could not contribute to building such a town.

In addition to requiring the approval of the town for the admission of a new inhabitant in a given town, the prospective settler needed to have a certificate from the governor. Direct notice of these certificates is rarely found in town records, but on 16 November 1637 the Newbury town clerk entered seven such records, of which we present a sample:

> Thomas Moulton being licensed by the Governor to live in this jurisdiction was admitted into the town of Newberry as an inhabitant thereof, hath expressed under his hand that he will be subject to all lawful orders that shall be made by the town.
> Nicholas Busbe being licensed by the Governor to live in this jurisdiction was admitted into the town of Newberry as an inhabitant thereof & hath here promised under his hand to be subject to any lawful orders that shall be made by the town.
> Abraham Toppan being licensed by Jo[hn] Endicott Esq. to live in this jurisdiction was received into the town of Newberry as an inhabitant thereof & has here promised under his hand to be subject to any lawful order that shall be made by the town.

The town had already instituted the office of selectman, for on 2 October 1637 we learn that

> This day were five more deputed by the town to manage the town's business & to settle the accounts in the town, who did generally by the erection of hands consent to what was done & approve of the same. It was likewise desired by the general consent that the same persons, to wit, Edward Woodman, Jno. Woodbridge, Henry Short, Christopher Hussey, Richard Kent, Richard Browne & Richard Knight, who were chosen by papers, should perform the same service for one quarter longer

The significance of the "five more deputed" is obscured by the loss of the first two years of the town's records. The number of seven selectmen was common at this period, but the brief term of office of only three months was not. For a number of years Boston selectmen served for six months [GMN 8:17], but in many other towns they served for a full year.

From October 1637 until October 1638, a general town meeting was held almost every month, and the selectmen met more often that that. Much of the business at these meetings related to the granting of land, but there was also discussion of taxation and the work of the constable, the maintenance of the highways, the management of woodlots, and similar town business.

On 19 November 1638, a general town meeting included the following notice:

> It was ordered that Edward Rawson shall supply the place of Mr. Woodbridge & be the public notary and register for the town of Newbury.

At the end of this meeting, the transcriber entered the following observation:

> Here commences the transcript of Mr. E[dward] Rawson's handwriting who succeeded J[ohn] Woodb[ridge].

At this point the nature of the recordkeeping changes dramatically. With few exceptions, we are no longer given the dates of individual meetings, whether of the whole town or of the selectmen. Rawson simply made one entry after another, almost all regarding the granting and transfer of lands. And with increasing frequency we find embedded within the records deeds from one owner to another, giving more detail than was found in the example cited above from 4 October 1637.

By the early 1640s Rawson had returned to the earlier practice of organizing the records by town meeting, and dating each meeting. Then, after a meeting of 17 May 1647, the transcriber informs us that

> The preceding extract from the Old Book closes all that can be found in the handwriting of Edward Rawson. In this year, 1647, he was chosen Secretary of State, & in 1651 was chosen Recorder for the County of Suffolk after Mr. Aspinwall. His successor as Town Clerk of Newbury was Anthony Somerby, who filled the office 38 years & died July 31, 1686.

NEWBURY LAND RECORDS

Although, as we have seen above, the bulk of the business transacted at town and selectmen's meetings involved the granting of land, the town of Newbury, like most other early New England towns, maintained a separate volume devoted solely to the recording of land records, called in this case, as in most others, the proprietors' records.

This volume, for the most part in the handwriting of Anthony Somerby, begins with the following rubric:

> The several grants of lands granted by the town of Newbury in New England (out of that portion of lands which the General Court kept then at New Towne in the year of our Lord one-thousand six-hundred thirty & five granted unto them) to particular persons to enjoy to them and their heirs forever as followeth.

Immediately below this heading, the remainder of the first page is devoted to a list of the parcels of land granted to "Mr. John Spencer," one of the wealthiest and most prominent of the early settlers of Newbury. The list begins with a houselot of four acres, a farm of four hundred acres, thirty acres of salt marsh and three acres of upland. These items were not dated, but the fifth item, for "a mill lot of fifty acres of upland," does bear the date 20 October 1637. Reverting to the town minutes, we find no meeting with that date, and no record of the grant of a mill lot to John Spencer. This tells us that not all town business was recorded in the original book, or perhaps that the transcriber omitted some items.

Furthermore, if we assume that the first four lots were granted to Spencer prior to the granting of the mill lot, then those grants were probably made in 1635 and 1636, a period for which the town meeting minutes do not survive. Those four grants do constitute the usual basic compliment of lands granted to proprietors in all New England towns: a houselot (which carried with it the proprietary rights); some marsh or meadow land; some upland or planting ground; and, in the case of the more affluent settlers, a farm, meaning at that time a large, remote parcel of land which the grantee could lease out to someone lower on the socioeconomic scale.

The page for John Spencer continues with a 1650 record of a sale of land by Spencer to Henry Sewall, a grant of sixty-nine acres of dividend land, and a 1654 acknowledgement that Spencer had sold the dividend land.

Other pages might contain the records for more than one man, for not every Newbury resident was so well blessed with land grants as was John Spencer. Folio 17, for example, contains the records for John Cheney, Henry Travers, Robert Pike and George King, just two or three items for each man.

In our discussion of the town meeting minutes above, we noted that Edward Woodman was granted a houselot on 10 July 1637, at a time when we expect that he would already have been granted a houselot, presumably upon his arrival in 1635, but that he was not required to relinquish to the town the houselot granted earlier.

When we turn to the page for Edward Woodman (Folio 22), we find that he did indeed have two houselots, "an houselot of four acres" and "another houselot of an acre." Unfortunately, the grant of a houselot on 10 July 1637 does not give the size of the parcel, but the second houselot in the proprietors' records likely represents the 10 July 1637 grant. Perhaps Edward Woodman had performed some special service for the town which resulted in the grant of the second houselot. The list of his lands fills the front side of the folio and spills onto the reverse, with multiple grants of marsh and meadow, of upland and planting ground.

There should be much overlap between the town minutes and the proprietors' records, and it should be possible to correlate hundreds of grants of land made by the town or the selectmen with the corresponding entries in the proprietors' records. On the other hand, it should also be possible, by a process of comparison and elimination, to compile from the two sets of records a reasonably good list of the grants of land made during the first two years of the town's existence, in the period for which the town minutes are lost.

NEWBURY CHURCH

The story of the founding of Newbury church begins to take shape in early 1634. On 14 May of that year, John Winthrop reported that

> Mr. Parker, a minister, and a company with him, being about one hundred, went to sit down at Agawam, and diverse others of the new comers [WJ 1:158].

"Mr. Parker" was Thomas Parker, a highly-educated minister from Newbury, Berkshire, who sailed to New England on the *Mary & John* in 1634 [GM 2:5:367-70]. Most of the passengers on that ship were from the adjacent counties of Hampshire and Wiltshire, and most of the "company with him, being about one hundred," probably sailed on the same vessel.

They went together to the new settlement of Agawam [Ipswich] and a number of them joined the young church there. On 3 September 1634, "Mr. Tho[mas] Parker, Mr. Nicholas Easton, Mr. James Noise" were admitted freemen of Massachusetts Bay Colony, the three names appearing together on the list of freemen for that date [MBCR 1:370]. James Noyes was also a minister, from Cholderton, Wiltshire, who had also sailed on the *Mary & John* and was first cousin of Thomas Parker [GM 2:5:282-86].

In his account of James Noyes, Cotton Mather gives us a brief synopsis of the activities of Noyes and Parker in 1634 and 1635 [Magnalia 484-85]:

> Mr. Parker and Mr. Noyes, and others that came over with them, fasted and prayed together many times before they undertook this voyage; and on the sea Mr. Parker and Mr. Noyes preached or expounded, one in the forenoon, the other in the afternoon, every day during the voyage, unless some extraordinary thing intervened, and were abundant in prayer.
>
> When they arrived, Mr. Parker was at first called to preach at Ipswich, and Mr. Noyes at Medford, at which places they continued nigh a year. He had a motion made unto him to be minister at Watertown, but Mr. Parker and others of his brethren and acquaintance, settling at Newberry, and gathering the tenth of the churches in the colony, and calling Mr. Noyes to be the teacher of it, he preferred that place; being loath to be separated from Mr. Parker, and brethren that had so often fasted and prayed together, both in England and on the Atlantic sea.

Curiously, Winthrop did not take notice of the founding of Newbury church in 1635, as he did with so many other congregations. This may have been because Newbury was one of only two early Massachusetts Bay churches organized on Presbyterian principles, the other being Hingham. The most important distinction between the church government of these two churches and the developing Congregational Way of all other Massachusetts Bay churches was that in the latter the church was organized by a small group of laymen, who then chose and ordained their minister [Robert Wall, *Massachusetts Bay: The Crucial Decade, 1640-1650* (New Haven 1972), 160].

Winthrop and other civil and church leaders would not have approved of the Newbury way of choosing a minister, which would not have included broad participation by the laymen, and so he may have chosen to take no notice of the founding of Newbury church. As with the manner of the founding of the town itself, the prominence of some of the earlier settlers may also have protected the church from higher interference in this matter of church government.

Another wrinkle in the early history of Newbury church was the brief presence in town of Rev. Stephen Bachiler, who had an unfailing talent for disturbing anything he became involved in. Bachiler had arrived in New England in 1632 as the leader of the Plough Company and, as noted above, would have been associated with Richard Dummer in that episode.

Bachiler and his associates attempted to found a church at Lynn, but were rebuffed by the General Court. Bachiler tried again, and apparently did create his own congregation, at Lynn but not of it, as another, more "official," church had been organized in the interim. Bachiler's church took up an itinerant existence, moving to Ipswich and Yarmouth, then making a brief appearance at Newbury in 1638 before moving on to Hampton. While in Newbury, Bachiler appears to have baptized at least four children of members of his "congregation" [HampVR 1:3]. As we wrote in an earlier *Newsletter*, "we feel that a strong case can be made that for much of his time [in the 1630s] Stephen Bachiler carried his church around with him, and was not tied to one town as were all other churches" [GMN 3:20-21].

RECENT LITERATURE

Joseph C. Anderson II and Priscilla Eaton, "The English Origin of Nathan[1] Lord of Kittery: With an Account of the Conley Family of Cranbrook, Kent, England, and the Ancestry of Abraham[1] Conley of Kittery," *The American Genealogist* 84 (2010):81-94. The authors first explored the Lord family, discovering a baptism at Rye, Sussex, in 1633 for a Nathan Lord. They then found that this Nathan Lord's father was buried just a few months after Nathan's baptism, and the widow then married at Wittersham, Kent, Abraham Conley. Within a few years, and no later than 1638, Abraham Conley, his wife, and his stepson Nathan Lord had moved to Kittery.

John E. D'Anieri, "When Was John Lyford Born?," *The American Genealogist* 84 (2010):176. By analyzing Oxford University records for Rev. John Lyford of Plymouth and elsewhere [GMB 2:1214-17; TAG 83:174-78], D'Anieri produces a more accurate estimate for his year of birth, suggesting that this event occurred in about 1578 (and perhaps even a few years earlier).

Patricia Law Hatcher, "The Peirce Family of Norwich, England, and Watertown, Massachusetts," *The American Genealogist* 84 (2010):177-84. The original passenger list for the family of John Peirce of Watertown tells us that he came from Norwich in Norfolk, but gives us no more detail than that. Hatcher has collected evidence which shows that this immigrant married Elizabeth Trull in 1610 at St. Edmund's parish in Norwich, and that nine of their children were baptized there, and a tenth buried (but not baptized) in that parish. The author also addresses the difficult question of the dates of arrival of family members in Watertown, not all of them having come in the same year. Finally, she provides information on the Trull family.

Myrtle Stevens Hyde, "Empson Ancestors, in England, of Child and Goddard Families in New England," *The American Genealogist* 84 (2010):185-89. Following up on work published more than two decades ago [TAG 63:17-28], Hyde delineates the family of Thomas Empson of London, whose daughter Ellen married in 1690 Wolstan Child. This latter couple were the parents of EPHRAIM CHILD {1630, Watertown} [GMB 1:349-53]. She also supplies some additions and corrections to the earlier article on these families.

John C. Brandon and Leslie Mahler, "The Parentage of Rev. Edward[1] Norris of Salem, Massachusetts: With a Descent from Edward I, King of England," *The American Genealogist* 84 (2010):200-11. The authors present the evidence for the English origin and parentage of Edward Norris, who arrived in New England in 1639, including his baptism at Alderley, Gloucestershire, in 1583. The authors then document a descent of this immigrant from Edward I through the De Clare, Despenser, Arundel, Browne and Poyntz families.

Brent M. Owen, "Elizabeth[2] (Dickerson) (Owen) Mountjoy of Salem, Massachusetts, and Southold, Long Island, and Her Children, John[3] Owen and Mary[3] Mountjoy," *The American Genealogist* 84 (2010):213-20. Previously published studies of the family of PHILEMON DICKERSON {1637, Salem} have not determined the fate of all his children. Owen makes a convincing argument that, although the Dickerson family had moved to Southold, Long Island, in 1650, daughter Elizabeth remained in or returned to Salem, where in 1670 she married Morgan Owen, who died within a few years. Still in Salem, the widow soon married Walter Mountjoy, who himself died in 1683. The author then argues that the twice-widowed Elizabeth, with two young children, one by each husband, then moved to Southold, presumably to be close to other family members there.

William W. Hough, "The Cheshire Home and Family of William Hough, 1640 Immigrant to New England," *The New England Historical and Genealogical Register* 164 (2010):245-49. Building on a clue entered in Saybrook, Connecticut, records in early 1703 by a son of the immigrant, the author presents a strong case for the origin and parentage of William Hough who came to New England in 1640, identifying the father of the immigrant as Edward Hough of St.-Mary-on-the-Hill, Chester, Cheshire.

John C. Brandon, "Reinterpreting the Vital Dates of William[B] Hawes and His Wife Ursula From Their Memorial Brass," *The New England Historical and Genealogical Register* 164 (2010):250-53. Brandon examines a memorial brass and thereby recalculates the years of birth for the paternal grandparents of EDMUND HAWES {1635, Duxbury} [GM 2:3:247-50].

Gale Ion Harris, "The Brothers William[2] and Daniel[2] Harris of Middletown, Connecticut," *The New England Historical and Genealogical Register* 164 (2010):281-91. In this second installment of a multipart article, Harris compiles accounts of the families of Daniel Harris, son of THOMAS HARRIS {1630, Winnissimmett} [GMB 2:864-66], and of the two eldest of Daniel's four sons.

Eugene Cole Zubrinsky, "Carpenter-Verin," *The New England Historical and Genealogical Register* 164 (2010):296-97. Zubrinsky provides evidence that JOHN GREENE {1635, Boston} [GM 2:3:141-48] and WILLIAM CARPENTER {1635, Salem} resided briefly in Salem before they removed to Providence.

Zachary McLeod Hutchins, "Building Bensalem at Massachusetts Bay: Francis Bacon and the Wisdom of Eden in Early Modern New England," *The New England Quarterly* 83 (2010):577-606. Hutchins argues that, contrary to claims made by Perry Miller, a number of New England Puritan intellectuals of the first generation of settlement were influenced by "Francis Bacon's grand schemes for recovering prelapsarian perfections," that is, for recovering the edenic knowledge lost at the time of Adam's fall. Most prominent of these was Rev. John Cotton.

(continued from page 2)

Turning to the Newbury records, we find the first direct evidence of a William White in that town in 1642. The Newbury proprietors's records have inventories of the land-holding of the earliest settlers of that town, that is, those who arrived in the late 1630s, and there is no entry for a William White.

William White does appear on a page of the proprietors' records dated 7 December 1642 and listing ninety individuals, mostly men, but with a few widows. These persons were all said to be "acknowledged to be freeholders by the town and to have proportionable right in all waste lands," and the list was compiled "for the managing of all things that concern the ordering of the new town" [Newbury Proprietors' Records 1:44v]. On 22 June 1642, six men were admitted to Massachusetts Bay freemanship, including a William White [MBCR 2:292]. Five of them, other than White, are known or thought to have been Newbury residents, and so this freemanship would appear to be for the Newbury man.

On 6 July 1650, Thomas Jones of Charlestown stated that "William White, lately of Newbery," sold land in Newbury to Jones, which Jones "long since in the year 1641 or 1642" sold to William Ilsley [ILR 1:146]. A deposition of 1679 shows that this land was first laid out to William Eastow, who then sold to William White, who sold to Thomas Jones, who sold to William Ilsley [EQC 7:194]. Finally, a deed of 1650 demonstrates that by this date (and certainly earlier) this William White resided at Haverhill [ILR 1:53].

In his will of 2 January 1683[/4?], "William White of Haverhill" made bequests to "my grandson John White" and to "Sarah my present wife" [EPR 304:265-67]. The grandson was son of John White, who had predeceased his father and left a will naming his son John [EPR 2:108-9].

There are many other interesting twists and turns to this story, which will be laid out in the completed sketch, but the final picture is clear. The various records relied on by Savage and Pope, along with many other bits of evidence for which there is not space in the present account, show the presence in early Essex County of two men named William White. The first, who may be identified with the 1634 passenger on the *Mary & John*, settled at Ipswich in the year of his arrival and remained there until his death in 1684. He had two wives, one whose given name we do not know, and the second the widow of JOHN JACKSON {1635, Ipswich} [GM 2:4:25-28]. With his first wife he had a son James.

The second William White was certainly in Newbury by 1642, and probably in 1639, but removed soon after 1642 to Haverhill, where he died in 1690. He also had two wives, Mary Ware, whom he married in late 1639 or early 1640 [WP 4:168], and Sarah, the widow of Renold Foster. This William White had an only son John.

Great Migration Newsletter

Vol. 20   April-June 2011   No. 2

COMMISSIONER TO END SMALL CAUSES

Among the county and local offices listed in the *OFFICE-HOLDING* section of Great Migration sketches, most are familiar or self-explanatory, even if they no longer exist in modern times. We have a good idea of the duties of a constable or a fenceviewer, and modern New Englanders know very well what a selectman does. Less familiar, however, may be the office of "commissioner to end small causes."

By 1635 Massachusetts Bay Colony had grown to the point that the colony courts held in Boston were no longer able to handle efficiently all the business brought to their attention. So, on 3 March 1635/6, the General Court instituted the system of Quarter Courts, to be held at four stated times a year at each of four towns: Ipswich, Salem, Cambridge and Boston. These courts were to try "all civil causes, whereof the debt or damage shall not exceed £10, & all criminal causes not concerning life, member, or banishment" [MBCR 1:169]. Each of these four courts had jurisdiction over the town where it sat and also over one or more neighboring towns; this arrangement was the precursor to the county system which was erected in 1643.

Before long, however, the authorities learned that even this expanded court system could not process all the cases that were brought before them. Therefore, on 6 September 1638, the General Court ordered as follows [MBCR 1:239]:

> For avoiding of the country's charge by bringing small causes to the Court of Assistants, it is ordered, that any magistrate, in the town where he dwells, may hear & determine by his discretion all causes, wherein the debt, or trespass, or damage, &c., doth not exceed 20s.; & in such town where no magistrate dwells, the General Court shall from time to time nominate 3 men, two whereof shall have like power to hear & determine all such actions under 20s.; & if any of the parties shall find themselves grieved with any such end or sentence, they may appeal to the next Quarter Court, or Court of Assistants, &c. And if any person shall bring any such action to the Court of Assistants before he hath endeavored to have it ended at home (as in this order is appointed), he shall lose his action, & pay the defendant costs. If no appeal be put in the day of sentence upon such small actions, the magistrate or the said 2 men shall grant execution.

The court then proceeded immediately to appoint three men for this office in each of four towns: Watertown, Weymouth, Hingham and Newbury. The General Court continued to make annual appointments of these commissioners, generally at the annual court of elections in May or June [see MBCR 1:263, 328-29 for appointments in 1639 and 1641].

A procedural change was made at the General Court of 26 May 1647 [MBCR 3:105]:

> It is ordered by the authority of this Court, that henceforth such as keep house of entertainment, clerks of the writs, & commissioners for small causes, shall be licensed at the County Courts where they live, or at the Courts of Assistants, to avoid trouble to this court.

Within a few years after this order, appointments of the commissioners to end small causes disappear from the colony courts and are found in the county court records. In the case of Edward Woodman of Newbury, for example, he was appointed to this office by the colony court on 18 June 1645, 8 May 1646 and 23 May 1650 [MBCR 3:31, 64, 194], but on 25 March 1651, and for many years thereafter, the appointment was made and recorded at Ipswich court [EQC 1:219]. John Upham, during the years that he resided at Weymouth, was appointed commissioner in 1639 and 1644, and on both occasions the record is in the county courts [MBCR 1:281, 2:73]. About 1651 he moved to Malden, and

(continued on page 10)

EDITOR'S EFFUSIONS

Three years ago, we experienced the First Great Migration Tour to England, conducted from 5 to 15 August 2008. The tour, based in Chelmsford, Essex, followed the lives and times of four ministers (Thomas Hooker, John Eliot, Thomas Weld and Roger Williams) as they were hounded out of England by Bishop William Laud of London.

We now announce the Second Great Migration Tour to England, to be held from 15 to 25 August 2012. We will be based in the ancient market town of Bury St. Edmunds, Suffolk, and will concentrate on the planning, equipping and recruiting of passengers for the Winthrop Fleet, which left for New England in 1630.

With the emphasis on the Winthrop Fleet, a prime destination for the tour will be the village of Groton, Suffolk, the home of Governor John Winthrop and a number of other 1630 emigrants. We will also visit Sudbury, Suffolk, the home parish of Rev. John Wilson, and Boxted, Essex, where Rev. George Phillips was minister. Wilson and Phillips were recruited for the voyage by John Winthrop and became the ministers at Boston and Watertown upon arrival in New England.

We will travel to a number of other parishes in Suffolk and Essex which had connections to the Winthrop Fleet, and also make excursions to Shakespeare's Globe Theatre in London and to Boston, Lincolnshire, which also supplied prominent passengers in the Winthrop Fleet.

In conjunction with the tour, we will be revising and updating those sketches from *The Great Migration Begins: Immigrants to New England, 1620-1633*, which pertain to Winthrop Fleet passengers. These augmented sketches will be published as a single volume just before the dates of the tour itself.

Based on the success of the 2008 tour and advance interest already expressed in any future tour, we expect the registration list for this event to fill very quickly. If you are interested in registering, please send an e-mail to Josh Taylor, Director of Education and Programs at NEHGS <jtaylor@nehgs.org>.

Robert Charles Anderson, FASG   Editor
Jean Powers, Production Assistant

The Great Migration Newsletter is published quarterly by the Great Migration Study Project, a project of the New England Historic Genealogical Society, 101 Newbury Street, Boston MA 02116
www.AmericanAncestors.org
www.GreatMigration.org
GreatMigration@nehgs.org

Copyright © 2011
New England Historic Genealogical Society

(continued from page 9)

for a number of years in the late 1650s and in the 1660s his appointment to the office may be found in the Middlesex court records [MCR 1:118, 150, 192, 217].

On 11 November 1647, the General Court ordered that

> in all towns within the jurisdiction where there is no magistrate, the 3 men appointed to end small causes under 40s. shall, from time to time, keep a true record of all such causes as shall come before them to be determined; & every plaintiff shall pay 18d. for every case so tried, toward the charge thereof; & the times of the meeting to be published, that all men may take notice thereof that are concerned therein.

This court also ordered that upon appointment, these commissioners were to take the oath of office from the town constable [MBCR 2:208-9].

There does not seem to have been a separate order recorded which raised the upper limit for this court's jurisdiction from 20s. to 40s.; the change simply appears here as a *fait accompli*. In his study of early Massachusetts law, George Lee Haskins, in a chapter on the English antecedents of colonial practice, noted that "the forty-shilling limit on cases which might come before the commissioners' courts for small causes in Massachusetts parallels the similar limitations imposed by statute on the jurisdiction of manorial courts, and suggests that the colonists may well have thought of the latter as a rough equivalent of their own courts for small causes" [George Lee Haskins, *Law and Authority in Early Massachusetts: A Study in Tradition and Design* (New York 1960), 275, footnote 12].

Despite the General Court order requiring that records be maintained for these lesser courts, very few records of the proceedings before these commissioners have survived. As noted above, however, cases heard before the commissioners could be appealed to the county courts, and when this happened copies were taken from the local court records and submitted to the county court along with other documents. We will examine three instances in which such extracts from the commissioners' court at Newbury have come down to us.

On 30 September 1662, at a county court held at Ipswich, "Rich[ard] Doell" sued "Samuell Plumer," on "appeal from the commissioners of Nubury" [EQC 2:436]. Among the loose papers for this court appears the following:

> Meeting of the commissioners of Newbury on Aug. 27, 1662, Mr. Woodman, Capt. Gerrish and Nicholas Noyes being present.
> Samuell Plumer, attorney for his father, Francis Plumer, v. Richard Dole; for cutting and carrying away hedging stuff from the land of Francis Plumer.
> Richard Dole acknowledged that he cut some brush wood from the land in controversy.

(continued on page 16)

Focus on Milford

THE FOUNDING OF MILFORD

Among the ministers who arrived in New England in 1637 were Rev. John Davenport and Rev. Peter Prudden. After spending the winter of 1637-8 in Massachusetts Bay, and considering various offers to settle in one or another of the Bay towns, these two ministers, and the families who had come with them, decided to join forces. They removed in 1638 to the Quillipiac (or Quinnipiac) region on Long Island Sound, where they founded the town of New Haven.

For nearly two years these two groups lived together in the new town, and in some ways behaved as one community. Most importantly, as we shall see, most of those known to be associated with Peter Prudden were granted land at New Haven in the same manner and the same amounts as were those who came with John Davenport. (For much more detail of this early settlement process, see Isabel MacBeath Calder, *The New Haven Colony* [New Haven 1934]. See also GMN 6:3.)

The two groups must, however, have known from the time they arrived in New Haven that one town would not hold both of them. The New Haven records begin on 4 June 1639, about a year after the arrival of the two parties in the new settlement, and in those earliest records there are very few references to any of the Prudden party.

The great exception to this latter statement was the inclusion of many of the Prudden party in the early list of estates, compiled at New Haven in late October and early November of 1640 [NHCR 1:91-93; GMN 6:4-5]. This list contained 123 entries, each representing a proprietary share in New Haven land. About sixteen of these individuals would make the move to Milford [GMN 13:11]. In fact, most were already residing at Milford when this list was compiled.

The oldest surviving book of Milford town records has the following inscription on its cover:

> Milford third Booke of Records
> With a Transcript of the most Nessisary
> Things Contayned in the two Former
> Books Transcribed by Major Robert
> Treat Thomas Welsh George Clarke
> John Stream Nicholas Campe
> Thomas Samford and Samuel
> Eells any four of them being
> A Commitie Chosen by the
> Towne. Samuel Eells
> Appoynted to write
> The Same as per
> Towne order
> January the 7th
> Anno Dom
> 1677

The first record is dated 20 November 1639, and lists "Those persons whose names are here underwritten [worn] to be free planters having for the present [worn] in the choice of public officers for the [worn] public affairs in this plantation" [MilfordTR 1:1]. There follow the names of forty-four men who would settle Milford. (As we shall see below, this meeting was almost certainly held at New Haven.) Of these forty-four men, about a third, as noted above, were of the Prudden party and had been residing for a year or more at New Haven. The remaining thirty or so were divided about equally between those from other towns, such as Wethersfield (where Prudden had briefly preached) and Roxbury, and those who were making their first New England appearance at Milford.

After this list is an order that "the persons settled in the church to choose persons [worn] to divide the lands into lots." This is followed by the names of eight more men, who would later appear as inhabitants of Milford, but some not for a few years, indicating that this part of the record at least did not properly date from 20 November 1639. Finally, "William Fowler, Edmond Tappe, Zachariah Whitman and Richard Miles are chosen for judges."

The formal acquisition of the land from the Wepowaug Indians took place on 12 February 1639/40 [Calder 57], and on 9 March 1639/40 there was "A General Meeting held of Wepowage [Company for?] the Ordering of Civil Affairs" [MilfordTR 1:1]. On 24 November 1640, "with common consent and general vote of the freemen the plantation is named Milford" [MilfordTR 1:2].

The meetings of the town were known as "General Courts" and for the first few years of its existence Milford was in effect an independent colony. This was a time when there many such minimal sovereign units throughout New England, which we have termed elsewhere "City States" [GMN 4:17-18-24]. At their first meeting, on 7 September 1643, the commissioners of the United Colonies of New England, as their first action, "upon a motion made by the commissioners of New Haven Jurisdiction, it was granted and ordered that the town of Milford may be received into combination and as a member of the Jurisdiction of New Haven, if New Haven and Milford agree upon the terms & conditions among themselves" [PCR 9:9-10].

On 23 October 1643, a General Court at New Haven noted that "this court was now informed, that of late there have been some meetings and treaties between some of Milforde and Mr. Eaton, about a combination," and proceeded to debate the issue, whereupon "it was, by general consent and vote, ordered that the consociation proceed in all things according to the premises" [NHCR 1:110-11]. Milford thus became a part of New Haven Colony, and remained so until the union with Connecticut Colony in 1665.

MILFORD CHURCH

Rev. John Davenport and Rev. Peter Prudden were the leaders of two independent "clerical companies." A "clerical company" was a grouping of a few dozen families, from a small number of neighboring parishes in England, who had gathered around a strongly charismatic Puritan preacher, and chose to come to New England in his company [Roger Thompson, *Mobility & Migration* (Amherst, Massachusetts, 1994), 44-55, 186-89, 260-62; GMN 6:3].

Perhaps the best evidence for the claim that the Davenport and Prudden parties knew from the earliest days that they would not remain together as one town is the dating of the foundation of New Haven and Milford churches. On 4 June 1639, Rev. John Davenport and his associates began the process of establishing their church, which, on 21 or 22 August 1639, became the First Church at New Haven [NHCR 1:11-18; Calder 84].

Rev. Peter Prudden and his followers must have entered into the same process at about the same time, for the first volume of Milford church records opens as follows:

> The Church of Christ at Milford was first gathered at New Haven upon Aug[ust] 22 [1639].
> The persons first joining in the foundation were these whose names [worn].
> Peter Prudden. William Fowler. Edmund Tapp. Zachariah Whitman.
> John Astwood. Thomas Buckingham. Thomas Welsh.
> The church covenant that they entered into is hereunder written [Milford ChR 1:1].

Immediately after the text of the covenant (which was identical with that adopted on the same day at the foundation of New Haven church) began the list of

> Persons after added and children baptized

The admissions to church membership were entered in a column on the left side of the page and the baptisms in a narrower column on the right side of the page. For many of the admissions, there are later annotations of deaths, dismissals to other churches, and, in some cases, later marriages. (Unfortunately, the early pages of this volume of church records are badly worn and stained and are difficult to read in places. Donald Lines Jacobus transcribed and published the admissions through 1687 [TAG 16:28-38].)

Over the winter of 1639-40, six men and women were admitted to the new church: Richard Miles and James Prudden on 13 October; Joannah the wife of Peter Prudden on 8 December; Richard Plot [i.e., Platt] on 29 January; and Francis Bolt and Hannah wife of Thomas Buckingham on 9 February. These six names were followed by the statement that "These were added to the church in New Haven."

The next admission reads

> March 8 [1639/40] William East joined at Milford

Henceforth admissions and baptisms were at Milford.

This was followed by the ordination of Peter Prudden on 8 April 1640:

> I Peter Prudden was called to the office of a pastor in this church & ordained at New Haven by Zachariah Whitman, William Fowler, Edmund Tapp designed by the church to that work, Zach[ariah] Whitman being the moderator for that meeting in a day of solemn humiliation.

This sequence of events forms part of the support for the conclusion that the first record in the town minutes, dated 20 November 1639, took place at New Haven as well. Note also that the second recorded town meeting, dated on 9 March 1639/40, was just one day after the admission of William East to the church at Milford, but that Peter Prudden states that he was ordained at New Haven a month later. Some few of the Milford settlers may have overwintered on the site of the new town, but most of the migration would have taken place in the spring of 1640, with much coming and going between Milford and New Haven.

MILFORD LAND GRANTS

There are a number of general orders about the granting of land scattered through the first few years of the town meeting minutes, but the first accounting of lands held by the inhabitants was made on "November 22th 1643 & December [worn]," when it was ordered that

> whosoever in Milford is entertained into possession of either meadow, house lots or home lots, that he or they all and every one for every acre of house lot or home lot or meadow, or part of acre, of which he is possessed shall pay after the rate of 4s. per acre provided a man shall be accounted to have so many acres of meadow as his proportion came to by the rule of persons and estates [and] according to the variation from the aforesaid number of acres, caused by reason of the different quality of meadow [Milford TR 1:4].

We see here the usual New England practice of fitting the size of the grants of land to the preexisting socio-economic status of the grantee and to the size of his or her family, the "rule of persons and estates," although the rule used in Milford is not stated explicitly, as it is in some other towns.

This town order is followed immediately by a list of the land already granted to forty-four men and one woman. There was also an entry for the "Mill Lot." The list was arranged in three columns, giving the acreage of the house lot, of upland and of meadow [Milford TR 1:4-5].

The size of the house lots ranged from seven and a half acres down to one and three-quarters acres. Five men received the largest size house lots: Zachariah Whitman, Mr. Edmond Tapp, Mr. Peter Prudden, Mr. William Fowler and John Astwood. These were the minister and four of the five men appointed to the first board of selectmen. The smallest house lot was granted to Jasper Gunn.

The "rule of persons and estates" cannot be divined from this list, as the grants do not seem to follow any regular formula. The five men who received the largest house lots each received a different amount of upland and meadow, ranging from fifty-five to thirty-three and a quarter acres of upland and from thirty-one to twenty-three acres of meadow.

Of the forty-four names in the 1639 list of those intending to settle at Milford, forty-two also appear in the 1643 list of lands granted. The two men missing were Thomas Baker and Nathaniel Briscoe. These two men had not, however, left town, for they held land in Milford soon after 1643. Three new names appear in the 1643 list: John Smith, John Fowler and Martha Beard. Based on these two lists only, the turnover in the population of Milford during its first four years was not very large.

In the town meeting minutes of the next few years, much of the business involved the granting and reassigning of land, a few examples of which we provide here. On 7 February 1643/4, the town "agreed that brother Thomas Baker shall be attended for satisfaction for land with the first opportunity" [MilfordTR 1:6]. On 27 March 1645, "upon debate about and concerning ten acres of meadow formerly given to Mr. Peter Prudden lying at the West River, [it] is now confirmed upon him by order of court" [MilfordTR 1:8]. On 15 December 1645, it is "agreed that William Roberts shall have a lot adjoining to William Slow" [MilfordTR 1:9].

MILFORD LAND INVENTORY

At "A General Court at Milford, December 24th, 1646," the town of Milford

> Ordered that all and every part and parcel of every man's land, both upland, meadow and house lots, shall be recorded in a book kept for that purpose, and whatsoever part or parcel of any man's land shall be sold or alienated or exchanged or given, from time to time, or at any time hereafter, it shall be brought, by either he or they who bought the land or meadow, unto him appointed to record, to be entered in the said book of records, and by both the parties who so exchange, or he that hath it a gift, before the particular court, next after such exchange or alienation [Milford TR 1:12].

The top half of the seventy-seventh page of the first volume of Milford records continues the chronological sequence of town meeting minutes, finishing with the meeting of 11 May 1663. Following the brief record for this town meeting, a line was drawn across the full width of the page, and then a different hand began a separate series of entries:

> A Transcript of the long narrow Book of Records Appointed by the town to be Transcribed by Rich[ar]d Bryan December the 23d 1700

(The date of this entry seems to conflict with the title page of this volume. A transcript made in late 1700 should not appear in a volume that was itself a transcript made in 1677. Closer examination of the entire volume might resolve this

apparent conflict, but our immediate interest is in the inventory of landholding which begins on this page.)

(The date of the entry also conflicts with the date of the town order which led to the creation of the book, but this may simply be one of the usual vagaries of record-keeping. Whatever the date on the volume, it could not have been compiled in a single day.)

Another line, somewhat lighter, was then drawn across the page, and the transcript of the "long narrow Book of Records" commenced, in the same new hand:

> December 28 1646: A Book of Records of all the upland house lots and meadow in Milford that is laid out to every man with the several bounds of every part and parcel and also the quantity or number of acres that every parcel doth amount unto or lie for.

This appears to have been the original title of this volume, and may have been written on a page of its own, perhaps even on the cover of the book.

The volume begins with a "Fundamental Agreement," a detailed exposition of the rules which the town adopted in an attempt to make the distribution of the land as equitable as possible. Since such agreements are not always preserved in the records, we here reproduce the entire document:

> It is a Fundamental Agreement that all lands whether upland, meadow or homelots, should be made equal, that if it was not equal to other men's in the quality of it, it should be made up in quantity, or if it were unequal in distance of place it should be made equal in quantity also, so that where you find any parcel to exceed in number of acres, more than it is charged with rates or any distant parcel that is not charged with rates, you may know that it is allowed for satisfaction to equal his land to other men's. And if it be a distant parcel that is not charged with rates you shall know it by this word (note) which part or parcel is never for time to come to be charged with any rates, except the owner of the land do exchange or give the [blank] parcel upon that condition & then for so much he is to be deducted out of his other parcel. Also where any land or meadow is found less in quantity than it is charged with rates, you must know that the quality of such land or meadow did and doth and forever shall be charged with rates as other men's land or meadow is for quality of such land or meadow doth equalize it to other men's.

Taken in isolation, this document would seem to indicate that Milford engaged in a more egalitarian regime for distributing land than did other New England towns in the immigrant generation. But we have seen above, in the order of 22 November 1643, that the town did employ a "rule of persons and estates," meaning that the proprietors would most certainly not receive equal-sized land grants. The equalizing spoken of in the "Fundamental Agreement" was more limited than that, simply ensuring that if a person was to receive eight acres of meadow, the tract assigned to that person should actually have eight usable acres of meadow, while a person who was to receive four acres of meadow should have four usable acres of meadow.

The "Fundamental Agreement" filled the remainder of the seventy-seventh page. Pages seventy-eight through ninety-nine contain the full inventory of Milford landholding as of 1646. Because this surviving version of the inventory is a transcript made more than half a century after the list was originally created, we should not expect that the transcript pages have maintained a one-to-one correlation with the pagination of the original, and there are many clues that no such correlation existed.

Page seventy-eight has a "header," as we would say in this modern world of word-processing, that declared the subject matter to be "Milford Records 1646," with the same header on the following twenty pages. This "header" appears to have been created at the time of the 1700 transcript.

Next on the page are the words "Home Lots," centered on the page. This is followed by the descriptions of the house lots of nine men and covers just over half the page. Then again centered on the page are the words "Home Lots 1646," followed on the remainder of the page by the descriptions of six more lots.

At the top of page seventy-nine are descriptions for two more home lots, then the centered words "Home Lots 1646," then descriptions of eight lots, then the centered words "Home Lots 1646," then the descriptions of four more lots, and so on through the remaining nineteen pages. In the latter pages the centered words refer to other types of land beyond just the home lots. We propose that these centered words represent the original page breaks, as created in 1646.

The listing of Home Lots begins at the top of page seventy-eight and ends about a third of the way down page eighty-two. The heading "Home Lots 1646" appears seven times, but in one instance was apparently not carried over by the 1700 transcriber. In most instances, each of these original pages had entries for about eight Home Lots, but in this one case the heading was followed by the descriptions of seventeen Home Lots, suggesting that this portion of the record had originally been two separate pages.

The standard form of an entry in this section is now given, using as examples the first two items on the list, at the top of page seventy-eight:

> Capt. Astwood hath seven acres and a half be it more or less being bounded with a highway to the east and north with the common to the west and Richard Baldwin's lot to the south

> Richard Baldwin hath three acres be it more or less bounded with a highway to the east Capt. Astwood's to the north the common to the west and Benjamin Fenn's to the south

The inventory continues in this manner, grouping the Home Lots in sequences directly reflecting their actual layout on the ground. John Astwood's lot was a corner lot, with unallocated land in his backyard and Richard Baldwin as his immediate neighbor to the south. Baldwin in turn had Astwood to the north and Benjamin Fenn to the south, and so on.

These descriptions allow one to reconstruct the original arrangement of the streets in town. The original first page of the inventory shows that one north-south "highway" had on its west side the five lots of John Astwood, Richard Baldwin, Benjamin Fenn, Samuel Coley and John Peacock, followed by a cross-street. South of the cross-street were four more lots, those of Henry Stonehill, Nathaniel Baldwin, James Prudden and Thomas Uffott (or Ufford), whose southern boundary was common land.

Interestingly, the first eight of these nine names appear in the same sequence in the founding document of 20 November 1639, being the eleventh through the eighteenth names in that list. Thomas Uffott appeared much later in that list. On the other hand, only two of these men had home lots of the same size as what they were credited with in the earlier list of 22 November 1643. John Astwood had seven and a half acres and Thomas Uffott had four acres. The other seven men on this original first page had in 1646 Home Lots slightly smaller than what they were said to have had in 1643. This may reflect the "equalization" process described above. However, all five of the men with the largest Home Lots in 1643, the seven and a half acre lots, had Home Lots of that same size in 1646. None of them had been "equalized."

On the last of the original pages of Home Lots, at the bottom of page eighty-one of the transcript and the top of page eighty-two, the regularity of the entries breaks down. The first two entries are for Mr. Peter Prudden and Mr. William Fowler, two of the leading men in the town, given their full seven and a half acres. These certainly continue the sequence of original Home Lots as given on the previous pages.

The remaining five entries, however, are more problematic. In one of them, "William Brooks hath bought of Thomas Bayly three acres," and in the entry following that, "William Camp hath one small home lot that he had upon exchange with William Tyler containing half an acre." These entries are not original grants from the town. Also, they do not constitute part of a regular series of lots on the ground, as we find on the preceding pages. This bottom half of the last of the original pages of Home Lots has the appearance of having been used after 1646 to record later changes in landholding. This is partially masked from us by the fact that this is a transcript and the hand appears to be uniform, but, as we shall see in the next installment of this investigation, the pattern repeats itself on many later pages of the inventory, and helps explain some seeming chronological problems in the record.

In the next issue of the *Newsletter*, we will examine this land inventory of 1646 in more detail, attempting to determine the usual package of grants of land made to each proprietor, and tracing from 1639 to 1646 the holder of each proprietary share, so far as possible.

RECENT LITERATURE

Jonathan A. Shaw, "George[1] Barrell, Emigrant to Boston in 1638, and His Children and Grandchildren," *The New England Historical and Genealogical Register* 165 (2011):5-14. George Barrell arrived in New England in 1638 and settled at Boston. The author has discovered that he was baptized at Cratfield, Suffolk, on 12 November 1581, son of George Barrell. In this first installment of a two-part article, Shaw has prepared sketches of the immigrant's father, of the immigrant himself and of the immigrant's daughter Anne.

Leslie Mahler, "The English Ancestry of Elizabeth Usborne, First Wife of Abraham[1] Cruttenden of Guilford, Connecticut," *The New England Historical and Genealogical Register* 165 (2011):15-26. Abraham Cruttenden, his wife Elizabeth and their six children came to New England in 1639 and settled at Guilford. After an extensive search in English wills, Mahler has discovered that Elizabeth, wife of Abraham, was the daughter of Thomas Usborne of Staplehurst, Kent. The author has prepared sketches for five generations of her Usborne ancestry and for the family of Peter Bridgeland, whose daughter Ann was the wife of Thomas Usborne.

David Butler Cummings, "Isaac[1] Cummings (1601-1677) of Watertown, Ipswich, and Topsfield, Massachusetts, and His Ancestry," *The New England Historical and Genealogical Register* 165 (2011):35-41. Isaac Cummings had four children baptized at Mistley, Essex, between 1629 and 1635 and then came to New England in 1636, where he settled at Watertown. The author has demonstrated that Isaac was baptized at Easthorpe, Essex, on 5 April 1601, son of "John Commin," and has prepared a sketch of John's family.

Gale Ion Harris, "The Brothers William[2] and Daniel[2] Harris of Middletown, Connecticut," *The New England Historical and Genealogical Register* 165 (2011):62-67. In this final installment of a three-part article, the author treats the families of William[3] Harris and John[3] Harris, sons of Daniel[2] Harris.

John C. Brandon and Leslie Mahler, "The English Ancestry of Joan Barton, Wife of Richard[1] Smith of Narragansett, Rhode Island," *The American Genealogist* 84 (2010):257-64. Richard Smith was in New England by 1638, settling first at Taunton. After sojourns at Portsmouth, Rhode Island, and New Amsterdam, he lived out the rest of his life at an isolated trading post in the Narragansett Country. Brandon and Mahler have identified Joan Barton, wife of Richard Smith, as the daughter of William Barton of Thornbury, Gloucestershire, and have prepared an account of his family.

Paul C. Reed, "The English Origin of Hezekiah[1] Usher, of Boston, Massachusetts, and His Brother Robert[1] Usher of New Haven and Stamford, Connecticut," *The American Genealogist* 84 (2010):265-77. Hezekiah Usher settled in Cambridge by 1638, but soon moved to Boston, where he became the colony's first book seller and publisher. He was

followed to New England by his younger brother Robert, who became an inhabitant of Stamford, Connecticut. Reed has demonstrated that the two brothers were baptized at Maidstone, Kent, sons of William Usher, and has prepared detailed sketches for the families of William Usher and his father John Usher.

Clifford L. Stott, "Thomas[1] Tibballs of Ellesborough, Buckinghamshire, and Milford, Connecticut," *The American Genealogist* 84 (2010):308-15. Stott argues that Thomas Tibballs, who came to New England in 1635 and eventually resided at Milford, was born at Ellesborough, Buckinghamshire, in 1613 and was baptized at the neighboring parish of Great Hampden. The author also demonstrates that Tibballs came to New England on the *Truelove* with a number of other families from the same part of Buckinghamshire, including Zachariah Whitman, the brothers John and Thomas Stream, Ralph Tomkins, Richard Hawes, William Preston, Edward Howe and Samuel Grover.

Joan A. Hunter, "William[1] Holton of Hartford, Connecticut, and Northampton, Massachusetts: With Discussion of His Prior History and Probable English Origin," *The Genealogist* 25 (2011):3-28. Hunter first presents evidence in favor of the argument that the William Holton baptized at Nayland, Suffolk, on 20 October 1610 was the same man as the passenger to New England on the *Francis* in 1634 named "William Haulton," and further that this passenger was identical with the early Hartford settler named William Holton. She then presents an account in standard genealogical form of the family of this immigrant.

Priscilla Eaton, "The Descendants of Nathan[1] Lord of Kittery and Berwick, Maine," *The Maine Genealogist* 33 (2011):20. A recent article co-authored by Priscilla Eaton established the English origin of Nathan Lord as Rye, Sussex. In the present article, Eaton has set forth details of the life of Nathan Lord and prepared an account of four generations of his descendants.

Caleb H. Johnson, "Troubles with the *Little James*: Edward Winslow's Depositions at the High Court of Admiralty," *The Mayflower Quarterly* 77:51-55. Johnson narrates the troubled history of the *Little James*, which was built in England for the use of the company of colonists at Plymouth and made the voyage to New England in 1623 along with the larger *Anne*. After calamitous adventures in the Narraganset region and at Damariscove, the ship returned to England, where a lawsuit was entered in the High Court of Admiralty by some of the London investors. Johnson then produces full transcripts, in part translated from the Latin, made before the Admiralty court by Edward Winslow in 1624, in which Winslow related his direct knowledge of the behavior of some of the crew of the *Little James*, first in negotiations with Governor Bradford, and then in their interactions with some of the fishermen at Damariscove when the ship was dashed upon the rocks there and sunk.

(continued from page 10)

Thomas Colman, aged sixty years deposed on Aug. 14, 1662, that the fence that was set up at the lower end of his house lot in Merrimack street was set up in the bounds of the said house lot and that the said lot was eight rods broad and four score rods long. Sworn before Samuell Symonds.

John Emery, Sr., testified the same.

Copy of the foregoing record made by Anthony Somerby, cleric.

The loose papers also contain the copy of a record regarding the town grant to Francis Plummer of seven acres of meadow, also copied by Anthony Somerby. This is then followed by the notation that "The commissioners found for the plaintiff. Richard Dole, defendant, appealed to the next Ipswich court" (that is, the court of 30 September 1662) [EQC 2:436].

Richard Dole then entered at the Ipswich court his reasons of appeal, listing three points in his favor. Samuel Plummer replied with his answer, responding to each of Dole's three points. The county court upheld the decision of the commissioners, entering "verdict for the defendant."

The county court at Ipswich held on 29 March 1664 heard two separate appeals made by Richard Kent, complaining of decisions made by the Newbury commissioners [EQC 3:126-30]. In both cases, the defendant was Lt. John Pike, attorney for the town of Newbury. On 10 February 1663/4, the town had issued a summons to Kent for "not paying for his horses that went on the dry herd commons."

Kent went before the Newbury commissioners on 10 February 1663/4 and again on 2 March 1663/4. The keepers of the dry herd entered depositions and a copy of their agreement with the town was brought forward. Several other Newbury residents made depositions as well. In both cases, the commissioners found for the town. Kent appealed both times; in the first of the two cases the county court came to a "verdict for plaintiff; the former judgment reversed," while in the second case they entered "verdict for defendant. Court did not accept this verdict." These two decisions seem to be in conflict, and, as is so often the case, we are unable to determine the final resolution of the dispute.

These glimpses of legal proceedings on the local level remind us of the constant stream of local disputes with which the authorities had to contend on a daily basis. The commissioners clearly attempted to follow procedures very much like those that obtained at the higher courts, taking written evidence from the contestants, including depositions from witnesses. While we are thankful for those local records which have survived, we can only bemoan the much larger loss of local records which, were they still extant, would undoubtedly answer many of our outstanding genealogical questions.

Great Migration Newsletter

Vol. 20   July–September 2011   No. 3

HOUSEHOLD GOODS - PART I

Eleven years ago in the *Great Migration Newsletter* we discussed the value of probate inventories to our genealogical research [GMB 9:9, 16-18]. That article took a broad point of view, laying out the overall structure of a probate inventory and naming some of the items that might be found in such a document. In the present article, we will take a narrower approach, looking in detail at some of the moveable items found in various rooms in the dwelling house of the deceased, with special emphasis on those possessions with names no longer familiar to us. (We will not in the present article have anything to say about real estate, livestock, or objects found in any outbuildings, including implements of husbandry.)

We will begin in the kitchen. Although the inventory of the estate of John Warner of Farmington, presented at court on 4 December 1679, does not explicitly state which goods were in which rooms, we can make some reasonable guesses [HaPR 4 (probate):27]. The estate was valued at £123 3s., with the goods arranged in eighteen groups, of which four consecutive groups all appear to pertain to the kitchen:

> a brass kettle, skillet & iron pot & kettle & trammel, tongs
>   & slice £4
> pewter 16s.
> a warming pan, chests, boxes, bellows & the books £1 13s.
> table, tubs, chairs, barrels, pails £1

A separate line at the end of the inventory also contains items which are normally found in the kitchen, along with items usually seen elsewhere:

> hive of bees, yarn & wool, cards, platters, dishes,
>   collander, trenchers, trays, kneading trough, flax hemp,
>   2 hoes & 2 sacks £4

The hive of bees was presumably in the yard and not in the house at all. Most of the other items appear to be the kinds of household goods which might be kept in the lean-to, a small extension off the back side of the house. The lean-to would usually be accessible from the kitchen and, in a smaller house, could serve many purposes, including use as a pantry.

Many of the items named in this simple inventory are familiar to us, such as kettles, skillets and pans. A *trencher* was a plate, often wooden; the word is now semi-obsolete, seen most often in the somewhat comic word *trencherman*, denoting a hearty eater. The reading of *slice* is uncertain, but may be intended for *slicer*, that is, an implement for slicing food. A *kneading trough* was a vessel for kneading the dough for bread.

Some of the terms refer to the implements and tools kept around the hearth for maintaining the fire and manipulating the cooking vessels. In the present instance the *bellows* and *tongs* would be in this category. A *trammel* was a part of the apparatus upon which a cooking pot was suspended over the fire. The trammel was, however, only one part of the apparatus, and the other parts are not named here. We will soon see, in a more detailed inventory, a more complete list of these fireplace items.

The inventory of the estate of Christopher Cane of Cambridge, taken 15 March 1653/4, does list all of his possessions room-by-room, with many more items than were listed for John Warner [Rodgers 1:132, citing MPR Case #3916]:

> In the Kitchen
>
> three potting dishes 2s.
> five pewter platters and some other small dishes £1
> four "chenne" dishes and two salts 1s. 6d.
> one bed pan and a frying pan 5s.

(continued on page 18)

EDITOR'S EFFUSIONS

With the completion of the second series of Great Migration volumes, covering the years 1634 and 1635, the Project is in a transitional phase. Part of our energies for the immediate future will be devoted to planning for the 2012 Great Migration tour, which will focus on the Winthrop Fleet of 1630. At the same time, we will be preparing a volume of sketches of the immigrants in the Winthrop Fleet, revising and updating the appropriate sketches which were initially published fifteen years ago in the three volumes of *The Great Migration Begins*.

Beyond this, however, and at the same time these projects are moving forward, we will be preparing for the future of the Great Migration Study Project by compiling a complete checklist of all those immigrants who came to New England from 1636 until the early 1640s. With this checklist in hand, we will have a clearer idea of how much work remains to be done to accomplish the original goals of the Project.

The compilation of this checklist will proceed in three stages. First, we will need to gather an inventory of all records created in New England from 1636 to about 1643. This will include town, church, colony and private records.

Second, we will compile a preliminary database by extracting from these many sources all names of early New England residents who have not already been covered in the volumes published to date. This database will likely contain many thousands of entries.

Finally, we will need to examine this rough database carefully, in order to combine those entries which belong to the same person. Even during these few years, individuals will appear multiple times in town and colony records. As part of this merging process, we will make a special effort with the most common names, to see just how many John Smiths or William Browns are among the immigrants.

In the Great Migration volumes published to date, there are about two thousand four hundred sketches. We think there are about as many more to be written in order to complete the Project. With this checklist in hand, we will have a more precise number of the sketches remaining to be composed, and will be better able to plan the future of the Project.

Robert Charles Anderson, FASG   Editor
Jean Powers, Production Assistant

The Great Migration Newsletter is published quarterly by the Great Migration Study Project, a project of the New England Historic Genealogical Society, 99-101 Newbury Street, Boston MA 02116
www.AmericanAncestors.org
www.GreatMigration.org
GreatMigration@nehgs.org

(continued from page 17)

one spit one pair of tongs one trammel 7s.
one great iron pot and two lesser pots £1
one brass kettle 17s.
one iron skillet one brass skillet 4s.
three axes 5s.
one sword and bandoliers 6s.
two pair of pot hooks 2s. 6d.
one bill hook and old iron 3s.
two water pails 8s.
one small table, cupboard and two forms 8s.
one powdering tub and tray 2s.

Potting was the act of "preserving of butter, meat, fish, etc., in a sealed pot or similar container," so a "potting dish" was employed in canning and preserving food. *Chenne dishes* were China dishes, this being one of several variant spellings of the time. A *salt* was a salt-cellar (or salt shaker). *Powdering* was "the act of seasoning or preserving food with salt or spice," so one will see a powdering tub or tray or trough.

A *pot hook* was "a hook suspended over a fireplace on which a pot or kettle might be hung." The *Oxford English Dictionary* gives an example from a 1630 inventory from Maldon, Essex, in old England: "In the little buttery, 1 iron hook to hang at the end of a trammel." Thus, the pot hook and the trammel could both be involved in hanging cooking vessels over the fire.

A *form* was "a long seat without a back, a bench," frequently found in the kitchen and used for seating at the table at mealtime.

A *bill-hook* was "a heavy thick knife or chopper with a hooked end, used for pruning, cutting brushwood, etc." Note that there were also "three axes" in the kitchen, so Christopher Cane apparently kept his tools for cutting wood in the kitchen.

As seen here, one often finds that the weapons maintained for service in the train band were kept in the kitchen; in this case, a sword and bandoliers. Why the bed pan was in the kitchen is hard to say.

When Henry Dunster died his estate was worth nearly £1000. The inventory was taken on 7 and 8 June 1659, and was very carefully arranged. The listing of items in the kitchen covered twenty-seven lines, and we will list here only a few of these items, not seen in the inventories we have already looked at [Rodgers 1:397-98; MPR 1:219-26]:

1 mortar and pestle £1, 1 grid iron 4s.
1 jack and 2 weights £1 10s.
2 old posnets 1s. 6d.
1 old kettle 18d., 1 brass mortar & pestle 7s.
3 old sieves, 1 churn, 2 washing tubs 6s. 6d.
2 brass scummers, and a brass ladle 5s.
2 glass platters 1s.
2 China dishes 12d., 2 cheese fats 18d.

(continued on page 24)

Focus on Milford

In the first installment of *Focus on Milford*, we began the examination of the earliest Milford land records. We first looked at some of the land grants as entered in the minutes of the town meetings between 1639 and 1646. We then began our investigation of what had originally been a separate land record book, which began with an inventory of lands granted as of 1646. To this point we have examined only the grants of houselots from that volume. We now proceed to look at the 1646 land inventory more broadly, in order to determine how the lands were actually granted, and also to see how much turnover there was in proprietary shares between 1639 and 1646.

1646 LAND INVENTORY

We have already demonstrated in our discussion of the Home Lots that the copy of the 1646 land inventory that has come down to us does not retain the original pagination. The copyist did insert centered headers that seem to represent the original pagination, although on occasions he failed to insert these headers, and two or more original pages have been run-on [GMN 20:14].

As already noted, the listing of the Home Lots covered page 78 through the top of page 82 in the copied inventory. Then, in the middle of page 82, we find the centered header "West Field, the Creek Shot, 1646." This denoted the beginning of what had been a new page in the original. There are eight land grant entries, after which the same centered header is repeated, followed by eight more entries, carrying over to page 83 of the copied inventory. There is then a new centered header, again indicating a new page in the original, and another seven entries of land grants. The inventory continues in this way until the middle of page 99, where there is a centered header saying simply "1647," indicating that the 1646 land inventory had come to an end.

A number of points about this arrangement demand discussion. First, there is the word "shot." This describes a subdivision of a larger piece of land, in this case the West Field. "Shot" is used in this context in the same way as "furlong," when the latter is employed in reference to area rather than distance. The West Field must have been quite large, as it contained seven "shots": The Creek Shot; the Cove Shot; the Pond Shot; the Meadow Shot; the Fence Shot; Poconock Point Shot; and Poconock Creek Shot. There were eleven other Fields, Plains or Meadows, some large enough to be divided into shots and some not.

As with the Home Lots, the copyist did not always remember to include the centered header indicating a new page in the original, so we cannot always be certain that we can assign a specific parcel to the correct division of land. For example, toward the bottom of page 90 of the copied inventory is the centered header "East Field, the East River Shot,

1646." This is followed by twenty entries of land grants, ending near the bottom of page 91.

There are a number of indications that this sequence of entries covered two pages in the original inventory, even though the copyist did not insert a header along the way. First, twenty entries are far more than are seen on other pages where the inserted headers seem to have been entered in the correct manner.

Second, there are clear indications that among these twenty entries are some that were entered at a later date. The first twelve entries were for grants made to the top ten or so leading citizens, who were always grouped together. The next entry is the grant of a Home Lot to James Pringle. A Home Lot should not have been entered in this section of the inventory, and James Pringle is not otherwise seen as a resident of Milford by 1646, suggesting strongly that this entry was added at a later date, in the blank space at the bottom of a page.

The sequence of twenty entries continues, on what we argue was a new page in the original, with three more grants to the leading citizens. These three grants were followed by five more, some being grants of Home Lots, to men not otherwise seen before 1646, including some who were sons of the early settlers, again suggesting that some blank space was used for later entries.

This same pattern appears in a number of other places. For example, at the bottom of page 83 of the copied inventory is the centered header "West Field, the Pond Shot, 1646," followed by seven entries. The first four of these were to men who had received several grants by 1646. The last three were to Joseph Northrupp (a Home Lot), Simon Lobdell and Walter Smith. The latter two men are not seen in Milford records as early as 1646, and their date of arrival in Milford will have to be determined by other records.

PROPRIETARY SHARES

We conclude by tracing the Milford proprietary shares from 1639 through 1646, by comparison of three lists. First, we take the 2 November 1639 list of those intending to settle Milford. The main portion of this list contains forty-four names, which are listed in order. (The 1639 list is immediately followed by nine other names, added at an uncertain later date. Those names will be discussed after we have examined each proprietary share.)

Second, we then enter after each name the three parcels of land granted to each of these persons on 12 November 1643. By the time of this 1643 list, three additional proprietors had been admitted, numbered 45, 46 and 47 below.

Third, and finally, we enter the lands actually granted to these and other persons between 1643 and 1646, and shown in the land inventory dated 1646.

(To save space and avoid some repetition, we have omitted the word "acres" after the number giving the size of each lot. The meadow lots were often measured in acres and poles, so "5¾ & 8 poles meadow" should be read as "5¾ acres & 8 poles meadow." An acre was equal to 160 poles; one rood was a quarter of an acre or 40 poles. We have also not taken note of the "shot" within each field.)

THE PROPRIETORS

1) **Zachariah Whitman**: 1643 allotment of 7½ houselot, 44½ upland and 20 meadow. In 1646 held 7½ houselot, 12½ in East Field, 11 in The Meadow "and exchanged with Mr. Fowler two acres in all thirteen acres" and 13 in North Meadow.

2) **Thomas Welsh**: 1643 allotment of 4½ houselot, 16¼ upland and 10 meadow. In 1646 held 4½ houselot, 4 in East Field, another 12¼ in East Field, 1 in The Meadow, another 4 in The Meadow and 5 in East Meadow. ("Thomas Welch bought of Mr. William Fowler" 2 in The Meadow.)

3) **Thomas Wheeler**: 1643 allotment of 3 houselot, 12¼ upland and 5¾ & 8 poles meadow. In 1646 held 3 houselot, 3 in East Field, another 9¼ in East Field, ½ in The Meadow, another 2½ in The Meadow and 2¾ & 8 poles in East Meadow.

4) **Edmond Tapp**: 1643 allotment of 7½ houselot, 55 upland and 31 meadow. In 1646 held 7½ houselot, 13½ in East Field, 41½ in Stubie Plain, 10½ in The Meadow, 15½ in East Meadow and 4 in Harbour Meadow.

5) **Thomas Buckingham**: 1643 allotment of 3 houselot, 17½ upland and 8 meadow. In 1646 held 2¾ houselot, 4 in East Field, another 13¼ in East Field, 1 in Stubie Plain ("this is not to be charged with rates"), 4 in The Meadow, 4 in East Meadow and another 1½ in East Meadow.

6) **Richard Miles**: 1643 allotment of 6 houselot, 39¾ upland and 21 meadow. By 1646 this propriety had been acquired by Robert Plumb, who held 5¾ houselot, 10 in East Field, another 29¾ in East Field, 10½ in The Meadow, 10½ in East Meadow,

7) **Richard Platt**: 1643 allotment of 4½ houselot, 27½ upland and 13 meadow. In 1646 held 4¼ houselot, 6¾ in East Field, another 20¾ in East Field, 4½ in The Meadow and 1 in Harbour Meadow. ("George Clark Senior hath bought of Richard Platt" 6 in East Meadow.)

8) **Thomas Tapping**: 1643 allotment of 6 houselot, 37 upland and 19 meadow. By 1646 this propriety had been acquired by Edmond Tapp, who held 1¼ & 20 poles houselot, 9 in East Field, another 13 in East Field, 19 in Stubie Plain, 1½ in The Meadow, another 8 in The Meadow, 9½ in East Meadow and 2 in East Meadow.

9) **Peter Prudden**: 1643 allotment of 7½ houselot, 33¼ upland and 29 meadow. In 1646 held 7½ houselot, 8¼ in East Field, another 25 in East Field, 7 in The Meadow, 9 in East Meadow, another 3 in East Meadow and 10 in North Meadow.

10) **William Fowler**: 1643 allotment of 7½ houselot, 41½ upland and 25 meadow. In 1646 held 7½ houselot, 10½ in East Field, another 31 in East Field, ¾ in The Meadow, another ¼ in The Meadow, and 12½ in East Meadow. ("Thomas Welch bought of Mr. William Fowler" 2 in The Meadow. "Henry Botchford hath bought of Mr. William Fowler" 4 in Great Meadow.)

11) **John Astwood**: 1643 allotment of 7½ houselot, 42½ upland and 23 meadow. In 1646 held 7½ houselot, 21¼ in West Field, another 21¼ in West Field, 10 in Stubie Plain and 23 in Great Meadow.

12) **Richard Baldwin**: 1643 allotment of 4½ houselot, 14½ upland and 8 & 32 poles meadow. In 1646 held 3 houselot, 7¼ in West Field, 11 in Stubie Plain and 8 & 32 poles in Great Meadow.

13) **Benjamin Fen**: 1643 allotment of 4½ houselot, 19½ upland and 10 & 32 poles meadow. In 1646 held 2¼ & 13 poles houselot, 1½ in West Field, another 9¾ in West Field, 13 in Stubie Plain and 10 & 32 poles in Great Meadow.

14) **Samuel Coley**: 1643 allotment of 3 houselot, 6 upland and 2 & 96 poles meadow. In 1646 held 2¼ & 20 poles houselot, 1 in West Field, another 3 in West Field, another 3 in West Field, 3 in Adding Plain and 2½ & 16 poles in Great Meadow.

15) **John Peacock**: 1643 allotment of 3 houselot, 11¼ upland and 5 & 68 poles meadow. In 1646 held 1¾ houselot, 5¾ in West Field, another 5¾ in West Field and 5¼ & 28 poles in Great Meadow.

16) **Henry Stonehill**: 1643 allotment of 4½ houselot, 17½ upland and 10 meadow. In 1646 held 2½ & 20 poles houselot, 8¾ in West Field, 14¾ in West Field ("six acres of this is not to be charged"), and 10 in Great Meadow.

17) **Nathaniel Baldwin**: 1643 allotment of 3 houselot, 5½ upland and 2 & 48 poles meadow. In 1646 held 2 houselot, 2¾ in West Field, another 2¾ in West Field, ¾ in Adding Plain, and 2¼ & 8 poles in Great Meadow.

18) **James Prudden**: 1643 allotment of 3 houselot, 6 upland and 2 & 96 poles meadow. In 1646 held 2 houselot, 3 in West Field, another 3 in West Field, 3¾ in Mill Neck, ¾ in Adding Plain, and 2½ & 16 poles in Great Meadow.

19) **Thomas Baker**: Not in 1643 allotment list. In 1646 held 3½ houselot, 7½ in Adding Plain, and 3½ in North Meadow.

20) **George Clarke Sr.**: 1643 allotment of 4½ houselot, 13½ upland and 6 meadow (as "George Clarke carpenter"). In 1646 held 4½ houselot, 3 in West Field, another 4 in West Field, another 21½ in West Field ("sixteen acres of this is not to be charged with rates") and 6½ & 16 poles in New Meadow. ("George Clark Senior hath bought of Richard Platt" 6 in East Meadow.)

21) **George Hubbert**: 1643 allotment of 4½ houselot, 12½ upland and 7 meadow. In 1646 held 4½ houselot, 2¼ in West Field, ½ in West Field ("this is not to be charged with rates"), another 1½ in West Field, another 4 in West Field ("this is not to be charged with rates"), another 3 in West Field, another 6¼ in West Field, 1 in Mill Neck and 7 in New Meadow.

22) **Jasper Gunn**: 1643 allotment of 1¾ houselot, 12 upland and 5 & 32 poles meadow. In 1646 held ¾ houselot, 10 in Mill Neck ("three acres of this is not to be charged with rates"), 6 in Adding Plain, 5 & 32 poles in Great Meadow and ¾ in New Meadow ("this is not to be charged with rates").

23) **John Fletcher**: 1643 allotment of 4 houselot, 17 upland and 8 & 32 poles meadow. In 1646 held 2¾ & 30 poles houselot, 8½ in West Field, another 8½ in West Field, ¾ in Mill Neck ("this is not to be charged with rates"), 1½ in Adding Plain, 8 & 32 poles in Great Meadow and ¾ in New Meadow ("this is not to be charged with rates").

24) **Alexander Bryan**: 1643 allotment of 2¾ houselot, 8½ upland and 3 & 96 poles meadow. In 1646 held 4 & 25 poles houselot. This was not, however, the houselot he had been allotted in 1643; by 1646 his propriety had been acquired by John Baldwin, who held 2¼ & twenty poles houselot, 4¼ in West Field, another 4¼ in West Field, 2 in Adding Plain, 3½ & 16 poles in Great Meadow and ½ in New Meadow ("this is not to be charged with rates").

25) **Francis Bolt**: 1643 allotment of 2¾ houselot, 5½ upland and 2 & 48 poles meadow. In 1646 "Francis Bolt or now Phillip Bolt widow Sarah Bolt and Susanah Bolt" held 2¼ & 20 poles houselot, 2¾ in West Field, another 2¾ in West Field, 1½ in Adding Field, 2¼ & 8 poles in Great Meadow and ½ in New Meadow ("this is not to be charged with rates").

26) **Micah Tomkins**: 1643 allotment of 2¾ houselot, 8 upland and 3 & 48 poles meadow. In 1646 held 2¼ & 20 poles houselot, 4 in West Field, another 4 in West Field, 2½ in Adding Plain, 3¼ & 8 poles in Great Meadow and ½ in New Meadow ("this is not to be charged with rates").

27) **John Birdsey**: 1643 allotment of 4 houselot, 5½ upland and 2 & 48 poles meadow. In 1646 held 2¾ & 20 poles houselot, 2¾ in West Field, another 2¾ in West Field, 1½ in Adding Plain, 1¼ & 8 poles in New Meadow and another 1 in New Meadow. ("John Birdsey bought of Roger Terrill" 4 in New Meadow.)

28) **Edmond Harvey**: 1643 allotment of 4 houselot, 15 up-land and 8 meadow. By 1646 this propriety had been acquired by Timothy Baldwin, who held 2¾ houselot, 7½ in West Field, another 7½ in West Field, 2 in Adding Plain and 8 in Great Meadow.

29) **John Lane**: 1643 allotment of 2¾ houselot, 10 upland and 4½ meadow. In 1646 held 2½ & 20 poles houselot, 4½ in West Field, another 4½ in West Field, 1½ in Mill Neck ("this is not to be charged with rates"), ¾ in Adding Plain, 4½ in Great Meadow and 1½ in New Meadow ("this is not to be charged with rates").

30) **William East**: 1643 allotment of 2¾ houselot, 5½ up-land and 2 & 48 poles meadow. In 1646 held 2¾ houselot, 2¾ in West Field, another 2¾ in West Field, ½ in Mill Neck ("this is not to be charged with rates"), 1½ in Adding Plain and 2¼ & 8 poles in Great Meadow.

31) **Thomas Lawrence**: 1643 allotment of 2¾ houselot, 5½ upland and 1 & 96 poles. In 1646 "William East hath bought of Thomas Larance" 2 houselot. "Thomas Laranc" held 1 in West Field, another 1¾ in West Field, another 1¾ in West Field and 1½ & 16 poles in Great Meadow.

32) **Thomas Samford**: 1643 allotment of 2¾ houselot, 16½ upland and 7 & 68 poles meadow. In 1646 held 2¾ houselot, 8¼ in West Field, another 8¼ in West Field, 4 in Adding Plain and 7¼ & 28 poles in Great Meadow.

33) **Timothy Baldwin**: 1643 allotment of 4 houselot, 15 upland and 8½ meadow. In 1646 held 4 houselot, 7½ in West Field, another 7½ in West Field, 2 in Adding Plain and 8½ in Great Meadow.

34) **George Clarke Jr.**: 1643 allotment of 6 houselot, 32½ upland and 18 meadow (as "George Clarke husbandman"). In 1646 held 4¼ houselot, 3 in West Field ("this is not to be charged with rates"), another 16¼ in West Field, another 42 in West Field "and bought of Timothy Baldwin half an acre of meadow" ("six and twenty acres and one rood of this is not to be charged with rates"), 7 in Great Meadow, 6¾ in New Meadow, another 4 in New Meadow ("this is not to be charged with rates") and 4 in Poconock Creek Meadow.

35) **John Burwell**: 1643 allotment of 3 houselot, 15½ up-land and 6 & 48 poles meadow. In 1646 held 2 & 20 poles houselot, 1 in West Field ("this is not to be charged with rates"), another 7¾ in West Field, another 6 in West Field ("this is not to be charged with rates"), another 19¼ & 20 poles in West Field ("eleven acres a half & 20 poles of this is not to be charged with rates"), 1¾ in Mill Neck ("this is not to be charged with rates"), 3 in New Meadow and 3¼ & 8 poles in Poconock Creek Meadow.

36) **Henry Botsford**: 1643 allotment of 3 houselot, 6 up-land and 2 & 96 poles meadow. In 1646 held 2½ houselot, 3 in West Field, another 7½ in West Field ("four acres and a half of this is not to be charges with rates"), 1 in New Meadow and 1½ & 16 poles in Poconock Creek Meadow. ("Henry Botchford hath bought of Mr. William Fowler" 4 in Great Meadow.)

37) **Joseph Baldwin**: 1643 allotment of 3 houselot, 11 upland and 4 & 96 poles meadow. In 1646 held 2¼ & 20 poles houselot, 5½ in West Field, another 14 in West Field ("eight acres and a half of this is not to be charged with rates"), 2¼ in Mill Neck ("this is not to be charged with rates"), 2 in New Meadow and 2½ & 16 poles in Poconock Creek Meadow.

38) **Philip Hatley**: 1643 allotment of 4½ houselot, 9½ upland and 5 meadow. In 1646 held 3¾ & 20 poles houselot, 4¾ in West Field, another 4¾ in West Field, 1 in Mill Neck ("this is not to be charged with rates"), 2 & 32 poles in New Meadow and 3 in Poconock Creek Meadow.

39) **Nicholas Camp**: 1643 allotment of 4½ houselot, 25 upland and 12 meadow. In 1646 held 6¼ & 20 poles houselot, 1 in West Field ("this is not to be charged with rates"), another 8 in West Field ("this is not to be charged with rates"), another 33¾ in West Field ("one and twenty acres and one rood of this is not to be charged with rates"), 4 in Mill Neck ("this is not to be charged with rates"), 6 in New Meadow and 6 in Poconock Creek Meadow.

40) **John Rogers**: 1643 allotment of 3 houselot, 6½ upland and 2¾ meadow. In 1646 held 1¾ & 20 poles houselot, 3¼ in West Field, another 8 in West Field ("four acres and three roods of this is not to be charged with rates"), 1¼ & 24 poles in New Meadow and 1½ in Poconock Creek Meadow.

41) **Thomas Uffott**: 1643 allotment of 4 houselot, 16¼ upland and 10 meadow. In 1646 held 4 houselot, 10 in West Field, another 10 in West Field, 9½ in Great Meadow and 1½ in New Meadow.

42) **Nathaniel Briscoe**: Not in 1643 allotment list. In 1646 held 3 houselot, 4 in West Field ("two acres of this is not to be charged with rates"), another 2 in West Field and 2 in North Meadow.

43) **Thomas Tibballs**: 1643 allotment of 3 houselot, 3 upland and 1 & 48 meadow. In 1646 held 1½ & 20 poles houselot, 1½ in West Field, another 2¼ in West Field, another 1½ in West Field ("this is not to be charged with rates"), another 6 in West Field ("two acres and one rood of this is not to be charged with rates"), 1¼ & 8 poles in New Meadow and 2 & 32 poles in North Meadow.

44) **John Sherman**: 1643 allotment of 4½ houselot, 20 upland and 9½ meadow. No holdings in 1646 inventory.

45) **John Smith**: Not in 1639 list. 1643 allotment of 2½ houselot, 3 upland and 2 meadow. In 1646 held 1¾ & 20 poles houselot, 1½ in West Field, another 1½ in West Field and 2¼ & 8 poles in Poconock Creek Meadow. ("John Smith hath bought of William Slow three acres and the town hath given him one acre in all four acres.")

46) **John Fowler**: Not in 1639 list. 1643 allotment of 3 houselot, 3½ upland and 1 & 96 poles meadow. In 1646 held 1½ & 20 poles houselot, 1¾ in West Field, another 4¼ & 20 poles in West Field ("two acres a half and twenty pole of this is not to be charged with rates"), ¾ & 20 poles in Mill Neck ("this is not to be charged with rates") and 1½ & 16 poles in New Meadow.

47) **Martha Beard**: Not in 1639 list. 1643 allotment of 6 houselot, 37½ upland and 19 meadow. In 1646 held 4¼ houselot, 1 in West Field ("this is not to be charged with rates"), another 18¾ in West Field, another 18¾ in West Field, another 20 in West Field ("this is not to be charged with rates"), 6 in Mill Neck ("this is not to be charged with rates") and 19 in New Meadow.

48) **The Mill Lot**: 1643 allotment of 10 upland and 20 meadow. By 1646 William Fowler had acquired this lot and held 10 in East Field and 12 on Housatonnack River.

49) **Roger Terrill**: Not in 1639 or 1643 lists. In 1646 held 2¾ & 20 poles houselot, 16 in West Field, 1 in New Meadow and 5 in Poconock Creek Meadow. ("John Birdsey bought of Roger Terrill" 4 in New Meadow.)

50) **Andrew Benton**: Not in 1639 or 1643 lists. In 1646 held 3 houselot, 7½ in West Field ("three acres and three roods of this is not to be charged with rates"), another 3¾ in West Field and 3 in New Meadow.

51) **Edward Riggs**: Not in 1639 or 1643 lists. In 1646 held 3 houselot, 5½ in West Field, and 2 in Poconock Creek Meadow.

52) **John Brown**: Not in 1639 or 1643 lists. In 1646 held 3 houselot, 6½ in West Field ("three acres and one rood of this is not to be charged with rates"), another 3¼ in West Field and 2 in North Meadow.

53) **William Brooks**: Not in 1639 or 1643 lists. In 1646 held 3 houselot, 5½ in West Field ("two acres and three roods of this is not to be charged with rates"), another 2¾ in West Field and 2 in North Meadow "and bought of Thomas Bayly two acres in all four acres."

54) **Thomas Bayly**: Not in 1639 or 1643 lists. In 1646 held 3 houselot. ("William Brooks hath bought of Thomas Bayly" 3 houselot.)

55) **Robert Denison**: Not in 1639 or 1643 lists: In 1646 held 3 houselot, 3½ in Adding Plain and 2 in North Meadow.

56) **William Roberts**: Not in 1639 or 1643 lists. In 1646 held 3 houselot.

57) **William Slow**: Not in 1639 or 1643 lists. By 1646 he had "bought of Joseph Northrupp" 3 houselot, 3½ in Adding Plain and 2 in North Meadow.

58) **James Prime**: Not in 1639 or 1643 lists. In 1646 held 3 houselot and 2 North Meadow. (By 1646 he had "bought of Thomas Read" 3 houselot and 2 North Meadow.)

An analysis of all the proprietary shares will be published in the next issue of *Great Migration Newsletter*.

RECENT LITERATURE

Eugene Cole Zubrinsky, "A Fresh Look at the Parentage of *Mayflower* Passenger Joan (Hurst) (Rogers) Tilley: With Her Mother's Identity and Family of Origin," *The American Genealogist* 85 (2011):1-8. Building on earlier research by Robert Leigh Ward, Zubrinsky gathers and interprets evidence which confirms that Joan (Hurst) (Rogers) Tilley, wife of Thomas Rogers and of John Tilley of the *Mayflower*, was daughter of William Hurst of Henlow, Bedfordshire. Zubrinsky also identifies the wife of William Hurst as Rose Marshe, daughter of John Marshe of Chipping Barnet, Hertfordshire.

Leslie Mahler, "The English Origin of George[1] Abbott of Rowley, Massachusetts," *The American Genealogist* 85 (2011):26-28. Mahler demonstrates that George Abbott, an early settler of Rowley, was baptized at Chappel, Essex, on 24 November 1586. Abbott was married at Great Tey, Essex, on 5 October 1624 to Mary Felstead, and their first five children were baptized at Chappel between 1625 and 1632.

Jane Fletcher Fiske, "Pyle Connections," *The New England Historical and Genealogical Register* 165 (2011):121-33. The author has compiled accounts of William Pyle of Clyffe Pypard, Wiltshire, born perhaps about 1490, and of his three sons Thomas, John and Richard. Thomas Pyle was grandfather of GEORGE LUDLOW {1630, Dorchester} [GMB 1208-11] and of ROGER LUDLOW {1630, Dorchester} [GMB 1211-13]. Richard Pyle was grandfather of RICHARD KENT SR. {1634, Ipswich} [GM 2:4:140-42], of STEPHEN KENT {1638, Newbury}, and of Mary Kent, the first wife of NICHOLAS EASTON {1634, Ipswich} [GM 2:2:396-403].

Jonathan A. Shaw, "George[1] Barrell, Emigrant to Boston in 1638, and His Children and Grandchildren," *The New England Historical and Genealogical Register* 165 (2011):141-49. In this concluding part of a two-part article, Shaw presents standard genealogical summaries of John[2] Barrell and of his children Hannah Barrell (wife of Daniel Turrell Jr.), William Barrell and John Barrell.

Austin W. Spencer, "The Yeo-Condy Family of Marblehead, Massachusetts: Some Proposed Corrections to Torrey," *The New England Historical and Genealogical Register* 165 (2011):165-72. Samuel Condy of Marblehead and his widow Ann both died in 1678, leaving complicated and obscure wills. Spencer analyses these wills carefully, and arrives at new conclusions about the identities of some of the legatees. As a consequence, he offers revised versions of the entries created by Clarence Almon Torrey for the marriages of ten members of the Condy, Green, Hooper, Reed, Salter, Taynour and Yeo families. (Although none of the individuals described in these ten entries were Great Migration immigrants, several of them were born in the 1630s, and undoubtedly had connections with Great Migration immigrants. Samuel Reed's second wife, Jane, was widow of Henry Stacey, whose father John had arrived by 1639.)

Leslie Mahler, "The English Origin of Robert[1] Rand of Charlestown, Massachusetts," *The New England Historical and Genealogical Register* 165 (2011):183-86. Robert Rand arrived in New England by 1635, settling at Charlestown, where he died in 1649 [GM 2:6:1-5]. Mahler has located the marriage of this immigrant at Ridgewell, Essex, in 1622, and the baptismal and burial records for several of their children between 1624 and 1634. The author has prepared genealogical accounts of the families of the immigrant and his father.

Jillaine S. Smith, "The Two Richard Taylor Families of Early Yarmouth, Massachusetts," *The New England Historical and Genealogical Register* 165 (2011):187-99. Gabriel Whelden had arrived in New England by 1639 and soon settled at Yarmouth. Two of his daughters married men named Richard Taylor, one of whom was a husbandman and the other a tailor. In this first part of a multi-part article, Smith lays out the problem and then argues that Richard Taylor, tailor, of Yarmouth, or possibly another Richard Taylor, tailor, of Boston, probably married Mary Whelden, while Richard Taylor, husbandman, probably married Ruth Whelden. The author then presents an account of the family of Richard Taylor, tailor, of Yarmouth.

Caleb H. Johnson, "*Mayflower* Passenger Humility Cooper," *The Mayflower Quarterly* 77 (2011):126-28. Gathering together all known records for Humility Cooper, Johnson constructs a connected narrative of what is known of her life. She returned to England and probably died there, apparently unmarried.

Katherine A. Grandjean, "New World Tempests: Environment, Scarcity, and the Coming of the Pequot War," *William and Mary Quarterly*, Third Series, 68 (2011):75-100. The literature on the causes of the Pequot War is extensive, but no consensus has been reached. Grandjean offers a new explanatory narrative, incorporating elements of older accounts with added emphasis on other factors. She describes the "lack of provisions" throughout New England in the years around 1635, especially in the three Connecticut river towns (Hartford, Windsor and Wethersfield) and in the settlement at the mouth of the river, Saybrook. She takes note of the pressures placed on the limited food supplies by the hurricane of 1635 (which affected everyone, but the English more than the Indians) and by the increased pace of new English immigration in 1634 and later. Many writers in the seventeenth century and ever since have ascribed the war to retaliation by the English against the killing by the Indians of Captain John Stone and his party in 1634 and of John Oldham and others in 1636. Grandjean admits the importance of this, but notes that, as coastal traders, Stone and Oldham were instrumental in the attempts to supply the recent Connecticut settlers with corn and other provisions. The author points to the raiding of the Indian corn harvests as part of the war efforts. She argues that much of the motivation for the actions of the English was hunger.

(continued from page 18)

One normally expects to see a *mortar and pestle* in an apothecary's shop, but this combination of implements is frequently seen in the kitchen, being used in the processing of food. Dunster was affluent enough to own two mortars and pestles, one explicitly stated as being made of brass, so the other was probably porcelain, although it could have been wooden.

Glass platters, or, for that matter, anything made of glass, are not often seen in seventeenth-century inventories, so this is another measure of Dunster's high economic status.

A *jack* was "a machine for turning the spit in roasting meat; either wound up like a clock or actuated by the draught of heated air up the chimney." In the Dunster household, this would have been a clockwork mechanism, driven by the *weights*.

A *scummer* is "a shallow ladle or sieve for removing scum or floating matter from the surface of a liquid," most likely grease in the normal operations of a kitchen. A *posnet* is "a small metal pot or vessel for boiling, having a handle and three feet." A *fat*, as in *cheese fat*, is "a cask or barrel to contain dry things." (In the context of a container for liquids, "fat" and "vat" could be used interchangeably.) A *gridiron* was "a cooking utensil formed of parallel bars of iron or other metal in a frame, usually supported on short legs, and used for broiling flesh or fish over a fire."

We close our exploration of the kitchen with an example from a much simpler inventory, that of Thomas Carter of Charlestown, taken 25 June 1652, in which there is only one entry clearly relating to the kitchen [Rodgers 1:95, citing MPR Case #4043]:

> In brass, pewter, iron vessels, and furniture in the kitchen with lumber in the chamber £6

The *brass, pewter, iron vessels* would comprise many of those items listed in more detail in other inventories, used in the preparation and consumption of food.

Furniture in the kitchen might seem to refer to the chairs, tables and cupboards that one would expect in this room, but at the time the word "furniture" usually meant what we now describe as "furnishings," and could be a brief way to include the hardware of the hearth, such as andirons, pot-hooks and trammels.

Lumber in the chamber does not mean that there were pieces of wood in the room above the kitchen. "Lumber" in the seventeenth century described miscellaneous, usually worn or obsolete items, which could be of wood or earth or metal. Another way to convey the same idea would be to say "odds and ends in the junk room."

In the next installment of this article we will examine the bed chamber and other rooms on the upper floor.

Great Migration Newsletter

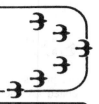

| Vol. 20 | October–December 2011 | No. 4 |

MILFORD PROPRIETORS

In the last two issues of the *Great Migration Newsletter*, we have published extensive details on the earliest granting of land by the town of Milford, Connecticut [GMN 20:12-14, 19-22]. We are now in a position to answer a number of more general questions about this process.

First, we will examine the mechanics of the land granting process itself. How close did the actual size of the land grants conform to the 1643 list of proposed grants? What differences were there in the granting of houselots, upland and meadow? How did the land granters deal with land of unequal quality?

Second, we will look at the stability of the population of proprietors from the founding of the town in 1639 until the creation of the 1646 list of landholding. How many of the founders of 1639 were still in Milford in 1646? How many new heads of household had arrived by 1643, and by 1646?

When the 1643 list of land grants was compiled, the assigned houselots came in a limited number of sizes:

Acres	Number of lots
7½	5
6	4
4½	10
4	5
3	12
2¾	7
2½	1
1¾	1

As noted in our earlier discussions, when the compilation of actual grants was made in 1646, it turned out that all five of the men who had been granted the largest houselots received the full complement of seven and a half acres [GMN 20:12-14].

Those with smaller lots, however, did not fare so well. None of the four proprietors who had been assigned six acres received that a lot of that size. Richard Miles was given five and three-quarters acres, while George Clarke Jr. and Martha Beard each had four and a quarter. Thomas Tapping received only one acre and a quarter and twenty poles; as we shall see, this may have been the consequence of the sale of his proprietary share to Edmond Tapp.

Some of those who had been assigned smaller houselots in 1643 received their full allotment in 1646 and some received less. Even Jasper Gunn, who was given the smallest grant in 1643, an acre and three-quarters, was reduced in 1646 to a mere three-quarters of an acre. In only one case was the 1646 holding greater than the 1643 grant; for reasons that are not at all apparent, Nicholas Camp was originally granted four and a half acres, but in 1646 held a houselot of six and a quarter acres and twenty poles.

Not surprisingly, the houselots were laid out in one piece. The 1643 grants of upland and meadow, though, were in almost all instances laid out in two or more parcels, these parcels often being some distance from one another.

Exploring the grants of upland first, we find in the case of John Peacock a very simple example. In 1643 he had been allotted eleven and three-quarters acres. He appears in the 1646 list holding two pieces of upland: five and three-quarters acres in the "West Field the Cove Shot" and the same amount in the "West Field the Fence Shot." Thus, although all his upland was in the West Field, his grant was still divided into two segments. This was done by the simple expedient of giving him two pieces of equal size, but apparently this arrangement was not always possible.

(continued on page 26)

EDITOR'S EFFUSIONS

The process of revising and updating the Winthrop Fleet-related sketches from *The Great Migration Begins* is now well underway. The new volume, to be titled *The Winthrop Fleet*, will contain about two hundred and twenty sketches.

The first step was to take an old electronic file of *The Great Migration Begins* and select those sketches of persons who came on the Winthrop Fleet in 1630 (as well as a few who had been sent ahead in 1629 by the organizers of the fleet). This file had been transferred from one format to another in the fifteen years and more since originally created. So, many hours were expended in cleaning up the files and reinstating the standard Great Migration style.

Over the decade and a half since the sketches were first compiled, much new research has been published which establishes the English origins and other new information on a number of these families. In addition, many readers of the original volumes have contributed useful corrections and suggestions. The incorporation of this new material and the corrections will occupy us for the next few months.

In addition to these steps, all of which were anticipated when this volume was first planned, an unexpected bonus has emerged. Although the precise English origins of many of these passengers remain unknown, the process of concentrating on just this limited group of immigrants is revealing many interconnections among these passengers. The Winthrop Fleet was organized from the top down, with a number of Puritan lords and London merchants each sending several servants to New England in 1629 and 1630. Much of this information is already contained in the sketches as written in 1995. At the time these sketches were originally composed, however, the full range and import of these connections was not noticed. As a result, we will be able to present a much clearer and more informative narrative of the process of recruitment of the Winthrop Fleet passengers.

Due to space pressures and to the shortage of appropriate material, this issue of the *Newsletter* will have an abbreviated **Recent Literature** section. Also, the second installment of the article on **Household Goods** will be deferred until the first issue of Volume 21.

Robert Charles Anderson, FASG   Editor
Jean Powers, Production Assistant

The Great Migration Newsletter is published quarterly by the Great Migration Study Project, a project of the New England Historic Genealogical Society, 101 Newbury Street, Boston MA 02116
www.AmericanAncestors.org
www.GreatMigration.org
GreatMigration@nehgs.org

Copyright © 2011
New England Historic Genealogical Society

(continued from page 25)

In the case of Thomas Welsh, for example, the 1643 grant was for sixteen and a quarter acres of upland. The actual holding in 1646 was four acres in the "East Field the East River Shot" and twelve acres and one rood in the "East Field the East River Shot." The two pieces added up to the precise amount of the original grant, but in this case the two pieces were of unequal size. The two segments were in the same shot of the same field, but with the holdings of three other men intervening.

In many instances, however, the holdings of upland in 1646 were many acres greater than in the grant of 1643. Henry Stonehill was assigned seventeen acres and a half of upland in 1643. In the 1646 list he held two parcels of upland: eight acres and three-quarters in the "West Field the Meadow Shot" and fourteen acres and three quarters in the "West Field the Fence Shot ... six acres of this is not to be charged with rates." Note that if the "six acres ... not to be charged with rates" is deducted, Stonehill had two upland parcels, each of eight and three-quarters acres, which adds up to seventeen and a half acres. This then falls in the category of those recipients, like John Peacock, who had their original grant laid out in two equal halves. The extra six acres, not to be taxed, may be in compensation for the poor quality of some of the land actually laid out. This would have been part of the "equalization" process discussed in an earlier installment of this article [GMN 20:13].

Other cases are not so neat. Jasper Gunn was granted twelve acres of upland in 1643. In the 1646 list he had two parcels totalling sixteen acres: ten acres in the "Mill Neck the Pond Shot ... three acres of this is not to be charged with rates" and six acres in the "Adding Plain the East Shot." Once the three acres not subject to tax are deducted the total is thirteen acres and not twelve; no explanation has been found for this discrepancy.

And there are even more complicated examples. William East was assigned five acres and a half of upland in 1643. In the 1646 list he has four parcels: two acres and three-quarters in the "West Field the Creek Shot," two acres and three-quarters in the "West Field the Meadow Shot," half an acre in the "Mill Neck the Pond Shot ... this is not to be charged with rates," and one acre and a half in the "Adding Plain the East Shot ... this is not to be charged with rates." The first two parcels, in the West Field, equal precisely the amount of the 1643 grant. The other two pieces, both to be free of taxes, must, then, have been part of the "equalization" process.

Although not every proprietary share has been examined in this detail for all the upland grants, the pattern seems to be that the principal grants of upland were made in the West Field and the East Field, and that most of the parcels in the Adding Plain, the Stubbie Plain and the Mill Neck were employed to make up for the deficiencies of land in the West Field and the East Field.

(continued on page 30)

Focus on Massachusetts Quarter Courts

by Randy A. West

This article will provide additional insight into the Quarter Courts which were created in 1636 by the Massachusetts General Court. The following order, issued on 3 March 1635/6, established the Great Quarter Court and four inferior Quarter Courts [MBCR 1:169]:

> Further, it is ordered, that there shall be four Courts kept every quarter, 1, at Ipswich, to which Neweberry shall belong; 2, at Salem, to which Saugus [Lynn] shall belong; 3, at Newe Towne [Cambridge], to which Charlton [Charlestown], Concord, Meadford, & Waterton shall belong; 4th, at Boston, to which Rocksbury, Dorchester, Weymothe, & Hingham shall belong.
>
> Every of these Courts shall be kept by such magistrates as shall be dwelling in or near the said towns, & by such other persons of worth as shall from time to time be appointed by the General Court, so as no Court shall be kept without one magistrate at the least, & that none of the magistrates be excluded, who can & will intend the same; yet the General Court shall appoint which of the magistrates shall specially belong to every of the said Court[s]. Such persons as shall be joined as associates to the magistrates in the said Court shall be chosen by the General Court, out of a greater number of such as the several towns shall nominate to them, so as there may be in every of the said Courts so many as (with the magistrates) may make five in all. These Courts shall try all civil causes, whereof the debt or damage shall not exceed 10£, & all criminal causes not concerning life, member, or banishment. And if any person shall find himself grieved with the sentence of any of the said Courts, he may appeal to the next great Quarter Court, provided that he put in sufficient caution to present his appeal with effect, & to abide the sentence of the magistrates in the said great Quarter Court, who shall see that all such that shall bring any appeal without just cause be exemplarily punished.
>
> There shall be four great Quarter Courts kept yearly at Boston, by the Governor & the rest of the magistrates; the first, the first Tuesday in the 4th month, called June; the second, the first Tuesday in September; the third the first Tuesday in December; the fourth, the first Tuesday in the 1st month, called March. The inferior Courts shall be kept the 1st, the last Tuesday in June, & the rest the last Tuesday in every of the said months.

Prior to this date, the General Court had met four times a year, and, between sessions of the General Court, there were meetings of the Court of Assistants. This arrangement was in accord with the original charter of the Massachusetts Bay Company.

GREAT QUARTER COURT

In addition to the semiannual General Courts, there are other court sessions recorded in the first volume of Massachusetts Colony records and in the copy of early Massachusetts Colony records which indicate they were held at Boston and began the first Tuesday in June, September, December, or March. Although none of these sessions explicitly so state, these are meetings of the Great Quarter Court, described in the last paragraph of the court order transcribed above.

The Massachusetts Colony records contains sessions for terms from June 1636 through September 1641, inclusive, that begin on the prescribed first Tuesday of the month [MBCR 1:176, 184, 193, 197, 202, 218, 219, 232, 234, 245, 248, 265, 268, 283, 285, 296, 298, 310, 314, 316, 334]. All but five of these twenty-two sessions have headings that indicate they were for a "Quarter Court" and were held at Boston.

The 5 September 1637 session records only the order that "the Quarter Court was adjourned till the 19th of this 7th month [September]." At the 15 November 1637 session of the General Court "it was ordered, that the Courts, both the General and the Quarter Courts, should be kept at Newetowne [Cambridge], until this Court do take further order" [MBCR 1:209], and at the 8 June 1638 session of the General Court it was ordered that "the Courts are transferred to Boston" [MBCR 1:232]. As a result, three sessions (5 December 1637, 6 March 1637/8, 5 June 1638) indicate they are Quarter Courts held at Cambridge [MBCR 1:218, 219, 232]. These actions were taken at the height of the Antinomian Controversy, in an attempt to insulate the courts from the many Boston adherents of Anne Hutchinson and Rev. John Wheelwright.

The 4 September 1638 session indicates it was held at Boston and was a Court of Assistants. The 3 December 1639 and 3 March 1639/40 Quarter Court sessions are further qualified as a Court of Assistants. Thus, these twenty-two court sessions are for the Great Quarter Court, which is the same as the Court of Assistants, the court made up of "the Governor & the rest of the magistrates" and not the general membership of the Massachusetts Bay Company.

While performing research for this article it was found that some missing portions from the first two volumes of Massachusetts Colony records have been published on pages xix-xxiv of William H. Whitmore's *A Bibliographical Sketch of the Laws of the Massachusetts Colony, from 1630 to 1686, ...* (Boston, 1890) [hereafter cited as Mass Laws]. The original source for this missing material is the copy of early Massachusetts Colony Records known as the "Barlow Manuscript" [Mass Laws vii, ix-x; RCA 2:iii].

The "Barlow Manuscript" of early Massachusetts Colony Records contains, in addition to the twenty-two court terms mentioned above, ten more terms from December 1641 through March 1643/4 inclusive [RCA 2:115, 117, 120, 123, 125, 128, 130, 132, 134, 138]. The June 1643 term does not have a session for the first Tuesday of the month, but instead the heading for this term is "At a Quarter Court at Boston the 10th of the 4th Month [June]" which is the second Saturday of the month. This session was probably a delayed opening of this court or an adjournment from the first Tuesday session that was unrecorded.

The General Court ordered on 17 October 1649 "that whereas there hath been four Quarter Courts held at Boston . . . henceforth there shall be but two only, vizt., that in the first month [March] and that in the seventh month [September]" [MBCR 2:285-86]. This order explains why the surviving book for this court with the title "Court of Assistants, Second Book of Records, Begun the 3d of March, 1673," only contains March and September terms.

The early surviving sessions of the Great Quarter Court indicate that it acted not only as a "superior court" in the modern sense, but it also dealt with judicial matters that would have been handled by the Inferior Quarter Courts, such as the acceptance of wills and inventories for probate. For example, at the 5 December 1637 session "the inventory of Joan Drake [of Boston], with a copy of her will, was presented to the Court" [MBCR 1:218] and at the 4 June 1639 session "the will of of Mr. Abraham Mellows [of Charlestown] was delivered in" [MBCR 1:268].

Other wills and inventories not mentioned in court session books were accepted at this court. For example, the will of "John Perry of Roxbury" was "witnessed by Phillip Eliot to be the will of John Perry before the Court at Boston the 7 of 1 [month, i.e. March] 1642 or 1643" [SPR 1(copy):18] and the inventory of "Thomas Blogget [of Cambridge]" was "deposed by Gregory Stone before the Court the 8 of the 1 month [March] 1642/1643" [SPR 2(copy):25-26] (it is assumed that the 8 March is the second day of the court session that began on 7 March).

INFERIOR QUARTER COURTS

Records exist for sessions of the inferior Quarter Courts of Salem and Ipswich but not for the inferior Quarter Courts of Boston and Cambridge. The records for Salem and Ipswich survive in court books and "waste books" [EQC 1:vi-vii]. It will be shown below that a separate court for Cambridge was not established until 1649.

The sessions of the Salem court are almost complete beginning with the first term in June 1636. A transcription of the first court book for Salem [EIHC 7:17-19, 87-90, 129-132, 185-192, 233-240, 273-280; 8:63-64, 123-128, 189-191] shows the clerk made note of the term number, e.g. "The 16th Quarter Court Begun 31 of 1 mo. [March] 1640 At Salem."

The surviving records for the Ipswich court consist of two sessions recorded in the first volume of Ipswich town records, one for 28 [illegible] 1641 and one for 29 March 1642 [GMN 15:8], and continuous sessions in court and waste books beginning with a record in a waste book dated 4 November 1645.

At a 2 June 1641 session of the General Court it is ordered that "after these next Quarter Courts shall be ended at Salem & Ipswich, two of these Quarter Courts to be kept at Salem & the other 2 at Ipswich, the first Court to be kept the last third day [Tuesday] of the 7th month [September] at Ipswich, (& the rest at the same time the former Courts were,) the next quarter at Salem, the 3d quarter at Ipswich, the 4th at Salem" [MBCR 1:325]. Therefore, after the June 1641 session Ipswich would only have terms in March and September and Salem only in June and December.

The published extracts of Essex County court records state that the month for the 28 [illegible] 1641 Ipswich session is "probably December" [EQC 1:37] without indicating the reasoning for this conjecture. This conclusion may have been based on John Goffe's will which was dated 4 December 1641 and grouped with this court session [EQC 1:38] and the 28th day of December being the last Tuesday of this month.

The month for this session could only be for March, June, or September based on the 1641 General Court order. As the last Tuesday for these three months in 1641 was the 30th, 29th, and 28th respectively, this 1641 term was more likely for September, although this month would be in conflict with the date of John Goffe's will. As the earliest surviving volume of Ipswich town records and the manuscript and published copies of it do not always agree on the sequence of the pages [GMN 15:3-5, 8], September may actually be the month for this court session and John Goffe's will presented for probate at a different court, possibly the 29 March 1642 session.

Freemen

At the 18 May 1642 General Court session "There is power given to every Court within our jurisdiction that hath two magistrates to admit any church members that are fit to be free, & to give them the freemens oath, & to certify their names to the Secretary at the next General Court" [Mass Laws xxiii-xxiv]. The record of the 27 December 1642 court session at Salem indicates that "Walter Price, Robert Gutch, Georg[e] Gardner, Richard Prence, Robert Leoman, Thomas More, Thomas Tresler, and W[illia]m Robinson, all of Salem, and Hugh Cawkin of Lynn, made free and sworn" [EQC 1:38] and these same men are recorded as freemen in the Massachusetts Colony records [MBCR 2:292].

"John Dolitle, Natha. Hanforth, Thomas Hudson, Timothy Coop[er], all of Lynn, and John Hathorne of Salem, made freemen" at the 31 December 1644 session of the Salem court [EQC 1:74-5], but these men are not recorded as freemen in the Massachusetts Colony records. Therefore, there might be those who were made freemen at an inferior court session in which the record of that session does not survive and their freemanship not recorded in the colony records. One possible candidate might be Richard Littlehale of Newbury and Haverhill who should have been a freemen based on his holding the office of town clerk, yet no freemanship records survives for him [GM 2:4:294-6]. As Newbury belonged to the Ipswich court jurisdiction, he may have been made a freemen at one of the missing sessions for this court.

Having the freemanship of an individual recorded in two different places can aid in resolving the identity of a name. On 9 July 1684, "Edw[ar]d Walker, Jno. Holden, Joseph Pierce, Sam[uel] Nogget, and Phineas Upham," apparently all of Woburn, were listed together as being admitted as freemen [MBCR 5:543], but the Nogget surname does not exist in Savage for early New England. At the 16 December 1684 session of the Middlesex County Court there are fourteen men "who presenting certificates under the Secretary's hand for their allowance at the General Court, took the Freemen's Oath" and five of them are "Edward Walker, Samuel Bloggett, John Holden, Joseph Pierce, and Phineas Upham" [Pulsifer 4:138]. Clearly, the Samuel Nogget in the colony record should be Samuel Bloggett, a resident of Woburn.

Associate Judges

The 1636 General Court order states that associates to the magistrates of the inferior Quarter Courts will be chosen by the General Court from those nominated from the towns. On 25 May 1636, the General Court named the "magistrates & other gent[lemen] as are deputed to keep the p[ar]ticular Courts" at Salem, Ipswich, Cambridge, and Boston [MBCR 1:175]. Associates were named only for the courts at Salem, Ipswich, and Cambridge at the 17 May 1637 General Court [MBCR 1:197].

At a session of the Court of Elections for the years 1638 through 1645, the General Court only named associates for the courts at Salem and Ipswich [MBCR 1:232, 261, 290, 328; 2:14, 35, 68, 110]. In 1642 and 1645 the General Court did not appoint the associates for Salem and Ipswich by name but only stated that those from the previous year were to continue. It would be reasonable to assume that if the inferior courts at Boston and Cambridge existed in these years the General Court would have named associates for these courts as well, even if only to reappoint those from the previous year.

Recorders

At the 7 October 1640 session of the General Court it was ordered "that there shall be one appointed at Ipswich, for which Mr. Samu[el] Symonds is chosen for that Court to enter all such bargaines, sales, &c, of all lands, &c, within the jurisdiction of that Court; & Mr. Emanuell Downing is chosen in like sort for the jurisdiction of the Court of Salem; & all the rest to be entered by Mr. Stephen Winthrope, the recorder at Boston" [MBCR 1:306-7]. One would assume that a recorder for the Quarter Court at Cambridge would be appointed for this task if this court had existed.

Boston Small Court

The following record from the 9 September 1639 session of the General Court created another court to be held at Boston [MBCR 1:276]:

> Forasmuch as the businesses of the ordinary Court of Assistants are so much increased as they cannot be dispatched in such season as were fit, it is therefore ordered, that such of the magistrates as shall reside in or near to Boston, or any 5, 4, or 3 of them, the Governor or Deputy to be one, shall have power to assemble together upon the last 5th day [Thursday] of the 8th [October], 11th [January], 2th [April], & 5th [July] months, every year, & then & there to hear & determine all civil causes whereof the debt or trespass & damages shall not exceed 20£, & all criminal causes not extending to life, or member, or banishment, according to the course of the Court of Assistants, & to summon juries out of the neighbor towns; & the marshal & other necessary officers are to give their attendance, as at other Courts.

Sessions for the October 1639 through January 1643/4 terms of this court are recorded in the same volumes as for the Great Quarter Court [MBCR 1:282, 285, 287, 297, 309, 313, 315, 334; RCA 2:115, 117, 118, 120, 122, 125, 127, 131, 134, 137]. All eighteen of these terms began on the prescribed last Thursday of the month except the January 1643/4 term which was held on 16 February. The headings for the 31 October 1639 and 30 April 1640 sessions further qualify these courts as for "small Causes" and the heading for the 28 July 1642 session states that it is a "Small Court at Boston." On two occasions, these sessions were called "Particular Courts" [MBCR 1:287, 309].

At the 27 September 1642 session of the General Court it was ordered "that Boston small Court shall have power to end any cause under 100£, as Salem & Ipswich have" [MBCR 2:28]. Although it was granted authority to handle civil suits, the court sessions only record criminal, administrative, and probate matters.

Most of the cases brought before this court dealt with residents of towns that were associated with the inferior courts at Boston and Cambridge.

County Courts

At the 10 May 1643 session of the General Court, the colony was divided into four counties: Essex, Middlesex, Suffolk and Norfolk [MBCR 2:38]. It appears that the court structure for Massachusetts did not change for many years after the establishment of counties.

The County Court for Essex evolved from the Quarter Courts at Salem and Ipswich as evidenced from their records, although they maintained a separate set of court books. The first Salem session to state that it was a County Court was 29 November 1659 [Salem Court Record Book, 1655-1666, folio 33v; Family History Library (FHL) Film 877,427] and the first for the Ipswich court was 25 March 1684 [Ipswich Court Record Book, 1682-1692, folio 16r; FHL Film 877,433 Item 2].

The General Court created county courts for Norfolk and Middlesex at a March 1647/8 session at the request of these two counties [MBCR 2:227]. The first session for Norfolk was held on 26 September 1648 [EQC 1:149] and that for Middlesex was on 30 October 1649 [Pulsifer 1:1]. Since Middlesex encompassed the towns that were to be associated with the inferior Quarter Court at Cambridge, it should not have been necessary to create this county court if this Quarter Court had already existed. (Note also in this connection that until 1649, Middlesex deeds and probates were recorded in the Suffolk volumes.)

The creation of the Suffolk County Court is not very clear, but on 22 May 1650 the General Court stated "Whereas the County Court at Boston, by order of the General Court, have begun to be kept upon the last Thursday in July, October, January, and April, it is now for some reasons by this Court ordered and appointed, that from henceforth they shall always begin upon the last Tuesdays of every of the said months, as all other Courts do" [MBCR 4:1:5]. As the Boston Small Court held sessions on the last Thursday of these months, it seems that the Suffolk County Court evolved from it.

SUMMARY

It appears that the 1636 General Court order creating four court jurisdictions was not followed. The courts at Salem and Ipswich clearly existed as indicated by the surviving court sessions and references to these courts in other records. The inferior courts at Boston and Cambridge may have existed for a year or two as evidenced by the appointment of associate judges in 1636 and 1637, but almost certainly did not exist beyond those years. Until the advent of the county courts in the late 1640s, the towns associated with the quarter courts of Boston and Cambridge were served by the Great Quarter Court and Boston Small Court.

Randy A. West is a longtime subscriber to the Great Migration Newsletter *and joins the short list of guest contributors to the* Focus *section. (Previous guest contributions may be found at GMN 6:19-25 (Patricia Law Hatcher, "Members of the First Church of Roxbury"), 7:3-6 (Melinde Lutz Sanborn, "Reverend James Allen's Church Census of 1688"), 7:19-22 (Melinde Lutz Sanborn, "Middlesex County Court Papers"), 8:27-30 (George F. Sanborn Jr. and Melinde Lutz Sanborn, "Focus on Salisbury"), 18:19-22, 27-30 (Patricia Law Hatcher, "Focus on Rowley and Ezekiel Rogers' Company"). Readers are reminded that the abbreviated citations embedded in the text here refer to the* Key to Titles *section in the front of each volume of* Great Migration *sketches.*

(continued from page 26)

Before addressing the grants of meadow land, we need to endure a brief course in the arithmetic of land measurements. In Milford, as in many other New England towns, the sizes of tracts of land were given in acres, roods and poles.

As a linear measure, a pole is sixteen and a half feet. (Rod and perch are synonyms for pole, but a rood, as we shall see, is different from a rod.) As a measure of area, a pole is equal to a square which is sixteen and a half feet on a side. One hundred and sixty square poles make up an acre.

There are four roods to an acre, so a rood is the same as a quarter of an acre, and is also the same as forty square poles.

(As an aside, a long narrow strip of land which is one hundred sixty linear poles on its long side and one linear pole on its short side would be equal to one acre in area. As it happens, one hundred sixty linear poles is equal to half a mile. This is why some towns, such as Watertown when laying out its Farms, began by dividing the land into large parcels half a mile in breadth and many miles in length. They could then survey a grant of so many acres by measuring along the length as many linear poles as there were acres in the grant. The distribution of land under these conditions was like cutting different-sized slices from a loaf of bread.)

Having laid down this background, we may now return to a consideration of the granting of meadow lands at Milford. As with the upland, many of the proprietors received their allotments of meadow in two or more pieces. However, because the grants of meadow were generally smaller than the grants of upland, the final allotment might only be in one piece.

A simple example of the granting of meadow would be that of Nicholas Camp, who was allotted twelve acres in 1643. In the 1646 list, we find him with two parcels: six acres in the New Meadow and six acres in Poconock Creek Meadow. Here again we see the realization of the original grant as two equal pieces.

A straightforward but less symmetrical situation is found with Rev. Peter Prudden, who in 1643 was given twenty-nine acres. In 1646 there are four entries for him in various of the town meadows: seven acres in "The Meadow the West Side," nine acres in "East Meadow the Indian Side," three acres in "The Harbour Meadow" and ten acres in "The North Meadow." These four different-sized parcels add up to the originally granted twenty-nine acres.

In other cases the proprietor received all his meadow in one piece. In 1643 Nathaniel Baldwin was granted two acres and forty-eight poles. In 1646 he was credited with "two acres one rood and eight pole" in the Great Meadow. And now we get to use our newly acquired arithmetic skills. The forty-eight poles of the original grant are now expressed as one rood and eight poles. Remembering that one rood equals forty square poles, we see how the transformation is accomplished. In like manner, James Prudden had a 1643 grant of two acres and ninety-six poles, and in 1646 is listed as holding "two acres a half and sixteen pole." In this case, the ninety-six poles have been parsed into eighty poles and sixteen poles, the eighty poles being equal to two roods or half an acre.

As with the grants of upland, there were also instances in which some of the parcels of meadow included bits of deficient land, which again required the application of the "equalization" process. In 1643 John Fletcher was granted eight acres and thirty-two poles of meadow. The 1646 list shows him with two parcels of meadow: in the Great Meadow "eight acres and two and thirty pole" and in the New Meadow "three roods … this is not to be charged with rates." The grant in the New Meadow apparently compensated for something lacking in the grant in the Great Meadow.

With the various examples of land grants discussed so far in this article, the reader should be able to interpret the particular details of the earliest land granting process in Milford for any one of these founding proprietors as recorded in the 1643 and 1646 lists.

We can now move on to the second group of questions, regarding the persistence in residence of the earliest proprietors.

There are forty-four names in the list of those who signed up for the settlement of Milford in late 1639, at which time most of them were still residing at New Haven. Of these, thirty-six also appeared in the 1643 list of grants of houselots, upland and meadow, and were still listed in 1646 as being in possession of the full range of grants:

Zachariah Whitman	Jasper Gunn
Thomas Welsh	John Fletcher
Thomas Wheeler	Francis Bolt
Edmond Tapp	Micah Tomkins
Thomas Buckingham	John Birdsey
Richard Platt	John Lane
Peter Prudden	William East
William Fowler	Thomas Samford
John Astwood	Timothy Baldwin
Richard Baldwin	George Clarke Jr.
Benjamin Fenn	John Burwell
Samuel Coley	Henry Botsford
John Peacock	Joseph Baldwin
Henry Stonehill	Philip Hatley
Nathaniel Baldwin	Nicholas Camp
James Prudden	John Rogers
George Clarke Sr.	Thomas Uffott
George Hubbert	Thomas Tibballs

Two other men, Thomas Baker and Nathaniel Briscoe, were in the 1639 and 1646 lists, but not granted land in 1643. They do not seem to have resided elsewhere between 1639 and 1646, so this omission in 1643 may be a simple oversight. We have, then, thirty-eight of the forty-four (or more than four-fifths) who remained in residence over this span

of seven years. Even over such a short period, this level of persistence is remarkable during the first generation of New England settlement. In the town of Dedham, Massachusetts, for example, between 1636 and 1642, the proportion of those who persisted as compared to those who moved on was just the reverse.

Of the remaining six names on the 1639 list, five were also present in 1643 when the initial grant of lands was made, but had been bought out by the time of the 1646 list:

> Robert Plum purchased the proprietary share of Richard Miles, who returned to New Haven.
>
> Edmond Tapp purchased the proprietary share of Thomas Tapping, who moved on to Southampton.
>
> John Baldwin purchased the proprietary share of Alexander Bryan, who remained in Milford, although owning only a houselot in 1646.
>
> Timothy Baldwin purchased the proprietary share of Edmond Harvey, who moved on to Fairfield.
>
> William East purchased the proprietary share of Thomas Lawrence, who died shortly after the making of the 1646 list.

Note that two of those who sold their land (Bryan and Lawrence) did not actually leave Milford. Note also that three of the purchasers (Tapp, East and Timothy Baldwin) were already proprietors, and so were simply expanding their landholding, and that a fourth, John Baldwin, was a brother of several other proprietors. These circumstances reinforce the conclusion of a high level of persistence of the early Milford proprietors.

Finally, John Sherman, who was in the 1639 and 1643 lists, had by 1646 returned to New Haven where he became the minister. The fate of his proprietary share has not been learned.

In the 1643 list of grants were only three names that had not appeared in the 1639 list: John Smith, John Fowler and Martha Beard. These three were the only additions in these first four years to the original list of proprietors, again an indication of the stability of the population of Milford in this period.

Between 1643 and 1646 ten other men were granted land, some just a houselot and some the full range of types of land: Roger Terrill, Andrew Benton, Edward Riggs, John Brown, William Brooks, Thomas Bayly, Robert Denison, William Roberts, William Slow and James Prime. Presumably all ten of these were admitted as inhabitants and proprietors in that three year period.

To conclude our coverage of Milford land records, we note that the 1639 list had an addendum of nine names beyond the original forty-four. Some authors have claimed them as 1639 proprietors, but as most of them first appear as proprietors in the interval between 1643 and 1646, these nine names are almost certainly a late addition to the 1639 list and not contemporaneous with its creation.

RECENT LITERATURE

Adrian Benjamin Burke, John Blythe Dobson, and Janet Chevalley Wolfe, "The Exhurst Ancestry of the Stoughton Siblings of New England," *The New England Historical and Genealogical Register* 165 (2011):245-60. In this first installment of a two-part article, the authors examine the ancestry of Mary Exhurst, wife of Edward Stoughton. This latter couple were grandparents of Rev. Thomas Stoughton, who was father of four New England immigrants: Thomas Stoughton, Israel Stoughton, Judith (Stoughton) (Denman) Smead and Elizabeth (Stoughton) (Scudder) Chamberlain [GMB 1773-79].

Doris Schreiber Willcox, "Proving the Identity of Deliverance, Wife of Samuel[2] Legg of Boston, as Deliverance Sandys," *The New England Historical and Genealogical Register* 165 (2011):261-72. Samuel Legg of Boston was son of the 1631 immigrant John Legg of Salem [GMB 1166 -68]. By following up on clues in probate records and a marriage contract, Willcox identifies Samuel's wife Deliverance as a daughter of Henry Sandys, who had settled in Boston by 1638. The author then compiles accounts of the families of Henry Sandys and Samuel Legg.

Roger Thompson, "The English Origins of Captain Francis Norton of Charlestown, Massachusetts," *The New England Historical and Genealogical Register* 165 (2011):273-39. Thompson, as part of his detailed explorations of early Charlestown history, has discovered that Captain Francis Norton, who had arrived in New England by 1637, was baptized at Caddington, Bedfordshire, in 1602. The author has also prepared genealogical summaries of the families of Francis Norton and his father John Norton.

Gary Grieve-Carlson, "John Winthrop in *The Maximus Poems*," *The New England Quarterly* 84 (2011):655-695. Charles Olson, who died at Gloucester, Massachusetts, in 1970, compiled a three-volume cycle of poems, *The Maximus Poems*, published in 1960, 1968 and 1975. A main theme of these poems is the settlement of New England, and the tensions between the Puritan settlers, led by John Endicott and John Winthrop, and the not-so-religious fishermen and other early settlers of the northern New England coast, represented by the likes of Roger Conant and Thomas Morton. Grieve-Carlson explores Olson's treatment of the conflict between the strictures of Puritan discipline and the more carefree life of the fisherman and their ilk. Grieve-Carlson also discusses the unresolved interplay of history and myth in Olson's poetry. Olson had sought an advanced degree in American Civilization at Harvard, and undertook extensive historical work during the writing of these poems.

INDEX OF SUBJECTS

INDEX OF PLACES

INDEX OF SURNAMES

James 62
Mary 62
BLOSSE see BLOIS
BLOTT
_____ Goodman 107
BLOYCE see BLOIS
BLUMFIELD
John 132
BLYSS see BLISS
BOINTON see BOYNTON
BOLLES
Hannah 41
BOLT
Francis 140, 149, 159
Phillip 149
Sarah (_____) 149
Susanah 149
BONNER
Isabell 32
Robert 32
_____ 69
BORDEN
Joanna (Hooker) 119
John 119
BOTSFORD/BOTCHFORD
Henry 148, 149, 159
BOULTER
Mary 87
BOURNE
Hannah (_____)59
Nehemiah 59
BOWEN
Richard 120
BOWERS
Benanuel 70
BOWLES
Dorothy (Bedle) 20
Hannah 41
John 20
BOYDEN
Thomas 43
BOYLSTON/BOYSON
Thomas 50
BOYNTON/BOINTON
Ellen/Helen (Pell) 93
John 93
William 83, 92, 93
BOYSE/BOYES
Grace (Moxom) 84
Hester 101
John 84
Joseph 101
Mary (Gleadston) 84
Matthew 83, 84
_____ (_____)84
BRACEY/BRACY
Phebe (Bisby) 7
Raberge (Salmon) 7
Thomas 7
BRADBURY
Elizabeth (Whitgift) 15
Thomas 15

BRADFORD
John 94
Robert 101
William 143
BRADLEY
Mary 83, 86, 91, 94
BRANDON
John C. 95, 119, 135, 143
William 12
BRAYTON
John Anderson 22, 32
BRECK
Anna 127
Edward 127
BREMER
Francis J. 98
BREWEN see BRUEN
BRIDGELAND
Ann 143
Peter 143
BRIDGES
Alice (_____) 84
Edmund 84
Robert 58, 59
BRIGGS
Clement 12, 27, 30
BRIGHAM
Constance 91, 94
Mary 91, 94
Mary (_____) 91
Mary/Marie (Fawcett) 91, 94
Sebastian 91, 94
Timothy 91, 94
BRISCOE
Daniel 102, 105
Nathaniel 141, 150, 159
William 59, 102, 105
BROADHURST
Phyllis (Cogswell) 47
BROCK
Henry 105, 109
John 105, 109
BROCKETT
Richard 60
BROCKLEBANK
Jane (_____)91, 94
John 91, 94
Samuel 91, 94
William 91
BROCKWAY
family 55
Wolston 47, 55
BROOKE/BROOKES/BROOKS
William 142, 150, 159
BROOKS see BROOKE
BROWN/BROWNE
family 135
Abraham 78
Edward 58, 60
George 45
James 118, 125
John 150, 159

Mary 78
Mary (Healy) 115
Richard 44, 45, 133
Robert 120
Thomas 115, 117, 124
William 54, 58
BRUEN/BREWEN
Obediah 110
BRYAN
Alexander 149, 159
Richard 141
BUCKINGHAM
Hannah (_____) 140
Thomas 140, 148, 159
BUCKLEY see BULKELEY
BUGBEE/BUGBY
Edward 44
Sarah 44
BULFINCH
John 101
BULKELEY/BULKLEY/
BUCKLEY
Edward 79
John 102, 105
Mary 79
Peter 79, 102, 105
BULLARD
Bettris (_____) 60
George 60
Margaret (_____) 60
BULLEN see BULLIN
BULLIN/BULLEN
Mary 61
Mary (_____) 61
Samuel 61
BUNKER
Nick 120
BURBAGE
family 39
BURBANK
Ann (_____) 93
John 83, 93
BURDON
George 62
BURGE
John 14
BURKE
Adrian Benjamin 160
BURNELL
family 103, 111
Samuel 103, 111
William 103
_____ (son of William) 103
BURNHAM
James 119
Mary (Kinsman) 119
Thomas 119
BURRAGE/BERIDGE
John 107
BURRELL
John 28

INDEX OF FIRST NAMES